NORTH ATLANTIC RUN

The Royal Canadian Navy and the Battle for the Convoys

NORTH ATLANTIC RUN

The Royal Canadian Navy
and the Battle
for the Convoys

Marc Milner

UNIVERSITY OF TORONTO PRESS

Toronto Buffalo London

© University of Toronto Press 1985
Toronto Buffalo London
Printed in Canada
Reprinted 1985, 1986

ISBN 0-8020-2544-7

Printed on acid-free paper

Canadian Cataloguing in Publication Data

Milner, Marc.
    North Atlantic run

    Bibliography: p.
    Includes index.
    ISBN 0-8020-2544-7.
    1. World War, 1939-1945 – Naval operations,
    Canadian.   2. Canada. Royal Canadian Navy –
    History.   3. World War, 1939-1945 – Campaigns –
    Atlantic Ocean.   I. Title.
    D779.C2M54 1985   940.54'5971   C85-098024-0

Charts on pages 42, 92, 135, 162, and 211 by William R. Constable and
Julie F. Sommerville.
Chart on page 286 from J. Rohwer, *The Critical Convoy Battles of March
1943* (Annapolis, Md: U.S. Naval Institute Press 1977), 39, gratefully
reproduced by permission of the author.

This book has been published with the help of a grant from the Social
Science Federation of Canada, using funds provided by the Social
Sciences and Humanities Research Council of Canada, and a grant from
the Andrew W. Mellon Foundation to the University of Toronto Press.
Publication has also been assisted by the Canada Council and the Ontario
Arts Council under their block grant programs.

For my parents

The land man's troubles and hazards are only during
a short fight ... whereas the work and labour and hazards
are most of them constant to a seaman, besides what he
meets in a fight.

Samuel Pepys

Contents

Charts

Illustrations

Foreword

There used to be a rather pompous old naval saying, 'The impossible can be achieved at once; the miracle takes longer.' Looking back at the RCN's contribution to the Second World War, one cannot but conclude that the impossible was achieved but the miracles remained elusive. How else can one account for the fantastic expansion from a handful of officers and men in 1939 to ninety-six thousand at the end of the war? The rate of expansion was fifty to one, compared with eight to one for the Royal Navy, fourteen to one for the Royal Australian Navy, and twenty to one for the U.S. Navy. Who could be surprised that there were teething troubles in the RCN? The struggle to reach acceptable standards of efficiency in the face of many difficulties is the subject of Marc Milner's book.

The speed of Canadian naval expansion was never understood by the British Admiralty, and I do not believe that even NSHQ in Ottawa realized the size of the task which had been undertaken. If it had it would not have ordered Tribal-class destroyers to be built at Halifax in 1940 – ships unsuited to the work of escorting convoys and full of complexities for the builders. Poor communication at the outset led to a number of misunderstandings between the RN and the RCN, which did not contribute to smooth operation.

Milner's book covers the period 1939–45, with a special focus on the crucial convoy battles between July 1942 and June 1943, when the Atlantic battle came to a climax of near defeat in March with a sudden change to complete victory in June. It was an unfortunate freak of fate that convoys escorted by Canadian groups were more often attacked by German wolf packs in the winter of 1942 than were convoys escorted by British groups, and there can be no doubt that the losses sustained by the Canadian groups were comparatively higher. The one American group involved also took disproportionate losses, but that is another story. However, results generally were bad, and when a new and tough commander-in-chief, Admiral Sir Max Horton, joined Western Approaches Command in November 1942, he surveyed the general scene with much dissatisfaction. He came to the conclusion that all the ships of the command needed a marked increase in efficiency, and he initiated several measures, more time for training between convoy passages and a new group-training scheme centred on HMS *Philante* being the most important. He also concluded – and this was agreed to by his air opposite number – that aircraft needed the same increase in efficiency.

Statistics showed that the Canadian groups had a worse record than the British – Marc Milner describes some of the convoys of this period and comments sagely on the results. Horton believed that tough measures were needed, and a drastic action was taken with these groups; they were switched to a base at Londonderry, where the training facilities were excellent, and moved from the mid-Atlantic convoys to those to Gibraltar.

Canadian corvettes which had been sent to the Mediterranean for operation TORCH had already shown that the RCN could contribute good results when the training was adequate and stability of teams was present. The shift to Londonderry and the subsequent blitz on training did have excellent results, and Canadian groups quickly came up to adequate standards of training with the equipment they carried. Steps were also taken to install as much new equipment as possible during their periods in harbour. As a result the ships were returned to the North Atlantic run, but, by complete chance, the Canadian groups missed the great convoy battles of April and May 1943, when the turn of the tide came. They were naturally disappointed, especially as they had borne a long and arduous burden for so long in the mid-Atlantic.

What were the reasons for the Canadian deficiencies? As Milner points out, there were three main reasons: first, as already mentioned, the enormous expansion, which resulted in ships being manned by inexperienced officers and men who were moved from ship to ship too often; secondly, inadequate equipment, particularly in the fitting of HF/DF and 10-centimetre radar, which were vital to the defence of convoys; and thirdly, insufficient training of ships and escort groups. The standard of personnel was high – higher I believe than in the British ships – but miracles could not be managed.

In particular, it seems not to have been appreciated that long periods of operating, often with no incidents except bad weather, resulted in more need for training – ships got into bad habits, and I believe that during quiet periods, when Ultra showed that there were few U-boats in the Western Atlantic, opportunity should have been taken to thin the escorts and give more training.

NSHQ must be held responsible for all this. In the understandable wish to contribute the maximum number of ships to the battle, the needs of the ships to prepare for the conflict were underestimated. In particular, the Naval Staff at NSHQ took a great time to understand the vital need for both 10-centimetre radar and for HF/DF sets for detecting U-boats.

The reasons for the shortcomings at NSHQ are clear, though Milner does not touch on such a delicate point. The average standard of the staff officers at Ottawa was not high enough – there were simply not enough first-rate staff brains to go around, and the ships had to be manned as well as the naval bases and the training establishments. I think that the Royal Navy could have helped more, though here again there were not enough high-class brains available. It is certain that the RCN tried to do too much and thus the miracles were not achieved, but that must be blamed on the politicians as well as the sailors. Milner makes this very clear.

I am full of admiration for Marc Milner's book. It is thoroughly researched and misses no important factors which affect the specialist subject of the part played by Canada in the mid-Atlantic war. In addition, the reader is given a mini-history of the Royal Canadian Navy, without which the nub of the book cannot be understood. I found it difficult to criticize the author's main findings, and his grasp is firm; he raises a few moot points, but above all the balance is right in what has become a very controversial issue.

After June 1943, the general standards of efficiency were satisfactory; training improved markedly, and in the flare-up on the convoy routes in the autumn and winter of 1943, Canadian groups performed with distinction. It is apt to be forgotten that escorts faced the menace of the acoustic torpedo and the dangers of the Snort-fitted U-boats after the main victory had been gained, and that life was hard and very high standards of training were needed to cope with the enemy. By 1944 the RCN was carrying the main burden of the mid-Atlantic war, and well she did it.

VICE-ADMIRAL SIR PETER GRETTON, KCB, DSO, CBE, DSC, MA
Oxford
April 1984

Preface

The popular impression of the Battle of the Atlantic is one of blazing merchant ships, prowling U-boat 'packs,' and weather-beaten escort vessels locked in an endless engagement. As an image it reflects conditions in 1940–3, when battles were most intense, and it focuses on that stretch of open water between Newfoundland and Ireland – what the Canadians called the 'North Atlantic Run.' Indeed, it was there, far from land-based aircraft, that the classic confrontation between escorted convoy and U-boats took place. For this reason, the mid-Atlantic was the decisive theatre of the campaign and the focus of all subsequent accounts. Most works on the Battle of the Atlantic actually end with the Allied victory in mid-ocean in 1943.

Both the popular image and the historical shape of the struggle for the North Atlantic sea lanes are accurate. There is, however, a serious flaw in what has become the standard version of the Battle of the Atlantic. The part played by the Royal Canadian Navy – a vitally important one – has been all but ignored. Admittedly, the Canadians resigned themselves to a supporting role in the beginning, but by early 1943 fully half of all the escorts operating between New York and Britain were RCN. In spite of this the saga of embattled escorts and perilous convoy crossings has been replayed time and time again in books, films, documentaries, and articles, with scarcely a nod in Canada's direction.

There is, of course, a very simple reason for this omission. The British, Americans, and Germans have produced well-documented accounts of the parts played by their navies in the crucial struggle for the main trade routes. The Canadian official history of operations, by contrast, was intended to foster public interest in the exploits of the wartime navy. *The Far Distant Ships* is not so much about the war as it is about the RCN itself, recounting the often colourful activities of Canadian sailors and warships in many theatres. The story of RCN participation in the decisive campaign of the Battle of the Atlantic – the navy's most prestigious commitment – therefore forms only a small part of the official history. Unable to reconcile this lone Canadian account with more analytical British and American histories, subsequent popular historians have been content to portray the RCN, if at all, as a benign or even negative element in the war.

But the RCN was a major factor in the story of the North Atlantic run, and uncovering its involvement in the battle to master the U-boat packs has been a labour of love. It was an attempt to measure Canada's contribution to the Battle of the Atlantic that prompted this project eight years ago, and what began as an undergraduate paper on the role of the RCN in the final crisis of 1943 has mushroomed into a full-scale study of a service at war. Apart from explaining Canada's contribution to the mid-ocean war, what follows makes at least three modifications to the standard version of the struggle: it portrays the RCN as a dynamic element – for better or for worse – in the war at sea, and not merely an appendage of the Royal Navy; it identifies the crisis of Canada's own war at sea, that learning experience which other Allied navies went through and prospered from; and it measures the RCN's contribution to the actual defeat of the U-boat packs, as distinct from the essential work it did to protect shipping.

Although this is essentially a story of battle, it does open new avenues of research for those interested in wartime Canada. For the most part Canadian historians have been content to write of the war as if it had been fought entirely on some remote battlefield. But final victory would not have been possible without the successful defence of the sea lanes. A crucial part of that achievement was the conduct of a major campaign in the Atlantic, by a Canadian service, drawing directly on manpower and resources from Canada. No years of training on Salisbury Plain here: ships and men sailed directly and regularly from Canadian ports into battle, and some of their corpses came ashore within a few hundred miles of Quebec City. Problems which historians have previously considered largely domestic in nature, such as industrial planning and manpower management, also profoundly affected the course of events at sea. No other major battle was so directly affected by distinctly Canadian issues.

This is also a case study of coalition warfare. It presents a small but militarily and industrially strong nation in a subordinate role and attempting (not always successfully) to apply its own resources to defeat of the enemy. The adoption of such a role had a considerable impact on the development of the navy and forms a crucial part of the story.

But in the end this book is, more than anything else, about men thrown into totally unfamiliar surroundings with inadequate training and equipment to fight a deadly enemy. As such, it is seldom a flattering tale. One senior RCN officer candidly admitted, at the height of wartime expansion, that 'most escorts are equipped with one weapon of approximate precision – the ram'! The operational efficiency of the Canadian navy not only seriously affected the outcome of RCN battles; it ultimately affected the disposition of the escort fleet as well, and it therefore forms a central theme of the story. In the eyes of some highly authoritative historians, the RCN and the Canadians who manned the escort fleet did not measure up to the required standards. For forty years they have borne that stigma. They deserve better.

Acknowledgments

The following study is the work of many years and owes a great deal to the kind co-operation, encouragement, and efforts of many people. Mr L.C. Audette, Mr P. Beesly, Captain E.S. Brand, RCN, Mr John Burgess, Rear Admiral H.G. DeWolf, RCN, Rear Admiral J. Charles, RCN, the late Rear Admiral H.F. Pullen, RCN, Vice-Admiral Sir Peter Gretton, RN, Dr Michael Hadley, Rear Admiral D.W. Piers, RCN, and Vice-Admiral B.B. Schofield, RN, endured both interview and subsequent correspondence. Many others answered my letters: Rear Admiral K.F. Adams, RCN, Rear Admiral P. Burnett, RN, Rear Admiral J.C. Hibbard, RCN, Mr J. Lamb, Mr C.S.J. Lancaster, Rear Admiral H.N. Lay, RCN, the late Rear Admiral E.R. Mainguy, RCN, Mr H. Revely, the late Captain S.W. Roskill, RN, and Captain J.M. Waters, USCG. Dr Jürgen Rohwer, of the Bibliothek für Zeitgeschichte, Stuttgart, fielded numerous inquiries and helped to locate suitable photographs. I would also like to add a special thank you to Mrs J.D. Prentice for her insightful comments on her late husband.

I naturally owe a great debt to staffs of various archives. In Canada my heartiest thanks go to the staff at the Directorate of History, National Defence Headquarters, both for their help during the long research period and for assistance and encouragement during the preparation of the final manuscript. In particular, I would like to thank Dr Roger Sarty for his tireless efforts in tracking down obscure facts and files and for his invaluable insights into the nature of the anti-submarine war during 1944–5.

Miss B. Wilson and Mr D. Smith of the Public Archives of Canada guided me through their massive and ever-changing collections. I am most grateful to Mr Justice A. Macdonald for permission to use his father's papers, and to Dr B. Cuthbertson, Public Archives Nova Scotia, for help in gaining access to them. Dr A.W. Tickner, of the National Research Council of Canada, kindly aided me in securing material from the NRC library.

In Britain my debt is equally great. The late Captain S.W. Roskill, RN, graciously allowed me access to his papers at Churchill College, Cambridge, while Mr C. Barnett and his staff helped me with those of others. The staffs at the Imperial War Museum and the Public Records Office provided invaluable assistance, for which I am grateful. Mr R. Coppock, Naval Historical Branch, London, gave very generously of his time in the midst of a move to new offices.

Dr D.C. Allard, Head of the Operational Archives, Washington, DC, kindly forwarded copies of specific documents and made my visit to his archives a most successful one. The staff at the U.S. National Archives, particularly Mr F. Purnell, were very helpful. Lieutenant Colonel N. Borchgrevink, of the Norwegian Centre for Defence History, answered my questions about the Royal Norwegian Navy.

The help of a support staff is crucial to any major undertaking, and this was no exception. The Imperial Order Daughters of the Empire supported the early research, while assistantships and travel grants from the University of New Brunswick helped me to keep body and soul together and made many research trips possible. The Military Studies Program at UNB was particularly helpful in defraying travel costs, and the Department of National Defence Fellowship saw me through the final stages of research and writing. Expenses were also mitigated by Mr L.C. Audette, Mr and Mrs P. Oulton, and, in particular, Mr and Mrs W. McAuley, all of Ottawa, who provided me with room and board on many occasions – and often for protracted periods. Without their help it would simply have been impossible to undertake the research required. Mr and Mrs John O'Connor, of Old Windsor, England, made my periods in Britain most memorable and enjoyable.

In addition, I am most grateful to the members of the History Department at UNB, who offered constant encouragement and interest, and to the departmental secretaries, Mrs Carol Hines and Mrs Phyllis Miller, who graciously undertook to type the text at a very late hour. I would also like to thank Mr Ken Jones for his insights on Angus L. Macdonald; Mr David Zimmerman for sharing his findings on RCN equipment; Dr David Charters, of the Centre for Conflict Studies, UNB, for his help during the preliminary stages; Dr J.A. Boutilier, RRMC, for his constant encouragement; Dr D.M. Schurman, RMC, for his comments on the draft;

my editor, Gerald Hallowell, of University of Toronto Press, for his encouragement and assistance; and my copy-editor, Susan Kent, for her diligence and enthusiasm.

Mr Ken Macpherson of Toronto, Dr H.A. Vadnais of the Curator Branch, USN Operational Archives, Mr Mel Lundy, Canadian Forces Photo Unit, Ms Marilyn Smith of the Maritime Command Museum, Halifax, and the staff of the National Photograph Collection, PAC, were extremely helpful in tracking down photos. I am grateful also to William R. Constable and Julie F. Sommerville, who prepared the maps.

I owe an enormous debt of thanks to Dr W.A.B. Douglas, director of the Armed Forces Directorate of History, Ottawa. His kind help and encouragement were crucial to the successful completion of this project. Dr Douglas's knowledge of the RCN and the war at sea kept me from many pitfalls.

My heartiest vote of thanks and appreciation must go to my long-time mentor Dr D.S. Graham. His quiet counsel and probing intellect have been a constant source of inspiration and guidance for many years. Those who know Dr Graham and his work will find his unmistakable and invaluable imprint on this work. His full support and intense interest in the project from the outset made the whole process extremely rewarding.

There are, finally, two special acknowledgments to make. The late Kenneth N. Windsor, that eccentric, erudite professor of history and student of humanity so cherished by countless UNB students, had a crucial influence on my early training as an historian. The many hours he devoted to proof-reading drafts and to clarifying difficult issues will never be forgotten. His enthusiasm and encouragement were largely instrumental in my decision to pursue the present subject.

The last, but never least, debt of thanks I owe to my wife, Barbara Jean. While I spent years on a challenging and extremely interesting chase through archives in many cities, she soldiered on at home and at work, bore two children, and provided a stable environment for all. Any plaudits for endurance and perseverance arising from this work must accrue to her. If the RCN's wartime escorts had enjoyed a similar measure of support, this story would have reached a different conclusion.

Abbreviations

A group	American escort group
AA/SSB	Allied Anti-Submarine Survey Board
ABC I	American-British Conversations I
ABC 22	American-Canadian appendix to ABC I, dealing with command arrangements in the Western Atlantic
ACI	Atlantic Convoy Instructions
A/CNS	Assistant chief of Naval Staff, RCN
ACNS (T)	Assistant chief of Naval Staff (Trade), RN
AMC	Armed merchant cruiser
A/S	Anti-submarine
ASW	Anti-submarine warfare
A&WI	Atlantic and West Indies (Squadron), RN
B group	British escort group
BAD	British Admiralty Delegation, Washington
BDienst	German radio monitoring and decryption service
BdU	Befehlshaber der U-boote (commander-in-chief, U-boats)
C group	Canadian escort group
C-in-C, WA	Commander-in-chief, Western Approaches, RN
CCCS	Commodore commanding, Canadian Ships (UK)
CCNF	Commodore commanding, Newfoundland Force
CNEC	Chief of Naval Engineering and Construction, RCN
CNES	Chief of Naval Equipment and Supply, RCN
CNO	Chief of Naval Operations, USN
CNS	Chief of Naval Staff, RCN
CO	Commanding officer
COAC	Commanding officer, Atlantic Coast, RCN

COMINCH	Commander-in-chief, USN
CTF-24	Commander, Task Force Twenty-four, USN
DA/S	Director, Anti-Submarine, RCN
DA/SW	Director, Anti-Submarine Warfare, RN
DCOS	Deputy chief of staff
DHist	Directorate of History, National Defence Headquarters, Ottawa
DNP	Director, Naval Personnel, RCN
DOD	Director, Operations Division, RCN
DOP	Director of Plans, RCN
DSD	Director, Signals Division, RCN
DTD	Director, Trade Division, RCN
DWT	Directorate of Warfare and Training, RCN
EG	Escort group
FONF	Flag officer, Newfoundland
FSL	First Sea Lord
HF/DF	High-frequency direction finding
HMCS	His Majesty's Canadian Ship
HMS	His Majesty's Ship
HN or MS	His Norwegian Majesty's Ship
HX	Fast eastbound convoy
MF/DF	Medium-frequency direction finding
MOEF	Mid-Ocean Escort Force
MTB	Motor torpedo boat
NEF	Newfoundland Escort Force
NHB	Naval Historical Branch, London
NHC	Naval Historical Center, Washington, DC
NMCS	Naval member, Canadian Staff, Washington
NRC	National Research Council, Ottawa
NSHQ	Naval Service Headquarters, Ottawa
ON	Fast westbound convoy
ONS	Slow westbound convoy
PAC	Public Archives, Canada
PRO	Public Record Office, London
RDFO	Radar officer
RPV	Revised patrol vessel (eg, a corvette with modifications)
R/T	Radio telephone
SC	Slow eastbound convoy
SNEM	Supervising naval engineer, Maritimes

SO(A/S)	Staff officer, Anti-Submarine
SOE	Senior officer, Escort
SWIC	Surface warning, First Canadian (Radar)
USCG	United States Coast Guard
USNA	United States National Archives, Washington
VCNS	Vice-chief of Naval Staff, RCN
VLR	Very long range
V/S	Visual signalling
WA	Western Approaches
WACI	Western Approaches Convoy Instructions
WLEF	Western Local Escort Force
WSF	Western Support Force
W/T	Wireless telegraphy

NORTH ATLANTIC RUN

The Royal Canadian Navy and the Battle for the Convoys

Prologue

Nothing of an efficient character could be built in a quarter or half a century. Was there any need for this costly or hazardous experiment?

Sir Robert Borden, 1911

On Christmas Day 1942 the slow convoy ONS 154, forty-five ships, most in ballast, was pounding its way through heavy seas six hundred miles due west of Ireland. The winds and high seas confronting the convoy and its meagre Canadian escort had much battered and delayed previous westbound convoys along northerly routes. Largely for this reason, ONS 154 was routed south towards the Azores, where merchant and escort sailors could enjoy a respite from the vile North Atlantic winter. Yet to the men on the spot, struggling through the tail-end of a hurricane, the good intentions of routing authorities meant little, for it was a grim and foreboding day. It was doubtless with a note of irony and cynicism that someone pencilled a cheery 'Merry Christmas' across the top of HMCS *Napanee*'s log as that tiny corvette corkscrewed her way through the oncoming seas. For the hundreds of men in ONS 154 it was not to be a very merry Christmas; for 486 of them it was to be their last.

On Christmas Day the convoy actually altered course from southwesterly to due south, in order to avoid a U-boat concentration which lay across its path. The new course carried ONS 154 deeper into the mid-Atlantic gap between the maximum ranges of land-based air power, and farther from ready reinforcement of any kind. In the event, it only delayed the inevitable. Searching U-boats from group 'Spitz' located the convoy on Boxing Day, and in the early hours of 27 December the first torpedoes struck – a thousand miles from the nearest Allied air base. By sunrise three ships had been sunk, and a fourth, already hit and straggling, followed shortly thereafter. Over the next four days some twenty U-boats from two 'wolf packs' were sent to attack ONS 154, and as many as twelve were in contact at any given time. The five Canadian escorts of group C 1, hopelessly outnumbered and badly equipped, proved incapable of either preventing losses or (apparently) exacting payment from the enemy for his successes. By the night of 30–31 December, with the escort grievously reduced as ships parted company to seek fuel, it appeared that ONS 154 was in for what the Senior Officer of the escort described as the 'final carving.' Little stood between the convoy and complete annihilation, and Commander Guy Windeyer, RCN, invited all ships with large passenger complements to escape if in their judgment they had an opportunity. Fortunately, the ranks of ONS 154 held, and miraculously the U-boats, also exhausted and scattered by the battle, did not return for the final blow. On New Year's Eve reinforcements arrived from Newfoundland, and the long ordeal of ONS 154 was over. With the reinforcements came a new Senior Officer, and Windeyer, who not surprisingly had begun to see torpedoes at every turn, was put to bed by his medical officer.

For the poorly equipped and ill-prepared Canadian escorts of the Mid-Ocean Escort Force (MOEF) and for the RCN as a whole, the battle of ONS 154 was an unmitigated disaster, the last in a long string of defeats dating back to September 1941. Moreover, it came at a time when the capability of the RCN was being directly challenged by the British. By the end of 1942 the latter felt that Canadian escort groups were no longer able to handle duties in the heavily embattled mid-ocean, and their point was driven home by the inept defence of ONS 154. This realization proved a bitter pill for the RCN to swallow and in the short term affected the operational deployment of Canadian escorts. But more importantly, the whole crisis of late 1942 forced the professional navy to re-evaluate its expansion policies and address the outstanding shortcomings in the auxiliary fleet – the reservists' war. In short, the battle for ONS 154 marked the end of the beginning for Canada's wartime navy.

The presence of a Canadian escort group in the mid-Atlantic shepherding a mercantile convoy was a remarkable development, and this helps to explain why the Canadians performed so badly. As recently as the fall of 1940 the RCN had had no plans whatsoever to use its burgeoning corvette fleet as ocean escorts. But what is perhaps even more remarkable is that there was a Canadian navy at all. Its establishment in 1910 as a separate national service, albeit with close ties to the Royal Navy, occasioned stormy debate. Many Canadians, like Sir Robert Borden, considered it a 'costly and hazardous experiment' and preferred a direct contribution to the imperial fleet. Twenty-nine years after its birth, on the eve of the Second World War, the navy was still tiny, and its existence in the interim had always been precarious.

In its infancy domestic political wranglings left the RCN stunted. By the First World War, after four years of argument, frustration, and cancelled plans, the RCN amounted to only two creaky old cruisers acquired as training ships. The war itself did nothing to elevate the navy from its obscurity. Only once, during a brief period in early August 1914, did the RCN capture the public's imagination. HMCS *Rainbow*, the sole naval presence on Canada's west coast, was at sea as war clouds gathered over Europe, and as tensions mounted, she turned back to Esquimalt to load high-explosive shells. On 5 August, while still at sea, *Rainbow* was ordered south to search for Admiral Graf von Spee's powerful squadron, which was known to be off Mexico. Armed with little more than solid shot, badly outclassed in all respects by the modern German cruisers, but spurred on by Ottawa's admonition to 'remember Nelson and the British Navy,' *Rainbow* searched in vain. On at least one occasion the cruiser actually passed within about fifty miles of the Germans, but von Spee was able to make good his 'escape.' *Rainbow*'s sorties were indeed in the best of British tradition – both Trafalgar and the charge of the Light Brigade – and had she found *Leipzig* or *Nürnberg* the outcome would hardly have been in doubt. West-coast defence soon passed to modern British and Japanese cruisers, while von Spee, after annihilating Admiral Craddock's squadron off Coronel (during which the RCN suffered its first fatalities), was eventually destroyed by the RN off the Falklands in December.

Luckily for *Rainbow* and her crew, the RCN had to find other means of establishing a gallant tradition, and it would have to wait for another war. The Canadian government's policy of fielding a large expeditionary force in Europe kept the RCN from making a significant contribution to the war at sea during 1914–18. By the latter date, the navy's strength stood at only nine thousand all ranks. Its vitally important work in trade control, intelligence, and the 'East-Coast Patrol' (of small armed yachts and trawlers) did nothing to bring the RCN public notice, particularly in light of the signal accomplishments of the Canadian Corps on the Western front.[1] For Canada, military tradition meant battalions, not ships. Germany supplanted the United States as the nation's principal enemy, and the RN's firm grip on the North Atlantic allowed the wholesale transfer of Canada's continental military tradition to the new land frontier of the Rhine.[2]

Anti-war sentiment, isolationism, and serious economic difficulties haunted the navy's inter-war years. Immediate post-war planning for a sizeable Canadian fleet came to naught. Although Canada acquired one modern cruiser, two destroyers, and several submarines as gifts from Britain, by 1922 the fleet was reduced to one destroyer and two trawlers per coast. The bare minimum – a 'two-ocean navy' that became the butt of much jesting within Canada and, in particular, within the Royal Navy – saw the RCN through the twenties. As the decade drew to a close, there was reason for quiet optimism. In 1929 the government of W.L. Mac-kenzie King doubled the navy estimates, which allowed the construction of two new destroyers. *Saguenay* and *Skeena*, the first warships ever built specifically for the RCN, were commissioned in 1931 and held the promise of better days. However, just two years later, at the height of the Great Depression, the navy's fortunes reached their nadir. In 1933 the chief of staff, Major General A.G.L. McNaughton, acting in response to the realities of Depression economics, suggested that one service be abandoned to preserve the others. Clearly the army would have to remain, and in the new age of air power and the air exploration of Canada's last frontiers the air force too was vital. By simple elimination it was proposed to cast the RCN 'out of the sleigh to save the other two.'[3]

Fortunately, the idea of scrapping the navy never gained ground, but the solution to the financing problem offered by Treasury Board was nearly as bad. Naval appropriations would simply be cut from two and a half million dollars to a half-million – enough to starve the RCN to death. The navy responded by threatening to pay off the fleet. The idea of a navy with no ships proved sufficiently embarrassing to allow the appropriations to pass, but clearly the navy never forgot its brush with extinction. The desire to build and maintain a credible naval service provided much of the impetus behind the RCN's wartime expansion. Better days lay ahead, in any event, when Mackenzie King was returned as prime minister in 1935 and the RCN – the child of an earlier Liberal administration – enjoyed favour as one of two services which could insulate Canada from growing world tensions.

It was shortly after this brush with extinction that then Captain Percy W. Nelles, RCN, the officer who was to lead the navy through most of the war, took over as chief of the Naval Staff. Born the son of a brigadier general in Brantford, Ontario, in 1892, Nelles did his early training in the fisheries-protection cruiser *Canada* just prior to the founding of the

RCN. His First World War experience was almost exclusively aboard British cruisers involved in trade protection in the Atlantic and Caribbean. Most of his post-war service was also with the RN, culminating in command of HMS *Dragon* of the America and West Indies Squadron in 1929. His first RCN command was HMCS *Saguenay*, which he took over upon her commissioning in 1931. After spending 1933 at the Imperial Defence College, Nelles was appointed acting chief of the Naval Staff on 1 January 1934. Promoted to commodore seven months later, he was confirmed as CNS in November, and there he remained for ten years.

The job of chief of the Canadian Naval Staff during the pre-war years was not an onerous one. As one later CNS observed, Nelles took on the task 'when it wasn't much.' A diminutive and rather dour man, his long face adorned by small round glasses, Nelles resembled the senior clerk of an old family firm, and his duties in the 1930s were not dissimilar. Undoubtedly the social responsibilities of being CNS outweighted the professional ones. Not surprisingly, then, Mrs Nelles was considered a more formidable character than her husband. Rear Admiral H.N. Lay, RCN, recalls in his *Memoirs* that when Naval Service Headquarters sought to expand in the early months of the war, it was considered prudent to search for accommodation off premises rather than tilt with Mrs Nelles and ask the Naval Officers' Wives to vacate the offices they occupied.

Whatever might be said about the impact of naval wives on the development of the RCN (and Mrs Nelles was not an isolated case), Nelles made a good job of his tenure as CNS. An anglophile, and later described as an 'Imperial Navy man,'[4] by 1938 he was the youngest rear admiral in the British Commonwealth and had built the RCN into a respectable service. Strength at the time of the Munich Crisis stood at six modern destroyers – a half-flotilla – enough for the defence of one coast at least, though the force had to be split between two. *Saguenay* and *Skeena* were joined in 1937 by two former Admiralty C-class destroyers, *Fraser* and *St Laurent*, purchased from the RN. Two more destroyers of the same class, renamed *Ottawa* and *Restigouche*, were purchased in 1938. Negotiations were also under way to acquire a seventh destroyer, the leader HMS *Kempenfelt*. Arrangements were completed by October 1939, and the ship commissioned into the RCN as *Assiniboine*. These River-class destroyers formed the backbone of the RCN until well into 1943. Significantly, none of them was built in Canada. A modest attempt was made to give Canadian yards some experience at building warships in the minesweeper program of 1938. Despite the dispersal of the contracts for four Fundy-class ships (two per coast and all in different yards), the

Canadian shipbuilding industry was unprepared for the demands wartime construction was to make of it.

The acquisition of a few modern destroyers and a small number of purpose-built minesweepers did not mark the end of pre-war expansion plans. In January 1939 the government, reacting to the Munich crisis, announced its intention to proceed with building a fleet capable of defending Canada's two coasts. The expansion plan, when completed, would give the RCN a strength of eighteen modern destroyers, sixteen minesweepers, and eight anti-submarine vessels, the numbers split evenly between Pacific and Atlantic commands, and a flotilla of eight motor torpedo boats (MTBS) for the east coast.[5] Not surprisingly, little came of this plan before war broke out. In fact, by May the government had sharply cut the navy's estimates. The 1939 building program (four anti-submarine vessels and two motor torpedo boats) was scrapped, and there was just enough money left to acquire the necessary plans. It is, however, significant that the RCN's expansion plans were actually laid down in the last days of peace. Later developments thrust a new form of expansion on the RCN, one more easily attainable in wartime than a fleet of destroyers, yet one which did not conform to the long-term goals of the professional navy.

The January 1939 expansion plan belied the fact that the RCN was a traditional, gun-oriented navy. The experiences of the First World War and technological developments since had confirmed the sanctity of the gun as the pre-eminent naval weapon. Admittedly, the threat from Germany's U-boats in 1917 had been grave. But her indiscriminate use of the submarine had brought the United States into the conflict on the Allied side and (or so it seemed) therefore cost Germany the war. It was felt that in future no nation would risk the sanction of a world coalition by resorting to 'piracy' on the high seas. But even if Germany, or any other nation, turned once again to unrestricted submarine warfare on merchant shipping, the means of defeating the threat lay at the fingertips of the Commonwealth navies – convoy and 'asdic.'

The adoption of mercantile convoys in 1917 had saved the Allies from collapse. Hitherto, German submarines had been free to rove their patrol areas with impunity. Operating primarily on the surface and using their precious torpedoes sparingly, U-boats had sunk most of their poorly armed targets with gunfire. With the introduction of convoys, the seas were cleared of these easy targets, and the proximity of the naval escort forced the U-boat either to fight an unequal surface battle or to operate submerged. As a consequence, the convoy system made the oceanic routes safe, but any 'success' in defeating the submarine menace was partly illusory. Ships continued to sail independently and unescorted to and from convoy-assembly ports in Great Britain, and U-boats resorted to submerged tactics inshore. Although they never again threatened Britain with defeat, losses to shipping from U-boats remained high for the balance of the war largely because of the immunity of a submerged submarine.[6]

With the U-boats relegated to nuisance status through the use of convoy, their final telling defeat simply awaited the perfection of a reliable underwater-detection device. The Allied Submarine Detection Investigation Committee was established in 1918 to resolve this problem, but it was not until the early twenties that an effective underwater sound locating and ranging set (now called sonar) was in use. 'Asdic,' as the British called the device, was felt to spell the doom of the submarine. As late as 1936 the First Sea Lord of the Admiralty, Admiral A.E.M. Chatfield, claimed that the RN's anti-submarine measures were 80 per cent effective. With location no longer a problem, it was believed that destruction of a submarine by a few well-placed depth charges would follow with equal certainty.

On the eve of the Second World War the submarine was therefore considered by the RN to be a manageable problem. The same held true in the RCN. In a pre-war analysis of the threats to trade and possible countermeasures, Commodore Nelles summarized Canadian reaction to the submarine in two brief paragraphs:

If international law is complied with, Submarine attack should not prove serious.

If unrestricted warfare is again resorted to, the means of combating Submarines are considered to have so advanced that by employing a system of convoy and utilizing Air Forces, losses of Submarines would be very heavy and might compel the enemy to give up this form of attack.[8]

Nelles went on to point out that the RCN would provide anti-submarine equipment and mines 'for prosecution of offensive measures against submarine attack.' His choice of words illustrates clearly the thinking of his naval contemporaries on how best to deal with submarines – offensive action. The countermeasures outlined by the CNS indicated that some lessons had been drawn from the previous war, and in the long term the combination of convoy, air power, and aggressive anti-submarine warfare proved more than a match for the U-boats. Unfortunately, Britain and her allies lacked the necessary means for a very long time, and the resilience of modern submarines proved a surprise to virtually everyone.

If anything, Canadian planners, like those elsewhere, were absorbed by the unknown dangers of air attack on trade (particularly on convoys) and by the very real threat of powerful enemy surface raiders. Both of these also presented Canada with the only real threat of direct enemy action. The RCN was therefore charged with defence against surface and air attacks on Canada and on trade in adjacent waters – the two were really inseparable. The 'forms and scales of attack to which Canada would be subject,' as anticipated in 1939, reflected the preoccupation with surface and air threats.[9]. Bombardment by a single battleship and / or one or two large cruisers, by armed merchant cruisers (AMCs), or even by heavily gunned submarines was felt likely. Attacks could also be expected in the form of MTBs launched from larger ships, mines, small assault parties, or aircraft carrying torpedoes, bombs, or gas. Indeed, it was thought that aircraft launched from remote points along the Canadian coast might penetrate as far inland as Toronto. Certainly, the major coastal centres were in danger of quick and unexpected raids.

The expansion plan of January 1939 was naturally intended to counter these threats. To make good its intentions, the navy hoped to acquire the most powerful destroyers then in service, the Tribal class. The Tribal's high speed and heavy armament (eight 4.7-inch guns and four torpedo tubes) made it a veritable 'pocket' cruiser, and several acting in concert posed a credible threat to a lone battleship. Not surprisingly, the RCN pursued its policy of acquiring Tribals throughout the Second World War, eventually absorbing dockyard space, resources, and trained manpower which could have been better used to maintain the escort fleet.

The RCN also shared the RN's cautious attitude towards the need for mercantile convoys in any future conflict. Although the Commonwealth made elaborate preparations for the establishment of trade convoys, many believed and most hoped that it would be unnecessary to undertake the enormous responsibility they represented. As in the First World War, the British government of the 1930s was under pressure from shipping lobbies to follow a trade-as-usual policy in time of war. 'I can assure the House,' the parliamentary secretary to the Admiralty told the British Commons in 1935, 'that the convoy system would not be introduced at once on the outbreak of war.'[10] A similar attitude prevailed in the RCN. Convoys were well down the list of protective measures outlined by Nelles in 1939, coming after diversive routing, provision of AMCs to cruise the sea lanes, control of navigational aids and wireless, and *ruses de guerre*. Even then convoys were to be established only 'if and where necessary.'[11]

The remarkable thing about British and Canadian attitudes towards convoys and submarines is that both were largely substantiated by developments in the first year of the war. Thus planning in the RCN and the RN was based on sound contemporary considerations. That they failed to anticipate what the submarine and its directing authorities were capable of owed more to a preoccupation with Germany's surface fleet and a measure of wishful thinking than to service intransigence.

The navy's concern for traditional naval tasks was also reflected in its training. With the exception of individual ship exercises and familiarization with home waters, the RCN's real training took place alongside units of the RN's Bermuda-based America and West Indies (A&WI) Squadron. During the first months of each year the navy gave up the cold northern climate for the azure blue of the Caribbean. In those placid waters the Atlantic and Pacific destroyers of the RCN were brought together and trained in fleet tactics. Invariably, the Canadian warships formed a portion of a destroyer flotilla and busied themselves with screening the battle line, laying smoke, or launching massed torpedo attacks on the 'enemy' fleet.[12] All of this was good basic naval training, though it bore virtually no resemblance to the type of war the Canadian navy was about to fight.

Finally, the resources available to the RCN, in both manpower and material, were wholly inadequte to meet even the most basic of home-defence tasks in 1939. A study by the director of Naval Intelligence and Plans, dated October 1938, revealed that the RCN was 434 officers short of the 684 required to establish the eight defended ports and their associated staffs as outlined in the mobilization plan.[13] As a result of this enormous shortfall, new reserve programs, such as the Fisherman's Reserve were instituted. But here, too, little was achieved by the outbreak of war. In March 1939 Nelles informed the British admiral at Bermuda that he should not rely on Canadian personnel to bring his ships up to wartime establishment. The RCN would do well, the CNS explained, to see to its own needs.[14] If such was ever official RCN policy, it died a quick and silent death very early in the war.

1

The Road to the Isles

It is worth recalling here that building ships is a slow business, the training of sailors even slower. Armies are improvised much more rapidly than Navies, and a coast which is undefended in peacetime will be undefended in war.

C.P. Stacey, *The Military Problems of Canada* (1940)

The first year of the war at sea developed as Allied planners had anticipated. Germany's U-boat fleet was small and remained so. Its operational strength of forty-six submarines (only twenty-two of which were capable of deep-sea work) was far short of the three hundred U-boats that Rear Admiral Karl Dönitz, *Befehlshaber der U-boote* (BdU; commander-in-chief of U-boats), estimated he needed to sever Britain's supply lines.[1] Moreover, the U-boat fleet was initially circumscribed by Allied control of the exits from the North Sea. In the early months of the war U-boat captains generally obeyed their strict instructions not to anger neutral opinion by rash and illegal acts, despite the torpedoing of the liner *Athenia* on the first day of the war, which suggested that Germany would adopt unrestricted submarine warfare. So the Allies concentrated on Germany's powerful surface fleet, on her commerce raiders lurking in disguise on the oceans of the world, and on hapless offensive anti-submarine (A/S) sweeps.

Until the winter of 1940–1, when Germany began to make good use of the excellent new bases in France and adopted new U-boat tactics, nothing shook the belief that the U-boat had been mastered by a combination of asdic, convoys, and air power. Indeed, in a book on *Modern Naval Strategy* published by Admiral Sir Reginald Bacon, RN, and F.E. McMurtrie, two well-respected naval theorists, in mid-1940,[2] submarine attack on an escorted convoy was given little chance of success. Supposing the submariner could find the convoy in the first place, his distorted view of the world through a periscope was considered a grave handicap. With a periscope exposed in broad daylight – the only time, the authors believed, that an attack was possible – the submarine invited swift retribution from both escort and merchant ship alike. Moreover, it was still generally believed that once a submarine was locked in asdic's grip, destruction would follow easily from a few well-placed depth charges. This view of anti-submarine warfare (ASW) was utterly shattered by the Germans' resourceful use of U-boats in the second winter campaign on the sea lanes.

By May 1941 the U-boat threat to Atlantic trade routes was clearly the most dangerous, a fact confirmed by the tragic sortie of the *Bismarck*. The loss of that great ship on her first operational cruise effectively ended German hopes of maintaining a credible surface threat to Britain's main trade routes. In a little less than two years the fundamental character of the war at sea was changed. Plans laid down in an era when surface fleets were the major opponent now had to be modified to meet a new, unorthodox form of naval warfare. All of these developments had a marked effect on the RCN. Its desire to plan and build a conventional navy based on powerful destroyers was admirably suited to the first months of the war. However, before the RCN could put these expansion plans into effect, the U-boat campaign on Allied shipping came to dominate events at sea, and the RCN's auxiliary fleet of small ships was called upon to carry the burden of operations against the enemy.

By 10 September 1939, when the Canadian government officially declared war on Germany, the Second World War was already a week old. The RCN, in fact, had been 'at war' longer still. The first mobilization calls went out on 28 August as the navy established its coastal defences and defended ports. The fleet too was placed on a war footing at the end of August, and by the time the country was legally at war, all sections of the RCN, including the reserves – 3684 all ranks – were either on duty or on their way to the coast.[3] Among the first tasks which faced the naval staff was the disposition of the fleet. Two-thirds of it was deployed on the west coast, in deference to the more evident threats from imperial Japan. Immediate steps were taken to rectify this situation. *Fraser* and *St Laurent* were despatched on 31 August to join *Saguenay* and *Skeena* on the east coast. The navy also sought to place the east-coast destroyers at the disposal of the commander-in-chief, A&WI, the nearest British flag officer. This was a natural course of action for the RCN, since its fleet was too small to ensure proper defence of Canada and its peacetime links with the squadron were strong. Operating directly under the C-in-C, A&WI, the navy would also have been assured of the type of duties for which it had been trained: fleet work, or sweeps in search of raiders. However, while this all made good sense to naval officers, it was not in keeping with the government's intention that Canada should play an independent military role. The notion that the navy should participate in some form of Commonwealth force was rejected, and the RCN was instructed to keep its ships home. Bowing to the inevitable, the RCN began using its powerful and fairly modern destroyers to escort trade convoys in the approaches to Halifax harbour.[4]

In the government the navy actually had a friend, as it discovered when planners began to submit estimates for expansion. As the late Admiral L.W. Murray, RCN (in September 1939 the director of Operations and Training), recalled, the navy was given carte blanche to plan its growth over the succeeding four or five years. When in February 1940 Murray and the deputy minister presented the first wartime naval estimates before the Finance Committee of the cabinet, they passed despite a 'fine-tooth comb' inspection.[5] The fact was that the navy's expansion and its attendant shipbuilding programs suited the government's intention to profit materially from what was seen as a limited European war. The prime minister, W.L. Mackenzie King, was steadfastly opposed to fielding yet another large army in Europe, which might lead to high casualties and a call for conscription. Rather, his government sought to channel Canada's war effort into the sinews of war and into much less personnel-intensive services such as the air force and the navy.[6] Both of these services also offered excellent opportunities for the development of Canadian industry.

The link between industrial and naval expansion also went deeper than simply the building of ships. In July 1940 the expansion of the navy was given impetus by the appointment of a separate minister of Defence for the Naval Service. King chose Angus L. Macdonald, former premier of Nova Scotia. Although once rather uncharitably described as 'lightweight,' Macdonald was extremely popular in his home province and a strong voice for Nova Scotia in Ottawa. Macdonald and two other prominent Nova Scotians, Colonel J.L. Ralston, the minister of Defence, and J.L. Ilsley, the minister of National Revenue, formed the right wing of King's cabinet – what J.W. Dafoe called the 'Tory imperialists.' All supported a full war effort, a position that led in 1944 to a bitter break between King and the two defence ministers over the issue of conscription. But apart from Macdonald's desire to see Canada fully represented at the front, he shared many of King's beliefs, including the notion that the preservation of the free world depended upon the retention of power in Canada by the Liberal party.

Macdonald also believed that Canada could and should progress industrially from the war. Long a crusader for the reindustrialization of Nova Scotia, he saw an opportunity to funnel some of government investment into his own province. There was, moreover, a direct link between industrial growth and a large navy. 'What use could it be to increase our agricultural production ... or to put forth the magnificent industrial effort that we have,' Macdonald asked in 1945, 'unless this food and these munitions could be got safely across the sea?'[7] Although in the end he failed to restore to Nova Scotia its past lustre, this was precisely the rationale used to justify the building of destroyers in Halifax during the war. In the most fundamental sense, then, the aspirations of the navy and the government coincided.

While the operational side of the navy chafed at the bit, the shore side got on with the daunting work of expansion. The first task was to provide both personnel and ships for the system of defended ports. Acquisition of the ships was a manageable problem, though the results were far from satisfactory. By the end of 1939 the RCN had managed to beg, borrow, or buy over sixty auxiliary vessels of all shapes and sizes, enough to fill out the minesweeping, anti-submarine, and harbour duties of the defended ports. Many of the ships were unreliable or unsuitable for their assigned roles and therefore badly needed replacement. In fact, few were worthy of long-term service in any but the most menial of tasks.

The bulk of the auxiliary vessels taken into the RCN came from other government departments. Manning them posed no problem because most of the ships' crewmen transferred to naval service, enlisting in the RCN Reserves, Special Service, which respected their peculiar skills (for example, ice clearance). Retired officers of the Royal Navy resident in Canada, of whom about forty were designated for duty with the RCN, also helped fill the gap in manpower.[8] With the dispatch of the second – and final – draft of volunteer reservists (RCNVR) to the coast on 10 September, the RCN exhausted its cadre of readily available and 'trained' personnel. The first plan for further mobilization was tabled on 17 September and called for an active strength of 5472 all ranks by the end of March 1940, rising to seven thousand by the same date in 1941.[9] As with other personnel projections in the early months of the war, this first one was based on the needs of home defence and the availability of ships. The RCN proved rather successful at cobbling together its auxiliary fleet, and the projections for March 1940 were surpassed much earlier. Yet, despite this early trend towards rapid growth, expansion in 1939 and 1940 was choked by shortages of every conceivable type. Sailors went without proper naval uniforms because no one foresaw, at the end of 1939, that the navy's strength would rise to ten thousand by September 1940. Further, until 1943 the 'key to expansion' – as the Naval Staff liked to call it – was the shortage of training staff, a shortfall which the RN proved unwilling to help alleviate.[10]

What the navy badly wanted were skilled men: men whom they were losing in large numbers to the other two services, particularly the air force. For the RCN did not even have the necessary housing to take in the throngs of eager and qualified volunteers waiting to join up. The problem occasioned debate at the first Naval Staff meeting in January 1940. The urgent need for temporary accommodation was stressed, 'in order that recruiting programme could be proceeded with before the new rapidly expanding RCAF seized all the best – and particularly skilled men.'[11] The RCN also found that it had to lower the minimum age of entry from twenty-one to nineteen in order to counter the ravages of the air force on available manpower.

Despite the struggle over manpower and the navy's reluctance to expand too quickly, the growth of the navy soon acquired a snowball effect which it seemed incapable – or perhaps undesirous – of firmly controlling. At the end of 1939 the Naval Staff anticipated a completed wartime strength (after three years) of 1500 officers and 15,000 ratings.[12] This figure was reached and passed in half the time. But the really hectic pace of expansion did not begin until after the fall of France and Norway. Up to that point the RCN planned a very deliberate and selective growth, as Vice-Admiral Nelles, CNS, explained to the minister of Defence, Norman Rogers, in January 1940.

Rogers had broached the subject of giving preferences in RCNVR commissions to members of prominent yacht clubs. In an illuminating statement Nelles made it clear to the minister what role 'Sunday sailors' would play in Canada's war at sea. 'The RCN is in need of many men before this war is over,' Nelles wrote, 'but the [types] of ships suitable to Canadian service conditions [Tribal-class destroyers or small inshore-patrol ships] are more suited to the employment of professional seamen than of amateur small boat yachtsmen.'[13] The CNS's comment was no idle remark on an easily dismissed subject. Earlier in the same day Nelles had received a memorandum from his director of Naval Personnel, who, no doubt responding to the minister's inquiry, refused to countenance the mythical value of 'Sunday sailors.' Yachting, the DNP reported to his chief, had about as much to do with the qualifications of a modern naval officer as kite flying had to do with the needs of the air force.[14] None the less, in order to find employment for these eager warriors, Nelles informed Rogers that he was prepared to release fifty young yachts-men to the RN 'to serve in the more interesting appointments overseas and represent Canada at the scene of active operations.'[15] His words suggest clearly what Nelles and the navy felt of keeping the fleet in home waters. In terms of manpower this option offered an alternative to simply turning recruits away, and they would not be lost to either Canada or the war effort. The loan scheme was approved, and it was initially decided to send all RCNVR recruits in excess of 4500 to serve in the RN. Though this plan was later drastically altered, the incident illustrates the selective nature of the navy's expansion before the fall of Western Europe, the desire to participate in the 'active' theatre, and the problems inherent in trying to expand from too small a base.

Fundamental to the whole problem of expansion was the availability of ships, and here too the RCN's plans in the early days were never reliable. To upgrade local defences, to replace decrepit auxiliary vessels, and to provide A/S 'strike forces,' the RCN had to undertake a modest shipbuilding program beyond that proposed in the pre-war plans. To round out local defences and the like it was decided in early September 1939 to build Bramble-class sloops and a small number of minesweepers. Further con-sideration was also given to the acquisition of Tribal-class destroyers. But the coming of war so early in the navy's planned expansion threw it into serious disarray. Tribals could not be built in Canada without considerable assistance from British firms, and with British industry now fully absorbed in war work little help could be expected. Unfortunately, the RCN rejected a very sensible British suggestion that it seek expertise in naval ship construction in the United States. The Canadian navy also failed, initially, to obtain permission to place orders for Tribals in British yards. Faced with an almost impossible dilemma, the Naval Staff hit upon the idea of bartering less-sophisticated Canadian-built warships for British-built destroyers. The scheme had all the advantages of speciali-zation. It permitted Canada to turn products from less-skilled manufac-turers into high-value, long-term investments. For the government it meant good business and the possibility of future orders. For the RCN it meant the fulfilment of its expansion plans.

As the Naval Staff sorted through the problems of destroyer acquisition, it also tackled the question of what type of auxiliary warship to build for its own purposes and what type to build for bartering. Initial hopes of building sloops were dashed by the news that Canadian yards were incapable of building even small warships to naval standards. As the problem was being discussed, basic plans for a much simpler auxiliary ship arrived at Naval Service Headquarters (NSHQ) from the National Research Council, which had acquired plans for 'whale-catchers' in July during a fact-finding trip to the UK. The whale-catchers immediately appealed to the Naval Staff as a workable substitute for sloops, given that they were intended to be auxiliary vessels for inshore duty. Moreover, their mercantile construction was ideally suited to Canadian yards, and British adoption of this class made them suitable for bartering.

Once agreed that corvettes (as the whale-catchers were called by early 1940) were to be built as the navy's primary A/S ship and as the means whereby larger vessels might be acquired, the Naval Staff had to decide how many to produce. For purely RCN purposes forty A/S vessels were needed over three years. Since some of the requisitioned ships were suitable for local duties, not all of the new vessels needed to be corvettes. It was also necessary to establish a rate of exchange if the smaller ships were to be bartered for Tribals. Quick resolution of these issues was essential if the full complement of the RCN's first expansion phase – two Tribals, twenty corvettes, and twelve minesweepers – was to be in commission by the spring of 1940, as the Naval Staff hoped.

The RCN did not get off the mark as quickly as it had wished. Detailed drawings needed to begin construction of corvettes did not arrive from Britain until early 1940. The placing of orders was also complicated by the requirement that the navy deal with contractors through a third party, the War Purchasing Board (later the Department of Munitions and Supply). In fact, the lack of official links to manufacturers and the interposition of another department between NSHQ and industry seriously complicated the process of modifying specifications in light of changing requirements. The first orders for corvettes to Canadian accounts therefore were not placed until February, when contracts were let for fifty-four. Of these, only twenty-four, or perhaps thirty-four (roughly the equivalent of the first expansion phase), were intended for the RCN. The remainder were to be bartered for destroyers. Ten more corvettes were ordered by the RCN before the end of the month as replacements for war-weary ships and to maintain a steady rate of construction. By the end of February the issuance of contracts for what became known as the first construction program was completed: sixty-four corvettes and twenty-four Bangor minesweepers (for which it was not possible to find enough contractors until August). Thus, when the barter scheme fell through in March 1940 because an exchange rate could not be agreed upon, the navy found itself 'holding contracts for considerably more corvettes than it intended to build.'

The vast majority of the orders, contracts for which had only just been signed, could have been cancelled. The size of the RCN program was actually reduced by transferring ten contracts to the British Admiralty, at its own request, for eventual commissioning into the RN. The total of corvettes still on order for the RCN – fifty-four – was only seven more than the number required for the full three-year expansion program. For this reason, as well as political and economic ones, the orders were allowed to stand. Indeed, in August a further six corvettes (and ten Bangors) were authorized in order once again to maintain a steady rate of construction in the shipyards.

What this embarrassment of riches meant was an acceleration of the navy's hitherto cautious expansion plans and the jamming of three years' careful growth into less than two. Small wonder, then, that the personnel requirements overtook projections. Despite this, it is doubtful that the prospect of commissioning extra auxiliaries troubled anyone at NSHQ, particularly when the failure of the barter scheme was followed by the news that the British would allow the construction of Tribals to Canadian accounts in UK yards. The latter ensured that the main thrust of fleet expansion would go ahead. Two Tribals were duly ordered in early 1940 and two more in early 1941, but none was completed in time to meet the requirements of the first expansion phase. As an interim measure the navy requisitioned three small liners, *Prince David*, *Prince Henry*, and *Prince Robert*, and converted them to armed merchant cruisers. The *Prince* ships remained the RCN's most powerful units until the first of the UK-built Tribals was commissioned in early 1943.[16]

The matter of building Tribals in Canada was never wholly abandoned. The navy was well pleased with its arrangements of a British supply, but long-term plans called for more than four. In April 1941 the subject of building Tribals in Canada was discussed once again by the Naval Council (the administrative and policy body of the naval service, chaired by the minister, with senior Naval Staff officers as members). The engineer-in-chief, Captain G.L. Stephens, advised against attempting such complicated building in Canada in the middle of a war. It was bound to be a long and expensive proposition, he warned, if for no other reason than that it was hardly worth tooling up industry to produce specialized steel plate and equipment for so small an order. Moreover, Stephens believed, construction of Tribals was likely to tie up manpower and resources which could be better used. Nelles agreed with his engineer's views but felt that if such ships could be built in Canada, the navy should not waste its time on smaller 'stepping stones.'[17]

The problem had also been considered by the government. Macdonald was under considerable pressure from politicians and the press in his home province to secure wartime capital investment in Atlantic Canada. Indeed, although Canada was prospering from the war, an incredibly small percentage of new capital investment found its way eastward (just 2.5 per cent by 1944).[18] Of the major wartime ship contracts let by May 1941, only three – all corvettes ordered from Saint John Ship Building and Drydock Company – were placed in the Maritimes. Mackenzie King wanted contracts for merchant ships let to Halifax shipyards, but Macdonald preferred destroyers. Without the latter, he explained in a letter to C.D. Howe, the dynamic minister of Munitions and Supply, the merchant ships would not get through. Macdonald wanted building in Halifax 'confined to destroyers,' which were, 'all in all, the best type of escort.'[19] Howe, who had survived the sinking of the ss *Western Prince* in December 1940 while on his first trip to Britain as minister of Supply, needed no convincing of the need for ships – or for escorts. Further, Howe, like Macdonald, wanted some construction undertaken soon in order to stabilize the employment situation for ship-repair workers, and thereby establish a pool of skilled labour for use in an emergency. Since the government was determined to build something, the navy was happy to support the construction of Tribals. Owing largely to the need to retool industry, it was not until September 1942 that the first keel was laid, and in the rush to complete the hulls the Tribals drained manpower away from essential ship-repair tasks: quite the opposite of the original intention, and precisely the fear expressed by the navy's senior engineer.

By the time plans for the acquisition of Tribals from all sources were finalized, the war had changed from a limited European conflict to an all-out war of survival for Britain and her Commonwealth allies. But even before German panzers arrived at the English Channel, the Canadian government had lifted some of the restrictions imposed on the employment of the fleet. By early 1940 Canadian destroyers were permitted to operate with the America and West Indies Squadron, thereby freeing cruisers to act as ocean escorts for convoys sailing from Halifax. Undoubtedly the alteration of this policy owed something to the stationing at Halifax of the RN's Third Battle Squadron, a force of aged battleships and light cruisers intended to provide anti-raider protection for mercantile convoys and more than sufficient to guarantee a credible deterrence along Canada's Atlantic coast. The alteration of the previous policy also inaugurated the principle of loaning ships to the RN, which became 'for a considerable period the dominant element of RCN policy.'[20]

The government's change of heart not only suited the navy's burning desire to join in the 'active operations' of more distant waters but was also perhaps a response to public pressure for a more active involvement in the war. In April 1940, before the invasion of Norway began, Mackenzie King confessed to his diary that the pride of the nation demanded that Canada increase its military commitment overseas from a division to a full corps. The slow expansion of the navy could not keep pace with the national desire to take up where the Canadian Corps had left off in 1918. Even Colonel Ralston, the minister of Defence, confessed that the military involvement in the war would have to grow, although 'we could have used our money more effectively if it had been confined to air and naval matters.' Canadians, the prime minister's private secretary wrote years after the war, remained remote from the war, 'despite the very large part Canadian airmen and sailors were taking in actual combat,' until the army landed in Sicily in July 1943.[21] The great irony of unpreparedness in peace was that it severely limited what could be done in war, and it has always been easier and faster to raise battalions than to build ships. It was a trap which Mackenzie King sought but failed to avoid. Indeed, the 'Phony War' was one of drudgery for the navy, aside from its participation in the capture of the German merchant ship *Hannover* in the Caribbean. Shuttling back and forth in the approaches to Halifax harbour, essential as it was, was hardly the work for which destroyers were intended.

For the eager warriors and adventurers of the RCN this tiresome duty was not destined to last. Even as the British Expeditionary Force fought to disengage itself and form a secure position from which to evacuate the continent, NSHQ received a formal request for assistance from the Admiralty. The fall of France left some senior Canadian politicians, Mackenzie King among them, more concerned than ever for the vulnerability of Canada's vast coastline. However, both the Canadian Chiefs of Staff and the British, including Prime Minister Churchill (by whose opinion Mackenzie King set great store), were able to convince the Canadian prime minister that Canada's first line of defence was the English Channel. At the end of May the destroyers *Restigouche*, *Skeena*, and *St Laurent* proceeded in company from Halifax to Britain, followed by *Fraser*, routed independently from the Caribbean via Bermuda. The three other River-class destroyers, *Assiniboine*, *Ottawa*, and *Saguenay*, were to follow after the completion of refits.[22]

From June until early fall Canada's destroyers formed part of the anti-invasion fleet based in the Channel. Here, working in flotillas or half-flotillas against a very real and well-understood threat, they found destroyer warfare at its most demanding. Four years later in the same waters the RCN's destroyers would earn a well-deserved reputation for excellence in such operations. In the interim, however, a very different kind of war had to be fought and won. The summer of 1940, then, represented a break in the continuity of convoy-escort work as begun in September 1939. This fleeting foray into traditional naval warfare assuredly whet the navy's appetite for more of the same and, at the same time, firmly established the policy of full aid to the RN.

Aside from the loss of *Fraser*, sliced in half by the cruiser *Calcutta* (RN) off the French coast in June 1940, the anti-invasion operations of the fleet were largely uneventful. Meanwhile, on the home front, the government was busy securing replacements for the destroyers dispatched overseas. Mackenzie King was involved from the outset in the famous 'destroyers for bases' deal, whereby the British traded base right in the Western Hemisphere for fifty First World War–vintage U.S. destroyers. The Americans were also pressing for base rights in Canada, and President Roosevelt wanted Canada to take over some of the destroyers assigned to Britain. The Canadian government was not about to entangle itself in the granting of base rights in exchange for a few ancient warships, but Mackenzie King made it clear to Roosevelt that Canada would entertain offers from the British.[23] While the three governments sorted out the details, the RCN was authorized to increase its complement in the event that some ships were forthcoming. The navy's reaction to the prospect of acquiring a handful of tired, outdated American cast-offs was less than enthusiastic. The ships were no suitable replacement for the River class now serving in British waters, and they were of no long-term value whatsoever. Rear Admiral H.G. DeWolf, who as an acting captain was director of Operations in Halifax in the late summer of 1940, recalls that the ex-American destroyers were only grudgingly accepted by the RCN after repeated Admiralty pleas that the Canadians take on more.[24] In the end the RCN commissioned six into service as HMC ships – *Annapolis*, *Columbia*, *Niagara*, *St Clair*, *St Croix*, and *St Francis* – and wholly or partially manned several others. At a time when any ship was better than none, Town-class destroyers (following the British decision to name them after town names shared by the U.S. and the UK – the RCN adopted the names of border rivers) filled a pressing need in the defence of Canada and her trade. Although seldom loved and more frequently hated by those condemned to sail in them, and ill-suited for modern ASW, the Towns eventually formed a crucial element of the fleet's escort forces by virtue of their high speed and heavy armament.

As the Towns were being taken into Canadian service, the navy's River-class destroyers returned to convoy-escort duties. With U-boats now operating from the Atlantic littoral and with the adoption of pack tactics, losses to convoyed shipping mounted during the late summer of 1940. From the outbreak of war until February 1940 only seven of the 169 Allied ships lost to enemy action had come from convoys. When, in August, U-boats began attacking convoys at night, the subs travelling on the surface in torpedo-boat fashion, losses from protected shipping skyrocketed. In September alone forty of the fifty-nine U-boat attacks on shipping were directed at convoy targets.[25] With the adoption of these tactics by the Germans the Battle of the Atlantic, as it captured the popular imagination and forms the basis of this study, finally began.

The intensification of the U-boat campaign on Allied shipping eventually forced a reallocation of ships to escort duty. Among the first to go were the five RCN destroyers still serving in UK waters: *Assiniboine*, *Ottawa*, *Restigouche*, *St Laurent*, and *Saguenay* (*Skeena* was refitting at Halifax). They sailed north to join the Clyde Escort Force in September, where they were briefly joined by *Fraser*'s ill-fated replacement, *Margaree* – lost by collision on her first convoy operation. Alone or in groups of two, and often in company with British warships, the destroyers escorted small outward-bound convoys to their dispersal point, roughly 12–15° west, and then shepherded an in-bound convoy through shallow waters to its UK destination. It was while escorting one of these convoys to the westward of Ireland that *Saguenay* was torpedoed by the Italian submarine *Argo*. She lost fifty feet of her bow and twenty-one crewmen, but eventually made port in Britain and, fortunately for the RCN, lived to fight another day.

The fall and winter of 1940–1 was a peculiar time for escort operations, and pre-war concepts of trade defence and ASW were under strain. Losses to convoys were high, and authorities were baffled about effective countermeasures. There was a strong lobby within the RN, supported by Churchill while he was First Lord of the Admiralty and after he became prime minister, that favoured offensive action against U-boats by even the slenderest of escorts. The two schools of thought, one favouring active pursuit of the enemy and the other the primacy of escort, were still matters for debate when the Canadians joined the Clyde Escort Force in late 1940. Through the winter the issue was finally resolved in favour of defence as the first priority.[26] However, in light of the subsequent Canadian tendency to pursue even the most tenuous contacts with zeal, it is questionable if this exposure to nascent British escort tactics did the RCN much good.

Through the rest of 1940 and the early months of 1941 the RCN's destroyer forces remained committed to escort operations in Britain's Western Approaches. By January all the River-class ships and four of the Towns – two having been held back by defects – were operating from the Clyde. During this second winter of the war there were also Canadian corvettes in the Clyde Escort Force participating in the crucial battles of the first phase of U-boat pack attacks. These corvettes were actually the ten of their class built in Canada to British accounts. All were completed before the freeze-up of late 1940, and the RCN assumed responsibility for their acceptance from the builders, commissioning into the RN and manning for passage to the UK. Once in England the ships were to be handed over to the Admiralty. Unfortunately, things did not go as planned, and the RCN ended up taking all ten of these corvettes into Canadian service.

The story of the 'British' corvettes and their transfer to the RCN is an important one, for it illustrates the kind of problem the RCN had when dealing with the RN. Because the ships were manned for passage only, their crews were the barest minimum, roughly assembled from spare hands, all of whom were designated for other duties upon completion of the crossing. Personnel from the first corvettes to go, for example, were assigned to HMCS *Dominion*, the RCN's depot in Britain. They were to form a manning pool for the destroyers already on operations in British waters. Those from the later passages were to return immediately to commission new RCN corvettes. All ten 'British' corvettes were in the UK by early 1941 (the ships were named after flowers, following the Admiralty practice: *Arrowhead, Bittersweet, Eyebright, Fennel, Hepatica, Mayflower, Snowberry, Spikenard, Trillium,* and *Windflower*), but from the outset it proved impossible to obtain the release of their crews. As early as October 1940 *Dominion* requested, on behalf of the Admiralty, that the crews of three recently arrived corvettes be allowed to remain aboard until the end of November. Reliefs for destroyer personnel, it was explained, could be drawn from the smaller ships (in the form of a 'floating' pool) and the ships turned over to the RN in piecemeal fashion. NSHQ concurred, but no British replacements were forthcoming, and the issue remained unresolved. The corvettes, meanwhile, began escort operations with the Clyde force.[27]

By February 1941 the delay in the release of men from the British corvettes began to affect planning of the RCN's own expansion. Commodore G.C. Jones, RCN, commanding officer, Atlantic Coast (COAC), complained that the men should be returned to Canada before the opening of navigation on the St Lawrence River deluged the navy with new ships. 'If our present commitments are to be met,' Jones observed, 'it is essential this personnel be available.' He was advised by NSHQ that the matter was under review and that a decision was pending. Yet the issue lingered. In April the Admiralty petitioned the RCN to allow Canadian crews to remain aboard 'so as to avoid impairing their efficiency by having to recommission them.'[28] Since the ships were now operational, concern for their efficiency was justifiable. That escorts manned by skeleton crews and lacking many essential stores should have been committed to operations says a great deal about the tremendous need for escorts of any kind. It also suggests that communications between the RCN and the RN were not what they should have been.

The misunderstanding over the nature of the RCN's commitment to the ten British corvettes was to have long and serious repercussions. For the moment, the Admiralty's concern for the efficiency of escorts operating in the embattled Western Approaches took precedence over all else. The Canadians were advised not to worry about the effect that losing these men would have on the buildup of the RCN's own forces in the Western Atlantic. 'It is considered,' the Admiralty's signal went on to read, 'that present circumstances justify some delay in these becoming effective.'[29] Faced with the inevitable, the RCN acquiesced, so long as the ten corvettes were comissioned HMC ships. The Admiralty agreed and undertook to cover the costs and arrangements for refits, maintenance, and alterations and additions to equipment. The RCN was to look after running costs, pay, victuals, and the like (a similar arrangement existed with other Allied navies that undertook to man British warships fully themselves).

The ten British corvettes were the second group of ships thrust upon a reluctant RCN by the British in less than a year. By RN standards the attendant manpower requirements for the sixteen ships was not large (about 1200 all ranks), but their acquisition represented a major expansion for the RCN. The means whereby the corvettes came into Canadian service also illustrates what was for the RCN a recurrent problem, that of obtaining the release of both men and ships lent to the RN. This first incident may well have been an absent-minded assumption on the part of many British officers that the RCN was committed to some form of Commonwealth navy. Yet the reluctance of the RN to release much-needed RCN personnel was indicative of the condescending and paternalistic attitude of the parent service towards what was often regarded as the 'kindergarten.'[30] In the event, the RCN put up an honourable fight, better than many of its later attempts. But once committed to the common cause, it had little choice but to turn in the direction where the powers that be deemed its efforts would achieve the most good. Perhaps more serious, with respect to the pending struggle for efficiency in the RCN's own corvette fleet, was the Admiralty's insistence that the Canadian navy could accept a delay in attaining that efficiency. Ironically, a few short weeks later the British urgently requested that RCN corvettes be committed to convoy operations in the Northwest Atlantic. If Canada's naval expansion seemed to lack firm direction, it is small wonder.

Provision of officers and men for the navy's new escorts was of course a primary concern as 1940 drew to a close. Much of the RCN's disposable manpower went into commissioning the six Town-class destroyers and ten corvettes taken over from the Admiralty – sixteen warships for which the navy had made no provision mere months before. Naturally this meant that the planning and assignment of personnel for the first wave of RCN corvettes was set back. Further, with virtually the whole fleet on active duty on the other side of the Atlantic, the navy had no ongoing access either to experienced personnel or to berths on operational warships which could serve as training posts for new officers and key non-substantive ratings. With proper management (by no means guaranteed), a modest interchange of new drafts and experienced personnel would have permitted a more orderly expansion of the fleet and shore establishments and would have softened the devastating impact of expansion in 1941. The navy considered this problem, and the Staff discussed the possibility of routing the occasional destroyer to a Canadian port where personnel could be exchanged. But the Naval Staff concluded that 'it would be a most unwise policy to relieve any large percentage of a ship's company when that vessel was acting in a War Zone.'[31] The first RCN corvettes to become operational therefore were commissioned with scratch crews. Although the navy kept its sound policy of not tampering with escorts in a war zone, the conditions which obtained over the winter of 1940–1 changed by the following spring. By then the fleet was operating closer to home and, technically at least, no longer in a war zone.

In late 1940 the RCN was faced with building up the manpower needed to commisison fifty-four corvettes, twenty-five minesweepers, and a small number of motor launches – about seven thousand officers and men. In addition, it was also necessary to find personnel to man new shore establishments. Indeed, by early 1941 the latter took precedence over the needs of the fleet. Although the navy remained committed to increasing the number of escorts assigned to its first operational priority, defence of North Atlantic trade lanes, the gradual extension of the war underlined the paramount need for bases. 'Our primary object from the Naval point of view,' a Canadian Chiefs of Staff 'appreciation' of May 1941 observed, 'must therefore be the extension of existing facilities and the provision of new ones to meet the ever-increasing demands of British – and perhaps United States – Naval Forces.'[32] The expansion fleet was then only one part of a much broader plan of support for North Atlantic naval operations. Moreover, actual planning for the commissioning and work-up of the new escorts took place as the fleet assumed new and more demanding tasks.

The concern of the Chiefs of Staff for facilities underlined the fact that even by the second winter of the war the navy's growth was still held in check by enormous shortages. In the fall of 1940, for example, when the Naval Council met to discuss manpower requirements for the next spring (when the bulk of the new construction would begin to commission), the situation looked grim. The director of Naval Personnel, Captain H.T.W. Grant, informed the council that the RCN needed three hundred RCNVR executive officers – none of whom had yet been enlisted – if the authorized commitments for the following May were to be met. This was no mean task in itself, but the Naval Council noted that the training establishments needed to prepare the men had to be built first. The final twist occurred when the minister advised that the navy must first take steps to acquire the necessary land![33] As Nelles later explained in a personal letter to Admiral Sir Dudley Pound, the First Sea Lord, the RCN was indeed making bricks without straw.[34] The truth was that the navy's initial modest plans for expansion, which amounted to using a limited European war as a means of fulfilling the naval program announced by the government in January 1939, had been overtaken by events. The primary need was now quantity in all aspects of naval endeavour – manpower, ships, and bases.

With existing training establishments choked and new ones still in the planning stages, the provision of personnel for the expanding fleet posed a serious problem. Urgency was added to Canadian planning in late 1940, when it became clear that Britain was involved in what Nelles described as 'a Naval Crisis equal [to] or greater than that which existed in 1917.'[35] The German perfection of U-boat pack tactics had apparently confirmed the worst fears of those who believed that convoys offered convenient, massed targets, difficult or even impossible to defend adequately. No clear solution to the problem was at hand. With the commissioning of the vast majority of the Canadian escort program unlikely before mid-1941, there was little the RCN could do to help. There was, however, one option that would aid the RN and ease the Canadian training problem: to formalize the existing arrangement for the loan of personnel to the British. The new scheme, authorized in early 1941, allowed the RCN to loan VR officers to the British for training at HMS *King Alfred*, the reservist training centre at Hove. The great irony of the scheme was that it proved virtually impossible to draw on this body of highly trained Canadian naval officers later on, when the RCN was badly in need of qualified personnel. Certainly, the *King Alfred* plan did nothing to resolve the shortage of qualified officers that crippled the fleet in 1941.

Another aspect of proper planning was work-up and operational-training facilities for the fleet, particularly with respect to ASW. As early as November 1940 the British complained of the poor state of A/S proficiency in Canadian destroyers operating from UK bases.[36] The Naval Staff were already aware of the problem, and the Naval Council agreed that one or two submarines were needed for the RCN as a useful 'adjunct to training.' But of course the navy had had none of its own since 1922, and now it lacked the expertise to man and maintain such craft. There was, however, one submarine currently operating on the east coast, the Dutch *O-15*, as part of the Third Battle Squadron. At the end of November the Naval Staff formally requested that *O-15* be made available for A/S training. For the moment the Admiralty refused, although some A/S exercises were conducted with her late in the year. Unable to obtain satisfaction from British sources, the RCN turned to the U.S., where preliminary investigations into acquiring an old USN submarine were made in early 1941. Commodore H.E. Reid, the naval attaché in Washington, raised the matter with the new Permanent Joint U.S.-Canadian Board of Defence and then set about beating the bushes in more obscure parts of the American capital. By the end of January it was clear that no submarines of any description would be forthcoming from American sources. The only gesture of assistance that the USN made was an offer to send a squadron of submarines (four boats) on a courtesy call sometime in the summer. The RCN was advised to prepare itself to make maximum use of two to three weeks of free asdic training time. It was a generous offer, but it did not provide the RCN with a long-term solution to the pressing problem of providing asdic trainees with proper targets. Probably for this reason and because of the fear that acceptance would prejudice negotiations still underway regarding the future of *O-15*, the RCN politely declined the American offer. A few days later the Admiralty signalled its consent to the use of *O-15* for A/S training.[37]

Acquisition of the Dutch submarine did not alleviate the need for training submarines – one was simply not enough. The shortage of training submarines remained a pressing problem until late 1943, when an infusion of Italian and Free French submarines was directed into the Western Atlantic in response to the need to train the large number of American-built British destroyer escorts commissioning from U.S. ports. Further, having secured the services of *O-15*, there was no reason not to return to the American offer of training time on U.S. submarines. That the RCN saw fit to reject direct USN assistance was perhaps the first example of what became a curious, closely guarded attitude on the part of the RCN towards the USN. Nor were training submarines the only answer to pre-paring escorts for battle with the U-boats. Had the RCN – and the RN, for that matter – been more attuned to developments in the war at sea and seen the U-boat pack for what it really was, a flotilla of submersible torpedo boats, motor launches would have formed an essential part of A/S training as well. These small craft offered an excellent substitute for a training submarine in exercises designed to simulate night attacks on convoys, but it was not until 1942 that the RCN began to use launches for that purpose. The continuing fixation with submerged targets was understandable, since training on an actual submarine was the only means of attaining and maintaining efficiency among asdic operators. It also illustrates the fervent desire of all the Allied navies to locate and destroy U-boats, a concentration which was frequently at odds with defence of shipping.

Aside from the escorts operating from the UK, RCN expansion hung fire during the winter of 1940–1. Obviously it would have been better to commission twenty corvettes into the RCN during 1940, as the Staff had originally planned. But when winter closed its icy grip on the St Lawrence River, only four were operational – *Chambly*, *Cobalt*, *Collingwood*, and *Wetaskiwin* – and the last, along with *Agassiz*, which commissioned in January, *Alberni* (February), and *Kamloops* (March), was on the Pacific coast. The first commissionings of April – *Chilliwack*, *Nanaimo*, and *Trail* – also took place from British Columbia yards. The last week of April brought the opening of the St Lawrence, and with the spring freshette came the expected deluge of new corvettes. *Orillia*, *Pictou*, and *Rimouski* commissioned before the month was out. In May ten more were accepted into service – *Chicoutimi*, *Dauphin*, and *Quesnel* on the west coast, *Arvida*, *Baddeck*, *Barrie*, *Galt*, *Levis*, *Matapedia*, and *Napanee* in the east – in addition to the ten Admiralty corvettes commissioned into the RCN. In a period of seven months thirty-three warships were added to the Navy List, slightly over half of the 1939–40 construction program.[38]

Had it been possible to build the fleet entirely on the Atlantic or Pacific coasts, the seasonal character of expansion would have been averted. But because of the heavy demand for repair work on east-coast yards after the fall of France, only three orders for corvettes were ever placed east of the St Lawrence River. All of these were much delayed, and the last to commission, *Moncton*, was not taken into service until April 1942 – two full years after the commencement of the program. Considerable foresight and careful planning would have avoided the harmful effects of such spurts of growth. Although these qualities were hardly in evidence during 1940 – particularly when the character of the war changed in mid-year – such planning as the Naval Staff undertook was quickly overtaken by events. Moreover, both the Naval Staff and the Naval Council were inundated by the trivia of expansion. The Staff, for example, pored over such mundane issues as the supply of woollen mittens and duffle coats. With so many immediate, practical problems to consider, planners found little time for the potential problems of the expansion fleet. For the time being NSHQ provided operational commands with the barest of support and direction, and left local officers to get on as best they could. It was hardly a satisfactory state of affairs, but then the same could be said for the course of the war at sea.

Staff preoccupation with a myriad of apparently non-essential matters also stemmed from the lack of any sense of urgency over the commissioning of the corvette fleet, at least for operational purposes. Despite Nelles's stated concern over a possible repeat of 1917, even the Admiralty advised in February 1941 that the RCN could accept a delay in the attainment of competence by its own corvettes. Further, although the navy ardently desired to play a full role overseas in what Nelles described as the theatre of 'active operations,' the Naval Staff decided in October 1940 that the products of the first construction program would go to meet home requirements first. Once fifty per cent of the latter were met, escorts would be sent to the Eastern Atlantic – the war zone – on an equal-priority basis.[39]

Despite the policy of sending auxiliaries overseas and the sure knowledge that the RN was already using its corvettes as ocean escorts, there is no indication that the RCN believed either that its corvettes would be called up for similar activities or that they required modification to make them more suited to an ocean escort role. In fact, Canadian escorts were primarily intended for inshore duty, as had been the original intention of the British as well. But the inshore role of Canada's corvettes was reinforced by defence arrangements made between the u.s. and Canada after the fall of Western Europe. In August 1940 the new Canadian-American Permanent Joint Board of Defence produced its first basic defence plan (Number 1) for North America. It adopted a worst-case scenario, the defeat of Britain by Germany, followed by a continued state of war between Germany and the Commonwealth, from which it took its sobriquet, Plan 'Black.' According to the terms of Black the RCN was to provide A/S 'strike forces' for its system of defended ports. In this role corvettes were to be deployed along the coast in detachments of five. Formed into two 'single hunting' groups of two ships each, or one 'double hunting' group of four (with one spare), corvettes were tasked with tracking down and destroying U-boats in the approaches to harbours or at the focal points of trade. It was expected that in some cases, notably off Halifax and Sydney, corvettes would conduct some local escort, though for Canadian purposes this was not their primary role.[40]

In addition to this offensive use of corvettes, the navy also looked forward to the commissioning of the first construction-program ships in order to proceed with many aspects of expansion, such as training. For the professional navy at least the corvette fleet was not the embodiment of naval expansion. Rather it was, as Nelles described it, a 'stepping stone.' Events at sea would soon change this, but it would be some time before that change affected attitudes in Ottawa.

While the RCN struggled with the physical and institutional constraints on growth and sought both to secure North America from intrusion and to participate overseas, the war at sea intensified and pushed farther westwards. During the winter of 1940–1 dispersal points for convoys under British A/S escort moved steadily into the mid-Atlantic. With the establishment of bases in Iceland in April 1941 the RN was able to provide A/S escort to roughly 35 degrees west. This move, in conjunction with a similar extension of air escort, proved initially successful. During April three convoys were attacked in the area previously uncovered by A/S escorts, and three U-boats were sunk in the ensuing action. The Germans, once again finding the climate around defended trade too unhealthy, simply pushed farther west. In May they struck at the Halifax-to-UK convoy HX 126 as it approached the limits of A/S cover. Before the escort could join, a U-boat pack of six attackers sank five ships. In the face of a continued threat the convoy was dispersed, which led to further losses. To forestall further German success, the gap in continuous A/S escort of convoys between the limits of local Canadian escorts and those of the RN based in Iceland needed to be filled.

The problem of providing end-to-end A/S escort in the North Atlantic was discussed by British and Canadian authorities during the winter. These talks were the first sure indication that RCN corvettes were likely to be used as ocean escorts (what the navy thought corvettes earmarked for the Eastern Atlantic were initially expected to do remains uncertain). In any event, the Anglo-Canadian discussions identified three factors crucial to the establishment of end-to-end A/S escort: the escorts must be available; they must have reached a reasonable state of individual and escort-group training; and the necessary bases must be available.[41] In May 1941 none of these factors obtained in the Western Atlantic. An insufficient number of new corvettes were in commission, and most of these only recently. The development of facilities was now a top priority, but support facilities outside of Halifax were virtually non-existent, and the standard of training was to prove inadequate, to say the least.

The natural place from which to stage escort operations in the Northwest Atlantic was Newfoundland. Although not part of the Dominion of Canada, the island was integral to Canadian defence, and its protection was assumed, in consultation with the British, as a Dominion responsibility in 1939. By early 1941, however, the Canadian armed forces had made only a modest contribution to Newfoundland's security, though more was planned under the terms of Plan Black. During 1940 the RCN had surveyed the coast for possible base sites and fleet anchorages and ordered a further ten corvettes for local defence. The navy had also seconded personnel to the Naval Officer in Charge, St John's, Captain C.M.R. Schwerdt, RN, the only naval establishment on the island. Until the latter was turned over to the RCN in early May 1941, the Canadian navy had no permanent presence in Newfoundland. For a number of reasons, not all of them enemy inspired, this low level of activity was destined to change. The absorption of Schwerdt's command into the RCN came as part of the integration of Newfoundland into the Canadian east-coast command system, and it mirrored similar army and air-force arrangements. But Canada was also engaged in an embryonic war of influence with the U.S. over the old colony. The establishment of American bases on the island, as a result of the destroyers-for-bases deal with the British, was attended by an agreement granting the U.S. rights to defend its new bases by operations in adjacent territory. The agreement was concluded despite strong protests from Canada and in spite of the prior Canadian claim to Newfoundland defence.[42]

The anxiety Canada felt over her position in Newfoundland was exacerbated by joint Anglo-American planning of a combined strategy for the defeat of Germany should the U.S. enter the war. For several weeks in early 1941 senior American and British staffs met in Washington to discuss a co-ordinated Commonwealth and U.S. plan. Neither Canada nor any of the Dominions was accorded official representation, although British delegates kept their Commonwealth allies informed of proceedings. The result of these meetings was an agreement, American-British Conversations 1 (ABC 1), whereby the world was divided into two basic strategic zones. The Americans were to assume responsibility for most of the Pacific and for the Western Atlantic, with the exception of waters and territory assigned to Canada 'as may be defined in United States–Canada joint agreements.'[43]

The Canadians were not pleased with their treatment in the Anglo-American discussions, and the Chiefs of Staff feared that ABC 1 was intended to oust them from Newfoundland. The issue was somewhat problematical, since the implementation of ABC 1 was dependent upon U.S. entry into the war. However, the resolution of such issues, which had a direct bearing on Canada's responsibilities as a sovereign state, did not accord with the national view of Canada as a full and independent partner in the war against Germany. Canada was already attempting to force recognition of that claim, at least with respect to North American defence, by the establishment of a Canadian Staff mission in Washington. While the battle to be heard and recognized went on, Canadian responsibilities under the terms of ABC 1 were worked out by the PJBD. These agreements, styled ABC 22 and appended to ABC 1, gave Canada responsibility for her own coastal waters (three miles) and for the commitment of five destroyers and fifteen corvettes to USN forces in the Western Atlantic. Under the terms of ABC 22 the balance of Canadian naval forces was to be sent overseas.[44]

In the strictest sense, should the U.S. enter the war, Canada had lost the battle for Newfoundland. But though the Canadians had earlier been prepared to place their forces unreservedly under U.S. strategic direction in the worst-case scenario of Plan Black, they considered ABC 1 and ABC 22 offensive plans. The Canadians therefore clung firmly to their right to exercise command and control of Canadian forces in Canada and Newfoundland, even should ABC 1 come into force. Further, actual command of forces, despite a strong American sentiment to the contrary, was to remain with the respective nations. Co-ordination of the military effort in a given area was to be by 'mutual co-operation.' Unified command of all forces under a single officer was allowed for upon agreement by the officers in the field or the Chiefs of Staff. The criteria for determining who was to command under such conditions were never clearly defined; however, the Canadians at least considered that the size of national contingent and the rank and seniority of its commanding officer were governing elements. It was Canadian practice, therefore, throughout the joint American-Canadian occupation of Newfoundland to keep Canadian strength above that committed by the U.S. and to ensure that the senior Canadian present outranked his American counterpart.[45] All of these considerations were foremost in the minds of the Canadian government and Staffs when Canada was asked by the British to base large escort forces at St John's in the spring of 1941.

Thus, aside from the very real operational importance of the task, it was not surprising that the RCN responded enthusiastically to the Admiralty's request of 20 May that the navy begin the escort of convoys from a base at St John's. NSHQ responded by declaring that it was prepared to commit all of its new construction and its destroyer forces as well – virtually the entire navy. 'We should be glad,' the Canadian reply read, 'to undertake anti-submarine convoy escort in the Newfoundland focal area.'[46] Naturally, command of the forces would rest with an RCN officer, and NSHQ suggested Commander E.R. Mainguy, RCN, an officer with experience in the Western Approaches who would be promoted to captain for the task. However, the Canadians agreed that the Admiralty, through the commander-in-chief, Western Approaches (C-in-C, WA), would assume 'direction of this force when necessary to coordinate its cooperation with those of the Iceland force.' Whether Canadian enthusiasm for the Newfoundland Escort Force (NEF) stemmed from a belief that a permanent, militarily and politically acceptable role for the burgeoning corvette fleet had been found remains a mystery. What is patently clear, however, is that both the British and the Americans considered NEF a stopgap measure. By the summer of 1941 it was becoming increasingly evident that the U.S. would get involved in the Atlantic battle under the guise of defending the neutrality of the Western Hemisphere. When that happened, the role of the RCN in the Western Atlantic would be governed by the accords of ABC I.

Whatever the final outcome of NEF, the commitment of the corvette fleet to ocean escort work marked a radical departure from the intended use of such vessels. The RN had used its corvettes for such duty from the outset and had begun piecemeal modification of the class to make the vessels more suitable for work on the open sea. The changes included extending the foc'sle to increase crew space so that extra crewmen could be accommodated and to make the ships drier. The bows were also strengthened to take the pounding of heavy seas. Corvettes of the first Canadian construction program, already delayed, might well have incorporated these changes while the ships were still in the builder's hands. Yet those being built for the RCN went ahead largely as originally planned. The major Canadian alteration of the original design reflected the corvette's inshore and 'jack-of-all-trades' role. In September 1940 the Naval Staff decided, in light of the shortage of minesweepers, to outfit the first fifty-four RCN corvettes with 'sweep gear. This involved considerable alteration of the quarterdeck – cutting back the engine-room casing to accommodate the steam winch, broadening the stern to fit both fairleads for the 'sweep wires and the depth-charge rails, and the addition of storage for the 'sweep gear. All of this delayed completion and may have hardened the Staff to any further delays occasioned by major alterations. Moreover, that the Naval Staff was not unduly concerned about the A/S performance of the corvettes is evidenced by the fact that the addition of a full mine-sweeping kit 'had an adverse effect on the operations of the A/S gear.'[47] The latter, as the Staff went on to observe, was carried forward and was affected by the corvette's tendency to trim by the stern when fitted for minesweeping. In practice, however, the original corvette design, when fully stored and armed, tended to trim by the bows, which also affected A/S efficiency. The addition of extra weight in the stern may unwittingly have compensated for the design fault.

More important in terms of seakeeping and habitability in deep-sea operations was the extension of the foc'sle. News of this major alteration reached NSHQ while most of the vessels of the first program were still in the builder's hands. Although the RCN did make allowances for more crewmen, better refrigeration, a more powerful wireless set, and more depth charges – all indications that corvettes were expected to go farther afield and stay longer – the navy did not act on this fundamental alteration in basic structure of its first sixty corvettes.[48] However, the Staff did recognize the value of the design improvements. These were embodied in a new class of corvette, the revised patrol vessel (RPV), which was much better suited to deep-sea operations. The RCN ordered ten RPVs in early 1941, and all were in commission by the spring of 1942. Unfortunately, it took some time for these purpose-built ocean escorts to find their way into mid-Atlantic operations. In the meantime, the RCN plodded along with escorts which, as late as the end of 1940, the navy still considered inshore auxiliaries. In any event, corvettes were still tied closely to the defended-port system under the terms of Plan Black. It is also arguable that the Staff's failure to extend the foc'sles of corvettes when it had the chance stemmed from the navy's need of ships to permit expansion really to begin, or from the increasing gravity of the war at sea. Whatever the case, it was a lost opportunity that would haunt the navy.

The RCN made other noteworthy modifications to the original design and outfit of corvettes. Aside from the 'sweep gear, the most visible alteration was the placement of the after gun platform. Because its original location ahead of the mainmast left the gun 'wooded' directly aft, the RCN adopted the practice of mounting the platform on the after section of the engine-room casing (this was not the case in the ten Admiralty RCN corvettes). This practice was maintained long after the mainmast was discarded. Secondary armament was in short supply in Canada, and two-pounder pom-pom guns, which the RN had adopted for the after gun platform by 1941, were unavailable. A number of .5-inch Colt and Browning machine guns were acquired from the U.S. and fitted in twin mounts – two in the aft gun position and one twin mount either side of the bridge. When the .5-inch became unobtainable, the previous practice (late 1940) of fitting twin Lewis guns on the bridge was reverted to. These .303-inch First World War–vintage guns also found their way to the after position, again in the form of two twin mounts. Both the .5 and .303 proved virtually useless as secondary armament.

Other differences between RCN and RN corvettes were much less noticeable but had a more important effect on the performance of the ships as deep-sea escorts. There was, for example, no provision in Canadian plans for a breakwater on the foc'sle. Without it water shipped forward was able to run aft and pour into the open welldeck – the crew's main thoroughfare. The British soon corrected this, but the RCN moved with incredible slowness on this simple matter, and as a result Canadian corvettes were unnecessarily wet. Canadian corvettes were also completed without wooden planking or some form of synthetic deck covering to prevent slipping in the waist of the ship, where the depth-charge throwers were fitted. Since this area was also constantly wet, the difficulties of loading charges can be imagined.

The most telling shortcoming of Canadian corvettes, and the one that was to cause the most difficulty in the struggle for efficiency, was the lack of gyro-compasses. The latter were at a premium in Canada, so the

Naval Staff decided to fit them to Bangor minesweepers, whose need for accurate navigation was paramount. The first Canadian-built corvettes (including those built to Admiralty accounts) were equipped with a single magnetic compass and the most basic of asdic, the type 123A. Even by 1939 standards the 123A was obsolete and in the RN was considered only suited to trawlers and lesser vessels. The 123A's standard compass, graduated in 'points' and not in degrees, made it equally hard for captains to co-ordinate operations between two ships or to undertake accurate submarine hunts and depth-charge attacks. The single binnacle and its attendant trace recorder were mounted in a small hut, above the wheelhouse. During an action it was impossible for the captain to be both in the asdic hut and outside on the bridge wings, the only place from which he could obtain an overall perspective on the situation. Nor was the needle of the standard compass stablized, a deficiency particularly noticeable in such lively ships as corvettes. As one officer wrote in 1944 when the issue of modernization came to a head, 'The problems of a corvette captain when attempting an accurate attack with a swinging magnetic compass are well nigh insoluable.' As a final point, it should be noted that the compasses were also susceptible to malfunction from the shock of firing the main armament, exploding depth charges, or simply from the pounding of the ship at sea. The tendency of the Canadians to launch inaccurate depth-charge attacks proved a source of continuous criticism from British officers.[49] It was, perhaps, because of this significant shortcoming that the Admiralty was happy to see its first ten Canadian-built corvettes transferred to the RCN.

In basic armament – number and mark of depth charges, the 4-inch gun, and the gently curving bow – the differences between RN and RCN corvettes were negligible. Yet in many other important respects the corvettes of the two navies parted ways from the start. In part, this was the result of a disparity of resources, but it also stemmed from the assumption of different roles. Not surprisingly then, Canadian corvettes were outclassed by their British counterparts as ocean escorts. Differences and delays in adopting standard British alterations and additions to corvettes arose from the confusion over what role the ships, and the navy itself, was to take in the North Atlantic. But the disparity between British and Canadian ships of the same class also owed something to misapplication of Naval Staff energies. Instead of laying down a basic policy for the engineer-in-chief to follow, the Staff haggled over every conceivable alteration to their corvettes. They insisted, for example, that inclining tests be done before .5-inch machine guns were authorized for the bridge wings, even though they knew full well that this practice had already been adopted for comparable British ships.[50] In the final analysis it would have been much better had the RCN continued its initial practice of calling its own corvettes 'Town class,' after its policy of naming them for small Canadian communities. Instead the practice was abandoned in deference to the Admiralty's choice of 'Town class' for the ex-American destroyers, and the RCN applied the British class name of 'Flower' to its corvettes. Had the RCN stuck to its distinctive class name, the tremendous differences between British and Canadian Flower-class corvettes, which were to prove so very important by 1942–3, might have been as apparent as they were real.

NSHQ's notion that the RCN was to provide convoy escorts for the Newfoundland 'focal' area suggests that the Naval Staff had not made the mental leap from the concept of locally based 'strike forces' to the idea of a regional escort force. In this they were not alone. The distinction between the two types of operation – one searching for submarines where shipping was plentiful, the other actually protecting the ships towards which the submarines were drawn – was never very clear in the early days. NEF was, none the less, admirably suited to RCN capabilities. It also met two other vitally important criteria: it supported the government's geopolitical aspirations and was at the same time fundamental to the war effort. So far, so good. But the westward advance of the war, which drew the RCN into the Northwest Atlantic, proved to be just another phase. In a few short months the focus of the war at sea and of Canadian operations shifted again, this time to the eastern seaboard of North America. In fact, during 1942 the navy's efforts were largely directed into developing escort forces along the Canadian and New England coasts. Operations closer to home would eventually ease the problems of building a service, but for the moment the RCN was not permitted to choose. The expansion fleet would have to be brought into shape in one of the most remote, barren, and bitter theatres of the war. With hindsight it may seem to have been a natural development, but it was something that no planner had foreseen in 1939.

The pre-war navy: *Skeena* (in the foreground), *Saguenay*, and *St Laurent* in Bermuda, 1937

Skeena (inboard), *St Laurent*, and *Restigouche* (aft) alongside at Plymouth,
2 June 1940, during the period when they were assigned to the English Channel
anti-invasion forces

Prime Minister W.L. Mackenzie King paying a visit to *Assiniboine* in October 1940,
during the brief period when she was commanded by Captain C.R.H. Taylor (seen
here to King's right)

Vice-Admiral P.W. Nelles, chief of the Naval Staff, and Captain H.T.W. Grant, director of Naval Personnel, on 14 May 1942. It was shortly afterwards that Grant made his unsuccessful attempt to check expansion and concentrate on consolidation.

Kamloops on the west coast in the spring of 1941. She epitomizes the changes made by the RCN to the original corvette design and incorporated into the first construction program.

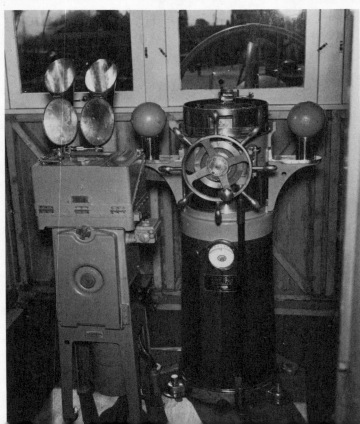

Depth charge and carrier leaving *Pictou*'s starboard thrower in March 1942. Despite the calm seas, the deck is awash. One of the two twin .5-inch machine guns fitted in the after position is just visible to the right.

OPPOSITE

The nerve-centre of the early corvettes. The magnetic compass, with the hand wheel used to rotate the asdic dome (under the keel), is to the right, the trace recorder to the left. Just visible through the window are the loops of the MF/DF set.

The open and barren harbour of Hvalfjordhur, March 1942. The ships to left of centre include a depot, four destroyers, and two corvettes.

St John's harbour, 26 September 1942. The recently completed naval-stores buildings in the centre foreground mark the site of the original NEF establishment. Naval facilities now stretch along the shoreline from the Newfoundland drydock, at right, to the harbour mouth. Despite this expansion, at least two accommodation ships are berthed at the head of the harbour, and the depot ship HMS *Greenwich* (with a destroyer alongside) remains anchored in the stream. Just out of the photo, below the position of the camera, lay the large new naval-barracks complex.

The corvette *Battleford*, travelling at her top speed, buries her bows in a swell while on escort duty in November 1941. Earlier photos in this series show her completely obscured by flying spray.

OPPOSITE

top Commander James Douglas Prentice, RCN, on the bridge of *Chambly* in May 1941. His distinctive rimless monocle (worn in the right eye) is barely discernible in the original print.

bottom Rear Admiral L.W. Murray, RCN, when he was flag officer, Newfoundland

Showing signs of North Atlantic operations, the corvette *Algoma* arrives in Ireland sometime during the winter of 1941–2. She carries SWIC radar at her masthead but no visible secondary armament on her bridge and has no breakwater on the foc'sle.

OPPOSITE

top The corvette *Levis*, her bows all but severed by *U74*'s torpedo, sinking astern of SC 44 on 20 September 1941

bottom *Assiniboine* arriving in St John's 9 August 1942, after her battle with *U210*

Survivors, probably from ONS 92, crowd the deck of *Shediac*.

OPPOSITE

top *Arrowhead* off Halifax in June 1942. She shows the partial modernization carried out on the RCN's 'British' corvettes and is fitted with both 271 (in the lantern abaft the bridge) and 286 (at the masthead) radars. *Arrowhead* was assigned to WLEF from the mid-ocean in March 1942.

bottom Rear Admiral G.C. Jones, RCN, when he was commanding officer, Atlantic Coast

Bangor minesweepers such as *Swift Current*, seen here in 1944, were the largest single class of escorts in WLEF, and their gyro-compasses and more modern asdics made them better ASW vessels than were the early corvettes.

St Croix, the only RCN Town-class destroyer with enough range and reliability to serve exclusively in the mid-ocean, seen here in June 1942

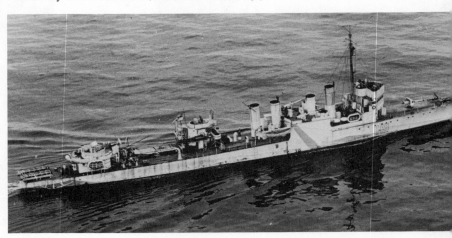

The corvette *Sackville*, about the time of the battle for ON 115. Her secondary armament is all twin Lewis guns, and she retains, under the tarp on her quarterdeck, the heavy steam winch for minesweeping. The antenna atop the foremast is for the SWIC radar.

ss *Belgian Soldier*, adrift in the fog astern of ON 115, as seen from *Sackville*

Replenishment at sea was crucial to German operations in the air gap during 1942–3. This is *U124*, a key player in Hecht's battles, preparing to take on stores.

U210 as seen from *Assiniboine* during their encounter near SC 94

U221, the U-boat that caused group B 6 so much trouble during the battle for SC 104

The bane of Allied escorts, the type VIIC U-boat. In this case it is *U94*, which was to operate so successfully against RCN and USN escorts in May and June 1942, seen leaving her French base. She was later sunk by HMCS *Oakville*.

A gallery of notable RCN officers aboard *Chambly* in St John's harbour, August 1942:
Rear Admiral L.W. Murray; Vice-Admiral H. Walwyn, RN, governor of
Newfoundland; Captain J.D. Prentice, who has just received his DSO; Mrs Prentice;
and behind Prentice, with the beard, Commander G.S. Windeyer, and to his left
Captain E.R. Mainguy

2

The Struggle Begins

At present most escorts are equipped with one weapon of approximate precision – the ram.

Captain (D), Newfoundland, September 1941

The completion of end-to-end A/S escort in the North Atlantic was only possible with the commissioning of sufficient numbers of Canadian corvettes. These 'cheap and nasties,' as Churchill called them, thus assumed a role for which they were never intended. But in May 1941 it was not just the ships themselves that were ill prepared for the rigours of the North Atlantic. The RCN was unable to provide either experienced or properly trained crews for the expansion fleet. 'The first Canadian corvettes were definitely not trained,' one senior RCN officer wrote in 1942; 'this was recognized by the Naval Staff at the time and they were only sent to sea in this condition on the urgent request of the Admiralty.'[1] One of the most vital factors controlling the establishment of end-to-end A/S escort was therefore not met by NEF.

In the spring of 1941 there was little reason to believe that training would come to a halt simply because escorts were assigned to operations. Clearly sea time and experience would add immeasurably to the level of efficiency. However, once committed to operations, the expansion fleet was moulded by forces far beyond the control of NSHQ: the school of hard knocks proved no panacea. That this motley collection of raw recruits and hastily built warships offered little threat to a skilful enemy is perhaps not so remarkable as the fact that none of the ships was lost through simple marine accident.

In the long term the quantity and quality of escorts and their equipment were not the decisive factors in the Battle of the Atlantic during 1941. That distinction goes to the excellent routing of convoys that was made possible by British penetration of the German U-boat cipher. From May 1941 – the month NEF was formed – through the balance of the year, every U-boat signal was read by British code breakers. Not all were read in time to be of immediate operational value, and there were still many problems with using precise intelligence in tactical situations. As a result, there were lapses in the effectiveness of convoy routing, such as occurred in early September, when SC 42 was heavily attacked. But the steady flow of excellent intelligence supplied to the Tracking and Routing Section of the Admiralty, coupled with the decision to raise the minimum speed for independently routed shipping – from which the U-boats had exacted a heavy toll – to fifteen knots, stabilized and subsequently reduced a growing loss rate among Allied shipping. Without improved routing and the inclusion of slower ships in convoys, Germany's attack on trade might well have driven Britain to peace in 1941. Indeed, the sharp reduction in ship losses was achieved despite a steady increase in the size of the U-boat fleet: from twenty-six operational submarines in April to ninety-one by the end of December. As one British official historian has written, 'It was only by the narrowest of margins that ... the U-boat campaign failed to be decisive during 1941.'[2]

While the object of the Admiralty's Trade Division was clearly the avoidance of the enemy, escorts of the Allied navies still faced the problem of dealing with U-boats when they were confronted. Through the winter of 1940–1 the issue of how best to apply available escort strength was hotly debated in British circles. Although the 1940 practice of concentration on offensive action even at the risk of exposing the convoy had gradually given way to a more defensive posture, total abandonment of offensive action was very unpopular. Even the British prime minister was known to favour the hunting and destruction of U-boats over apparently passive defensive measures. In February 1940 Churchill (then still First Lord of the Admiralty) voiced strong displeasure with the RN's inability to 'kill' U-boats on a decisive scale.[3] The realization that present escort strengths and the state of technology precluded simultaneously adequate defensive and offensive operations came hard to service and political interests alike. In May 1941 an Admiralty committee finally concluded that offensive action on a decisive scale against U-boats was not possible until shipping was properly protected.[4] In some measure the establishment of NEF helped meet the latter goal, and this, in combination with excellent intelligence, restored some flexibility to the use of escorts. However, by the summer of 1941 specialization of roles for escorts, defence for the close escort of convoys, and offence for 'support groups' were established theory. To what extent NSHQ was privy to these developments – or indeed, felt them applicable to the Western Atlantic – remains unclear.

Under the escort arrangements adopted with the formation of NEF, the new RCN force protected convoys between the West Ocean Meeting Point (WESTOMP) off Newfoundland (see map 1) and the Mid-Ocean Meeting Point (MOMP) south of Iceland. Both NEF and the British escort groups operating to the east of MOMP shared facilities at the advanced base in Hvalfjordhur, Iceland. These consisted exclusively of auxiliary support ships capable of sustaining life, not embellishing it. Oil, basic stores, water, food, and the most elementary of running repairs were available. The anchorage itself offered little respite to tired men and belaboured ships. When all-too-frequent gales swept down over the barren hills of Iceland, the layover period for escorts became even more demanding than life at sea. The poor holding ground of the fjord's bottom, the proximity of other ships, the rugged shoreline, swirling snow, and hurricane-force winds made a night on the open sea preferable to one at anchor in Hvalfjordhur.

Certainly, when winter came, the Iceland layover offered no rest and little haven for escorts. *Assiniboine* was nearly lost in early 1942 when a winter gale struck as she lay alongside the depot ship, with her boilers torn down for cleaning. Ralph Hennessy, the destroyer's first lieutenant, recalls receiving twenty minutes' warning of the impending storm. Feverish activity below decks to restore power was coupled with equally intense activity above decks to secure *Assiniboine* to the larger ship. In due course, and right on time, the gale descended on the anchorage, bringing howling winds, blinding snow, and freezing spray. Within minutes 'wires were just popping like pieces of spaghetti,' while the anometer on the depot ship 'blew off at 120 knots.' Despite the efforts of *Assiniboine*'s entire crew, within an hour she had blown clear of her moorings – just as the engine-room reported steam on one boiler. With both anchors down and occasionally with revolutions on for fifteen knots, *Assiniboine* held her place for over thirty hours and rode out the storm. During the ordeal Hennessy and the rest of the destroyer's crew watched in amazement as an American depot ship, which was unable to find good holding ground, was driven fifteen miles down the fjord, 'jigging back and forth' as she went through the crowded anchorage.

Hvalfjordhur was a dreary and unforgiving haven, by far the worst of those used by escort forces in the Battle of the Atlantic. For British sailors

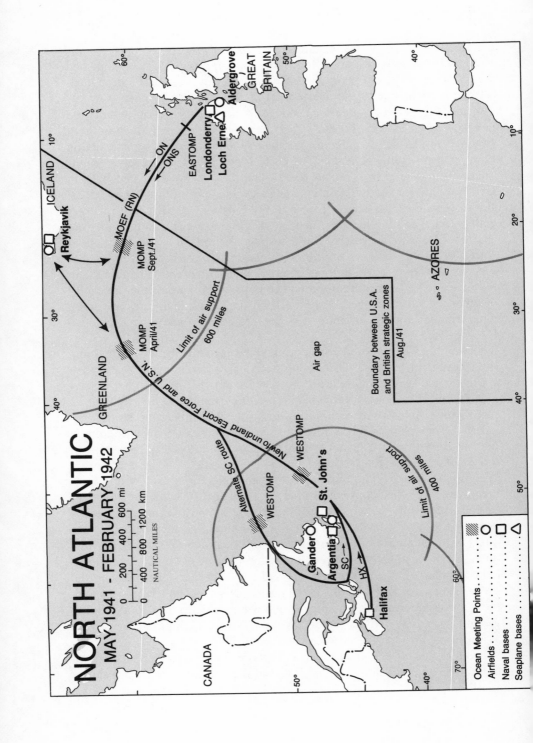

it represented the end of the most gruelling part of their convoy cycle. Departure from Iceland meant a short southwestward journey to pick up a convoy, followed by a passage down the prevailing wind to a well-appointed harbour in the UK. For NEF escorts, the barren, windswept shores of Hvalfjordhur were merely a prelude to the most arduous portion of the cycle. Departure from Iceland meant a long and laborious westward struggle against the elements, at the end of which lay the tiny cleft-like harbour of St John's.

It may seem unkind to compare the capital of Britain's oldest colony to a bleak Icelandic fjord, but for warships in need the two ports were equally barren. Facilities necessary for the support of a large fleet of escorts were almost totally lacking. Wharfs not integral to the commerce of the port were without exception dilapidated, and those which could be of service had already been leased to the U.S. Army by the spring of 1941. The lone drydock was fully employed with repairs to merchantmen and lacked both the equipment and manpower to do work to naval standards. It was, in any event, the only drydock for hundreds of miles. Priority was given to emergency repairs, and the need for these never slackened.

When it became clear that the RCN was to base a sizeable force of escorts at St John's, it took several months to iron out the details of base development. Legal niceties concerning title to land, financial responsibilities, and development direction were not settled until the late summer – months after NEF was operating. By then the unknown effects of USN participation in convoy escort in the Northwestern Atlantic had resulted in further delays. For these reasons and because both materials and labour were scarce, the RCN initially gave priority to construction of the base hospital, the wireless station, and the port war signal station. Work on support facilities for escorts was not totally neglected, despite delays in settling ownership and responsibility for the base. Even before the first Canadian warships arrived, local naval authorities had leased a stretch of waterfront in the southwest corner of the harbour near the Newfoundland drydock and had strengthened a wharf to take heavier weights.[5] Despite these early efforts, however, NEF's wharfs were sadly inadequate. Naval Minister Macdonald confided to his diary following his first visit to St John's in August that the wharfs were 'all pile and none seemed strong'[6]; much of the next two years was spent in rebuilding them. The one bright spot was a four thousand ton fuel-oil storage tank, nearing completion in the spring of 1941.

Although the RCN lacked the resources to add quickly to support facilities at St John's, the Admiralty provided that direct assistance necessary to conduct operations. The RN's fleet auxiliary oiler *Teakwood* arrived on

29 May, followed five days later by the British storeship *City of Dieppe*. A second RN oiler, *Clam*, arrived on 9 June, and on the fourteenth the new submarine depot ship HMS *Forth* cast her anchor in the harbour. *Forth* was replaced in September by HMS *Greenwich*, an older and smaller destroyer-tender more suited to NEF's needs. In contrast, the RCN's commitment was small. One of the *Prince* ships was detached to act as a temporary barracks towards the end of the year, and the oil barge *Moonbeam* was sent to augment the fuelling fleet. Canadian efforts were, in fact, directed into constructing the shore establishment at St John's, building it into a fairly large and wholly self-sufficient naval base.[7] This not only fit well with the Admiralty's vision of the importance of St John's; it suited Canadian interests, too. Protection of North Atlantic communications was Canada's first defence priority, while the establishment of a large operational base in Newfoundland lent credence to Canada's claim that the old colony fell within the Dominion's defensive arrangements. Although the RCN pushed development once the legal niceties and operational responsibilities were sorted out, it took two full years to bring support facilities at St John's up to standard. Unfortunately for the Canadian navy, these proved to be the two most important years of the Atlantic war.

The twenty-third of May 1941, the day that the first flotilla of corvettes left Halifax for St John's, marks an important turning point in the RCN's use of its expansion fleet. Certainly, the first escorts to arrive from Canada were inexperienced in the type of work which lay before them. The corvettes themselves – *Agassiz, Alberni, Chambly, Cobalt, Collingwood, Orillia,* and *Wetaskiwin* – were among the first to commission into the RCN and represented the disposable strength of the east-coast command. All of the ships had been worked up from scratch with new crews, and five of their commanding officers were naval reservists (RCNR), that is, professional seamen. One of the escorts, *Wetaskiwin*, was commanded by a lieutenant commander, Guy Windeyer, RCN, and another (*Chambly*) was under the charge of the group's commander and the Senior Officer, Canadian Corvettes, Commander J.D. Prentice, RCN.

'Chummy' Prentice, as his friends called him, was one of the real characters of the war and a driving force behind the RCN's quest for efficiency. Born in Victoria, BC, of British parents in 1899, Prentice had decided on a naval career by the tender age of thirteen. He wanted to join the infant RCN, but his father believed that the new naval service of Canada would become little more than another avenue for political patronage. If Prentice was to join the navy, it had to be the RN, so in

1912 he entered the Royal Naval College, Dartmouth, and later in the same year joined the RN as a cadet. His twenty-two years of service in the RN were undistinguished, the pinnacle reached when he served as first lieutenant commander of the battleship *Rodney*. When passed over for promotion to commander in 1934, Prentice realized that his future in the RN was limited, and he therefore took an early retirement. He returned to BC in 1937 to take a position as financial secretary of the Western Canada Ranching Company, and there he stayed until the outbreak of war in 1939.

The RN having no immediate employment for him, Prentice was placed on the list of officers at the disposal of the RCN. When the RCN mobilized, Prentice was offered a commission at his old RN rank, an offer he eagerly accepted, and he was posted to Sydney, Cape Breton, as staff officer to the Naval Officer in Charge. Although content with his lot, Prentice was rescued from this important but otherwise colourless duty in July 1940, when he was transferred to Halifax pending the commissioning of the corvette *Levis*, which he was to command. In Halifax Prentice came in contact with Commodore L.W. Murray, then Commodore Commanding Halifax Force, whom Prentice had first met at the RN's staff college. The two men shared many ideas and interests, and became fast and lifelong friends. Prentice soon found himself attached to Murray's staff as Senior Officer, Canadian Corvettes. It was a curious post, one which never fitted into the organizational structure of any command and soon became little more than titular. However, it did provide Prentice with a legitimate priority of interest in the affairs of Canadian corvettes, which he was to exercise constantly over the next three years.

As things turned out, Murray was soon posted overseas as Commodore Commanding Canadian Ships (CCCS), UK, but what was to become – for better or for worse – the 'dynamic duo' of the east coast was not long broken up. In the meantime, Prentice spent the winter of 1940–1 working up the few newly commissioned ships which managed to arrive in Halifax before the freeze-up. In late March he was finally given command of one of these, *Chambly*. All of this gave his fertile and often over-active imagination an opportunity for expression, for Prentice was an innovator and an original thinker. During his service in the RN he had produced numerous papers and essays for publication and competitions on a myriad of topics. Not surprisingly, he quickly developed ideas of what corvettes were capable of, how they could be used, and how their efficiency could be improved.

As a fairly senior officer in a rather junior service, one in which he had no long-standing presence or long-term ambitions, Prentice allowed his concern for efficiency to dominate his work. His combination of experience, seniority, and lack of vested service interest gave Prentice a freedom of expression which few if any other RCN officers enjoyed. By all accounts he used his position and influence wisely. In any event Murray was always interposed between Prentice and more senior (and, one might assume, less tolerant) officers and was therefore able to direct some of the heat generated by Prentice into more useful, if not always successful, directions. In many ways Prentice was Murray's alter ego, an energetic innovator paired to an efficient but somewhat uninspired administrator.

Prentice's eccentricities apparently did not keep him at arm's length from his fellow officers. More importantly, perhaps, his cigars, monocle, English accent, and sense of fairness positively endeared him to the lower decks. The story of Chummy Prentice and the monocle is probably apocryphal, but it illustrates the type of rapport he apparently had with the other ranks. It is said that once a whole division of *Chambly*'s company paraded wearing monocles. Without saying a word or altering his expression, Prentice completed his rounds and then took a position in front of the jesting crewmen. After a moment's pause, and while the whole crew waited for the dressing-down, Prentice threw his head back, flipping the monocle into the air. As the glass fell back he caught it between his eyebrow and the bottom lid – exactly in the place from whence it had been ejected. 'When you can do that,' Prentice is reputed to have said, 'you can all wear monocles.' Whether it is a true story or not, it makes the point. Prentice was an ideal commanding officer and admirably suited for the posts which he held. He was ruthless in his quest for efficiency at all levels of shipboard life, from gunnery to the welfare of the lower decks. A good measure of fairness and a well-developed sense of propriety seem to have governed his treatment of subordinates. He was, above all, enthusiastic about his work, and much of this rubbed off on those who came in contact with him. Although the RN apparently felt he had little to offer them, Prentice clearly found his calling in the small ships of the RCN.[8]

The first task assigned to Prentice and the embryonic NEF was the screening of the battle-cruiser *Repulse* as that great ship lay in Conception Bay following the hunt for the *Bismarck*. Screening *Repulse* was good basic exercise if nothing else, and the clear, unstratified waters of the bay returned good asdic echoes. The real work of NEF began shortly thereafter. Pending the arrival of a Canadian commanding officer for NEF, the escorts were placed under Captain C.M.R. Schwerdt, RN, the Naval Officer in Charge, St John's (whose establishment had in fact only just been transferred to the RCN). Schwerdt, in consultation with his trade officers, determined that NEF should attempt its first escort of an eastbound convoy in early June. The date of sailing, course, and so on could all be obtained through local trade connections, and a rendezvous with HX 129 was worked out by Schwerdt's staff. Word-of-mouth orders were passed to Prentice advising him of this plan and of the likelihood of very poor weather. The orders, which in effect stated 'If you have any reasonable hope of joining the convoy, proceed to sea,' gave Prentice the carte blanche he thrived on; foul weather only added to the challenge.[9]

On 2 June, the first NEF escort group to sail on convoy duty put to sea. The escorts *Chambly*, *Orillia*, and *Collingwood* rendezvoused with HX 129 within an hour of their estimated position. Although the convoy was not attacked, many stragglers and independents nearby were lost to enemy action, and the Canadians soon found themselves busy with rescue work. Two asdic contacts were also made, one each by *Chambly* and *Collingwood* while operating in company. Unfortunately, co-ordination of searches was hampered by the failure of visual-signalling (V/S) equipment in *Chambly*. The latter also had to stop engines twice to repair defects. Despite the breakdowns, lost opportunities, and general mayhem of this first operation, Prentice's spirits were buoyant. 'The ships behaved extremely well,' he wrote in his report of proceedings. Certainly all the COs in question, Acting Lieutenant Commander W.E.S. Briggs, RCNR, of *Orillia*, and Acting Lieutenant Commander W. Woods, RCNR, of *Collingwood*, went on to do well in the RCN. But one cannot help but feel that Prentice was writing about the corvettes themselves.[10]

The first operation of NEF pointed to the many problems which beset the expansion fleet, and yet Prentice was pleased with the group's performance. Having participated directly in the commission and work-up of these first seven corvettes, the SO, Canadian Corvettes, could be excused his pride in their initial foray into troubled waters. Other RCN officers maintained similar limited expectations of the expansion fleet. The British, on the other hand, entertained little sympathy for struggling civilian sailors. From the outset, RCN and RN officers displayed a tendency to view the expansion fleet from vastly different perspectives. To use an analogy, the RCN was, through the period 1941–3, like half a glass of water. From the Canadian perspective the glass was half full; the RN always considered it half empty. Though the Naval Staff was apparently informed of how ill prepared the early corvettes really were, this came as a rude shock to the more staid RN. Moreover, shortcomings manifested themselves even before the first major Canadian convoy battle.

In mid-May the Fourth Escort Group of the Clyde Escort Force, comprising the Canadian Town-class destroyers *Columbia* and *St Clair* and the corvettes *Eyebright, Trillium,* and *Windflower,* carried out A/S, wireless, and visual-signalling exercises off Moville, Northern Ireland. The results of the exercises showed a complete lack of understanding of what was expected of divisions within individual ships (the asdic team, depth-charge crew, gunners, and so on) and of ships operating as a group. The British found the Canadians keen, intelligent, and willing to learn. But no one, from the captain on down, had any conception of ASW, and this caused the British great concern. On the whole the destroyers came off better than the corvettes, which were found to be undermanned and poorly stored. Most disturbing was the training officer's criticism of the corvettes' commanding officers. He reported that they showed a great lack of initiative and relied entirely on the senior officer for instructions. 'No one would possibly question either their courage or endurance at sea,' the RN officer wrote, 'and they are fine seamen. Their lack of technical knowledge is their greatest difficulty and possibly due to their age they are slow to learn.' The RCNR commanders of Canada's first corvettes may also have had an understandable reluctance to jump too quickly when asked to do so by a young RN officer. None the less, Captain (D),* Greenock, who took exception to the above officer's dim view of Canadian COs, concluded bluntly that the low state of efficiency reached by these ships was 'attributable directly to inexperience and perhaps the age of their commanding officers.' Captain (D), Greenock, recommended that they be replaced as soon as possible by younger, more adaptable RCN or RCNVR officers with escort experience.

Although wireless communication among Canadian ships of the Fourth Escort Group was found to be good and bearings and distances of contacts were passed among them continuously and accurately, visual communication in both classes of escort 'was at times hopeless,' the training officer reported, 'and at best was barely adequate.' Similar remarks came from the commodore of the RN's escort work-up base at Tobermory, HMS *Western Isles,* where *Spikenard* and *Hepatica* trained in May. In compiling his remarks for his commander-in-chief, Captain (D), Greenock

* See page 50 for an explanation of Captain (D).

(who received reports on both training programs), even went so far as to draw extracts from the original work-ups of the Canadian corvettes to illustrate just how inefficient they really were.[11] Whether any of these officers knew that the ten 'Canadian' corvettes then operating in UK waters were manned for passage only seems unlikely. Operational and training authorities in Britain were clearly appalled by what they saw, and Captain (D), Greenock's memo was not intended purely for internal consumption. The RCN's expansion had got off to a poor start, and the foundations of a legacy of inadequacy and ineptitude were laid. No amount of hard work or improvement would shake it for some time.

As the above report made its way through channels and the ships of the Fourth Escort Group sailed to join NEF, things moved apace in Newfoundland. Commodore Murray, the Admiralty's choice for commander of NEF, arrived to assume the post of Commodore Commanding Newfoundland Force (CCNF) on 15 June. Murray was a native Nova Scotian with deep roots in rural Pictou County. He attended the first class of the Royal Naval College of Canada in 1912 as a boy and went on to serve in various warships of both the RN and the RCN. His first notable appointment was to the wardroom of HMS *Calcutta* as a young sub-lieutenant when that ship commissioned from the builder's yards in 1919. *Calcutta*'s first commanding officer was then Captain Dudley Pound, a man who was instrumental – as First Sea Lord in 1941 – in having Murray posted to St John's. Close links with the RN not only fostered personal connections; young Canadians also adopted many of the trappings of RN officers. Murray was not spared the effects of his long exposure to the traditions and habits of the parent service. Although he did not develop a British accent, it is unlikely that many Pictonians would have recognized him as one of their own in 1939. Yet Murray never lost his playful charm and his appreciation of his background. He was fond of sports and played a bruising brand of ice hockey. Among the few personal papers of his which were passed on to the Public Archives of Canada are a number of citations from his team-mates for wounds received in action on the ice. What exists of his diary confirms that Murray was a frequent visitor to the medical officer at Halifax during hockey season.[12] This rapport carried on throughout the war; ironically, his concern for 'his boys' has been cited as evidence that Murray was never capable of the type of dynamic command that his positions warranted. There is some truth in this. But few major naval commands during the Second World War were comparable to those of the RCN, where tact, diplomacy, and goodwill were essential to running an organization composed almost entirely of reservists. Murray was above all a competent and confident officer, an excellent ship handler (as his contemporaries attest), and an able administrator.[13]

Murray's task in Newfoundland was daunting. Not only were the facilities jury-rigged and totally inadequate; a whole administrative and support staff had to be assembled and adapted to conditions at St John's. Perhaps because the very long-term existence of NEF – as distinct from the base itself – was an open question in the summer of 1941, the development of its staff was slow. Murray, as CCNF, was charged with overall command of naval operations off Newfoundland. But the initial staff at St John's in May 1941 was wholly administrative, belonging to the port defence establishment. The first official record of HMCS *Avalon*, which appeared in the September 1941 *Navy Lists*, shows little more than Captain Schwerdt's port-defence and naval-control-of-shipping staffs. Newfoundland Escort Force's staff consisted of Murray, his chief of staff Commander R.E.S. Bidwell, RCN, and the commodore's secretary. A more accurate indication of NEF's supporting staff by mid-1941 was published in November. By then CCNF had added staff officers of Operations, Intelligence, and Signals and a secretary's staff. These staffs provided the vital elements of naval operations: the processing and collecting of intelligence, handling of heavy signals traffic, and the organization and management of operational forces.

The actual administration of the escort forces themselves fell to a separate 'Flotilla' staff under a 'Captain (D[estroyers]).' Traditionally Captain (D) was a seagoing officer, responsible in all respects, including operational efficiency, for a flotilla of ten to twelve destroyers. Administratively the system was applicable to escort forces, but the small size of their ships and the small size of escort groups made it inappropriate for Captains (D) to go to sea. As a result the main staff of escort forces such as NEF remained ashore, while the actual seagoing duties of Captain (D) were passed to the less senior commanders of escort groups.

Captain (D) was crucial to the performance of his forces. Through a staff of specialists he monitored and was ultimately responsible for the efficacy of escort groups, individual ships, and the important warlike functions within each ship. In the early days of NEF the latter problems overwhelmed those of group co-ordination and the development of and adherence to a suitable tactical doctrine, for which Captain (D) was also responsible. Initially, much-needed specialists in all but a few traditional naval functions were unavailable. During 1941 Captain (D), Newfoundland, had only two specialist officers, one for gunnery and one for signals. A torpedo officer, whose duties included depth charges, was not added until 1942, while the key posts of a/s, radar, and engineering were not filled until 1943. In an a/s escort force the delay in providing specialists to oversee the use of asdic, radar, and depth charges was serious. In the interim, St John's–based escorts had to draw on the expertise of the base a/s and radar officers (both well-qualified RN officers), whose duties covered maintenance and supervision of port defences as well. Fortunately, these men found time to devote to NEF. Yet what the escorts needed were officers exclusively assigned to their operations and problems. The RCN did what it could, but there simply were not enough qualified personnel to go around. The result was a serious deficiency in Captain (D)'s staff. In the context of a time when things were difficult all around, however, these weaknesses appear comparatively minor. Further, like the escorts themselves, Captain (D)'s initial shortfalls could be expected to diminish with time.[14]

There was another notable deficiency in Captain (D), Newfoundland's staff. Theoretically he was responsible not only for the material readiness of his ships, in conjunction with the local maintenance establishment, but also for the modernization of equipment – in naval parlance, 'additions and alterations' (As and As). At St John's simple maintenance was difficult enough, but the port also lacked facilities for any but emergency repairs, supplies of equipment, and even accommodation for extra staffs. As a result, only Captain (D), Halifax, had an As and As inspection staff. St John's–based escorts were required to make their requests to him and not to their own Captain (D) in order to qualify for new equipment.[15] Thus, there was nowhere in NEF's normal operational area where escorts could even be cleared to acquire new equipment, let alone fit it. Such a situation was highly unsatisfactory in a rapidly changing tactical environment. Further, a trip to Halifax – six hundred miles away – was a venture not to be undertaken lightly.

The organization and operation of NEF mirrored British practice and was initially organized as an extension of the RN's Western Approaches Command. The size and composition of escort groups, typically one destroyer and two to three corvettes in mid-1941, was identical, and NEF groups adopted numbers (14–25) following in sequence from those used by WA.[16] Similarly, NEF groups were expected to be more or less permanent in membership in order to foster teamwork, and, as was the British practice, sailed under their most senior officer (Senior Officer,

Escort, or SOE). The SOE fulfilled the duties of a Captain (D) at sea, conducting the group's operations and taking responsibility for its efficiency.

Detailing tasks, issuing sailing orders, and other related duties fell to CCNF's operational staff. It provided the link between actual naval forces and the trade and convoy organizations. The control and management of shipping was part of the bureaucratic war. The Commonwealth navies, through their trade divisions and naval-control-of-shipping (NCS) organizations, rationalized and systematized the movement of merchant ships, allowing them to be defended in one of two ways. On the basis of intelligence and under the indirect cover of battle fleets, shipping was routed independently along 'safe' routes. This form of protection, by far the most prevalent until 1943, was predicated upon the existence of British, and later Anglo-American, command of the sea. It was an effective form of defence when dealing with surface raiders, but it was never completely successful against U-boats, particularly as their numbers began to grow. The second type of naval defence of shipping was the raison d'être for NEF.

The organization and sailing of convoys was co-ordinated by the Admiralty's world-wide intelligence network, of which Ottawa was the North American centre. The assembling of shipping in convoy ports was the responsibility of local NCS staffs working in conjunction with the regional intelligence centre, through which all communication with other regional centres passed. The actual organization of the convoys, issuing code books, charts, special publications, arrangement of pre-sailing conferences, passing out sailing orders, and so forth, was all the work of the NCS. The latter also looked after the convoy commodores, usually retired RN flag officers. The commodore's task was similar to that of an admiral handling a fleet, except that the commodore's fleet usually consisted of a motley collection of merchant ships commanded by an independent breed of seamen. It was the commodore's responsibility to get this entourage to sea, form it up, ensure discipline on passage, and see that the ships broke ranks for their assigned ports in an orderly fashion. In large transatlantic convoys the commodore sailed front and centre, usually in a large ship which was well appointed for visual and sound communications with the rest of the convoy and equipped for direct wireless communication with shore authorities. The commodore was also the crucial link between the convoy and its escort. Although the escort commander was ultimately responsible for the safe and timely arrival of the convoy, in practice he and the commodore worked as a team. Depending on the size of the convoy, the commodore was also aided by vice- and rear commodores stationed in stern positions on the outer columns of the convoy. Each had his own staff, largely signallers (five for a commodore, less for others). Interestingly, the majority of convoy signallers in the North Atlantic by 1941 were RCN.[17]

Once the convoy cleared the outer defences of the harbour, it became the responsibility of the escort forces. Its routing, however, was laid down prior to sailing by the RN's Trade Division (shared with the USN after the American entry into the war), which prescribed a series of points of longitude and latitude through which the convoy was to pass. Minor tactical deviations within a narrow band along the convoy's main line of advance were permitted the SOE, but major alterations of course remained the prerogative of shore authorities. The ideal routing, one towards which the Allies moved much more slowly than they would have liked, was one simple 'tramline' along the most direct course between North America and Britain – the great-circle route. For a number of reasons tramlines were not feasible until 1943. For the greater portion of the period covered by this study the object of routing remained simple avoidance of the enemy, within the limits of air and sea escorts.

Finally, by the time NEF became operational there were two types of convoy plying the waters between Canada and Britain: fast and slow. The fast eastbound series, the famous HX convoys, originated in Halifax. Their westbound counterparts, the ON series (until July 1941 called the OB series), assembled from a number of British ports in the Irish Sea or the North Channel. In 1941 fast convoys included all ships capable of making no less than 9 and no more than 14.8 knots (those above were routed independently). Slow convoys, ships capable of speeds between 7.5 and 8.9 knots, began sailing to Britain from Sydney, Cape Breton, in August 1940 as a temporary measure. Their slow speed drew together a feeble and ponderous class of aged tramps, and there was initially no thought of convoying them through the storms of winter. Yet necessity dictated that all merchant shipping below a certain speed be convoyed. For the escorts it was a thankless task. Slow convoys were characteristically unruly. Their ships were prone to belching smoke, breaking down, straggling (falling out of station in the convoy, beyond the protective screen of escorts and accompanying ships), or even romping ahead if stokers happened upon a better-than-average bunker of coal. In the early days slow convoys more often resembled an organized mob than an orderly assemblage of ships, and their slow pace of advance made evasive action in the face of the enemy useless, if not altogether impossible.

By the time Murray arrived to take command of NEF it had grown to seven RN and six RCN destroyers, four RN sloops, and twenty-one corvettes, all but four of them RCN. The Admiralty would have liked even more committed to NEF. Indeed, in early July the Admiralty proposed to NSHQ that Halifax be virtually abandoned as an operational base and that the RCN's main effort be concentrated at St John's.[18] Naval Service HQ might have expected grander British plans for St John's when the Admiralty recommended that Commodore Murray command NEF instead of the RCN's initial choice, Commander Mainguy. For practical reasons, however, concentrating the fleet at St John's was impossible. In the summer of 1941 there were not enough facilities to support NEF, let alone the RCN's whole expansion program, and it would be a long time before this situation was reversed. The Naval Council did not debate long before the idea was dismissed as impractical. None the less, subtle British pressure to increase the RCN's commitment to NEF continued, in large part because the RN wanted to eliminate its involvement in escort operations in the Western Atlantic. In August, for example, the Admiralty advised the RCN that it preferred to deal with only one operational authority in the Western Atlantic, CCNF.[19] The pressure, in combination with a serious German assault on convoys in NEF's area by the late summer, proved successful. Despite growing USN involvement in convoy operations in the Western Atlantic, fully three-quarters of the RCN's disposable strength was assigned to NEF by the end of the year. In the spring of 1941, however, the RCN was unprepared to make such large-scale commitments.

One week after Murray assumed his post as CCNF, NEF fought its first convoy battle. Ironically, the confrontation was brought about by the increasing effectiveness of Allied convoy routing as a result of penetration of the U-boat ciphers in May. Excellent evasive routing so reduced the incidence of interception that the U-boat command, out of frustration, broke up its patrol lines and scattered U-boats in loose formation. This made accurate plotting by Allied intelligence much more difficult and consequently made evasive routing less precise.

On 23 June, HX 133, fifty-eight ships escorted by the destroyer *Ottawa* and three corvettes, *Chambly*, *Collingwood*, and *Orillia*, was sighted by *U203*. The U-boat was given permission to attack on the night of 23–24 June, and she easily penetrated the screen and sank one ship. The Senior Officer, Captain E.R. Mainguy, found it impossible to co-ordinate the escort either in defence or in a search for the assailant because the Canadian corvettes were not fitted with radio telephones (R/T) and their wireless sets were inadequate. In this first attack only *Chambly* received any signals from *Ottawa*, and she only got about half of them. Visual signalling was equally bad. When, on the twenty-sixth, *Ottawa* attacked a contact and two corvettes came to her assistance, Mainguy instructed the latter to stay behind to keep the U-boat down while the destroyer rejoined the convoy. The message, sent by light, was only partially received, and the corvettes, unable to pierce the inky darkness with the smaller signal lights, could not obtain a repeat and broke off the action. The escort was eventually heavily reinforced by British ships, and although HX 133 lost six ships, the RN escorts destroyed two U-boats. Canadian problems in the early going were lamentable, but hardly unexpected. As Joseph Schull, the RCN's official historian, concluded, 'no one could have expected it to be otherwise.'[20]

In the meantime Captain (D), Greenock's stern criticism of the Canadian corvettes found its way to NSHQ, accompanied by a covering letter from Captain C.R.H. Taylor, RCN, who had succeeded Murray in London as CCCS. Taylor noted that the poor state of readiness of the corvettes stemmed from the fact that they were manned and stored for passage only. Deficiencies could not be made up from the RCN's UK manning pool since most of the men who were committed to it were in fact still aboard the ships. Taylor also noted that the poor quality of officers, especially COs, had been pointed out in April and that they would never have been assigned if the ships had commissioned permanently. It was heartening to note, however, that *Hepatica*, *Trillium*, and *Windflower*, through remedial work and extra effort, were worked up 'to a state of efficiency which the Commodore *Western Isles* reported as surpassing many RN corvettes.'[21]

Naval Service HQ was therefore well braced when a follow-up letter from the Admiralty arrived several days later. The letter took a conciliatory view of Canadian difficulties, noting that these seemed to be 'essentially similar to those occasionally experienced with RN corvettes and trawlers.' To overcome these the Admiralty advised of three means employed by the RN. If the officers and men were competent and responsive, simply prolonging the length of work-up usually sufficed – as was the case with the three corvettes mentioned by Taylor. If the officers were incompetent or otherwise unsatisfactory, they could be replaced by new ones drawn from a manning pool. Similarly, inefficient or unsuitable key ratings could be replaced by men drawn from a pool maintained for this purpose. In its concluding remarks the letter cautioned that corvettes commissioning and working up in Canada were likely to display a wide variation in efficiency, and warned that at this point, with ships stretched to provide continuous A/S escort in the North Atlantic, 'no reduction in individual efficiency can be safely accepted.' This was true enough, but it contradicted what the Admiralty had said to the RCN in April, when the issue of manning the ten 'British' corvettes had been resolved.[22]

While the Admiralty clearly felt that it was offering the RCN a workable set of solutions, the suggestions contained few alternatives for the Canadians. In sum, the RCN was hard pressed just to find men with enough basic training in order to get corvettes to sea. Producing a surplus of specialists – of any kind – was out of the question. Nelles, in his draft reply to the Admiralty, pointed out that all experienced officers and men were already committed either to new ships or to the new RCN work-up establishment, HMCS *Sambro*, at Halifax. Future prospects looked equally grim. Spare HSD ratings (the highest level of asdic operator, of which there was to be one per corvette) would not be available until the spring of 1942, a prognosis even Nelles considered optimistic. And no trained RCN commanding officers or first lieutenants could be spared for some time to come. In short, a pool of qualified and disposable personnel was out of the question. If the RN wanted to loan experienced personnel until they could be replaced by the RCN, such help would be 'greatly appreciated.' The only other options were prolonged work-ups or some form of ongoing training. Aside from that, Canadian escorts had to make do.[23] RCN escorts sent to work up at Tobermory through 1941 continued to arrive in an unready state, though there is no indication that these were any worse off than corvettes retained for work-up in Canada. The state of ships arriving at Tobermory not only resulted in 'much excellent training [being] lost';[24] it did little to enhance the RCN's already tattered image within the parent service.

Although reports from both sides of the Atlantic indicated that the expansion fleet was badly in need of training and direction, its future looked bright in the summer of 1941. Corvettes operating from Sydney and Halifax as part of the Canadian local escort held up remarkably well to operations in the calmer months. A sampling of escorts based at Sydney in the months of August and September reveals startling statistics on the small amount of sea and out-of-service time logged by the new ships. Considerably less than half of their days were spent at sea, and this represented only about 56 percent of their seaworthy time. With so much time alongside, ships' companies were able to keep up with teething problems. In the ships in question all time out of service was devoted to boiler cleaning. For completion of the latter task by the crew alone, six days were allowed, or with dockyard help, four: one day to let the fires die, two to clean, and one to raise steam again. Later, as operations crowded available time and spare hands crowded the mess decks to provide extra watches for longer voyages, the shorter period became routine. But it is significant that until the fall of 1941 the corvette fleet enjoyed considerable slack, in which it could make good its defects.[25]

The easy routine extended to NEF as well and offered an opportunity to improve on the operational efficiency of escorts already committed to convoy duties. 'As the force is now organized,' Captain E.B.K. Stevens, RN, Captain (D), Newfoundland, wrote in early September, 'there is ample time for training ships, having due regard for necessary rest periods between convoy cycles.' It would be a year and a half, or more, before the same could be said again. Moreover, when the Canadian escorts did have slack time, the dearth of training equipment and expertise prevented good use being made of it. The available equipment at St John's was, as Stevens reported, 'a beggar's portion'; one wholly inadequate target borrowed from the United States Army and one MTU (mobile A/S training unit) bus suitable for training destroyers (although corvette crews could be and were trained on it).

Captain (D)'s concern for the languishing advance to full efficiency arose from recent gunnery exercises off St John's. 'It is noticeable,' NEF's gunnery officer reported, 'that everyone from the First Lt., who is Gunnery Control Officer, downwards put their fingers to their ears each time the gun fired.' Not surprisingly, this prevented the ship's gunnery officer from observing the fall of shot, since he could not possibly use his glasses with his hands thus employed. In addition, some of the guns crews were startled by the firing, and all of this contributed to a deplorable rate of three rounds per minute. Captain (D) drily concluded that 'At present most escorts are equipped with one weapon of approximate precision – the ram.' And so it remained for quite some time.[26]

What NEF really needed, of course, was a proper training staff, hard and fast minimum standards for efficiency, the will to adhere to them, and improved training equipment. A tame submarine would have been a distinct advantage, but by the time L27, the submarine assigned to NEF by Western Approaches Command, arrived from Britain later in the fall, there was no time set aside for training. Throughout 1941 only hesitant and largely unsuccessful attempts were made to rectify this situation. In August Prentice obtained permission from Murray to establish a training group for newly commissioned ships arriving from Halifax. The crews of these were found to be totally 'inexperienced and almost completely untrained.'[27] Unfortunately, as with other such attempts, Prentice's first training group was stillborn because of increased operational demands at the end of the summer. So long as the training establishment at Halifax produced warships of such questionable quality, operations in the mid-ocean suffered, and it would be some time before the home establishments switched their emphasis from quantity to quality.

Relief for the struggling escorts of NEF was in the offing from two directions as summer gave way to autumn. By the end of August 1941 nearly fifty new corvettes were in commission, including those taken over from the RN. More were ready, at the rate of five to six per month, before the end of the year. With the men, the ships, and a little time and experience, the nightmare of jamming two years of expansion into one would be ended. This optimistic view was enhanced by the increased involvement of the USN in NEF's theatre of operations and by the prospect that many of its responsibilities would be passed to the Americans.

The Americans had hardly been passive bystanders in the unfolding battle for North Atlantic communications. The westward expansion of the war threatened to bring an essentially European conflict to the Western Hemisphere. Certainly, it disrupted normal trade patterns. With the establishment of American bases in Newfoundland in late 1940 that island became for the U.S. what it was already for Canada – the first bastion of North American defence. But neither the U.S. president, Franklin D. Roosevelt, nor American service chiefs were content to rest on the Monroe Doctrine. Moreover, aside from the purely defensive character of U.S. involvement in Newfoundland, the Americans made an enormous moral, financial, and industrial commitment to the free move.nent of trade to Britain with the announcement of lend-lease in March 1941. A natural corollary to lend-lease was what Churchill called 'constructive non-belligerency,' the American protection of U.S. trade with Britain. While Britain would clearly have liked a more rapid involvement of the U.S. in the Atlantic battle, American public opinion would only stand so much manipulation. Therefore, it was not until August that Roosevelt felt confident enough to meet Churchill and work out the details of American participation in defence of shipping.[28]

A great deal has been written about Roosevelt's and Churchill's historic meeting at Argentia, Newfoundland, in August 1941. Here it is only important to note how the agreements directly affected the conduct and planning of RCN operations in the North Atlantic. The British and Americans decided, without consultation with Canada, that strategic direction and control of the Western Atlantic would pass to the U.S. as per ABC 1. Convoy-escort operations west of MOMP became the responsibility of the

USN's Support Force (soon redesignated Task Force Four), with its advanced base at Argentia. According to operational plans already worked out under the terms of ABC 1, the U.S. commitment to Support Force was large – including battleships, a large force of escort destroyers (forty-eight), and, in the event of war with Germany, fleet-class aircraft carriers. The intention of the Argentia agreements was to relieve the RN of the burden of the Western Atlantic, including defence of trade. As far as the escort of convoys was concerned, Support Force was initially responsible for protection of fast convoys only between WESTOMP (the limit of local RCN escorts) and MOMP. The RCN commitment to the Western Atlantic, outside of local duties, under the terms of ABC 22 and the operational orders prepared by the USN was five destroyers and fifteen corvettes. With these forces the RCN was to assume sole responsibility for slow convoys between WESTOMP and MOMP. All British escorts operating west of MOMP were to be withdrawn, and it was expected that when the USN had gained sufficient experience in the conduct of convoys, it would take over NEF's duties as well. In the interim, NEF passed from the operational control of C-in-C, WA, to that of Rear-Admiral A.L. Bristol, USN, Commander, Support Force, an officer whose nation was still neutral.[29]

The agreements reached at Argentia illustrate the Anglo-American tendency to take decisions affecting the operational deployment of the RCN without direct consultation with Canadians at any level. Canadians were not so petty as to resent active American involvement in the war in aid of the Commonwealth, nor did they underestimate the importance of firm direction of the war effort. But the imposition of an American admiral on to the fabric of an emergent Canadian naval commitment – and in the midst of an enormous expansion – had serious and lasting consequences. Admittedly, Canada's naval effort was just that, emergent, but the ill will generated by the failure to include Canada in decisions directly affecting her war effort could easily have been avoided. Murray was known to be particularly annoyed at this shoddy treatment, although his relations with Admiral Bristol were always cordial and efficient.[30]

Perhaps the most important long-term effect of American involvement in the Northwestern Atlantic in 1941 was the confusion it introduced into the RCN's plans and development. While much of this is difficult to document, it is clear that uncertainty over the future of the base at St John's delayed work on that base. In many respects the delay was more than compensated for by RCN access to the American naval-operations base at Londonderry in early 1942. More problematical was the effect of operations alongside the USN on developing RCN tactical doctrine.

While professional naval officers never lost their close ties with the RN, the more proletarian wartime navy felt greater affinity with its North American counterpart.[31] Left to deal with only one authority – for example, Britain's Western Approaches Command – it is likely that the RCN would have made quicker and surer advances towards the type of operational efficiency expected of them by the RN during 1942 – after the USN had largely withdrawn. But the infusion of the inexperienced USN into NEF's theatre brought a concept of ASW very different from that which developed in the RN, and this despite the interchange of such information.

By the spring of 1941 the RN had finally resolved its internal squabbling over the purpose of escorts in favour of defence. In April Western Approaches issued its famous 'Convoy Instructions' (WACIS), which set the doctrine for convoy escort down on paper. The first and primary task of the escort was to be the 'safe and timely arrival of the convoy.' All else, including pursuit of the enemy, was secondary to this aim. In practice WA Staff officers preferred to see safe and timely arrival tempered with aggressive pursuit of the enemy if time and circumstances permitted. But unless the escort could balance losses from its convoy with destruction of the enemy, it was best to push U-boats off and return to station in the escort screen. In contrast, the American concept of convoy escort had not progressed beyond the pre-war British belief in offensive escorting – that is, pursuit of the enemy and his destruction as the surest means of guaranteeing the defence of convoys. United States Navy 'Escort-of-Convoy Instructions,' in use in the fall of 1941, placed 'conduct of the convoy clear of the enemy' last on its list of escort priorities – exactly opposite to RN preference.[32]

In retrospect, the passing of NEF from RN to USN command could not have come at a worse time. The expansion fleet needed the guiding hand of a consistent and well-defined doctrine. The RCN did adopt WACIS as the basis of escort operation, but the British would argue (and have argued since the war) that the spirit of its escort sections – the primacy of safe and timely arrival of the convoy – was absent from Canadian operations. In this the RCN was at least consistent with its earlier aim to conduct 'offensive' ASW, through the provision of corvette 'strike forces' for example. It was natural, therefore, for the Canadian navy to exhibit such tendencies in its escort operations. Moreover, whereas Western Approaches Command was a specialized force tasked exclusively with trade protection, Canadian escort forces remained part of the mainstream of the RCN. The sharp distinction, as it was made in the much larger RN, between what the main fleet was to do and what was expected of trade escorts was never clearly delineated in the early days of RCN expansion. Escort of trade convoys was what the whole navy did. And yet, within that fleet there beat the heart of a more traditional service, one which aspired to cruisers and destroyer flotillas. Operations under the USN, whose escort doctrine in late 1941 was offensive, to say the least, simply reinforced the RCN's natural tendencies – to the detriment of the navy's image in British eyes. Indeed, British attempts during 1942 to reassert C-in-C, WA's command of convoy operations to WESTOMP were motivated in part by a desire to establish Western Approaches tactical doctrine firmly over the whole of the crucial central segment of the convoy route.

Although these considerations may have troubled some officers in the late summer of 1941, they were more than outweighed by the enormous benefit of American assistance in convoy operations in the Western Atlantic. What almost certainly caused Canadian officers consternation (as it did the British) was the division of labour resulting from USN participation in NEF's area. United States Navy destroyer forces were more suited, tactically, to the escort of fast convoys, where their high speeds allowed them greater flexibility. A corvette detached from a fast convoy for any length of time simply did not enjoy a sufficient margin of speed over its charges to regain station in the screen quickly. The different qualities of the two forces were recognized, and on 25 August the RCN agreed to assume responsibility for slow convoys between WESTOMP and MOMP.[33] Escorting slow mercantile convoys was a calling of dubious distinction. Later, operational research would reveal that ships in slow convoys stood a 30 per cent higher chance of being torpedoed than those in fast convoys. In the summer of 1941 this grim statistic remained to be proved, although it should have been obvious that slow convoys spent nearly 30 per cent more time at sea and this, in combination with their inability to respond to tactical situations, made them much easier targets.[34] It is also clear that to some extent the high loss rate in slow convoys was due to the fact that they were largely escorted by the RCN. It was unfortunate for both that the RCN continued to escort the bulk of slow convoys long after the sleek USN destroyers sailed for warmer climes.

A great many issues remained to be resolved, then, as the RCN began to build a service in the Northwest Atlantic. Even the choice of base sites was not the best in the summer of 1941. The RCN had settled on St John's but had actually considered Botwood, on the island's north coast, as a possible alternative. Although it seems a remote location, Botwood made more sense operationally in mid-1941 because convoys were being routed through the Straits of Belle Isle – at the opposite end of the island from St John's. The circuitous routing, problems plaguing new corvettes and the aged Town-class destroyers, weather and sea conditions, and the ever-present threat of enemy action conspired to give NEF's early operations a befuddled, occasionally comic quality. One such convoy operation from late August will serve to illustrate the character of those early forays and the trouble the Canadians managed to inflict upon themselves.

In the last week of August the Twenty-first Escort Group was detailed to escort convoy SC 41, scheduled to clear the Straits of Belle Isle on 27 August. Two days before the agreed rendezvous the corvette *Galt* departed St John's for Wabana, to escort a small joiner convoy to SC 41. The balance of the Twenty-first Group, the destroyer *St Croix*, Commander H. Kingsley, RCN, as SOE, and the corvettes *Buctouche* and *Pictou*, sailed the next day and made the rendezvous with the convoy on schedule. Relief of the local escort, the RN sloop *Ranpura* and the corvette *Matapedia* (RCN), was effected without difficulty, but SC 41 was badly scattered among icebergs, which, along with poor visibility, made effective screening impossible. When, by the next day, SC 41 had cleared the ice and fog, it was delayed because *Galt* and her charges failed to make their rendezvous. Nor were the two portions of the convoy in radio contact. In the early hours of the twenty-eighth *Buctouche* was detached to pass a wireless message to *Galt* via Halifax. While *Buctouche* was thus engaged, the fog that had once again beset the convoy lifted, revealing that the corvette *Pictou* was no longer in company. *St Croix* remained SC 41's sole escort until *Buctouche* rejoined, whereupon she was immediately detailed to repeat the exercise, since nothing had yet been heard from *Galt*. When it was finally clear that Halifax had repeated *Buctouche*'s message to the errant escort, she returned to SC 41. In the afternoon of the twenty-eighth the convoy received brief air cover before fog once again closed in. The night passed uneventfully, which was just as well for the two escorts of the screen. Part of the next morning was passed sinking canvas fishing floats, which provided some relief and some gunnery practice. But the highlight of the morning came when *Pictou* rejoined. She had spent most of two days battling a faulty magnetic compass and engine defects. Later, just before hands were piped to dinner and as *Buctouche* closed with *St Croix* to obtain medical supplies for a rating suffering from gonorrhoea, *Pictou* broke down again. *Buctouche* was detached to stand by, and when it was found that *Pictou* could only make four knots, she was ordered to return to St John's alone.

As one player left the stage, another lost soul made a much belated entrance. *Galt* and her charges, less one, were met before sunset on the twenty-ninth. The missing ship fortunately had not been lost to enemy action. As *Galt* reported to Kingsley, the motor vessel *Odorin* believed that she was not required to sail in convoy. When *Galt* closed to pass orders instructing her to do so, there had been a slight collision. Neither ship suffered damage, but *Galt* was unsuccessful in forcing the reluctant ship into her station. Rather like a jilted lover, *Galt* reported that *Odorin* was last seen in company 'with a Portuguese.'

On the morning of the thirtieth *St Croix*'s steam-powered steering developed a leak and she had to revert to manual, at least until a gale struck later in the day, when she effected emergency repairs simply by closing off the space into which the live steam was escaping. Later, her gyro-compass was knocked out of commission when a rating asleep on a nearby bunk was thrown on to it as his ship was lifted by a heavy sea. The convoy was reassembled following the gale on Monday, 1 September, and the next day an RN Town, *Ramsay*, joined the escort as it sailed into U-boat–infested waters. In the days that followed various U-boat contacts were made, but air cover from Iceland kept the balance in the escort's favour. The only equipment failure to occur before the Twenty-first Group left SC 41 for Hvalfjordhur was the asdic of *Buctouche*. She put her own set out of action by the shock of a depth-charge attack – an all-too-frequent cause of equipment failures in Canadian corvettes.[35]

The passage of SC 41 had all the flavour of NEF convoy operations in 1941: fog, collision, gales, ice, equipment breakdowns, lost escorts, reluctant and ill-disciplined merchant masters, and a small, poorly co-ordinated escort. All this was bad enough. But when this circus was beset by a pack of determined and skilled U-boats in a part of the ocean far from quick reinforcement, the result was a genuine nightmare. Such was the battle of SC 42.

3

Between a Rock and a Hard Place

The reputation of the RCN in this war depends on the success or failure of the NEF ...
Commodore L.W. Murray, RCN, October 1941

The enemy that NEF faced in late 1941 was its exact opposite in almost every conceivable sense. The U-boat fleet was still an elite force: well motivated, highly skilled, and very professional. To these qualities, the hallmarks of the pre-war service, could now be added two years of hard experience in war, experience gained at a time when Allied countermeasures were in the formative stages and mistakes by U-boat captains offered food for thought and learning, not the prospect of certain death. Admittedly, the British had scored great success against the U-boat fleet late in the second winter of the war. In March alone Germany lost one-fifth of her operational U-boat fleet and her three top U-boat aces: Prien, Schepke, and Kretchmer. These losses proved the wisdom of the convoy and escort system, its value as a strategic offensive. Escorted merchant shipping forced the U-boats to fight in order to fulfil their assignments. At the tactical level the escort's task, at least until 1943, was to 'hold' this strategic objective by waging a defensive battle. This was particularly so in the first four years of the war, when it was the U-boats, as attackers with the initiative, who determined the character of convoy battles.

By 1941, with new U-boats coming into service in increasing numbers and the seas around Britain largely barren of unescorted trade, German tactics finally became highly centralized. Their object now was to mass overwhelming strength against convoyed shipping. Finding and plotting operations against convoys in the broad Atlantic was no mean feat, particularly after the Allies penetrated the German naval ciphers in June.

But the requirements of concentrated attack also facilitated co-ordinated searches over vast stretches of ocean. By disposing a U-boat pack in a patrol line at right angles to the main convoy routes, BdU expected to ensnare a convoy, determine its position, course, and speed, and bring the pack down upon it. Failing the success of initial dispositions, the whole line could be moved in any direction or used to 'comb' the convoy lanes in search of targets or convoys which may have slipped through during darkness or bad weather. The longer the line or the greater the number of U-boats, the better the chances of interception and successful attack.

Admiral Dönitz had thought through the theory of pack attacks before the war. When he took command of Nazi Germany's first U-boat flotilla in 1935, Dönitz experimented with and perfected his theory. Initially he sought a local means of command and control of pack operations from a specially equipped U-boat. It was soon realized, however, that submarines were unsuited to the task of command. The easy elimination of the directing U-boat, even by an unwitting enemy aircraft or warship which forced it to submerge, made local command of packs impractical. The only alternative was shore-based control through the use of high-frequency, long-range wireless. Dönitz and his officers appreciated that regular or even frequent signalling presented the enemy with potentially useful operational intelligence. To minimize the danger, the Germans developed a system of standardized numerical and alphabetical codes representing regularly used phrases. They also developed high-speed automated transmitters which could send these small groups of figures almost instantly. The likelihood of successful enemy use of the actual signal traffic, (that is, the analysis of volume, location of transmitters, and so on, as opposed to reading the signals themselves) was considered minimal and in any event was outweighed by the practical advantages of central control. Signals were also considered relatively safe from enemy cryptanalysts. They were encoded and deciphered on a mechanical device, resembling a typewriter, the settings of which were changed daily, presenting the potential interloper with an astronomical number of possible combinations. The Germans were not so naïve as to believe that the settings, or individual signals, would never be broken. But the time-lag would inevitably prove much too long to affect operations.

The entire system of shore-based control and pack attacks on escorted convoys was tested in exercises immediately before the war and was found to work perfectly. Whether the Allies were aware of these exercises in the Baltic and the Atlantic remains unknown, but the tactics themselves were certainly not secret. Dönitz actually published a book in January 1939 outlining this method of submarine attack on trade. Its adoption in wartime was delayed by the sheer abundance of easy targets in the first year. Perhaps because of this delay, the British expressed surprise at the German adoption of pack attacks in late 1940.[1]

The key to the whole German system was, of course, use of wireless. In general U-boats observed strict wireless silence, but the instances in which they were called upon to communicate with BdU were numerous. Daily position reports were usually required of U-boats on station in a patrol line, and occasionally BdU wanted weather reports as well. U-boats were naturally charged with reporting major enemy naval units and all convoys, along with details of positions, course, and speed. In a pack operation against a convoy the first U-boat to intercept was directed to act as a shadower, maintaining contact and sending off periodic reports (on average, every two hours). Based on the intelligence provided by the shadower, BdU directed other members of the pack on to the convoy..In addition, BdU could also instruct the shadower – if it was not current operational procedure to do so automatically – to transmit periodic homing signals on medium frequency for the benefit of U-boats trying to join.[2]

Modifications to this system were made from time to time, such as allowing the shadower to attack, or holding off all the U-boats in contact until a large force was assembled. But the basic principles of central control, concentration, and (whenever possible) mass attack remained unaltered until late 1943. BdU's control of all phases, with one exception, was absolute. The exception was the actual attack itself. BdU gave permission for U-boats to launch attacks, but each commander then acted independently. Tactical co-ordination would have reaped handsome rewards, and the Allies frequently attributed German success to such co-ordination. In practice, however, the physical limitations of a Second World War submarine and the difficulties of attacking a seething mass of ships in the dark of night made co-ordination at the local level impossible. U-boat wolf-pack tactics therefore had an apt – and to the Allies, at least, sinister – appellation. On the long lead of wireless, BdU tightly controlled its packs until the signal to attack was given. From then until a night's action was over and the pack needed to be concentrated for another assault, the U-boats were turned loose on the convoy.

Canadian escorts had brushed with this enemy before, and of course NEF had been blooded by a pack as early as June. But the battle of SC 42 in September revealed that NEF was a very long way from having the measure of its enemy, a situation not peculiar to the RCN. Aside from its obvious significance as a major convoy battle, the story of SC 42 is important for two other reasons. The two nights during which NEF Group Twenty-four fought alone were the acid test of the expansion fleet, and the fleet failed. The reasons for its failure have been touched upon, but it is necessary to illustrate just how these shortcomings manifested themselves in the face of the enemy. The battle also brought the RCN's first U-boat kill of the war. This remarkable achievement tends to overshadow the tragedy of SC 42, and in fairness it was a positive accomplishment at a time when little seemed to be going right. But in no small way the sinking of *U501* was an aberration. It was natural for a young navy to forget its first bloody nose and revel in the triumph of its first victory. However, it was to be two more long years before destruction of the enemy took precedence over the safe and timely arrival of the convoy.

SC 42's ocean escort was Group Twenty-four.[3] Its Senior Officer, Lieutenant Commander J.C. Hibbard, RCN, in command of the destroyer *Skeena*, had served in UK waters during the winter of 1940–1 as part of the Clyde Escort Force and was therefore no stranger to escort operations. Two of the group's corvettes, *Orillia* and *Alberni*, were original members of NEF, and had sailed with *Skeena* on at least one previous occasion. The newcomer to the newly formed Twenty-fourth Group was the corvette *Kenogami*. She had commissioned at the end of May and had only just been assigned to NEF, replacing *Primrose* (RN) in Group Twenty-four. Thus, aside from *Kenogami*, the escorts of SC 42's screen were experienced – at least by 1941 standards – but hardly old salts when it came to dealing with a sustained pack attack.

Group Twenty-four met SC 42 just east of the Straits of Belle Isle at the end of the first week of September. Aside from bad weather, which plagued the convoy through most of its passage, reducing its speed to less than five knots, the first days were uneventful. As the convoy edged its way towards Cape Farewell, however, intelligence plotting of enemy movement indicated trouble ahead. The developing situation was watched closely in St John's, not least by Prentice, who was making preparations for sailing with his first training group. In view of the threat to SC 42, Prentice obtained permission from Murray to sail with *Chambly* and *Moose Jaw* (all that remained of the five ships originally assigned for training) on Friday, 5 September – four days ahead of schedule. Prentice planned to join SC 42 just about the time it fell afoul of the U-boats, and shaped his course accordingly. On the second night out Prentice received a garbled transmission from CCNF which, in the light of verbal orders passed to him before he had left St John's, he interpreted as an order to support SC 43, due to pass the straits on the eleventh. Instead of retracing his path to meet SC 43 off Newfoundland, Prentice held his position due east of Cape Farewell (roughly 60° N, 33° W) and waited for SC 43 to close up. In the interim *Chambly* and *Moose Jaw* conducted exercises.

Meanwhile, SC 42 forged along just south of Greenland. On 8 September, when the convoy was south-southeast of Cape Farewell, its course was altered to due north in hopes that it would pass around the U-boat concentration which lay across its path. Such a course would eventually have carried SC 42 on to the rocky shores of Greenland. Since no ship had been able to take a sighting for over a week, *Skeena* went on ahead to watch for the coast. Course was held as long as possible (twenty-three hours), until at 1900Z (Z: Greenwich time), on the ninth the convoy altered to 43°. SC 42 was still making only five knots in a moderate swell, with a sea state of five and strong winds out of the east-southeast. Three-quarters of an hour after SC 42 altered course towards Iceland, the moon, now four to five days after full, rose on the starboard (southern side). At about 2137Z the first torpedoes struck.

The torpedoes came from the dark (northern) side of SC 42 and hit the fourth ship in the outside port column, number 14,* ss *Muneric*. Laden with iron ore, she sank immediately, leaving no survivors. *Kenogami*, the port-side escort, began to search the dark quarter of the convoy and was rewarded with an asdic contact. The latter turned out to be false, but *Kenogami* soon obtained a U-boat sighting and engaged her target with the 4-inch gun. Firing the main armament without flashless powder, and unequipped with starshell, with which they might have illuminated the target, *Kenogami*'s crew was left temporarily night-blind, and they soon lost the U-boat. In the meantime *Skeena*, coming down from her post directly ahead of the convoy, attempted to find the U-boat by firing starshell over the area in which she thought the attacker to be. Unfortunately the opportunity for a co-ordinated search never developed. *Skeena* no sooner reached the scene of *Kenogami*'s action than she was called away by the convoy commodore (in the leading ship of the middle column, number 71), whose lookouts had sighted a U-boat on his port bow. Aboard *Skeena*, Senior Officer Hibbard instructed *Kenogami* to search for ten minutes and then resume her position on the convoy's port side, while *Skeena* set off to investigate the commodore's report.

At 2210Z the leading ships in the fifth and sixth columns reported

---

* Hereafter numbers following the name of a merchant ship indicate its position in the convoy (for example, first column, fourth ship = number 14).

sighting a U-boat, whereupon the commodore ordered an emergency turn to starboard. No sooner was the turn underway than number 61 reported yet another U-boat on the surface directly ahead. In the interest of general safety the commodore then ordered a return to the original course. An hour and a half later (2348Z) number 95 informed the commodore of a U-boat sighting off her starboard quarter. *Skeena*, in station just off the commodore's port bow, turned and passed down between the seventh and eighth columns to investigate the report. As she did so the commodore ordered an emergency turn to port – once again away from the general direction of the intrusion. The turn caught *Skeena* in the midst of the convoy doing a fair speed, and she had to manoeuvre wildly to avoid collision. As she did so, a U-boat passed up the convoy – also between the seventh and eighth lanes. The German submarine drew fire from all nearby merchantmen and continued to do so as she passed by *Skeena* on a reciprocal course, too close for the destroyer's guns to bear. Shortly after this fleeting confrontation the U-boat dived, but the tangle of wakes from the advancing convoy kept *Skeena* from relocating her adversary.

While the destroyer was engaged in saving herself from the very ships she was charged with protecting, two ships in the fourth column, *Baron Pentland* (45) and *Tahchee* (42), were struck in quick succession. The commodore, now fearing further attacks on his port side, ordered yet another alteration of course. The emergency turn to starboard put SC 42 back on its main course, while the escorts, thrown off by the breadth and frequency of the sightings and attacks, accomplished little.

Following this last flurry of activity, two quiet, suspense-filled hours passed before the enemy struck again. Astern of the convoy the real tragedy of such battles was acted out as men, numbed by cold and fear, struggled to save themselves and their ships. The corvette *Orillia* lingered astern to do what she could to help stricken vessels and survivors, while the last merchant ship in each column, the designated rescue ships, displayed an understandable reluctance to perform their assigned duties.

At ten minutes past two the port side of SC 42 was attacked again. The first ship to be hit, *Winterswijk* (25) was torpedoed twice, over an interval of several minutes, on her port side. Almost immediately *Stargard* (12) was also hit (by a single torpedo) on her exposed side. *Regin* (23) went to *Stargard*'s aid, engaging a surfaced U-boat as she did. *Skeena* immediately left her position ahead and began to fire starshell over the port side of the convoy. With the help of *Kenogami*, *Skeena* searched for the attacker, gained some questionable contacts, and dropped a few depth charges, but to no avail. Meanwhile, astern, *Orillia* began to salvage the damaged tanker *Tahchee*, which effectively eliminated the escort from further action in defence of SC 42. With three-fourths of the escort employed astern, the leading ship of the starboard column, *Sally Maersk* – more than five miles away – was struck on her outboard side. Moments later a U-boat was sighted by *Thistleglen* (91), and the commodore ordered another alteration of course to port. *Alberni*, the only escort left with SC 42, was ordered by Hibbard to investigate *Thistleglen*'s report, but the mass of turning merchantmen left *Alberni* little chance to act. Out of sheer frustration *Alberni* turned to rescue work, where at least she could accomplish something tangible. For the time being SC 42 carried on without any escort at all, and it was not until 0320Z that *Skeena*, having left *Kenogami* to rescue survivors on the port side, resumed her position ahead of the convoy. Up to this point the U-boats had launched three successful attacks on the port side and one on the starboard of SC 42. Although actual sightings of U-boats were plentiful, none of the enemy had been sighted by the escort in the act of closing on the convoy or launching an attack.

Moments before the attack on SC 42 was renewed in the early hours of the tenth, Prentice's training group, which had wandered southwestwards to rendezvous with SC 43, received orders to reinforce SC 42. Since the exact whereabouts of the convoy was unknown, a rendezvous in the area of 64° N, 32°10′ W was worked out and course set accordingly. During the tenth *Chambly* and *Moose Jaw* intercepted further signals which allowed them to estimate the position of SC 42 more accurately. But it was not until well after dark on the second day of the battle that the tiny force was able to come to the Twenty-fourth Group's aid. In the interim, the battle continued unabated.

At 0504Z on the morning of the tenth the *Empire Hudson* (21) was torpedoed on her port side. The attack was followed shortly thereafter by an eleven-minute alteration of the convoy's course to starboard. The main course was resumed at 0521Z, while *Skeena* did an asdic search around *Empire Hudson*, now still in the water but buoyed by her cargo of grain. The search was only just under way when *Skeena* was again called away by a report of a periscope from the commodore's ship. Nothing came of either search, nor of *Alberni*'s asdic contact on the starboard side an hour and forty minutes later. *Kenogami*, meanwhile, continued her work astern, which by now involved screening the intrepid freighter *Regin* as she went about her rescue work.

Attacks continued throughout the day on the tenth, and numerous periscopes were sighted by both the escort and the ships of the convoy.

At 1000Z one such sighting resulted in another emergency turn, while *Skeena* conducted an unsuccessful asdic search and dropped random depth charges in an attempt to keep the U-boat at bay. Proper course was resumed at 1030Z, but the alteration had served only to carry SC 42 on to another waiting U-boat, and about an hour afterwards *Thistleglen* (91) was struck on her port side. Two successive emergency turns to port were ordered as *Thistleglen*, drawn down by the steel and pig iron in her holds, fell out of station. The escort, which had been in WACI day-escort screen number 3 (one ahead and one on each beam), joined in line of bearing and swept to the northwest of the convoy, but no U-boats were contacted. At the end of this sweep a periscope was reported by ships in the stern of the convoy. It was soon sighted by all three escorts, and Hibbard took *Skeena* in to deliver a depth-charge attack by eye. As the destroyer opened range to renew contact and attempt a more deliberate attack, *Alberni* dropped charges on an asdic contact only two thousand yards away. This threw off *Skeena*'s asdic recorder trace (which was essential for timing in a deliberate attack), and her attempt was delayed. When a firm contact was finally regained by both *Skeena* and *Kenogami*, the latter was instructed to act as directing ship while the destroyer delivered a ten-charge pattern. The attack produced a large air bubble and some oil. Unable to regain the contact following this apparently successful attack, Hibbard considered the U-boat sunk and ordered the corvettes to resume their stations screening the convoy. *Skeena* lingered briefly to ensure that the U-boat was well and truly down, if not actually destroyed.

By early afternoon all the escorts were once again back on station (less *Orillia*, of course, who was busy salvaging *Tahchee*). Nothing notable occurred until 1805Z, when an aircraft from Iceland put in a brief appearance over the convoy. It dropped some flares on the port side of the convoy, indicating U-boat sightings, and a course alteration to starboard was ordered while the escort investigated. No U-boat contacts were obtained, and the main line of advance was resumed at 1820Z. All remained quiet until at 2057Z *Bulysse* (103) was hit on her port side. *Skeena* immediately began a starshell search of the starboard side. But in the deteriorated weather conditions (heavy swell and winds of force three to four), she was unable to locate anything untoward. While the convoy conducted an emergency alteration to starboard, the survivors of *Bulysse* were picked up by *Wisla*, the last ship in the tenth column and the designated rescue ship. But no sooner was the new course assumed than the *Gypsum Queen* (81) reported a U-boat on the surface off her starboard beam. On hearing the news *Skeena* abandoned her search in the wake of

SC 42 and turned to illuminate the starboard bow of the convoy. As she did this the *Gypsum Queen* was torpedoed and sank very quickly. Those who remained of her crew were picked up by *Vestland* (84), which also stood by her duty as rescue ship for the eighth column.

The pyrotechnics of this latest attack were seen by the lookouts of *Chambly* and *Moose Jaw*. During the tenth this small reinforcement had actually passed beyond SC 42's line of advance with the intention of closing the convoy from the dark side after moonrise. This provided the two escorts with the best opportunity of catching lurking U-boats silhouetted against the southern sky. It was a tactic which paid off, albeit in slightly different form. U-boats were present on the dark side all right, and at half past midnight *Chambly*'s asdic operator obtained a firm contact. The echo was confirmed as 'sub' by the A/S officer, but the corvette was almost on top of it – seven hundred yards distant, well inside the twelve hundred prescribed by current doctrine in depth-charge attacks. 'In view of the handiness and small turning circle of a corvette,' Prentice wrote in his report, 'it was decided to attack at once.' Fifteen degrees of helm were ordered, and this soon brought the contact dead ahead. The echo was classified as 'high' (referring to the doppler effect, the shift of pitch, between transmitted and received signals, that gives information on the speed of the target), and Prentice ordered a reduction in speed prior to attacking. Further classification of the target indicated that it was on a reciprocal course and therefore closing at a rate slightly faster than anticipated. For this reason and because the charges had already been set to a moderate depth (that is, more than one hundred feet), Prentice instructed that the five-charge pattern be laid a little early.

The order to fire was given at 0038z, just two minutes after the echo was first reported. But things did not go well on *Chambly*'s quarterdeck. The port thrower misfired, and the seaman at the port depth-charge rails – a relief man on his first trip to sea – missed his cue when the firing gong went. As a result there was a slight delay in firing the first and second charges, and when they did go, they went rather close together. All five charges were heard to explode, the first and second almost simultaneously. Upon completion of the attack *Chambly* swung round to port to regain the contact. But as she did so *U501* surfaced close by *Moose Jaw*. The corvette had followed *Chambly* in her initial turn to port and was passing through the scene of the attack (which would have spoiled Prentice's chances of quickly regaining the target). *Moose Jaw* promptly drew alongside the U-boat, close enough for the submarine's captain to step from his conning tower to the corvette's foc'sle without wetting his feet. Fearing further boardings, *Moose Jaw* withdrew, giving the U-boat the opportunity to get under way. As *U501* passed slowly across the corvette's bows, *Moose Jaw* rammed her and then, with gunfire, prevented the Germans from manning their deck armament. As the U-boat's crew began to assemble topside, Prentice put *Chambly* alongside and sent away a boarding party under Lieutenant Edward Simmons. After failing to pursuade *U501*'s crew, at gunpoint, to return below, Simmons and his small party gamely entered the submarine. Once inside they found the lighting system broken, instrumentation wrecked, and heard the tell-tale sound of inrushing water. All save one of the boarding party were able to clear *U501* before she took her final plunge. Stoker W.I. Brown and eleven of the German crew perished.

Before she sank, *U501* had been found to be missing her rear port hydroplane and to have a large dent about thirty feet abaft of the conning tower. Survivors reported that the U-boat had been driven downwards by two explosions, which wrecked all the ship's instrumentation and forced her to the surface. Prentice concluded that it was probably the poorly delivered first and second charges which had combined to do the damage. Thus skill and resolve on the bridge was enhanced by a healthy measure of luck. Once finished with *U501*, *Chambly* and *Moose Jaw* took their places in the screen of SC 42, port bow and starboard quarter respectively.

In the action around SC 42 which followed, five more ships were lost. *Stonepool* (111) and *Berury* (113) were both hit on the starboard side within minutes of one another. Two hours later (0210Z), *Scania* (43) and *Empire Crossbill* (44) were struck almost simultaneously (probably on the port side), followed at 0230Z by *Garn* (24), which was hit on her port side. The loss of the last three was due largely to the absence of *Alberni*, *Kenogami*, and *Moose Jaw*, all busy astern rescuing the crews of *Stonepool* and *Berury*, although Hibbard actually thought they were on station. Both *Skeena* and *Chambly* kept busy investigating asdic contacts and trying to prevent further losses. For all intents and purposes the battle ended in the forenoon of 11 September, when five destroyers, two corvettes, and two sloops (all RN) reinforced the escort, and the convoy moved within range of effective air support from Iceland.

The reasons for the loss of sixteen ships from SC 42 and for the escort's inability to deal effectively with the attackers were evident. As the Admiralty's assessment of the SC 42 disaster concluded, the 'slender escort' of one destroyer and three corvettes was painfully inadequate to protect the convoy from a pack of U-boats more than three times that number. It was widely recognized that Hibbard had made the best of a very difficult situation. Indeed, the surviving merchant captains 'unanimously and spontaneously' expressed their appreciation for the efforts of the Twenty-fourth Group and, on their arrival in Britain, made that sentiment known to Admiral Noble at once. Immediately following SC 42 the British asked the RCN to increase the strength of NEF's groups from the current four escorts to a minimum of six, two of which would now be destroyers. The Naval Council was quite prepared to accept this request, and the RCN could meet the increased commitment of smaller ships required (a minimum of forty-five corvettes based at St John's).[4] But the RCN simply did not have the fifteen destroyers needed to provide two (operational) with each of its six escort groups, nor were many of its Town class capable of mid-ocean operations.

Given that operations in the Western Atlantic were now an American responsibility, the RCN approached the USN for help with SC convoys. Commander F. Houghton, the director of Plans and Signals, who was in the U.S. to discuss the arrangements of joint operations in the North Atlantic, broached the issue with Admiral E.J. King, then commander of the U.S. Atlantic Fleet, and sent King's reply to Ottawa on 23 September. It was a flat no. 'I gathered that one of his difficulties,' Houghton wrote to Nelles, 'was the length of time his ships were not running due to refits and time in dockyard hands for fitting of new material.' Houghton's mission had little chance for success in any event. King was a notoriously obstinate and prickly character and a great burden on his peers. General Dwight D. Eisenhower, later the Supreme Allied Commander in Europe, confided to his diary that the whole war effort would have gone more smoothly had someone shot King. Eisenhower's Commonwealth colleagues would have agreed, and King's anglophobia proved a serious impediment to the Allied campaign in the Atlantic. King impressed on Houghton his belief that SC convoys were a joint RN-RCN responsibility – which was hardly the agreement reached at the Argentia meeting. It was, however, indicative of the American tendency to view the two Commonwealth navies as some form of joint entity (which, in fairness, they were). But King was also known to dislike the idea of escort groups of mixed nationality, a sentiment which, at least in so far as the USN was concerned, Canadian authorities shared. Faced with this obstacle, the Admiralty agreed to leave some of their destroyers in NEF, although this component of the force's strength fell from nine in September to five by October, where it stayed for the balance of the winter. The

Americans later agreed to help the RCN 'if the situation [became] more critical.'5

The ineffectiveness of SC 42's screen was also a function of the action of the escorts themselves. *Orillia's* detachment to salvage *Tahchee* and the tendency for inexperienced corvette commanders to busy themselves with rescue work contributed to further losses. While this was bad enough, the corvettes' failure to maintain proper communications with their SOE was even more unfortunate. Hibbard commented in his report that his use of radio had, by 1941 standards, been excessive. But in a tactical situation, when the whereabouts of the convoy was already obvious to the enemy and particularly with a new group, no amount of effective and efficient use of radio could be excessive. In fairness to Hibbard and the escorts of the Twenty-fourth Group, their task was a daunting one: to defend sixty-four ships in twelve columns spread out over thirty square miles in the face of at least fourteen U-boats. Further, it was hard enough to detect a U-boat travelling hull-down in the inky blackness of high latitudes, but the moderate-to-heavy swell and the slight spray from the wind on the wave-tops made the task well-nigh impossible. The prevalent surface conditions coupled with a near-full moon and otherwise good visibility (three to five miles) made ideal conditions for U-boat operations. At night they could easily see without being seen. On top of this, the escort was frequently called upon to make asdic searches for contacts reported inside the convoy. The turbulent waters in the convoy's wake made this task pointless, while the constant emergency turns rendered relative positions of sightings useless as the basis for starting searches. Unable either to prevent attacks or to deal effectively with intruders once sighted, the escorts turned to rescue work. Had they remained at their posts their deterrent effect might have saved some ships. It is plain, however, that the tactical necessity of maintaining the deterrence was poorly understood by the escorts, while their natural desire to help those in distress proved too strong. All of this points to poor training and a failure both to comprehend and to follow the WACIS sections on the conduct of escort.

The successful destruction of *U501* in the shortest possible action was an equal combination of skill, good luck, and inexperience on the part of the enemy (the U-boat had only commissioned in June). For the latter reason it was, perhaps, a fair contest for the RCN, but the action illustrated the accuracy which a good asdic team could bring to an attack. It also illustrated Prentice's preferred method of depth-charge attack by corvettes, one which he encouraged. The order to reduce speed upon attacking was in direct contradiction to the accepted British practice. The RN was trained to stalk a U-boat from an initial range of twelve hundred yards, tracking the U-boat at the ship's best asdic speed (which was usually about twelve knots) to the 'throw-off' point. At the latter point, still eight hundred yards distant from the submarine, speed was to be increased and the course altered to lay the depth-charge pattern ahead of the target. Increased speed allowed the corvette to close the distance to the target quickly, thus reducing the U-boat's time for evasive action. It also carried the attacking ship well clear of its own explosives. Prentice believed that the corvette's short turning radius (four hundred yards) coupled with the known limitations of type 123 asdic demanded more resolute action. He advocated a much shorter initial range, a steady speed for attacks (roughly equivalent to the best asdic speed), and a much closer throw-off point – half the distance of that prescribed by the RN. This allowed the target to be held by the asdic operator until the last possible moment, while the steady speed gave no warning to the U-boat of impending attack, thus reducing the likelihood of successful evasive action. Employing Prentice's method it was theoretically possible to launch a rapid series of accurate attacks. Prentice even went so far as to have a transparent 'rate recorder' (indicating the change of target distance) prepared and fitted to *Chambly*'s asdic to facilitate these short, quick depth-charge actions (such a rate recorder was later adopted by the RN as standard equipment, but there is no indication the idea was solely that of Prentice). Although the quick attack paid off handsomely against *U501*, it had a serious drawback. If the charges were set shallow or the escort lost too much momentum from the application of her helm at the throw-off point, there was a danger of damage from her own explosives. In one of the last depth-charge attacks undertaken by *Chambly* around SC 42, electrical fittings in the after portion of the ship were blown, and the engine- and boiler-room personnel reported being lifted six inches off the deck by the force of the exploding charges.[6]

The lessons of SC 42 were fairly obvious, and they suggested nothing of which the RCN was not already aware. Newfoundland Escort Force was organized into proper escort groups and had been since May. Teamwork would come with time and effort. Radios were either already fitted or on their way. Aside from a shortage of starshell, flashless powder, and searchlights (*Kenogami* was criticized for not illuminating her U-boat with a searchlight), the real equipment shortfall during SC 42 was the lack of effective radar.

The RCN was slow to appreciate the potential of radar for small ships.

Its uses in naval gunnery were understood, but none of the Canadian fleet warranted fitting such equipment in 1939–40. While future needs might require expertise in the field, sufficient instruction was available through the RN, where Canadians were exposed to larger ships and gunnery radar. Moreover, there was a great need for radar officers and technicians in Britain early in the war, and by 1941 Canada had been picked clean of her available expertise. The first training course for naval radar officers in Canada was actually inaugurated to meet the growing need overseas. The RCN had precious little to do with this first class, and when approached to provide $2500 to finance instruction of the eleven candidates, declined to do so. It is statement enough of the navy's lack of interest in radar that the first class, given by the University of Toronto, was sponsored by the local Kiwanis Club. All the candidates were successful, and the RCN belatedly granted them commissions in the RCNVR before sending them overseas to serve, on loan, with the RN.[7]

Towards the end of 1940 the RCN finally began to appreciate the need for radar personnel of its own, but by then the readily available manpower had been gobbled up by the army, the air force, and the RDF (radio direction finding) Imperial Forces Recruiting and Training scheme. It was now necessary to train men from scratch, and the RCN lacked both instructors and facilities. A few positions were available at the army's radar school in Halifax, but, as the Naval Staff noted rather quixotically, this was largely an army and air-force program.[8] In any event, radar policy remained undefined in early 1941, and until that of the Admiralty respecting escort vessels was ascertained, the Naval Staff took no action. News of British practice and policy reached Ottawa in February, at which time authorities in Ottawa took immediate steps to acquire radar for the fleet. They approached the National Research Council, also the navy's research and development establishment, to ask if the NRC could develop a radar for the detection of submarines on the surface at night. The navy requested specifically that the set be compatible with comparable British equipment. The NRC was already involved in radar and was working on a variation of the British ASV or 1.5-metre set, an airborne version of the RN's type 286 radar, the type then fitted in escort destroyers.

On 19 March 1941 a special meeting of the Naval Staff and NRC officials was held, during which the issue of radar was thrashed out. Dr C.J. Mackenzie, head of the NRC, explained that they were working on ASV and that this set was now being fitted to escorts of the RN. 'As the immediate requirement is locating submarines at night etc.,' Dr Mackenzie stated, 'this simpler set will be sufficient for our needs particularly as these can be produced at short notice in Canada.' The decision whether or not to build a new 1.5-metre set or simply to produce a Canadian version of the 286 was to be made following trials in April.

The NRC constructed the first Canadian submarine-control (CSC) radar with dispatch. It was ready for sea trials on 12 May, only fifty-four days after the RCN had made its initial inquiries. Interestingly enough, the first trial set went to sea in *Chambly*. There, under the careful, practised hands of NRC boffins and the watchful gaze of Prentice, the new radar performed admirably. The second day of trials, conducted in company with another corvette and the Dutch submarine *O-15*, revealed that the set worked very well indeed. The sub was tracked at ranges between 2.7 and one-tenth miles (there was no indication that the *O-15* proceeded with her deck casing awash in the manner of an attacking U-boat, and it is likely she was fully surfaced), and bearings were regarded as unerringly accurate. On 16 May further trials were undertaken, this time simulating an attack on a convoy. According to NRC personnel, naval authorities were completely convinced of the value of the set. On the twentieth the Naval Staff instructed that all escorts should be fitted, and the NRC agreed to provide the first fifty sets from their own laboratories. Further orders were placed with Research Enterprises Limited of Toronto.[9]

Once alerted to the need, the Naval Staff and Canadian scientists had moved with commendable speed. However, it is noteworthy that at the same time that *Chambly* was testing a new Canadian 1.5-metre set, HMS *Orchis*, also a corvette, was conducting trials in UK waters with a 10-centimetre set, the type 271 – the radar which was to contribute so greatly to successful escort operations in 1942.[10]

The production model of the Surface Warning, First Canadian (SWIC), as the CSC came to be known, differed little from the set tested in *Chambly* (which was removed following the trials – Prentice had to wait until February 1942 to get one of his own). It consisted of a masthead 'Yagi' antenna, comparable to the roof-top television antennas so common after the war, made of copper, from which signals were both emitted and received. The antenna was mounted on a steel shaft which, held in place by a series of bearing-lined brackets, ran down the mast into a gearbox fitted at the bottom, level with the foc'sle deck. From this main weight-bearing assembly the transmitter-receiver cable and a manually operated driveshaft ran to the forward port side of the deckhouse. In what had been the officers' water-closet a radar room was constructed, housing the set and a large handwheel and bearing indicator used to direct the antenna.

A cathode-ray-tube indicator gave the operator the necessary information on strength and character of echoes.[11]

Like all early radars, the SWIC was a fickle instrument. It had to be rested periodically and had to be started and shut down in a proper sequence to avoid damage to electrical components. Aside from requiring that such precautions be taken against overheating and improper procedures, the vacuum-tube technology of early radar – particularly Canadian-built sets – took constant maintenance and suffered greatly from the shock of depth charges, firing of the 4-inch gun, and general pounding of the ship at sea. The SWIC had other limitations. Its search area was limited to a narrow cone ahead and a very small 'back echo' astern of the antenna. The SWIC could 'sweep,' unlike the fixed British 286 set from which it was developed, but the rotation of the antenna was manual. If the set was not directed at a suspect target, the latter went unseen. The significant advantage of the 271 set just entering British service was that it did sweep a full 360 degrees automatically, although it took what now seems a rather prodigious amount of time (two minutes) to do so. Further, the first Canadian set, like its early RN counterpart, had a very long wavelength – 1.5 metres – much too long, in fact, to give a sharp definition to small targets among the clutter thrown up at sea level. The 271 set overcame this problem by using an extremely short wavelength of 10 centimetres, which returned a sharp echo.

Initial supplies of SWIC were disappointingly slow, and by the end of 1941 only fifteen RCN corvettes were fitted. In contrast, all the destroyers carried the British 286, and at least one of the ten 'British' corvettes was already equipped with the new type 271.[12] By the end of the winter all RCN escorts did have some form of radar, yet for all practical purposes the early radar sets made no appreciable contribution to escort operations, except perhaps to provide crews with experience in nursing a new technology under trying conditions. From August 1940 to February 1942 only four U-boats are known to have been detected on the surface with the aid of radar, and of this number only one was attacked. Even if this figure, which is based on admittedly incomplete data, is grossly inaccurate, doubling, tripling, or quadrupling it still produces an incredibly low number of contacts.[13] It may well be, as the commanding officer of *Orchis* reported after several months at sea with his new 10-centimetre set, that it took considerable time for both operators and bridge personnel to become adjusted to a radically new innovation. It is also true that both the 286 and the SWIC were failures as surface-warning sets, particularly against hull-down U-boats. Still, that the SWIC and its successor the SW2C proved to be unsuccessful under operational conditions tends to overshadow the remarkable achievement of the navy, industry, and science in fitting out the fleet with radar in much less than a year. Unfortunately, development and supply of a Canadian-built 10-centimetre radar did not go as smoothly, and this was to have important consequences at sea.

As the summer of 1941 gave way to the fall, any spare time previously enjoyed by NEF quickly evaporated. In part this stemmed from the simple increase in the basic size of escort groups. But it was also the result of factors well beyond the immediate control of RCN authorities. In mid-September the Mid-Ocean Meeting Point was moved eastward from 26–30° W to 22–26° W, following an agreement by RN and USN staffs, in order to free three RN escort groups for duty in the South Atlantic.[14] The extended length of passage for NEF and lack of any corresponding reduction in the convoy cycle eroded the escorts' harbour time. In addition, evasive routing drove convoys farther and farther north through later 1941, lengthening mileage logged and forcing escorts and merchantmen alike to endure the foulest weather the North Atlantic had to offer. NEF escorts were supposed to have twelve days of every convoy cycle free, but in practice spare time never approached this figure. *Chambly*, for example, averaged twenty-six of every thirty days at sea during the last three months of 1941 – barely enough time left over for boiler cleaning.[15]

By mid-October the increased amount of sea time logged by NEF led Captain (D), Newfoundland, Captain E.B.K. Stevens, RN, to send a strongly worded memo to Murray. In no uncertain terms Stevens chastised Murray for measuring an escort's endurance solely on its fuel capacity. He warned that unless immediate steps were taken to reduce the amount of sea time, 'a grave danger exists of breakdowns in health, morale, and discipline.' Murray was sympathetic and could see first hand the effect that strenuous operations were having on his command. Many of the escorts were still undermanned, and the general shortage of personnel kept him from forming a manning pool ashore to provide reliefs. The situation was so tight, Murray confessed, that he was forced to send defaulters back to sea, a sentence few can have thought lenient.[16] In any event, so long as schedules were left unchanged and escort groups were to sail at maximum strength, there was little Murray could do. Even the Americans were worried by mid-October. Captain M.L. Deyo, USN, destroyer squadron commander at Iceland, advised Admiral Bristol that the RCN was already near a breaking point:

As I understand it, they want to make quick turn around at this end in order to get more time in home ports. Having only 6 units, their cycle is 36 days with convoy intervals of 16 days. This gives them 10–14 days at home. The pinch comes when they have a maximum of 2 days which is often reduced to 36 hours or less and they are feeling the strain. The voyage out takes them 11 days. They arrive here tired out and the DDs [destroyers] barely just make it ... With winter coming on their problems will be more difficult. They are going to have breakdowns and ships running out of fuel at sea.[17]

In large part the problem of too-extensive layovers in Iceland, towards which Captain Deyo's remarks were largely directed, arose from the slightly unsynchronized convoy cycle. NEF escort groups were having to lie in Hvalfjordhur awaiting the next slow westbound convoy as it fought its way through prevailing winds and weather. The Americans were sympathetic to the Canadian plight, and on 9 October Admiral King authorized the assignment of westbound convoys to NEF on a priority basis. But with the onset of winter weather in the late fall, the pressure on NEF increased. Even the British admitted in late November that the Canadians were working twice as hard as Western Approaches escorts and suffered the added burden of almost totally inexperienced crews. Finally realizing just what a strain NEF was under, the Admiralty's director of Anti-Submarine Warfare apologized to Murray in December for being 'far too critical' in his assessments of recent Canadian actions.[18]

The harsh climate of the North Atlantic, coupled with the demanding task of escort operations in small ships, made proper rest for the crews an important element of operational efficiency. This was particularly the case when the gales of November set in. But even in the summer of 1941, USN officers were shocked by the ill-kept appearance of British escorts they encountered off Newfoundland. Initially Americans could not understand why ships' crews were not turned to with ardour to chip and paint ship during layovers. Once they were committed to operations in the North Atlantic, this wonderment ceased, and the USN, which had not yet undergone rapid wartime expansion, found the Newfoundland-to-Iceland run a serious impediment to operational efficiency. One American later wrote of the USN's impressions:

Escort operations in the North Atlantic were physically demanding because of the stormy weather, and emotionally enervating because of the need for constant vigilance in a tedious enterprise and the strain of making rapid decisions involving the fates of men and ships on the basis of incomplete information. The stress sometimes induced fatigue and irritability which had to be treated by rest, lest it lead to a nervous breakdown.[19]

The impact of these conditions on the smaller ships of NEF can be imagined. Small wonder that Canada's first corvette captains, more often than not the only qualified watch-keepers on their ships, were preoccupied with things other than maintenance and training during their brief layovers.

Even before NEF was beaten into submission by the North Atlantic, the slow march to efficiency animated both RN and RCN officers. In mid-September SC 44 lost four ships and the corvette *Levis* in one night's furious action. The British SOE of another convoy, SC 45, included a strong criticism of his Canadian escorts in his report of proceedings. Again Canadians were sloppy in signalling and reckless in their use of signal lamps by night. His conclusion, that 'their convoy discipline is not good,' was something of an understatement.[20] In action and out of it, the RCN's expansion fleet displayed an alarming propensity for ineptitude. In fairness, the escorts themselves were hardly to blame for most of this. The example of *Shediac*'s losing her convoy following an emergency turn and then searching for five days to no avail in an attempt to relocate it made professional naval officers' hair turn grey. In the case of *Shediac*'s misadventure, which happened in mid-October while she was escorting SC 48, no one thought to pass the alteration (arranged by flag while it was still light) directly to her. *Shediac* having no telescope with which to read flags, had a hopeless task, and the convoy simply sailed off the other way after dark. Rendezvous points with the convoy were unknown to *Shediac* for some inexplicable reason, and her wireless set was improperly tuned, so that transmissions were not received. No group of warships ever sailed so ill prepared for the most rudimentary tasks. When news of *Shediac*'s sojourn reached the Staff at Western Approaches, it was treated as more of the same. Admiral Sir Percy Noble, C-in-C, WA, minuted a bemused 'no action' on the report, while an unknown hand summed up the whole affair in five words: 'A sad state of affairs.'[21]

Losses continued to befall Canadian escorted convoys through October and November, and the prospects for the future looked grim. *Shediac*'s convoy, SC 48, lost three ships in two separate attacks while the convoy and the escort struggled to recover from a gale-forced dispersal. Reinforcement, in the form of five British and American destroyers and one RN corvette, arrived the next day, but even this enlarged escort could not prevent the loss of six more ships – which spoke volumes for the need to have properly co-ordinated teams defending convoys. In addition to merchant-ship losses from SC 48, one RN destroyer, HMS *Broadwater*, and the corvette HMS *Gladiolus* were sunk and the USS *Kearny* torpedoed in the fierce battle which surged around the convoy. Through October the packs moved further westwards, and by the end of the month the Germans had concentrated twenty U-boats off Newfoundland in an attempt to intercept convoys as they funnelled around the island. Group 'Mordbrenner,' of four U-boats, arrived on station off the Strait of Belle Isle on 16 October and was soon joined by 'Reisswolf' and 'Schlagetod,' both of which had pursued westbound convoys into Newfoundland waters. On 1 November, as Mordbrenner moved south to support attempts by Reisswolf to press home attacks on an American-escorted convoy, *U374* sighted SC 52 fifty miles off Cape Race. Operations against ON convoys were immediately dropped and the available U-boats (regrouped as 'Raubritter') sent to attack SC 52. Routing authorities, fully aware from special intelligence of the U-boat dispositions, altered the convoy's course to due north, while the German attack was hampered by poor radio conditions. Fearing heavy losses in a thousand-mile running battle, the British ordered SC 52 to return to Canada. Before it cleared the danger area, four ships were sunk by Raubritter, and a further two ran aground in fog when the convoy passed through the Straits of Belle Isle. Escorted by a scratch team of two RN destroyers and five Canadian, one British, and one Free French corvettes, SC 52 was the only transatlantic convoy driven back by U-boats alone during the entire war.[22]

The problem of strengthening close escort groups or providing them with rapid reinforcement was a vexing one in 1941. This was particularly so for the RCN, which had limited resources and which was bound, under the terms of the Anglo-American accord of August, only to provide escorts, not to manage the campaign. Any large-scale redistribution of escorts within NEF would have required at least the tacit consent of both the RN and the USN – though the RCN had every right to act in its own interest. Within this rather circumscribed adherence to gentlemen's agreements, the RCN did have some limited options and was never short of ideas. The idea of a training group which doubled as a reinforcement component of NEF was never abandoned, but some officers had even bolder ideas. One of them, Lieutenant Commander H.S. Rayner, CO of the destroyer *St Laurent*, advocated using NEF's destroyers to form five 'hunting groups' of four destroyers each to prowl the Newfoundland-to-Iceland route. With two such groups constantly at sea, Rayner believed that reinforcement on an effective scale would be readily at hand for any threatened convoy. The concept was not new, and American help in the Western Atlantic had given the RN sufficient slack to establish a number of these in UK waters.[23] But Rayner's suggestion would have left the actual escort work to corvettes alone and tinkered with an embryonic group system. Corvettes were considered unsuitable to act as SOE's ships, while the heresy of tampering with existing groups was obvious, and Rayner's plan was rejected. Conceivably, the ineffectiveness of massive destroyer support for SC 48 was still fresh in everyone's minds.[24]

The alternative of actually merging the USN's destroyer forces with NEF to provide a more equitable distribution of these effective escorts was considered, but never very seriously. Admiral King, as already noted, was opposed to such a scheme, as were senior officers of the RCN. Working with European navies-in-exile never presented a problem because they adopted British tactical doctrine and procedure. But the USN was the odd man out in the North Atlantic. Captain (D), Newfoundland replied negatively to just such a proposal in December, stating that amalgamation of USN and RCN escort forces was 'inherently inefficient.'[25]

The truncated battle of SC 52 in early November was watched closely in St John's by RCN officers who were concerned about the effects that inefficiency was having on operations. Although the retreat and dispersal of the convoy was not one of the major defeats of the battle of the Atlantic, it was a signal setback for NEF. It showed clearly that the ability of Canadian escorts to push trade safely through to MOMP was seriously doubted by senior operational authorities, both British and American. Concern among professional RCN officers manifested itself immediately in the form of a strongly worded memo to Captain (D), submitted on 4 November, the day after SC 52 altered course to return. The memo began by noting the rough handling recently meted out to Canadian escorted convoys in the Western Atlantic. It expressed doubt about the future of slow convoys and even suggested that they might have to be abandoned. If senior authorities planned to continue with slow convoys, the memo advised, certain steps had to be taken to bolster the expansion fleet's lamentable lack of A/S fundamentals. It was painfully clear that most corvette captains knew precious little of the basic principles of convoying or of ASW. Their ignorance stemmed not from an unwillingness to learn but rather from the failure of the training system at Halifax. Most important was the lack of emphasis on co-ordination and teamwork – essential qualities of effective defence. The RCN's manning policy was attacked, as were increased sea time and poor training facilities. Time, the memo admitted, was the crucial element: 'RCN Corvettes ... have been given so little chance of becoming efficient that they are almost more of a liability than an asset to an escort group.' The memo was signed by Prentice but carried the endorsement of Hibbard, Acting Commander H. Pullen, CO of *Ottawa*, and Lieutenant Commander G. Windeyer of *Wetaskiwin*.[26]

Stevens concurred fully with the complaints in the memo, which he forwarded directly to Murray. In his covering letter Captain (D) advised that 'written reports from other COs have not been called for. It is known they are substantially in agreement.'[27] Murray must have read the letter and the memo with concern. The situation in his command was now a source of considerable embarrassment to Canada's professional naval officers. Yet almost certainly he read it with satisfaction. Here at last was written proof from responsible men at sea that the policies adopted by the Naval Staff in Ottawa were adversely affecting NEF and the image of the service. Murray was particularly exasperated by the navy's manning policy, over which he had no control. Escorts sent from St John's to Halifax for repairs, common since dockyard space and time were at a premium in Newfoundland, returned to NEF with crews largely composed of new drafts. Yet, aside from being allowed time to store and raise steam, these ships were given no opportunity to integrate and work up the new men. Ships which one month were at least passably competent were reduced the next to the state of newly commissioned vessels and sent immediately back into operations. This Jekyll and Hyde character of the early expansion fleet must have been particularly baffling to RN officers.

Murray was well aware of the problem from very early on and had complained of it in August. In October he bitterly attacked Commodore G.C. Jones, the commanding officer, Atlantic Coast (COAC), and the manning officers at Halifax for condoning the manning policy. The latter he labelled 'pirates' and castigated for lacking the 'breadth of vision to see that the RCN's reputation in this war depends on the success or failure of NEF.' But clearly no action had been taken by November, so Murray, armed with Prentice's memo, appealed directly to the Naval Staff. In measured tones he condemned the manning policy for undermining the effectiveness of his command, endangering the lives of seamen, and ruining the reputation of the service. On four pages of foolscap paper, closely typed, Murray recounted the litany of efficient escorts reduced to incompetence as a result of visiting Halifax. One of the more damnable effects of this policy was that it worked the few good people who were available into near exhaustion. Lieutenant Briggs's *Orillia*, for example, had recently been ravaged by Halifax manning personnel, and Murray warned that she 'may be unfit for further duty at sea for some considerable period' following the completion of her latest passage. Briggs was now the only qualified watch-keeper aboard *Orillia*, and the corvette had spent twenty-eight days at sea during the month of October. 'We are asking a lot,' Murray wrote, 'of the morale of an inexperienced crew, to expect them to be happy, and remain in fighting trim and aggressive, in a ship in which they know their safety from marine accident, and not from any action of the enemy, depends upon the ability of their Captain to remain awake.' Murray also noted that recent strong criticism of NEF by the RN was unwarranted but that this did not matter. By all standards Canada's expansion fleet was dreadful, with few signs of rapid improvement. As one RN officer had informed a NEF counterpart, 'Canadian corvettes are only useful for picking up survivors.'[28]

Murray believed that it was possible to salvage the situation but that this required a radical alteration of the manning policy. All new commissions would have to work up from scratch, as the first corvettes had done. Permanence of crews and permanence of escort-group compositions were the touchstones of efficiency and should be adhered to as RCN policy. Murray offered to part with Prentice in order to upgrade the training establishment at Halifax. Unfortunately, his efforts came to naught. The RCN was quite prepared to accept a 'temporary' reduction in efficiency for the long-term benefits of producing a large cadre of experienced personnel. Murray and other senior operational commanders were informed of this policy in December.[29] Bluntly put, the Naval Staff was not concerned with the operational efficiency of NEF or indeed of the corvette fleet in general. Heavy drafting from escorts committed to operations (with the exception of destroyers) continued, and no firm policy on the length of work-up periods for either new commissions or ships suffering from a high proportion of new drafts was laid down. All of this was left to the discretion of Captain (D), Halifax, by then Captain E.R. Mainguy.

In light of events at sea, the navy's adherence to such a manning policy and its failure to establish firm guidelines for proper work-up of escorts seem reckless. Not only did the manning policy contribute to the legacy of incompetence which haunted the RCN's expansion from this time forward, but it had more serious consequences. Unlike inefficiency in many other forms of military or naval endeavour, inefficiency in escort forces meant destruction for the men and ships that the escorts were trying to protect, not for the warships themselves. During the battle of the Atlantic,

Allied merchant seamen paid for the RCN's inefficiency. It was this that embittered Murray and the RCN's most vociferous post-war critic, Captain Donald Macintyre, RN. Elevating this deplorable condition to the status of policy was tragic. Moreover, it seems difficult to comprehend such a manning policy in light of the Naval Staff's decision of 11 February 1941. At that time the Staff agreed that it was an 'unwise policy to relieve a large percentage of a ship's company when that vessel was acting in a war zone.' Ironically, the navy's sound policy remained unaltered, but so did its definition of war zones. The war had indeed moved westwards, but this extension had drawn the U.S. initially into proclaiming a 'security zone' west of 26° in March 1941, then into active naval operations in defence of trade in the same area by September. By the fall of 1941 NEF was actually operating under the direction of a neutral power in a zone determined by the British and Americans to be inactive. In these circumstances it was easy for NSHQ both to follow its manning policy with respect to the expansion fleet and to maintain the letter of the February statement. It would have been difficult, however, to convince anyone in NEF that its theatre was inactive in the fall of 1941.

Another reason for the Naval Staff's reluctance to abandon its manning policy was pressure to increase the size of NEF as quickly as possible – hence the need to commission the entire first construction program promptly and get it to sea. Indeed, in mid-October Murray was informed that all available corvettes were now to be sent to his command, not split among NEF, home waters, and overseas as originally planned.[30] Thus, despite active American involvement in trade escort in the Western Atlantic, NEF's responsibilities became the prime focus of RCN operations. By early December fully 78 per cent of the RCN's escort strength was assigned to St John's.[31] Newfoundland had become what the Admiralty had wanted it to be in June: the RCN's number-one operational base. Yet facilities remained meagre, and the incidence of missed sailings owing to defects increased as winter took its toll.

The dispatch of all available escorts and the arrival of NEF's first training submarine did offer Murray some glimmer of hope. The idea of a training group was resurrected in early December, this time with a slight difference. With the large number of escorts now available Murray proposed to form one additional group in order to permit operational groups to slip out of their cycle on regular intervals to conduct training. Prentice and *Chambly* were to be detached to form the nucleus of the new training establishment. Anti-submarine exercises were planned for Conception Bay in conjunction with the training submarine *L27*, following which the group would sail for a twelve-day cruise, 'in which all forms of attack, defence, and communications could be practised under ocean-going conditions.' Here at last was a promising scheme to speed the advance of the expansion fleet towards full competence, or so it was thought. Murray's letter to the naval secretary outlining the plan and requesting permission to implement it was dated 7 December 1941.[32]

By the time Murray's letter reached the crowded desk of Captain J.M. Cossette, RCN, the naval secretary, the war was in a new phase. Not only were escorts badly needed off the American coast, but the Japanese advance in the Pacific had also brought crippling losses. The U.S. Pacific Fleet's battle-line had been sunk at Pearl Harbor, followed shortly afterwards by Britain's 'Force Z,' HMS *Repulse* and *Prince of Wales*, off the coast of Malaya. By the end of the year the American Asiatic Fleet, a small, weak force based in the Philippines, was seriously exposed. Eventually it and the remnants of British and Dutch naval power in the South Pacific were lost in a vain attempt to defend Indonesia. The burden which the USN assumed in the North Atlantic with so much promise in the summer of 1941 therefore gradually fell back on the two royal navies. Cossette politely advised Murray that new priorities precluded the establishment of a training group. The Naval Staff recommended that the whole idea be shelved until the spring or that training be conducted by senior officers during group layovers. The latter was a simply impossible plan, and its suggestion is evidence of the poor understanding the Staff had of conditions in NEF. Permanent groups and spare time had both fallen afoul of winter's fury. Murray, now a rear admiral with the title of flag officer, Newfoundland Force (FONF), scribbled a hurried 'no action at present' on Cossette's letter, and the matter was temporarily laid to rest. For all intents and purposes NEF's training group had been sunk by Japanese bombs.

Fortunately for the escorts and merchants ships plying the main trade routes, the last two months of 1941 brought a lull in German activity in their area. Despite Dönitz's protests, most U-boats were now sent to operate off Gibraltar and in the Mediterranean in response to British naval success against Axis supply lines to North Africa. During early 1942 emphasis switched to the U.S. east coast, and for more than half a year convoys were largely spared the nightmare of pack attacks. For Allied sailors on the milk run, life on the North Atlantic – even without the Germans – was dangerous, demanding, and debilitating. In December *Restigouche* was crippled and nearly lost in a gale. Flooded fore and aft, foremast down across her deck and one funnel crumpled, she rode the storm eastwards to a safe harbour in Britain. In the same month the corvette *Windflower* was rammed by a merchant ship in a heavy fog. The inrush of seawater detonated one of her boilers, and those nearby thought she had been torpedoed. Sixty men were saved. The constant strain of operating a tiny escort in proximity to the often-invisible hulks of convoys was devastating.

During that first winter professionalism took second place to a rough pride in the ability to withstand suffering. Hal Lawrence, then serving on *Moose Jaw*, described it as a 'macabre and desolate winter' of 'sleet, snow, rain, ice a foot thick on the forward superstructure: four hours on watch, two hours chipping ice, sleep and eat in between.'[34] All corvette sailors remember their ships as a source of numbing fatigue and indescribable discomfort. Conditions were aggravated by overcrowding since by 1941 corvettes already carried twice the crewmen allowed for in the original plans. Men slept where they could: on lockers, table-tops, or in some dark, special place that offered a little warmth. Even in moderate seas the ships pitched and rolled violently, and most men spent their first weeks desperately ill.

Water dominated a corvette sailor's existence. It permeated the entire ship, soaking the men and even their food. 'An almost constant cataract of water ... poured across the focsle and down into the well-deck amidships,' William Pugsley wrote after the war.[35] It was simply impossible to bring food from the galley (aft of the wheel-house) through this torrent to the mess-decks forward. The men of the escorts survived on a diet of hard tack, pickled beef, and lime juice – Nelson's fare, but the only diet that would endure the hardships of corvette life. At action stations men were continuously drenched in spray, while water cascaded down into living spaces through hatches left open to permit access to magazines. Water covered the decks inside and out and dripped incessantly from condensation on the deckhead. Once a sailor was wet, it was impossible to get dry again. Men 'just wore their clothes wet till they dried in the wind.' Perhaps the final indignity was the straight pipe which ran from the toilets to the open sea. Harry Shorten, a telegraphist aboard *Dundas* in 1942, recalls that if you happened to be sitting on the seat 'and she rolled, you got a four-inch jet of icy Atlantic up your stern.'[36]

The suffering of men was perhaps greatest during the first winter, when few were inured to the sea and the corvettes had not yet received the most rudimentary improvements. A year later the ships were much the same but the weather was worse and the mess-decks even more crowded. If the Americans found the North Atlantic in winter a difficult place to maintain a professional service, it was unlikely that the RCN would have much luck building one there.

Dönitz hoped the U-boat war would spread quickly following the American declaration of war, but it was not to be. His initial hopes for a rapid descent of the U.S. coast were forestalled by the German naval high command, which wanted pressure in the Mediterranean maintained. It was not until early January 1942 that the first five U-boats were freed for action in the Western Hemisphere. They made a purposely quiet passage, hoping to take the Allies by surprise, but their movements were watched closely by Allied intelligence. Despite this foreknowledge, American preparations to meet the threat were grossly inadequate, and the first German campaign in the Western Atlantic was highly successful. From 12 January until the end of the month forty ships, all sailing independently, were sunk by U-boats west of 40°. This figure continued to rise in February and March, until in excess of 90 per cent of all shipping lost in the Atlantic fell off the American coast.[37] To the British and Canadians, American failure to introduce convoy seemed inexplicable, particularly in light of the free access to Commonwealth experience extended to the USN for years previously.

It was inevitable that many of the escorts needed to protect shipping along the American coast would have to come from the mid-ocean. Yet so long as the convoys adhered to diversive routing into very high latitudes, the extended passages and heavy storm damage to escorts prevented the transfer of some of their numbers to the now-embattled southern routes. Actually, Admiral King had long considered the circuitous routing of North Atlantic convoys a waste of resources. In November 1941 he recommended to Admiral H.R. Stark, chief of Naval Operations in Washington, that the convoy route be pulled straight and the extra escorts produced thereby used to kill U-boats. King was frustrated with the emphasis on evasion and wanted the whole basis of the system changed. He was not alone in his desire to establish a 'tramline' in the North Atlantic. Just a week after Pearl Harbor the British proposed changes that would have tied slow convoys to the great-circle route and had NEF escorts call at Londonderry as their eastern terminus. Further, the British also wanted all escort operations for slow convoys placed under C-in-C, WA, once again, including the Canadians. Naturally, King supported the idea of using the great-circle route, but he informed Stark (on Christmas Day) that the command arrangements were to remain unaltered.

King followed his comments on the British proposals with a plan of his own.[38] Foul winter weather, he observed, was making escort operations 'untenable.' In addition, the bases from which the USN was operating – Argentia and Hvalfjordhur – King considered too exposed. It is also plain that the commander of the Atlantic Fleet was displeased with the damaging effect that operations from the two advanced bases were having on USN efficiency. For this reason the eastern terminus for USN escorts was switched to Londonderry at the end of January, something Murray had attempted but failed to do for NEF in November. In early February King finally made an official proposal to the Admiralty to alter convoy and escort arrangements along the lines already discussed. By sailing all convoys along the great-circle route it would be possible to reduce the strain on escort forces and in fact to eliminate one whole force (the RN's UK-to-Iceland section). And if the limits of local Canadian escorts were pushed a little farther eastwards, it would be possible for escorts to take convoys all the way from Newfoundland to Ireland. Under the new arrangement NEF – as an ocean escort force – ceased to exist (its title passed to local Newfoundland forces). From the second week in February all escorts operating between Newfoundland and Ireland became part of the new Mid-Ocean Escort Force (MOEF). Escort groups also received new designations. The old NEF numbering system (and that of the British groups committed to MOEF) was changed to a letter-number combination in Commonwealth usage (for example, C 1 for the first Canadian escort group), while the USN designated all groups operating in its zone by task-unit numbers as part of Task Force Four (for example, C 1 was TU 4.1.11).

Aside from the fairer weather of more southern latitudes, the appeal of Northern Ireland was strong. The Americans were already at work on a large naval base at Londonderry, and the same port held excellent RN escort facilities. Maintenance and training services were up to date and ideally suited to the types of problems faced by the RCN. In the Western Atlantic, British (or B) groups began to call at Newfoundland. They did not, however, make St John's their port of call except in an emergency. Rather, RN escort groups were granted access to the American base at Argentia, where conditions were much less congested. Ironically, the RCN had just begun to avail itself of the same facilities, largely for repair purposes, following an American invitation the previous fall. Eventually, growing British use of Argentia forced the RCN out, a development which was perhaps compensated for by new Canadian access to facilities in Ireland.[39]

At the time that Admiral King obtained British agreement for the restructuring of the escort and convoy system, he also informed the

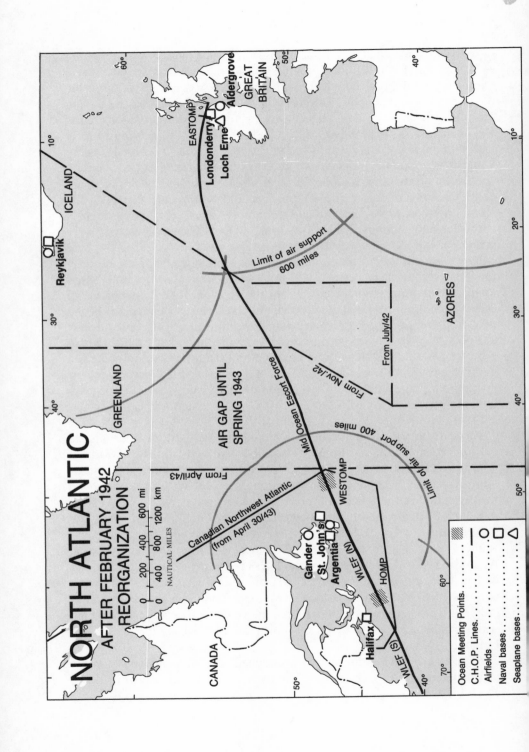

NORTH ATLANTIC
AFTER FEBRUARY 1942 REORGANIZATION

ICELAND

Reykjavik

GREENLAND

CANADA

Gander
St. John's
Argentia
WLEF (N)
HOMP
Halifax
WLEF (S)

Canadian Northwest Atlantic
(from April 30/43)

WESTOMP

Mid Ocean Escort Force

AIR GAP UNTIL
SPRING 1943

From April/43

Limit of air support 400 miles

From Nov./42

From July/42

Limit of air support
600 miles

AZORES

GREAT BRITAIN

Aldergrove
EASTOMP
Londonderry
Loch Erne

0   200   400   600 mi
0   400   800   1200 km
NAUTICAL MILES

Ocean Meeting Points.........
C.H.O.P. Lines................
Airfields.....................
Naval bases...................
Seaplane bases................

Admiralty of his intention to sail the American groups of MOEF directly to Boston at the end of each convoy cycle in order to provide the ships with much-needed maintenance and repairs.[40] How King justified the time that would be lost in light of the clear need for efficient use of escort time is uncertain. It does illustrate, however, that the Americans were quite prepared to balance operational demands and those of the fleet. NEF, of course, was in much the same condition. So many Canadian warships lay at St John's suffering from defects in December that Admiral Bristol, commander of Task Force Four at Argentia, considered that Canadian strength was all on paper, and that the RCN's effort was on the verge of collapse.[41] It is not known if Murray ever considered seeking permission for his ships to call in at Halifax between passages in order to obtain access to better facilities. Since the Naval Staff would not permit the establishment of a training group, it is unlikely that it would have sanctioned trips to Nova Scotia. Indeed, given Murray's estimation of the manning staff at Halifax, it is inconceivable that he would have encouraged any use of the RCN's most important base unless in case of emergency or regularly scheduled maintenance. In February the effects of visiting Halifax were every bit as bad as they had been the previous fall. *Chambly* went to refit during February and came back into operation seventy-two hours after recommissioning with 80 per cent of her crew new drafts.[42]

Whether Murray harboured any resentment against Jones in Halifax (or vice versa) as a result of the disputed manning policy is unclear. Jones was Murray's contemporary; indeed both were members of the Royal Naval College of Canada class of 1912. Their careers were virtually identical, and they had stayed even in promotions. By 1941 Murray and Jones were at the top of the list to succeed the first generation of senior RCN officers. Those who knew both men well recall that their personalities were quite different. Jones was ambitious and, unlike Murray, an indifferent ship handler. That limitation earned him the nickname 'Jetty Jones' after his ship, *Ottawa*, struck the Halifax-to-Dartmouth ferry in a fog and she was forced to remain alongside at the dockyard when the rest of the River class sailed to Europe in June 1940. Jones was none the less well liked by those who served under him. William Sclater, a member of intelligence staff at Halifax in 1942, later published a glowing eulogy to Jones, describing him as the father of the wartime navy.[43]

Those who served in Newfoundland in 1941–2 would disagree, if for no other reason than that the Halifax and Newfoundland commands were at cross purposes during those crucial years. This alone might have set

Jones and Murray at loggerheads, but their bitter rivalry was of long standing and was well known in the pre-war navy. When Jones was due to give up command of *Assiniboine* in September 1940 to become commanding officer, Atlantic Coast, Murray was scheduled to replace him. But since it was unthinkable that command could pass directly from one to the other, Commander C.R.H. Taylor had to take over the destroyer for a few weeks. Officially, Murray and Jones got along well enough, but their relationship could not be described as friendly. Certainly, Murray always resented Jones's promotion to rear admiral on 1 December 1941, one day ahead of himself. In the end, both reached career pinnacles suited to their respective temperaments. Jones eventually became CNS but was publicly overshadowed by Murray, the navy's foremost (and still best-known) flag officer.[41]

For most of the first year of operations, NEF and its successor, the Canadian component of MOEF, were caught between the bitter North Atlantic and a hungry, growing service at home. Even if Murray did not actively discourage the sending of ships to Halifax to effect repairs, maintenance suffered from another, more insidious conspiracy within the escorts themselves. Under continuous pressure from operations through the latter part of 1941 and on throughout the winter, chiefs, petty officers, and even officers manipulated defects lists in order to ensure time for rest for their men. Neglected maintenance was complicated during 1942 by ever-greater operational demands and more missed refits. The cumulative effect would haunt the RCN until 1944.

The ambiguity which affected RCN escort operations in the North Atlantic during the fall of 1941 clearly had an impact on the orderly development of the expansion fleet. Certainly NEF and its notable characters found much to learn from the lessons of SC 42 and other convoy battles. But for the navy as a whole, escort operations in late 1941 were not the learning experience which a similar exposure to enemy action had been to the RN the previous winter. The Naval Staff was too preoccupied with the everyday affairs of expansion, with the development of bases and the simple commissioning of ships. It was too intent upon building a large service quickly to concern itself overly with the plight of reservists serving in the 'stepping stones' of the fleet-development program. Indeed, had the Americans fulfilled their promise, NEF would have evolved into a purely local force and Canada's naval war effort would have been directed overseas. By January 1942 the war, which the Naval Staff never conceded to have infested NEF's area of operations, leapt the escort forces based at St John's and fell, in full fury, on the American east coast. While the departure of American forces in large numbers eventually placed more responsibility on RCN mid-ocean escorts, the new danger area lay off the Nova Scotia and New England coasts. It was natural for the RCN to shift its priorities accordingly, and the establishment of the Western Local Escort Force (WLEF), the new link between western convoy ports and MOEF, became the primary objective in 1942. With this development the fleet was pushed even harder, and the opportunities needed to make good the defects, both material and professional, revealed in the battles of 1941 were lost.

4

New Priorities and a Certain Balance

As attackers, we held the initiative, and by rapid switches of the
main weight of our attack from one focal point to another we
could confuse and surprise the enemy. The Americans, obviously,
could not provide adequate protection for all the focal points at
all times, and they would be compelled to follow us from one to
another. In this way it seemed likely that we could compel the
enemy to a real dispersal of his defensive forces.

Admiral Karl Dönitz, *Memoirs*

American entry into the war gave promise of eventual Allied victory.
But until her mighty resources could be mobilized and put into the field,
U.S. participation as a combatant opened vast new areas for Axis attack
and placed enormous strain on available forces. The burden of carrying
America through her mobilization was not unforeseen. The RCN realized
that the broadening of the war would seriously stretch Canadian resources.
It was also evident to the Canadians – junior partners that they were –
that there was precious little the navy could do about this. 'Relieving the
RN and the USN of duties and the loan of ships,' Plans Division warned
Nelles in late January 1942, 'depends on circumstances outside the control
of the RCN.' The determining factor was the Allied nations' naval position
relative to that of the Axis. Any deterioration in that situation was likely
to 'be reflected in increased demands on the RCN by their Allies.'[1]

Even before the Germans launched their offensive along the U.S. east
coast, the RCN felt the weight of the expanding war. By January the
Ottawa Trade and Intelligence Centre was straining in its efforts to fill
the gap in control of merchant shipping caused by America's precipitous
entry into the war. The USN's naval-control-of-shipping organization was

still embryonic, and Ottawa formed a vital communication link between it and the extensive Commonwealth system. In addition, for the first six months of 1942 Ottawa ran the tracking and routing duties for the area west of 40 degrees and north of the equator. These were heavy responsibilities, ones for which NSHQ was not prepared. None the less, they were handled efficiently until the USN was ready to take over its rightful duties in the early summer.[2]

Further direct aid to the Americans and the British in the form of escorts was expected as NSHQ resigned itself to generous support of the Allied naval effort. But increased demands on the fleet did not absolve the navy from responsibility for its maintenance and readiness for action. Certainly, despite the spread of the war in early 1942, neither the RN nor the USN was willing to compromise fully on quality. Admiral King had already insisted in February, even as the Allies scrambled for more escorts, that American MOEF groups lay over in Boston at the end of every cycle. By May, when the scramble was even more intense, an American officer sent to report on British A/S training noted with surprise that the RN found 'time for this instruction somehow.'[3] The contrast with Canadian priorities in early 1942 could not have been sharper.

Yet, in the context of the pandemonium of mounting losses and the advent of new theatres of war, NSHQ's acceptance of new responsibilities and the resulting reduction – in both absolute and relative terms – of the RCN's commitment to MOEF are comprehensible. Through the winter of 1941–2 the development of local Canadian forces gradually overtook the practice of sending every available escort to St John's. The shift in effort was given a push by the establishment of the Halifax-based Western Local Escort Force in February, which gave a new form and importance to a hitherto nebulous force of almost non-combatant escorts. The RCN also received substantial assistance in the establishment and operation of WLEF from the RN, which sent twelve aged but very well-equipped short-ranged destroyers to serve with Halifax-based groups. Even more significant to the development of the RCN were the many highly skilled and experienced North Atlantic veterans who commanded the RN escorts of WLEF. Several of these men were to linger on in key RCN staff posts until the end of the war.

Although chronically under strength until 1944, Halifax-based escort groups became responsible for one-third of the main ocean trade routes. Fortunately they were spared sustained enemy pressure and were always under the lee of the coast of North America. But in 1942 WLEF was every bit as important to the RCN as its commitment to MOEF. Though for a number of reasons WLEF was never as prestigious as its mid-Atlantic counterpart, its expansion and development dominated RCN activities in this crucial stage of the war.

Intially, MOEF strength was not affected by the build-up of forces closer to home, since newly commissioned ships were simply redirected to Jones's command at Halifax. By February the RCN's corvette commitment to MOEF was still at its January peak of fifty. RCN destroyer strength, however, was down from eleven to eight. The decline was not the result of need in WLEF but stemmed from the now greater operational responsibilities of MOEF over those of NEF. The Town-class destroyer escorts *St Clair*, *Columbia*, and *Niagara* simply lacked sufficient endurance to operate between Newfoundland and Ireland and were therefore relegated to WLEF.[4] The loss of three RCN destroyers was thus an indirect result of the shift of escort strength southwards, but the effect on C groups was no less real. Canadian MOEF destroyer operations were now restricted to six pre-war River class (*Assiniboine*, *Ottawa*, *Restigouche*, *Saguenay*, *Skeena*, and *St Laurent*) and two long-range Towns (*St Croix* and *St Francis*). The balance of destroyer complements in Canadian groups was made up of whatever destroyers the RN chose to assign, invariably aged Town-class ships even less reliable than comparable RCN escorts.[5] The weakening of the RCN's destroyer commitment to MOEF and the navy's inability to redress the situation from Canadian resources held serious consequences for the war in the mid-ocean and the success of Canadian operations there.

March 1942 brought the first sizeable reduction in Murray's command when five operational corvettes (*Arrowhead*, *Kenogami*, *Matapedia*, *Nanaimo*, and *Snowberry*) were assigned directly to WLEF. One other corvette, *Spikenard*, was lost to enemy action, though her place in the ranks was filled briefly by *Sudbury*. In some measure the impact of this first major shift was offset by the fairer weather of early spring and the lower latitudes now prevalent in convoy routing. But much of whatever slack existed was needed to fill the growing gaps in American MOEF groups. By March the five A groups contained only a token force of USN destroyers or Coast Guard cutters. The balance of group strength was now made up of RCN (A 1–3) or RN (A 4–5) corvettes. Thus the mixed groups which both the RCN and USN had feared in late 1941 came to be.

The progressive withdrawal of American escorts from MOEF did little to stem the rising tide of losses along the u.s. coast because the USN steadfastly refused to adopt convoy. To the British and Canadians this failure was both perplexing and exasperating. The Commonwealth navies had shared two years of hard-won experience with the USN, and yet the Americans seemed to have missed the fundamental defensive importance of convoys. It was particularly frustrating to see ships escorted safely to Halifax and then lost in large numbers in waters that, by virtue of their proximity to land, should have been safe. The Americans argued that shortage of escorts kept them from instituting a system of coastal convoy. In truth, the USN had enough escorts to begin convoys, but not enough of the type they liked – destroyers.[6]

The establishment of a convoy system also required a considerable act of will, and it may have been American exposure to NEF in late 1941 which set them against inadequately escorted convoys. 'It should always be borne in mind,' the USN's Board on the Organization of East Coast Convoys reported in March 1942, 'that effective convoying depends upon the escort being in sufficient strength to permit their taking offensive action against attacking submarines ... Any protection less than this simply results in the convoy's becoming a convenient target.'[7] In many ways the board was correct in its assessment, at least in so far as a convoy beset by a large pack in the mid-Atlantic was concerned. But these conditions hardly obtained where air cover could be provided or where inshore waters limited U-boat operations. More importantly, the object of the exercise was defence of shipping, not the conduct of offensive action against the enemy. Convoying trade fulfilled both objectives, since with the ocean otherwise clear of ships the U-boats must of necessity be drawn to the convoy, where the defender could assemble in force. The value of convoys as a strategic offensive proved a difficult pill for all professional naval men to swallow and demonstrated how unwilling the USN was to learn from its allies.

While the USN sought ways of inflicting defeats on the U-boats without resorting to convoys, Admiral King, in his capacity as commander of the Western Atlantic, instructed the RCN to establish a convoy system between Boston and Halifax. The shuttle began in March and became a WLEF responsibility. As the U-boats extended their attacks farther south and losses in the Pacific mounted, more USN escorts were withdrawn from MOEF. The result was a transfer of groups A 4 and A 5 to British control and the renumbering of the groups to B 6 and B 7 respectively.[8] The Americans also withdrew completely from two other groups, A 1 and A 2, which had RCN corvette complements. Because no Canadian destroyers were available as replacements, A 1 and A 2 were simply disbanded, leaving Murray with eight additional escorts. The resulting sizeable reduction in MOEF's strength forced a major rearrangement of convoy cycles in late April. But for the moment, the combination of spring weather, better routing, and elimination of American groups gave Murray much-needed leverage within his command.

The shorter route and fairer weather had already brought relief to the C groups by the end of March, at least enough to allow reconsideration of the establishment of a training group at St John's. The initiative to get operational training under way off Newfoundland came from the new Captain (D), Captain E.R. Mainguy, RCN. Mainguy was an affable character, well respected by officers and men alike for his professional skill and fairness. He had joined the navy in 1918 and followed a typical RCN career pattern, alternating between Canadian and RN postings. In October 1939 he took command of *Assiniboine*, his first command, upon her transfer to the RCN. After nearly two years of escort duty off Canada and in the Western Approaches (largely in *Ottawa*, which he took over in April 1940) Mainguy was appointed Captain (D), Halifax, in June 1941, moving to the same post at St John's in early 1942. Although even by 1942 he was an experienced North Atlantic veteran and was viewed as an innovator during his later tenure as chief of the naval staff, Mainguy is best remembered for his intense interest in the welfare of sailors. His tendency to be people oriented contrasts sharply with the more businesslike manner of his RN counterparts, and certainly during 1942 Mainguy was not on the same wavelength as staff officers at Western Approaches.

On the last day of March 1942 Mainguy passed a memo to Murray proposing that *Chambly* and Prentice be withdrawn from operational duties to form the nucleus of an operational-training establishment. Mainguy suggested the formation of one additional group in order that units could be trained in rotation. It was, in fact, the very scheme shelved at the end of 1941. Murray wasted no time informing NSHQ of his intention of going ahead with the plan 'as soon as operationally possible.'[9] He also emphasized, lest the Naval Staff seek to nip his plans in the bud, that the scheme was quite different from the type of individual escort instruction provided by HMCS *Sambro* in Halifax. Murray might also have added that group training was precisely what the navy's operational escorts now badly needed.

There were a number of reasons why Murray did not attempt to restate his case in any greater details. The most obvious is that his position was already on record. Further, when NSHQ rejected the original request in December 1941, Murray was told to wait until the spring. When the latter rolled around, Murray therefore simply announced his intention to go ahead with delayed plans. Moreover, by March 1942 the focus of U-boat operations was well to the south of St John's, not, as it had been from September to November 1941, in Murray's theatre. The need for training was still as great, but the efficiency of St John's–based escorts was for the moment not a crucial issue.

Naval Headquarters offered no objection, and Prentice began operations on 6 April. On that day *Chambly* went to sea in company with *Buctouche*, *Cobalt*, and *Rosthern*. Shortly after they cleared the approaches to St John's the corvettes were joined by the destroyer *St Francis*, and the ships divided into two divisions to conduct manoeuvring exercises. No sooner were the latter under way than Prentice received a signal ordering him to investigate a U-boat sighting 'close to the West of Cape Race.' Prentice rearranged his group in line of bearing and swept the area, but to no avail. The group passed a quiet night at sea and was joined the next morning by the corvette *Dunvegan* (WLEF). Throughout the seventh the six ships participated in towing, screening, depth-charge, and gunnery exercises. In the afternoon the anti-aircraft crews of the corvettes were given practice on air bursts put up by *St Francis*. By 1930 local time on the second day of the program all of the escorts were secure alongside at St John's, their brief foray as a training group completed.

The exploits of the first group were an auspicious start, and certainly a quantum leap forward from anything Murray's command had enjoyed before. But the additional group needed to make a regular rotation possible never materialized. Instead, Prentice busied himself with exercising operational groups as they made their passage from St John's to WESTOMP. It was not until 20 May, six weeks after the first training cruise, that Prentice was able to arrange a training program once again. The corvettes in this second group (*Camrose*, *Galt*, *Sackville*, and *Wetaskiwin*) were all fresh from refit. Like the first group they were exercised in towing, manoeuvring, gunnery, depth charges, and anti-aircraft. But they also were given time with the training submarine, *P514*, in Conception Bay, the only place near St John's where water conditions permitted effective asdic training. The second training program was also the longest of any given by Prentice: five days. It concluded with operations 'in the vicinity of Convoy "ON 95." '¹⁰ The final supporting operation nearly ended in tragedy, illustrating again the problems of trying to train off Newfoundland, where the Labrador Current and Gulf Stream combine to produce almost perpetual fog.

Returning from exercises on the last day in a thick fog, one of Prentice's group obtained an asdic contact. 'Action stations' were sounded, followed almost immediately by a report from *Sackville* that she too had obtained a target. In pursuit of these contacts the group soon split up. Each escort was equipped with SWIC radar, but since the sets needed to be directed towards a suspected target, keeping track of nearby corvettes was impossible without good bearings. None the less, the sounds of action, such as *Sackville*'s depth-charging of her contact, could be heard clearly through the fog. In the best of naval tradition Prentice ordered *Chambly*'s helmsman to steer to the 'sound of the guns.' In a very short time *Chambly* passed through waters heavily laden with dead fish – silent testimony to the problems of target classification. The real excitement, however, soon followed when *Sackville* suddenly emerged from the fog on a reciprocal course, obviously bent on dealing the enemy another blow. The untimely demise of both ships was only narrowly averted when they turned in the same direction. Parallel courses were assumed 'close enough for each ship's respective thrower parties to almost shake one another's hands.'[11]

All that Prentice was able to achieve with the fifteen or sixteen escorts which passed through his 'group' was doubtless of great value. However, in hindsight there is cause for concern about the emphasis of his training philosophy. Canadian escorts needed to know the basics of co-operation and teamwork, but they also needed to know how to conduct a good defence of convoys. The latter problem, as distinct from learning the principles of teamwork, was largely untouched by Prentice's training exercises. His emphasis was on effective anti-submarine warfare, a goal towards which Prentice was a tireless worker. Moreover, the offensive strike-force concept also lay at the base of the navy's ASW doctrine and had since before the war. The specialization in safe and timely arrival of the convoy which characterized the RN's Western Approaches Command – and formed the basis of the escort sections of WACIS – was never taken up by the RCN, nor did it find a home in any of the separate RCN commands, for the period covered by this account. Shielded by the wing of U.S. strategic and operational command in the Western Atlantic, the RCN was allowed to pursue these tendencies, which were in any event identical to those of the USN. It was a situation watched with considerable and growing interest by the Staff at Western Approaches.

In fairness to both Prentice and the RCN, the future character of the U-boat campaign on Allied trade was by no means certain in the first half of 1942. Individual U-boats now operated inshore, relying extensively on their guns. The uncertain future of U-boat warfare was noted by the Canadian Chiefs of Staff at meetings with senior British and American officers in Washington in January 1942.[12] But while U-boat tactics might change and alter the nature of defence against them from time to time, there was one constant and vexing problem: how to deal effectively with a cornered U-boat. Driving U-boats off was an effective means of defending trade and could be readily understood by all. But perfecting the business of sinking U-boats with certainty took long hours of hard practice. Not surprisingly, then, there was a tendency to concentrate on the offensive tasks of convoy escort – pursuit of nearby U-boats and hunting them to destruction. The idea was right, but in early 1942 it needed to be balanced with an equal measure of defence.

There is another aspect of this issue which warrants examination in light of the failure of C groups to meet British standards of performance in the latter half of 1942. In large measure the RCN's most important battle was one for survival. Laurels were won by destroying the enemy – a point driven home to the RCN by its own minister in late 1943 – and this could only be done by efficient ASW ships. Further, the navy's long-term goals required the preparation of good all-round naval officers, men who could man the post-war navy. Training programs therefore stressed the traditional basics of gunnery, seamanship, and navigation. This was fine. But although the RCN was primarily an A/S navy by 1942 (indeed, if not sooner), it had not yet begun to think like one. None of this meant that losses to shipping were inconsequential. The disaster of SC 42 was a nightmare to be avoided. Yet even Murray wanted his groups strong enough to take offensive action when threatened, and of course a good limited offensive was the best means of breaking up a pack attack. Unfortunately, the mere size of a group was no measure of the effectiveness of offensive action.

Finally, there is a geographic determinant which separated North American and British views of Atlantic convoy battles. Both the Canadians and the Americans were prepared to accept a certain scale of losses from convoys in 1942, provided that the escort displayed an aggressive spirit in the face of enemy attack. For the Canadians and Americans, North Atlantic convoys were 'operational' in the same sense that the Murmansk or Malta convoys were to the British. For the British, the main Atlantic convoys were the lifeline of the nation, a perspective which gave a very different tone to their assessments of convoy battles. It is inconceivable, in any event, that the languishing state of efficiency and even of equipment in the escort fleet would have continued had Canada's fate hung in the balance.

Despite the best intentions of Murray and the efforts of Prentice, the operational-training scheme was never fully developed. The reason, of course, was the continued expansion of commitments. By the end of

April – as the British abandoned Burma and the Japanese extended their grip on the Solomons – USN participation in MOEF was down to one group, A 3, containing a token force of U.S. Coast Guard cutters – the very large, modern, but slow Treasury class – and a balance of mostly RCN corvettes. The reduction of USN commitment to MOEF finally forced a major reorganization of the force and convoy cycles. From the end of April 1942 onwards the escort of convoys between WESTOMP and EASTOMP fell to eleven groups, six British (B 1, 2, 3, 4, 6, and 7 [B 5 was on loan to the USN in the Caribbean]), four Canadian (C 1–4), and A 3.[13] It should be noted, however, that the national designation of each escort group was often nominal. One, A 3, was mixed, and within the four C groups there was actually one full British group on loan (usually concentrated in C 2) and initially several Free French corvettes. B groups frequently contained escorts from other European navies in exile; B 6, for example, comprised two RN destroyers, but its corvettes were all Norwegian. Fortunately, all except the USN followed British operational procedures. The lack of a common escort doctrine in MOEF was largely overcome by September 1942. By then the commander of Task Force Twenty-four (CTF-24, as the former commander of Task Force Four became in March) had begun to see the wisdom of British insistence on safe and timely arrival, while the new 'Atlantic Convoy Instructions,' issued as a replacement for WACIs in September, included USN screening diagrams.[14] Thus, a meeting of minds was gradually effected in MOEF throughout 1942. But the continued existence of different procedures in A 3 made it difficult for Allied captains to adapt quickly to working with the Americans.

This meeting of minds was still some time off when the first convoy to sail under the new eleven-group arrangement departed in late April. Ironically, although American involvement in the escort of trade in the Northwestern Atlantic was now just a token, the USN retained operational control of convoys west of the CHOP (change of operational command) line (roughly 26° W) agreed to at the Argentia conference the previous August. Command continued to be exercised by CTF-24, now in the person of Vice-Admiral R.M. Brainard, who replaced Bristol following the latter's untimely death on 30 April. Like his predecessor, Brainard was a very capable officer with a wide and varied service career. His most recent posts had included those of deputy chief of staff to Admiral King and, in March, commander of Amphibious Force, U.S. Atlantic Fleet. The latter job lasted barely a few weeks before Brainard was promoted to the rank of vice-admiral (temporary), which gave him sufficient seniority over the Canadian admirals at Halifax and St John's, and was sent to replace Bristol.

The continued existence of CTF-24 meant that Atlantic convoy operations straddled two commands. It also meant that all Canadian naval operations outside the three-mile territorial limit (which in effect meant all of them) remained under a foreign admiral with few ships of his own. The incongruous situation of Canadian warships engaged against an enemy under the direction of a neutral commander now gave way to an equally incongruous situation. So long as the U-boats were busy elsewhere, the potential problems of dual control did not arise, and the Canadians were content to leave the command structure unchanged. The British, however, were never very pleased about the arrangement and sought to have it changed. They made an official request in January, but Admiral King was unprepared to tamper with something that was at least working at a time when so much else was going wrong. King's logic thus defeated initial British attempts to re-extend C-in-C, WA's control of escort operations once again to the shores of Newfoundland. For the moment the RN let the matter rest. However, the issue was aired internally at the Admiralty in May, when it was suggested, as a means of levering control from CTF-24, that the Canadians might be given responsibility for the area west of WESTOMP. It was only with 'considerable reluctance' that the British once again let the matter rest unchallenged.[15] In time the shifting pattern of the war would bring the necessary impetus for change.

There were several other noteworthy developments that resulted from the reduction of MOEF to eleven groups and the adoption of the great-circle route as the mean line of advance for convoys. The latter streamlined escort arrangements considerably, permitting the redistribution of forces to more active theatres. The dispersal was largely permanent. Coverage of the whole Newfoundland-to-Ireland stretch by a single escort force substantially reduced the tactical flexibility of escort groups, since they had to be cautious not to leave the convoy underguarded as a result of escorts' having to detach early to seek fuel. This severely limiting factor also hampered convoy routing, making the convoys more susceptible to interception. In early 1942 these considerations were overshadowed by the grave need for escorts in other theatres. As the year wore on, some measure of flexibility was restored through the introduction of refuelling at sea (never reliable in 1942), the formation of Western Support Force, and adjustments to WESTOMP. In the meantime, however, the enemy took considerable advantage of the inflexibility and scored some real successes as a result of the triumph of his ulterior strategy – dispersal of Allied escort strength.

For the time being all eyes focused on the plight of shipping along the U.S. east coast, and the redirection of Allied forces continued. Through April and May the Canadian contribution to MOEF was spared further large losses, though corvette strength was reduced to forty in April when *Chicoutimi*, *Sudbury*, and *Summerside* were sent to WLEF. *Baddeck* followed them in May, but her place was taken by *Sackville*, so the figure remained steady until the end of the month. However, further large reallocations of corvette strength were in the offing in May as a result of dwindling oil stocks in eastern Canada and Newfoundland. Nearly half of Canada's domestic oil supplies were imported by tanker from the Gulf of Mexico and the Caribbean, areas under heavy German attack by the late spring. Although the movement of traffic from the Caribbean to northern waters was ostensibly a USN responsibility, American inability to defend adequately tankers engaged in trade with Canada forced the RCN to consider the establishment of its own Halifax–to–West Indies convoys. To meet these and other WLEF commitments an additional eight corvettes (*Barrie*, *Cobalt*, *Fennel*, *Hepatica*, *Kamsack*, *Rimouski*, *Sorel*, and *Trail*) were assigned to WLEF from MOEF in early June.[16] But the Naval Staff wanted and needed more in order to put the oil convoys on a firm footing, and petitioned both Murray and Jones, suggesting two possible sources for yet more escorts.

One possibility was to curtail training by ending the practice of sending new commissions, three at a time, to the RN's escort work-up base, HMS *Western Isles*, at Tobermory, Scotland. It is noteworthy that NSHQ was quite prepared to use the negative effects of its own manning policy as a means of securing agreement for discontinuing the use of Tobermory. 'Due to the necessary rapid changes in personnel in RCN corvettes,' NSHQ observed, 'it appears that some of the value of this training is lost.'[17] The other alternative offered by NSHQ was to withdraw 'a number of RCN corvettes from C and A groups' which NSHQ maintained still had sufficient strength for 10.8 escorts per group. This was true, but only if allowance was made for inclusion of escorts undergoing refits.

Jones, whose command was increasing in size and importance, recommended that training at Tobermory be suspended, at least temporarily. 'Local training will continue,' he replied, 'and is of increasing value.' This was true enough, and Commander J.C. Hibbard (transferred from command of *Skeena* to Halifax as training officer in March) had managed to make considerable headway. But Murray was not so matter-of-fact about either alternative. In a long reply he advised the Naval Staff of the importance of proper training: 'Consider Tobermory training doubles morale and efficiency and cannot be duplicated elsewhere. Lack of training allows convoys to be attacked without consequent submarine losses.' As for reducing the size of his escort groups, Murray warned that 'groups should sail from St John's at full strength which should not be less than six ships and preferably eight if we are to avoid repetition of SC 42 losses.' The inequality of group size between WLEF and MOEF cited by NSHQ (WLEF averaged only half that of MOEF) was totally justifiable in Murray's opinion by virtue of WLEF proximity to both air and surface reinforcement. Moreoever, the operational strength of C groups was roughly equal to that 'which the Admiralty considers necessary for B groups employed in the same area.' As a parting shot Murray reminded NSHQ that the U.S. contribution to A 3 was not three destroyers but actually only two Coast Guard cutters – whose margin of speed over corvettes was almost negligible.[18]

Murray's concern for the continuance of Tobermory training was echoed by the director of A/S at NSHQ, Commander A.R. Pressey, RCN. Contrary to what was implied in Jones's reply, Pressey advised the Naval Staff on 1 June that facilities at Halifax were still inadequate, particularly with regard to training submarines, which were in short supply. In fairness to Jones, Hibbard was on the verge of some very important work, including realistic convoy exercises and development of the 'night-escort trainer.' The NET was a synthetic training device which simulated the bridge of an escort at night during a U-boat attack, right down to the occasional bucket of salty water hurled at a bridge mock-up by a member of the training staff. However, the training program at Halifax was still a long way from being adequate in the summer of 1942, and, in fact, few of the escorts which fought battles later in the year passed through Hibbard's command. In the event, the Naval Staff concurred with Pressey's assessment and instructed that the dispatch of corvettes to Tobermory not be tampered with. Instead the Staff settled on the second alternative. On 15 June Murray was asked to part with eight more corvettes – 16 per cent of his operational strength.

The genesis of this reduction lay in the unchecked spread of the U-boat campaign and was by no means unilateral on the part of the RCN. The British estimated that 280 ships – nearly half of them tankers – totalling 1,650,752 gross tons were lost to enemy action between January and May 1942, most of them in the Western Atlantic.[20] The British concern about American delays in establishing convoys was justified, as was their frustration at not being able to intervene effectively. Trade Division at Ottawa could have established an interlocking convoy system off the U.S. and in the Caribbean. The RCN had both the intelligence and the infrastructure at its disposal, although setting up such a system would have taken some assistance from American authorities. As things turned out, Ottawa contented itself with its routing and diversion duties, which included prohibiting the movement of all Commonwealth trade south of New York. Similar action was taken by the Jamaica Intelligence and Trade Centre, which routed all Commonwealth Gulf of Mexico and Caribbean traffic to Britain via Africa.[21]

German attacks on oil trade were most intense, and this factor more than any other finally forced American authorities to adopt convoy. Indeed, Dönitz hoped to cripple American industry by shutting off its supply of petroleum, a strategy which was very nearly successful.[22] Its effects were important in the long term, when the shortage of tankers threatened to restrict British industry later in the year. In the late spring of 1942 the heavy losses of tankers seriously disrupted the movement of oil to Allied consumers, including Canada, and forced both Commonwealth nations to take independent action to protect their own supplies. In early May B 5 began to escort oil convoys between Aruba, in the Dutch West Indies, and Trinidad for eventual passage to the U.K. via Sierra Leone. Faced with similar disruptions, the RCN began to escort tankers between Halifax and Trinidad on 22 May (switched to Aruba on 5 July).[23]

The gradual shifting of escort strength southwards did not lessen American appeals for aid. Even as the corvettes designated for the oil convoys lay in wait at Halifax, Admiral H.R. Stark, formerly chief of Naval Operations (the American equivalent of CNS), now commander of U.S. Naval Forces in Europe, petitioned the Admiralty for more escorts.[31] The British were in something of a quandary. They believed that the Americans' problems were largely organizational. They were also gravely concerned about the main trade routes between Newfoundland and Britain. Although these were still enjoying a respite from sustained attack, it was not expected to last. Moreover, the excellent intelligence which had proved so decisive in 1941 was no longer available since the introduction of a new cipher for North Atlantic U-boats in February. Operational Intelligence still enjoyed a wealth of data from other, more conventional, sources, but the plotting of U-boats and consequently the routing of convoys was now much less precise. This boded ill for future convoy operations beyond the range of effective air support, particularly in light of the continued rapid expansion of the U-boat fleet. Into this atmosphere of doubt and concern came the news that a convoy had been attacked in mid-ocean by a U-boat pack during the second week of May. This was a marked change from the attacks by individual U-boats on passage to the Western Hemisphere which had characterized the first months of 1942.

Thus, when the First Sea Lord, Admiral Sir Dudley Pound, turned to Stark's request for more aid, he found a strong opponent in the assistant chief of the Naval Staff (Trade), Vice-Admiral E.L.S. King, RN. The latter warned Pound that, in light of the recent attack on ONS 92, 'we shall have to face a renewal of attacks on these convoys.' Far from endorsing further loan of escorts to the Americans, the ACNS (T) wanted both B 5 and the Canadians, designated for oil convoys, returned to the North Atlantic. Stark persisted and on 20 May passed along a personal request from Admiral King, now commander-in-chief (COMINCH) of the USN, for fifteen to twenty corvettes. Undoubtedly sensing British discomfort over the prospects of distant relocation of forces, the Americans now suggested that British ships would be kept along the U.S. eastern seaboard – where they would be readily available for redeployment to the main trade routes – while USN forces moved farther south to counter the spreading U-boat campaign.

Pound replied to this latest American request the next day. In a lengthy letter the First Sea Lord outlined the stretched nature of British escort resources. He held firmly to the need to allow one-third of strength for necessary repairs and refits and for training. Of those committed to operations Pound noted that they were already averaging twenty-four of every thirty-eight days at sea. If the British now released B 7, as Pound proposed, the remaining RN groups of MOEF would have their average harbour time cut by three days. With MOEF reduced to ten groups, the present cycle could only be maintained so long as they were able 'to adhere closely to the Great Circle Route across the Atlantic and provided convoys [were] not delayed by bad weather.' The First Sea Lord advised King that he would not allow RN groups to log any more sea time 'unless both American and Canadian escorts are being equally hard worked.' To ensure that this was the case Pound had his reply to the USN repeated to Nelles in Ottawa, in hopes that the RCN was willing to work up to the standard proposed. If this was the case, Pound confided to COMINCH, the 'three of us' would find his twenty corvettes.[24]

Nelles's reaction to Pound's signal remains uncertain, but the RCN did send delegates to a conference convened in Washington in early June to discuss the issues raised in May. Among the Canadians present was Murray's chief of staff, Captain R.E.S. Bidwell. It was agreed at the conference that the matter of finding additional escorts could best be resolved by reducing the operational size of each MOEF group. The new minimum strength was set at six ships, preferably two destroyers and the rest corvettes. Murray's contention that his MOEF groups should not be tampered with because they met Admiralty standards now became the rationale for the transfer of eight ships to WLEF.

Canadian acceptance of the reduction of MOEF-group strength suggests that the RCN was working up to the standard set forth by Pound in his letter to King. Certainly, by July this was the case with C groups.[26] Without contemporary evidence it is difficult to say the same for WLEF. However, if the proportion of escorts assigned for refits is any indicator, the RCN as a whole was more than pulling its weight in 1942. By the spring less than 22 per cent of the navy's escort force (approximately eighty ships) was undergoing repairs, while the number of ships assigned to training or work-ups seldom exceeded three or four. This was a far cry from the one-third allowable, upon which both the British and the U.S. placed great emphasis. Moreover, the percentage of strength committed to necessary refits and repairs by the RCN continued to decline sharply as the year wore on. This was particularly the case with C groups, where by August fully 90 per cent of allocated strength was operational.[27] Under pressure from both the British and the Americans (not to mention the Germans), the RCN willingly accepted new responsibilities. In itself this was a heady potion for a service which had nearly disappeared between the wars, and it in no small way helps to account for Canadian zeal. Unfortunately, the navy's naïve eagerness to meet every request for escorts stretched the fleet to the point of collapse and, ultimately, brought a sour reward.

Although the rapid spread of the U-boat campaign in the Western Hemisphere was enormously successful and caused many anxious moments, the final outcome was never in doubt. Even Dönitz knew that it could not last. The intent of his campaign was first and foremost to sink the highest possible amount of tonnage per U-boat-day-at-sea. When this proportion came down, as it had to do with the extension of Allied countermeasures, new theatres would need to be exploited. As these in turn ceased to be profitable according to the formula set forth by Dönitz, the main convoy routes would once again come under seige.

The fear of a German renewal of pack attacks beyond the range of Allied air power formed the basis of Murray's concern over reduction of

C-group strength and the dread of another SC 42. His sentiments were echoed by Vice-Admiral E.L.S. King, the British ACNS(T), both in King's letter to Pound already cited and in his contribution to the 'Battle of the Atlantic Review' of May 1942.[28] It is noteworthy that in the latter Vice-Admiral King considered that high U-boat losses, not the rate of losses to Allied tonnage, would in the end determine Döntiz's strategy. But in contrast to the Americans, who thought the same way with respect to the importance of destroying the enemy, the ACNS(T) put his faith in convoy and escort. Once an effective defence was established, the review observed, U-boat losses would inevitably rise and Dönitz would be forced to seek new theatres. Among the areas in which King considered the Germans likely to strike was the mid-ocean, where the weakened escorts guarded vital shipping without air cover along easily intercepted routes. Moreover, the whole matter was compounded by the growth of the U-boat fleet, which allowed the Germans to attack widely separated areas in strength, and the intelligence black-out, which limited the effectiveness of evasive routing.

The ACNS(T) was also painfully aware that it was not possible for the Allies to be strong everywhere at the same time. Dönitz still held most of the cards. To win some advantage from the Germans the Allies needed to keep their resources as flexible as possible. But they also needed greater air support for convoys and a high level of training among the escorts. 'In fact,' the review read, 'it may be said that with adequate and efficient air escort the "Wolf Pack" attack on a convoy should be impossible.' In the absence of sufficient very-long-range aircraft, the elimination of the mid-ocean air gap would take nearly another year to complete. Training, at least for the RN, was more immediately solvable. Captain C.P. Clarke, RN, the director of the Admiralty's A/S Warfare Division, noted with relief in his remarks in the review that the RN had just come through a period of unprecedented expansion during which training standards were reduced to an unacceptable level. As a result of this experience the RN had adopted new minimum requirements for operational efficiency and had lengthened many of its hitherto shortened courses in order to overcome the ravages of expansion. British action in this regard contrasts sharply with that of the RCN.

Aside from good training, the key to convoy battles in 1942 was modern radar, the type 271. As Captain Clarke concluded, this was 'another corollary to the present U-boat surface night tactics.' The RCN was not unaware of the great potential of the type 271 or of the comparative failure of the first generation of escort radars. Complaints about the SWIC poured forth from Murray's office through the winter of 1941–2. In large part these concerned the frail qualities of the equipment under operational conditions, a situation not enhanced by the RCN's poor maintenance capabilities.[29] The latter were virtually non-existent in 1942, and as early as April Murray advised NSHQ that the failure of the SWIC was due primarily to poor operators 'rather than faulty equipment.' Proper radar mechanics (RDF 1s) did not become available in sufficient numbers until early 1943; in the meantime the radar rating of each escort (trained solely as an operator) and the wireless rating had to manage as best they could.[30]

The only vital element missing from the review's assessment of how the U-boat packs were to be mastered was high-frequency direction finding (HF/DF). The plotting of transmitters – and thus ships – was a well-developed science by early 1942. Much of the Allies' operational intelligence of U-boat activities was gleaned from the network of shore-based DF stations which ringed the Atlantic. The provision and use of commercial-wavelength (MF) DF sets in ships was never a problem for the RCN, and these were widely fitted to escorts by early 1942. MF/DF was potentially useful for locating the homing beacons of U-boats shadowing convoys. But for a number of reasons MF/DF never developed into an effective means of disrupting the assembly of a pack around convoys. Until the fall of 1942 the escorts themselves did not have sufficient manpower to monitor medium frequency constantly. This duty was therefore left to the MF 'guard ship' of the convoy, and with only one possible interception the precise location of the transmitter was never a sure bet. Moreover, proper classification of MF interceptions was always a problem.

Much more important from a tactical point of view were the U-boats' operational communications, particularly sighting reports of convoys, which were sent by HF. Because of the difficulty of plotting HF transmissions and their brevity when used with coded messages, HF communications were considered fairly secure. But the British pushed development of a shipborne HF/DF set during the winter of 1940–1, and in July 1941 the first set, FH3, went to sea. Like the first radars, the FH3 was not a runaway success. It operated much like the early sonars in that it was dependent upon the operator's ear as he sat with headphones on, monitoring suspect wavelengths. The FH4, in production by early 1942, displayed the intercepted transmission on a cathode-ray tube, which made classification and bearing determination much faster and easier.[31]

HF/DF, especially when operated in pairs, provided the escort with very accurate and vitally important intelligence of immediate value. A U-boat transmitting a sighting report was always within striking distance of the escort and hence could be forced down and driven away from its newly acquired target. In the absence of two sets it was still possible for a trained operator to differentiate between a signal received on the 'ground wave' and one intercepted after skipping off the ionosphere. Such knowledge provided relative distances and was therefore of some value to the escort. In short, so long as U-boats were dependent upon HF communication, HF/DF functioned much like a long-range radar. By the summer of 1942 the RN's escort destroyers were equipped with HF/DF (on average one per group), and many of the rescue ships which now began to accompany ocean convoys were also fitted.

All of this modern equipment was soon to prove vitally important, since the Allies' close adherence to the great-circle route did not go unnoticed by the Germans. Despite continued success along the U.S. east coast Dönitz also wanted to attack this highly predictable trade to the north in order to make better use of U-boats on passage to the Western Hemisphere and prevent the reallocation of Allied resources from the mid-ocean. As a result, BdU prepared the first of what was expected to be a series of sweeps along the great-circle route by groups of U-boats on their way to the Americas. It was, in fact, not the first such use of U-boats in transit: the American-escorted convoy ON 67 had been heavily attacked in February by a pack hastily assembled from U-boats in the area. The difference with group 'Hecht' was that it was a planned operation from the start, and when it took station in the Western Approaches in early May, Hecht constituted the first serious attempt to attack the main trade routes since the previous November.[32]

Hecht was on station for only a short time before the slow westbound convoy ONS 92 was intercepted. Its escort was group A 3: the US destroyer *Gleaves*, with Commander J.B. Heffernan, USN, as Senior Officer, the US Coast Guard cutter *Spencer*, and the RCN corvettes *Algoma*, *Arvida*, *Bittersweet*, and *Shediac*. In light of the group's poor performance with ONS 92, for which Heffernan would be blamed, it is interesting to note that A 3 had undergone group training, including night exercises with a surfaced submarine, just prior to sailing. What lay before A 3, therefore, was not unrehearsed. In fairness to Heffernan, though, his group was almost totally bereft of modern equipment. None of the escort was fitted with HF/DF (the American ships of A 3 were not fitted until October); only *Bittersweet* was equipped with type 271 radar, and her operators were inexperienced.[33]

The first four days of ONS 92 passed without note. Group Hecht was under orders to maintain radio silence until 14 May, when it was expected to be on station and ready for operations. However, on the morning of 11 May, as she was proceeding to join Hecht, *U569* sighted ONS 92.

U569's sighting report and subsequent signals from the U-boats of Hecht as they made contact with the convoy were detected and plotted by the HF/DF operator of the rescue ship HMS *Bury* (assigned to ONS 92). The presence of shadowing U-boats was also confirmed by an Admiralty warning on the eleventh. Heffernan took no action on *Bury*'s DF fixes but in the afternoon sent *Gleaves* and *Spencer* on sweeps ahead on either bow of ONS 92, with orders to return just after dusk. Less than an hour after *Gleaves* left her screening position to commence her sweep, lookouts obtained a U-boat sighting seventeen miles ahead of the convoy. After forcing the U-boat to dive, Heffernan began a series of depth-charge attacks lasting until 0100Z on the morning of the twelfth. While the SOE was far away on the starboard side of ONS 92, *U124* torpedoed two ships on the port side, *Empire Dell* (11) and *Llanover* (13). In contrast to SC 42 eight months before, ONS 92 held its course following this first attack. Illumination fired over the convoy revealed nothing, and the escort held its screening positions. *Gleaves*, meanwhile, stood towards the convoy, but as she closed, three more ships were hit, *Cocle* (58), *Mont Pares* (12), and *Cristoles* (31), two by *U124* on her second pass of the night and one by *U94*. Two emergency turns to starboard were immediately conducted, drawing the convoy away from the dangerous waters to the south. *Gleaves* finally regained the convoy as it settled into its new course. The latter was held for two hours until at 0355Z *Empire Clive* (91) sighted a U-boat and the original course was resumed by two emergency turns to port.

All five of the ships torpedoed during the night of 11–12 May sank. With the exception of *Gleaves*'s protracted pursuit of her contact and a doubtful sighting by *Algoma* following the first attack, the escort of ONS 92 had seen nothing except burning and sinking merchant ships. On the twelfth the two American escorts again swept forward on the flanks of ONS 92 in an attempt to put down U-boats trying to gain a march on the convoy. In the process *Spencer* forced two U-boats down, attacking one. *Gleaves* joined to assist in the hunt for the latter contact and remained in the area until well after dark in order to keep U-boats from surfacing and renewing their pursuit of ONS 92. Meanwhile the convoy made two large alterations in course in a vain attempt to shake off group Hecht. In the early hours of the thirteenth, while *Spencer* and *Gleaves* were still astern and while steering due south, the convoy was attacked again. At 0235Z *Tolken* (13) and *Batna* (22) were struck by torpedoes from *U94*. Because of bad weather this attack went unnoticed; no illuminants were fired, and the escort took no action. Later Heffernan admitted candidly that he 'did not know what was happening and neither did the convoy commodore.' This much was true, but the SOE's assumption that 'probably this is the usual situation' reflected how little he understood his task.

No further attacks developed on the night of 12–13 May, and no contacts with U-boats were reported. Hecht stayed in contact with the convoy, however, even though adversely affected by the severe weather. Six U-boats were still in contact on the fourteenth, when BdU ordered the chase abandoned because it considered ONS 92 beyond reach. The Germans were well pleased with the outcome. The attacks had been successfully and skilfully conducted, primarily by two experienced commanders, Mohr of *U124* and Ites of *U94*. Moreover, it was clear that the escort was no more capable of effective defence than it had been in the fall of 1941. The failure of A 3 was complete.

The fall-out from ONS 92 illustrates just how divergent were the views of various staffs and navies involved in MOEF's operations. Despite the loss of seven ships and the demonstrable inability of A 3 to exact retribution from the enemy, Heffernan – who was in command of a group for the first time – was happy with A 3's effort. 'The COs of all the escorts are entitled to credit for a highly satisfactory performance,' he wrote in his report. This comment, and those already cited, brought down howls of protest from all quarters of Western Approaches Command. The ire of the shore staffs was also fuelled by the comments of the convoy commodore and the captain of the rescue ship *Bury*. The latter noted that the failure of the Senior Officer to act on HF/DF bearings passed to him 'may well have contributed greatly to the loss of valuable lives and ships.' *Bury*'s sentiment was shared by the commodore, who noted laconically that *Gleaves* was never there when ONS 92 was attacked.

Officers at Western Approaches were shocked. Their opinion of the USN was already at a low ebb as a result of the carnage off the U.S. coast, and they were now apparently faced with similar problems in the mid-ocean. The staff officer, Anti-Submarine, Commander C.D.H. Howard-Johnston, a thoroughly experienced and imaginative A/S officer with a pungent pen, wanted to confront the USN directly over the handling of ONS 92. His equally able senior officer, Captain R.W. Ravenhill, the deputy chief of staff (Operations), was unsure and suggested withholding criticism of the Americans until it was needed to counter any the USN might make of British groups. While all this was being sorted out, the commander of Task Group 24.7, the senior American officer at London-derry, Captain H.T. Thébaud, passed along word of British reaction to ONS 92, and Heffernan was quietly moved to another command.

Criticism of the RCN arising from ONS 92 was of a more insidious kind, reflecting not so much on the escorts as on their shore staff at St John's. *Arvida*'s action in picking up survivors, for example, at the expense of pursuing a counter-attack on a U-boat was frowned upon by WA officers because she could have dropped a raft for the men in the water and pressed on with her attack. Commander Howard-Johnston found the commendation extended by both Murray and Mainguy to *Arvida* for her action incomprehensible. But worse still was the Canadian reaction to *Bittersweet*'s missed opportunity. While that corvette was stationed ahead of ONS 92, she obtained a radar contact closing rapidly on a reciprocal course only a half-mile away. Thinking it might be *Arvida*, which was supposed to be in station on the port beam, the officer of the watch altered *Bittersweet*'s course to avoid. As she did so a U-boat went racing past her port side and on into the darkness. 'This is quite bad enough,' Howard-Johnston explained in a staff minute, but 'both Captain (D) [Newfoundland] and FONF consider that *Bittersweet* took the correct action: this is awful.' Clearly, neither the RCN nor the USN held favour with WA Staff in the summer of 1942. Certainly the British opinion of the Canadians was unaltered from what it had been in 1941, however much the escorts might have improved since. The fact was that in the interim the war at sea had become even more demanding. Canadian failure to keep pace would become painfully obvious during the last half of 1942 as C groups bore the brunt of MOEF's battles.

The stiffening of Allied defences in the Western Hemisphere, coupled with the success of Hecht's initial battle, encouraged Dönitz to keep the group together. However, having pursued ONS 92 to the Grand Banks of Newfoundland, Hecht in its subsequent battles was seriously affected by fog and the proximity of land. On 20 May Hecht sighted ONS 94, escorted by B 7, but promptly lost it – for good – in heavy fog. After failing to locate the next ON convoy, the U-boats were directed to refuel from the tanker *U116* six hundred miles south of Cape Race. Once this was completed, Hecht re-established a patrol line six hundred miles southeast of Cape Farewell, where on 31 May ONS 96, escorted by B 1, was sighted. The convoy was pursued westwards in a strong westerly gale. Contact was finally abandoned in persistent bad weather and in proximity to Newfoundland. The friction of war thus prevented Hecht from attacking two British-escorted convoys. The Canadians and Americans were not so lucky.[34]

Towards the end of the first week of June ONS 100, escorted by C 1, was intercepted by Hecht.[35] Contact was intermittent in deteriorating weather but was firmly established on the eighth. C 1 had joined ONS 100 on 3 June, and aside from difficulties with a recalcitrant commodore, the first days passed without incident. The escort itself, ostensibly Canadian, was in fact anything but for this operation. Two of its RCN escorts, the Town-class destroyer *St Croix* and the corvette *Buctouche*, missed sailing owing to defects. *Assiniboine*, one of the River class, was the only Canadian member of C 1. However, her captain, Lieutenant Commander J.H. Stubbs, RCN, was the SOE. Other escorts with C 1 included the British corvettes *Dianthus* and *Nasturtium* and the Free French corvettes *Aconit* and *Mimosa*. C 1 was thus a very mixed group, but it was no scratch team. Five of the escorts had been with C 1 for at least two previous crossings, and Stubbs had gone to some length to mould it into a unit. These preparations would doubtless have been even more advantageous if C 1 had sailed with its full strength, particularly of destroyers.

By the early hours of 9 June ONS 100 was well out to sea, making seven knots on a west-southwesterly course. The escort was disposed around the convoy in accordance with WACI screening diagram NE5B: *Assiniboine* (286 radar) on the port bow, *Nasturtium* (271 radar) on the starboard bow, *Aconit* (271) and *Dianthus* (271) on the port and starboard quarters respectively, and *Mimosa*, whose radar was out of order, in the clean-up position directly astern of the centre column. The first warnings of U-boat contact came almost simultaneously. Shortly after 0200Z explosions were heard on the starboard quarter, followed by an Admiralty notice to Stubbs and the commodore that U-boats were shadowing the convoy. The former would probably have sufficed to convince the Senior Officer that the enemy had found ONS 100, but in the minutes which followed the mysterious explosions, none of the escort or the convoy reported anything untoward. Stubbs none the less concluded that an attack had been attempted and that the detonations had come from torpedoes exploding at the ends of their runs. His belief was reinforced by further explosions moments later and would have been confirmed as enemy action had *Aconit* reported her radar contact at 0215Z.

On the strength of the second explosions and in light of the fact that ONS 100 had already been reported by group Hecht, Stubbs ordered Operation 'Raspberry,' an illumination procedure laid down in WACIs for use when a ship in the convoy was torpedoed at night by an unseen assailant. Each escort had a pre-arranged pattern to steer in accordance with its position in the screen and was charged with illuminating a specific sector of the convoy for a prescribed time. The intention of Raspberry was to turn night into day and expose the attacker as he attempted to make good his escape on the surface. Nothing came of this first use of Raspberry in defence of ONS 100.

Dawn on the ninth revealed the absence of *Mimosa*, and it soon became apparent that something was amiss. Turning the escort over to *Dianthus*, *Assiniboine* raced astern to the convoy's 0215Z position, where Stubbs's worst fears were confirmed. In the water he found wreckage and only four survivors of the French corvette. From them Stubbs learned of the frantic night action and the destruction of *Mimosa* by two torpedoes from *U124*. Why this action was not reported to the SOE at the time and why *Aconit* waited until dawn to report her radar contact of 0215Z remain mysteries. At least in this instance fundamental failures by the escort were not paid for by the merchant marine.

Further U-boat warnings were received from the Admiralty on the ninth. But with no HF/DF-equipped ships Stubbs had no idea where the shadowers were lurking. The escorts therefore had to hold their positions around ONS 100 and wait, but the lack of precise information on the location of the enemy did not prevent the SOE from taking some precautions. In the afternoon of the ninth *Dianthus* and *Nasturtium* were ordered to visibility distance on the port and starboard beams in order to push away U-boats attempting to take positions ahead of ONS 100 in preparation for a night attack. Stubbs's use of this American innovation showed a sound appreciation of his situation: a number of U-boats known to be in contact while the escort lacked the necessary tactical intelligence – which could only be provided by HF/DF – to disrupt the pack's operations. In this instance the distant screens were largely effective. At 1515Z *Nasturtium* reported a U-boat on the surface and set off in pursuit. *Assiniboine*, which was alongside the ss *Empire Ocean* as Stubbs made arrangements to launch the one-shot Hurricane fighter mounted on the catapult over her foc'sle, immediately went to the corvette's assistance. While *Nasturtium* and the destroyer were busy attacking a now-submerged U-boat with depth charges, *Dianthus* – at visibility distance on the other side of the convoy – reported sighting a U-boat coming up astern of her position. Stubbs ordered her to drive it off to a maximum of thirty miles before returning to her station.

Dianthus's pursuit of her contact effectively eliminated her from C 1 for the next twelve hours. *Nasturtium* and *Assiniboine* rejoined ONS 100 just at dusk, at which time *Aconit* was ordered to conduct a brief sweep astern. By midnight the three remaining escorts were closed up in a variation of the screen for four ships as they awaited the return of *Dianthus* – *Assiniboine* on the port bow, *Nasturtium*, whose 271 was now out of service, on the starboard bow, and *Aconit* astern. When *Dianthus* regained the convoy, the two rear corvettes were to occupy the quarters. With the escort reduced by missed sailings, loss, and temporary detachment, ONS 100 was now very vulnerable. Regardless, Stubbs was rather pleased with the situation. The Admiralty had warned of at least three U-boats in contact, and two of these were known to have been driven off during the day. Unfortunately, the third shadower, which might have been expected to have been driven off as well, unseen by the distant screen, remained in contact. At 0139Z on the tenth, in heavy fog that reduced visibility to two hundred yards, Ites in *U94* slipped in behind *Assiniboine* on the port beam and sank *Empire Clough* (75) and *Ramsey* (15). The heavy fog also threatened to hamper C 1's attempts to search for the attacker. Indeed, had it not been for Stubbs's contingency plan for an organized search in low visibility without the aid of illuminants, the escort would have been reduced to inaction. In the event *U94* escaped unscathed, and survivors of the two ships were picked up by *Dianthus* as she came up astern of the convoy.

On the tenth ONS 100 enjoyed a respite as the U-boats lost contact in the heavy mist. German attempts to relocate the convoy were successful the next day, although *U94* and *U569* combined to sink the small steamer *Pontypridd*, which had straggled astern of the convoy. But by that time C 1 had received some very welcome reinforcement in the form of *Chambly* and *Orillia*. Stubbs immediately passed over command of the escort to Prentice, who then took his training group to sweep at visibility distance. Prentice's sweeps revealed nothing, although they may have held off *U96*, the U-boat which had regained contact with ONS 100 earlier in the day. They certainly did not deter Mohr in *U124*, who came across the convoy in the early hours of the twelfth. He successfully penetrated the screen and sank the *Dartford* (34) at 0119Z. *Gothland*, the rescue ship, picked up survivors, while a search by the escort once again failed to detect the attacker.

By the twelfth ONS 100 was well within effective air support from Newfoundland, and the escorts of C 1 began to leave for St John's. Prentice nevertheless continued to use his escorts offensively, pushing out advanced screens and sweeps on the beams. With the dispatch of *Dianthus* to St John's on the thirteenth and the arrival of *Bittersweet* and *Primrose*, which were temporarily assigned to Prentice, ONS 100 was under escort by the 'training group.' WLEF Group 24.18.8 joined the next day, but Prentice and his charges stayed on until the fifteenth, when they finally departed for Newfoundland.

Fortunately for ONS 100 and its poorly equipped escort of corvettes, the Germans terminated operations against the convoy on the thirteenth in the face of continued bad weather and the nearness of land. Two of these factors – poor visibility and lack of modern equipment – were largely to blame for the losses the convoy did suffer. Had the escort been fitted with HF/DF and 271 radar in working order, the limited visibility would have provided excellent opportunities to surprise U-boats operating around the convoy. As it was, with the exception of the incidents surrounding the loss of *Mimosa*, the escort performed very well. Stubbs used his limited resources skilfully on the ninth, when U-boats were known to be in contact. Even the highly critical Staff at Western Approaches were reduced to speculating on whether or not the sweeps were properly organized.

The absence of HF/DF with the escort was noted by the British and also formed the basis of a plea by Murray to NSHQ to have this equipment fitted to Canadian destroyers. The most important criticism to arise from ONS 100 was again directed at Murray and his staff. In commenting on *Nasturtium*'s report of proceedings, Mainguy wrote, 'It is considered that a certain U-boat [that is, a confirmed sighting] is well worth leaving the convoy unguarded.' Prentice would have agreed with this, and so too would the USN. But Howard-Johnston thought Mainguy's comment a 'rather rash generalization.' It was just as well for both Stubbs and the RCN that group Hecht had had such a difficult time mounting its attack. Certainly ONS 100 did nothing to restore confidence in C groups or their senior staff officers within the offices of Western Approaches Command.

The final operation of Hecht also fell largely on the RCN.[36] On 16 June, ONS 102 was sighted by the intrepid Oberleutnant Ites in *U94*. The convoy of forty-eight ships was escorted by A 3, now much more powerful than in its previous clash with Hecht in May. ONS 102's escort included the U.S. Coast Guard cutters *Campbell* and *Ingham*, the destroyers USS *Leary* and HMCS *Restigouche*, and the corvettes *Agassiz*, *Collingwood*, *Mayflower*, and *Rosthern*. The presence of four large escorts, two of them destroyers, gave A 3 an enormous edge, one which was greatly enhanced by the HF/DF set fitted in *Restigouche* (acquired through her commander's initiative during refit in the UK the previous winter). On the sixteenth *Restigouche* located five U-boats as they made sighting reports of ONS 102, and the escort was able to drive them all off. In the course of these actions *U94* and *U590* were both damaged. The escort was also aided by Prentice's training group, which sailed to support ONS 102 and ON 103 (C 2) on 16 June. On this occasion Prentice had specific orders from Murray not to join the close screens of either convoy but to keep his group as a separate unit. Because of his ostensible commitment to both convoys Prentice was able to resist repeated attempts by the Senior Officer of A 3, Captain P. Heineman, USCG, to draw *Chambly*, *Bittersweet*, *Chilliwack*, and *Orillia* into his fold. Eventually Heineman reluctantly accepted Prentice's insistence that he adhere to his orders 'to act as a striking force' and passed on the intelligence necessary to make the training group's operations useful. Over the next few days Prentice conducted sweeps during daylight hours and provided a distant screen for ONS 102 at night. Group Hecht was finally called off the pursuit on the eighteenth, but not before *U124* penetrated the screen in a daring submerged daytime attack and sank one last ship. With that parting shot the operations of group Hecht, overshadowed by more dramatic events to the south, were brought to a successful conclusion – twelve U-boats had sunk twelve ships at a cost of only two U-boats damaged.

Reaction to Hecht's string of convoy battles was mixed. For the Germans, who held the initiative in the war at sea, the results were more concrete. The success of Hecht and of group 'Endrass,' which operated concurrently along the UK-Gibraltar route, indicated that Allied countermeasures in the mid-Atlantic were largely unchanged from the previous year and that the prospects for further pack attacks were therefore good. The successful defence of ONS 102 by A 3, particularly the repeated interception of U-boats by HF/DF-directed sweeps, was put down to aggressive patrolling. Dönitz found nothing in the experiences of Hecht to indicate the existence of an effective shipborne (A/S) radar, initially believed to be the cause for the failure of the ONS 102 operation. The potential problem of DF fixes on sighting reports and homing signals was admitted, but a change of procedure was felt sufficient to make this essential traffic less vulnerable.

The Germans also believed that the apparent improvement in the defences of ONS 100 and ONS 102 stemmed from the fact that many of Hecht's U-boat commanders were inexperienced and that their rashness made operating around the convoys more dangerous than it normally was. Thus the Germans, too, suffered a decline in the efficiency of the fleet as it expanded. In July and August 1942 the RCN was able to exploit this weakness and destroy several submarines.[37] The increasing prevalence of inexperienced U-boat captains, coupled with sharply improved Allied countermeasures, would eventually bring about the collapse of Germany's mid-Atlantic campaign in 1943. In the meantime, however, Dönitz could still rely on officers like Ites and Mohr to find the gaps in Allied defences and press through with attacks.

Allied conclusions from the battles with group Hecht were much less certain. In part this stemmed from the late realization that a U-boat pack was actually operating along the convoy lanes and was not simply on passage to the west. The immediate problem was to reintroduce some flexibility in routing, which was possible in the fairer weather of the summer months. The technical and tactical lessons were by no means uniformly understood, particularly in the RCN. Murray and his staff appreciated the value and importance of good radar and HF/DF and now had solid operational evidence to back this up. But the understanding of the relationships between equipment and operations enjoyed by the navy's operational commands was not shared by NSHQ. When the Naval Staff discussed the merits of SWIC and 271 in mid-May, officers were reluctant to admit that the Canadian set was useless in an A/S role. Despite noting comments from Captain (D), Halifax, who considered SWIC 'disappointing' and the 271 'extremely satisfactory,' both the director of Anti-Submarine and the RDFO (radar officer) felt compelled to defend the Canadian equipment. They admitted that 271 was undoubtedly superior to SWIC but contended that the SWIC was better than the RN's type 286, from which it had been developed. So it was, but the relative merit of obsolete sets was hardly the point. Finally, the RDFO, after noting that the SWIC series was scheduled for yet more improvements, recommended that one hundred 271 radar sets be ordered from the Admiralty. Typically, the Naval Staff decided not to make a decision on the matter pending consultation with the Admiralty radar mission, which was then in Canada.

Prospects for the acquisition of a 10-centimetre radar set for the escort fleet were not promising. The Admiralty radar mission advised the Staff that the 271 would probably not be made available to the RCN and that the Canadian service should rely on North American sources. Canadian 10-centimetre equipment, the Staff was later advised, was still in the trial stage and would take a year or more to mass produce. Even then the distinctive character of such an exclusively Canadian radar presented maintenance problems for the far-ranging fleet. Moreover, U.S. supplies of 10-centimetre radar were likely to be wholly absorbed by the USN. At the next staff meeting the RDFO, having seen a trial of the Canadian 10-centimetre set, suggested that all decisions on the matter be deferred until the supply problem was resolved. The latter was settled much more quickly than the RCN had hoped when, at the end of May, the Admiralty offered to supply the RCN with 271 sets at a rate of ten per month until a domestic source of supply was available.[38] Unfortunately, before this assistance could be felt at sea, the C groups fought many more battles.

On the issue of HF/DF the Naval Staff's record was much less salutory. HF/DF was also discussed at the end of May, several weeks before Murray's submission of the reports from ONS 102 which so clearly illustrated the value of the equipment. In the absence of such hard evidence, the Staff's concern for the cost and delays entailed in fitting HF/DF is somewhat understandable. After all, RCN warships were already fitted with MF/DF, and the relative merits of the two remained obscure for some time to come. What was most alarming in these early discussions was the misunderstanding of the functioning of shipboard HF/DF by the Staff's would-be authorities on direction finding, the director of Signals Division (DSD), Commander G.A. Worth, and the director of Foreign Intelligence Section (FIS), Commander J.M.B.P. de Marbois (both of whom were involved in the RCN's own DF network). When considering a possible scenario for the use of HF/DF, both of these officers envisaged only a single set, which, it was noted, would give direction but not distance. 'Therefore,' they concluded, 'there was some question as to the practical application of this equipment.' That may have been the case at NSHQ. But had Worth and de Marbois been closer to the action, they would have known that operators of HF/DF equipment could distinguish between ground waves and skip or that two sets with the same convoy provided a wide enough base to determine distance by triangulation, just as the shore-based sets did. The example of Restigouche's lone set in defence of ONS 102 might here have shown the way, but the Staff remained remarkably unimpressed by HF/DF for many more months to come.

The need to re-equip the fleet, particularly the corvettes, and the extent to which Canadian corvettes lagged behind their British counterparts were well known to the Staff by late 1941, when the Admiralty began to extend the foc'sle, modernize the bridges, and fit 10-centimetre radar to its corvettes on loan to the RCN. Although this program was overtaken by events and not completed, the 'British' corvettes were the best-equipped escorts of their class in the RCN for most of 1942. The RCN would have liked to follow suit in the winter of 1941–2, but the enormity of the task and the dearth of accessible repair facilities in Canada precluded action. Moreover, the navy had not planned to make large-scale structural changes to the corvette fleet until 1943.[39] Once again the Naval Staff waited for a report, this time from the Admiralty A/S mission, which toured North

America in early July, before making a final decision on improvements to the corvette fleet. With the tabling of the report on the ninth the Staff, somewhat reluctantly, agreed that modernization was necessary. Yet, they remained intimidated by the sheer size of the job, and their decision was not matched by a will to proceed with the work promptly. All the requisite material to re-equip the seventy-seven obsolete corvettes, including much-needed gyro-compasses, was ordered immediately. But only one ship was to be taken in hand right away, in order to determine the costs and time required to complete the rest of the program.[40]

The great need in 1942 was for escorts of any description. The serious implications of obsolescence in the fleet were not apparent until later in the year. Meanwhile, at sea MOEF enjoyed nearly a month's respite following the recall of Hecht, and much of this period was uneventful. When, in mid-June, Murray reduced his escort strength by eight ships, it was perhaps indicative of his dislike of this reduction that all of the corvettes transferred to Halifax were either due to refit or badly in need of boiler cleaning.[41] Thus the immediate operational strength of C groups was not affected, at least not by the transfer to WLEF. The escort of ONS 100 had been understrength from the outset because of defects in two of its RCN escorts. Keeping the ships going continued to be a major problem, and this was not helped by the home establishment's concentration on expansion and new responsibilities. Although at least one key officer, Captain H.T.W. Grant, the director of Naval Personnel, wanted to check the growth of the navy in early 1942 in order to consolidate, his plea was overwhelmed by the operational emergency.[42]

The most distressing incident of the lull was the accidental sinking of the Newfoundland training submarine *P514* by the minesweeper *Georgian*. *P514* had lost her escort in a heavy fog while on passage from Argentia to St John's, and *Georgian*, acting as escort to a local convoy at the time, sank her instinctively when the submarine came across the 'sweeper's bows in the fog. Newfoundland was now once again without a training submarine until a replacement, *P554*, arrived in August. Other bad news for the training establishment at St John's came at about the same time, when the Admiralty requested the release without replacement of the RN A/S liaison officers at Halifax and Newfoundland. As Admiral Pound explained to Nelles, the need for these men in the UK was now great, and the CNS reluctantly agreed to let them go.[43] Luckily for the escorts based at St John's and for the RCN, Murray was able to retain Lieutenant Commander P.M. Bliss, RN, the port A/S officer, a former member of the staff at the RN's anti-submarine school and a valuable asset.

The success of group Hecht led BdU to lay plans for the renewal of pack attacks in the mid-ocean air gap. In the interim, however, the continued success of the inshore campaign in the Western Hemisphere required the main German effort to remain there for the time being. A logical reconciliation of the two lay in a repetition of Hecht: using U-boats on passage to America for pack operations. Plans went ahead accordingly, and by 13 July group 'Wolf,' nine U-boats all commanded by inexperienced captains, was in position six hundred miles west of Ireland. The scouting line had only just formed when a convoy was intercepted by the northern wing. Initially it was believed that the convoy was eastbound, and some of Wolf wasted time and effort in pursuit to the northeast. Attempts to obtain accurate information on the convoy's course and position failed, and on the nineteenth the operation was finally abandoned. Wolf was then instructed to sweep southwards, along the main trade routes. For the next three days the U-boats saw nothing but empty seas. But on 22 July, just as Wolf was due to rendezvous with a replenishment U-boat, BDienst (the German radio-intelligence service) located the position of a westbound convoy. Wolf was redisposed to intercept, and contact was made, according to plan, by *U552* on the twenty-fourth.

The convoy was ON 113, thirty-three ships under the escort of C 2: *Burnham* (RN) and *St Croix*, both Town-class destroyers, and the corvettes *Brandon*, *Dauphin*, *Drumheller*, and *Polyanthus* (RN).[44] The battle for ON 113 was destined to be short and balanced in its outcome. Very heavy fog beset the convoy during its first days at sea and continued to shroud it through most of its passage. The first indications of trouble came even before Wolf made its planned interception – on 23 July *Burnham* chased and attacked a lone U-boat (probably on passage) directly ahead. Nothing came of this first brush with the enemy or of *St Croix*'s first contact later in the day, and it was not until 0940Z on the twenty-fourth that the first Admiralty warnings of shadowing U-boats were received by ON 113. As a result of these warnings, Acting Commander T. Taylor, RN, CO of *Burnham* and SOE of C 2, ordered *St Croix* and his own ship to distant screening positions ten miles ahead. The move paid off, for at 1530Z Lieutenant Commander A.H. Dobson, RCNR, CO of *St Croix*, reported two U-boats on the surface, one to port and one to starboard. *Burnham* gave chase to the U-boat nearest her, but the interloper dived and avoided subsequent detection. *St Croix* meanwhile forced her contact to dive and then proceeded to deliver three quick and very accurate depth-charge attacks. As the Canadian destroyer turned to drop a fourth pattern, wreckage from *U90* was spotted on the surface, and *St Croix* shifted her effort to collecting the necessary flotsam needed to confirm a kill – the second of the war for the RCN.

The elimination of one U-boat did little to remove the threat of loss from ON 113. Shortly after *St Croix*'s destruction of *U90*, *Burnham* reported another contact ahead of the convoy, and while the two destroyers undertook the hunt, Taylor ordered ON 113 to alter course to due north, away from the known danger. No sooner was the course alteration under way than American convoy authorities (CONNAV), who now controlled the operation, ordered ON 113 to alter to due south after dark and hold that course for twelve hours. The commodore, mindful that such an action would carry the convoy back over the scene of recent U-boat contacts, effected a compromise. At dusk he turned ON 113 east and then at about midnight again to due south, in accordance with CONNAV's wishes. Half an hour after the southerly course was assumed and while both *Burnham* and *St Croix* were still away from the convoy, *U552* torpedoed *British Merit* (94) and *Broompark* (74). Attempts were made to illuminate the convoy, but these were frustrated by high winds. Moments after the two ships were struck, the steamer *Salsten* (64) reported a U-boat on the surface and engaged it with her armament. However, *U552* was able to make good her escape and no further attacks were attempted that night. The convoy held course until 1055Z on the morning of the twenty-fifth, when a westerly course (253°) was finally resumed. The convoy had lost a day's advance, turned a complete circle in the middle of the ocean, and suffered two ships heavily damaged as a result (*Broompark* later sank while in tow). The losses were not completely the fault of the escort, which, although it left the convoy exposed by prolonged pursuits of U-boat contacts, managed to destroy one shadower.

The twenty-fifth passed rather quietly; the only excitement came from *Burnham*'s pursuit of a U-boat detected following the passing of a transmission bearing from the convoy's MF/DF guard, *Pacific Pioneer*. The night also passed peacefully, at least until *Empire Rainbow* (91) was damaged by a single torpedo hit just one hour before sunrise. Searches by the escort, in what was by now very poor weather, revealed nothing. *Empire Rainbow* was able to proceed under her own power but was sunk by *U704* on the twenty-sixth as she made her way towards St John's. The deteriorating weather, which had greatly facilitated Wolf's already successful attacks, eventually led to the termination of operations against ON 113, as the pack found it difficult to locate and close the convoy. One further ship was lost from ON 113, however; on the twenty-ninth, while under escort by WLEF, *Pacific Pioneer* (41) was sent to the bottom in a skilful submerged daylight attack delivered by *U132*, which was operating independently off the Canadian coast.

The Germans later admitted that their failure to exact a heavy toll from ON 113 stemmed from three things: the inexperience of the U-boat commanders, poor weather conditions, and 'the movements of the strongly escorted convoy.' The first of these undoubtedly contributed to the high incidence of U-boat sightings by C 2. During the four days of the battle (23–26 July) there were at least seven and possibly eight separate sightings. In daylight this naïveté allowed *Burnham* and *St Croix* to drive the pack off and thereby keep all but two U-boats from penetrating the convoy itself. Poor weather conditions hindered attempts to establish and maintain contact with ON 113. Once in close contact, however, conditions were virtually ideal for pack attacks, particularly against an escort almost completely without modern radar. Indeed, given the absence of both 271 radar and HF/DF it would have been reasonable to expect even greater success than was actually achieved. In the final analysis it was the sweeps by the two destroyers – which were fast enough to make good tactical use of this practice – that kept the inexperienced U-boat commanders at bay.

The conduct of the escort by Taylor drew no criticism from operational authorities on either side of the Atlantic, although Dobson, CO of *St Croix*, noted in his report that the escort was reduced, on Taylor's orders, in order to pursue U-boat contacts on the night of 23–24 July – the first night of contact with the enemy. Taylor was indeed fortunate that no attack developed, since he had no certain means of knowing that the destroyers were dealing with all the shadowers. British concern was focused squarely on the course alteration ordered by CONNAV on the twenty-fourth, which the British considered responsible for the subsequent attacks and losses. The idea of a convoy turning a wide circle in the mid-Atlantic while the pack lay to the west was indeed difficult to accept without protest. Moreover, it was just the type of confusion over command and control of convoy operations which the British had sought to eliminate by reasserting C-in-C, WA's authority westwards to Newfoundland. The British considered the role of shore authorities to be that of advisers, leaving it to the man on the spot to decide what course of action to take in light of all the available intelligence. Much of the latter was simply not available either to Tracking and Routing Section at the Admiralty or to CONNAV in Washington. Admiral Brainard at Argentia appreciated the British position and was prepared to endorse it, but for the moment two fundamentally different procedures existed on either side of the CHOP line. The issue of drastic course alterations would arise from the next convoy battle. So too would the conduct of the RCN, despite the fact that, with losses low and the escort finally sinking U-boats, the C groups were able to bring a certain balance to their convoy operations.

5

An Acceptable
Rate of Exchange

The escorts left their convoy singularly unprotected by day.
However, they got their s/m and must receive their due for that.
Captain R.W. Ravenhill, RN, of ON 115

The battle for ON 113 heralded the start of the final German campaign in the mid-ocean. Over the next ten months the struggle between U-boat packs and MOEF built to a climax, culminating in the German defeat of May 1943. The period actually has two distinct phases. The first, from July to December 1942, has been treated as the warm-up for the main events of early 1943. But for the RCN this first phase was enormously significant. During the last six months of 1942 Canadian escorts in MOEF bore the brunt of the German assault on the main trade lanes. Eleven of the sixteen convoys which lost ships in the air gap from July to the New Year were escorted largely by Canadians (that is, C and A groups). Further, for a number of reasons the Germans were able to exert much more pressure on Canadian convoys than on those protected by B groups, MOEF's best-prepared escorts. Of the eighty ships lost in convoy in the mid-ocean during the last half of 1942, sixty were destroyed while under C- or A-group escort.[1] The story of MOEF in late 1942 therefore is the story of the RCN's own crisis: its learning experience and its coming of age.

The day before group Wolf made firm contact with ON 113, senior Canadian, American, and British officers met in Ottawa to discuss proposals for improving trade and escort matters in the Northwest Atlantic. The overriding issue affecting all discussion was the general shortage of escorts. More were needed to increase the movement of oil to Canadian ports, to increase the average size of WLEF groups from four to six escorts, and to provide for 'at least $\frac{1}{3}$ of the ships to be under repair.' WLEF, it was noted, was six destroyers and twenty corvettes short of its basic requirement. MOEF, by contrast, was still in much better shape. Its current cycle of twenty-four days at sea out of every thirty-eight was considered acceptable, but prospects for the winter looked grim. It was believed that with the onset of winter weather in November, eleven groups would be incapable of maintaining the thirty-eight-day cycle. A minimum of one additional group was therefore needed for MOEF by the fall, plus 'an additional 12 corvettes to allow for weather damage.' Thus, while MOEF strength and operating conditions were adequate in late July, the situation was not expected to hold even over the short term. To prepare for the coming winter MOEF required three more destroyers and eighteen corvettes.[2]

While the scale of needs was evident, no conclusions were reached on where to obtain the additional escorts. U-boat attacks in the Gulf of St Lawrence had forced on the RCN the establishment of yet another convoy route, and there is no doubt that by mid-1942 the Canadian navy was operating to the limit. Even the navy's minesweepers were pressed into escort work, leaving the RCN understandably anxious about the potentially paralysing effect of a German mining campaign. Moreover, the shortage of escorts was enormous. In June the RCN had only half of the 212 escorts the Naval Staff estimated it needed for the navy's commitments to WLEF, MOEF, the Gulf Escort Force, and the oil convoys if allowance were also to be made for one-third undergoing refits or committed to training.[3] The decision to do without the latter almost entirely and to use Bangor minesweepers as escorts eased the situation somewhat, but it must have left many officers extremely uneasy about the long-term effects of driving the fleet into a state of disrepair.

By mid-summer, then, MOEF, despite the reduction of its Canadian component alone by 50 per cent since January, was still in enviable condition compared to other RCN commitments. But that was cold comfort to Murray and his staff. His warning that MOEF and WLEF operated in vastly different theatres still obtained. Yet for the time being nothing could be done by the RCN to increase his strength. Indeed, his pleadings were probably undone by the series of successful – at least from the Canadian perspective – convoy battles that began that summer with ON 113.

While C 2's battle around ON 113 was still at its height, the next westbound convoy to be intercepted, ON 115 (ON 114, escorted by A 3, was not sighted), was just clearing the Irish coast.[4] Its escort, C 3, was the most stable and most successful of the C groups during 1942. *Saguenay,*

Skeena, and the corvettes *Galt*, *Sackville*, and *Wetaskiwin* had all been together since May, and the corvettes had been trained as a unit by Prentice. The two other members of C 3, *Agassiz* and *Louisburg*, were both relative newcomers, the former recently transferred from A 3 and the latter fresh from refit. Despite these additions, the group performed creditably in the forthcoming battle – although not everyone agreed.

The convoy received air cover briefly off Ireland on 26 July, but the aircraft reported no sign of the enemy. Just before noon on the same day, however, *Saguenay*, commanded by Acting Commander D.C. Wallace, RCNR, Senior Officer of C 3, obtained a doubtful contact directly ahead of the convoy. While *Saguenay* investigated and later attacked the contact, Wallace ordered the commodore to alter ON 115's course 90° to starboard to clear the danger area. The new course carried the convoy almost due north and was held for several hours. In the interim, Wallace received an MF/DF bearing from the commodore which indicated a U-boat astern of the convoy. Wallace abandoned his questionable underwater contact, instructed the escort to set MF watches, and took *Saguenay* to search to a depth of thirty miles in ON 115's wake. Again the search revealed nothing. *Saguenay* was able to regain her station in the screen four and a half hours later, at which time *Skeena* and *Wetaskiwin* were ordered to visibility distance on the beams of the convoy.

The first night in treacherous waters passed quietly, as did the early daylight hours of 27 July. The convoy once again received support from Coastal Command in the forenoon, and in the afternoon course was altered to west-northwest in accordance with instructions from Western Approaches. Five hours after the convoy assumed its new course (2300Z), *Wetaskiwin* obtained a firm radar contact. The corvette attempted to close the target, but it was able to outrun the escort, and the precise nature of the contact was never ascertained. At least the interloper had been driven off. Yet for some inexplicable reason *Wetaskiwin*'s commanding officer, Lieutenant Commander Guy Windeyer, RCN, a professional naval officer who should have known better, failed to report his contact to Wallace – who could have sent a destroyer to run down what was later believed to be a U-boat.

The second night also passed quietly. The twenty-eighth was marked by the interception of four homing transmissions by the convoy's MF guard, all of which bore aft (89°). These were passed to Wallace, as were three more interceptions, considered 'definitely German,' on the twenty-ninth. As a result of the latter Wallace ordered *Skeena* to sweep to a depth of thirty miles along the bearing; *Wetaskiwin* was pushed to visibility distance on the threatened side, and all escorts were once again ordered to set MF watches at dusk. In view of the evident U-boat activity around ON 115, *Saguenay* also swept the starboard quarter to a depth of thirty miles in the afternoon. None of these sweeps produced tangible results, and both destroyers were back in station with the screen by dusk.

Wallace's concern for the safety of his charges was justified, although the Germans did not make firm contact with ON 115 until the twenty-ninth. On that day *U210*, outward bound for the U.S., obtained the first firm sighting of the convoy, and six U-boats in the area were detailed to attack. Accordingly, MF homing signals (bearing 276°) were picked up by the convoy at dusk on the twenty-ninth and the commodore took evasive action, turning to course 168° in the early hours of the thirtieth. The new course actually took the convoy slightly eastwards until, at 0630Z, a westerly course (245°) was resumed. Meanwhile *Skeena* and *Saguenay* searched the bearings provided by the MF interceptions. Unable to locate any U-boats, Wallace took the two destroyers to positions immediately astern of ON 115 'so as to intercept any U-boats chasing.'

Again the night passed quietly, and at dawn on the thirtieth the escort resumed extended screening positions, with *Skeena* and *Wetaskiwin* deployed to visibility distance. On this occasion the extended screen paid off. *Skeena*, which in the course of her patrols had worked her way towards the convoy's starboard quarter, reported a U-boat on the surface at 1400Z. The destroyer turned immediately to prosecute the contact, while Wallace ordered *Galt* to assist, with the instructions that the corvette was to remain in the area whatever happened in order to keep the U-boat down. As *Galt* set off to help, *Skeena* attacked several underwater contacts in the area where the U-boat had submerged. By the time *Galt* arrived, virtually all hope of obtaining asdic contact on the U-boat was gone, and a co-ordinated search by the two ships failed to reveal anything other than a single doubtful contact. The latter was attacked but later reclassified as non-submarine. With that the search was abandoned; *Galt* was left to stand guard, and *Skeena* made her way back to the convoy.

While *Skeena* and *Galt* were thus engaged, *Saguenay* began a sweep to starboard a few hours before dusk, to which direction was soon given by MF bearings passed from the commodore. As Wallace took *Saguenay* to sweep along the bearings, the commodore conducted a pre-arranged course alteration to due south, which Wallace hoped would throw off the shadowers. He doubtless would have felt much better about the prospects for successfully shaking ON 115's pursuers had *Saguenay* remained in the vicinity of the convoy: Wallace later reported that smoke from the convoy could be seen clearly in the bright moonlight from fifteen miles away; the Germans would have little problem locating the convoy.

Both *Skeena* and *Saguenay* rejoined ON 115 just after dark and were no sooner in station than MF transmissions 'loud and apparently close' were DF'd on the starboard beam of the convoy. *Skeena* was ordered to search but found nothing. Wallace then instructed her to maintain a screening position seven miles distant on the threatened side. For the balance of the night U-boat homing transmissions bearing from 260 to 275 degrees (that is, to starboard) were intercepted by the convoy, but lacking effective radar (and HF/DF, which might have yielded more precise information on ranges), C 3 held its ground and waited. In time *Skeena* was again rewarded for her diligence by a U-boat sighting, and *Wetaskiwin* was ordered to her assistance.

Wallace's choice of *Wetaskiwin* as a partner in *Skeena*'s search was not chance. During the night Wallace had disposed his screen so that the two destroyers and the only corvette commanded by professional and experienced officers were on the threatened side. Moreover, Lieutenant Commander K.L. Dyer, RCN (in command of *Skeena*), and Windeyer (in *Wetaskiwin*) had recently conducted co-ordinated attacks on a submerged U-boat off Rockall and had since discussed the best methods for dealing with those which apparently had gone deep. Familiarity and professionalism were to come in handy in the forthcoming action.

It was nearly an hour before *Wetaskiwin* closed with *Skeena*, and in the interim the destroyer delivered a series of unsuccessful attacks on her target. Windeyer's arrival on the scene was marked by an exchange of signals in which it was agreed that Dyer, although actually junior to the corvette commander, should conduct the hunt from his better-equipped destroyer. A co-ordinated search then began to regain the contact lost after *Skeena*'s last depth-charge attack. Just before 0900Z the U-boat was relocated and *Wetaskiwin* dropped a pattern of charges. Contact was once again re-established at 0908Z, whereupon *Skeena*, directed by plotters in *Wetaskiwin* who provided a check for her own plots, delivered a full ten-charge pattern on the contact. These two attacks and one by *Wetaskiwin* twenty minutes later failed to produce results, and the U-boat eluded its hunters.

Having lost contact in the aftermath of the last attack, the two escorts began a deliberate search. *Wetaskiwin* remained in the area of the last firm echo, while *Skeena* conducted a triangular search to the north. Their persistence was rewarded an hour later when *Wetaskiwin* regained contact. She delivered two deliberate attacks before *Skeena* arrived, at which time the corvette stood off to direct the destroyer over the target for what proved to be the final attack. Again both ships kept accurate plots, and Dyer aboard *Skeena* was able to check his progress against the plot kept by *Wetaskiwin*. During the final approach it was decided to change the setting of the charges from 350 to 550 feet and to lengthen the interval between firing in order to compensate for the long descent time and the likelihood of evasive action. *Wetaskiwin* dipped her flag (indicating the point of firing) at precisely the same moment that *Skeena*'s plotters concluded that the firing point had been reached, and a five-charge pattern was delivered. Underwater explosions – distinct from the charges – were heard soon afterwards. The two ships were in the midst of another approach when debris was spotted on the surface. Boats were lowered to collect the grisly proof of a certain kill, and the ships then set course for ON 115.

To date C 3 had been both skilful and lucky. From the twenty-ninth to the early hours of the thirty-first the convoy had been shadowed by six U-boats. Even though Wallace was hampered by very imprecise intelligence, C 3 had driven the U-boats off one after another. In addition, *U558* was destroyed in a very professional and prolonged hunt – an uncommon opportunity in 1942. In the early hours of 1 August the last of the six shadowers lost contact with ON 115. The first phase of the battle was over, and it had been won by C 3.

But for ON 115 the worst was yet to come, and it was fortunate that the coast of Newfoundland lay near at hand. Having tracked ON 115 across the mid-Atlantic for no gain, BdU was still determined to mount an effective operation against it. In fact, the Germans had both time and resources. Loss of contact on 1 August was followed promptly by the formation of a new patrol line, 'Pirate,' directly across the convoy's path. To these six U-boats were added the replenished members of group Wolf, who lay in position to intercept ON 115. As a result of these hurried redispositions ON 115 was sighted again on 2 August.

By the time Pirate obtained contact with ON 115, the convoy's escort was much reduced. Wallace's aggressive use of destroyers during the early phase of the crossing left them short of fuel by the thirty-first, while the convoy was still more than five hundred miles from Newfoundland. *Skeena* requested permission to sail direct to St John's following her destruction of *U558*. She arrived two days later with barely 10 per cent of her fuel remaining. *Saguenay* departed within hours of *Skeena*, while *Wetaskiwin*, groping through heavy fog, was unable to relocate the convoy. Wallace therefore passed command of what remained of C 3 to

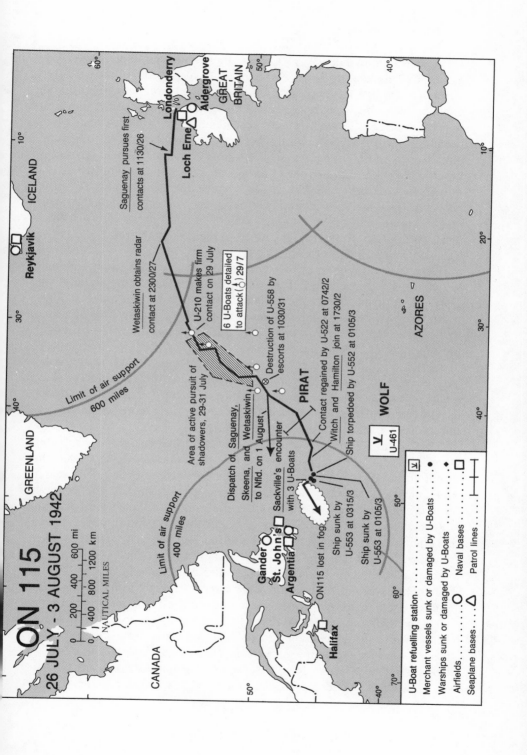

ON 115
26 JULY – 3 AUGUST 1942

GREENLAND

ICELAND
Reykjavik

Saguenay pursues first
contacts at 1130/26

Londonderry
Aldergrove
GREAT
BRITAIN
Loch Erne

Wetaskiwin obtains radar
contact at 2300/27

U-210 makes firm
contact on 29 July

6 U-Boats detailed
to attack ( ) 29/7

Limit of air support
600 miles

Destruction of U-558 by
escorts at 1030/31

Area of active pursuit of
shadowers, 29-31 July

PIRAT

Contact regained by U-522 at 0742/2
Witch and Hamilton join at 1730/2
Ship torpedoed by U-552 at 0105/3

Dispatch of Saguenay,
Skeena, and Wetaskiwin
to Nfld. on 1 August

AZORES

WOLF

U-461

Limit of air support
400 miles

CANADA

NAUTICAL MILES

Gander
St. John's
Argentia

ON115 lost in fog

Sackville's encounter
with 3 U-Boats

Ship sunk by
U-553 at 0315/3

Ship sunk by
U-553 at 0105/3

Halifax

U-Boat refuelling station....................
Merchant vessels sunk or damaged by U-Boats....
Warships sunk or damaged by U-Boats........
Airfields.......................
Seaplane bases.....................
Naval bases.............
Patrol lines............

Lieutenant Commander W.F. Campbell, RCNVR, the captain of *Louisburg*. Now reduced to three corvettes, C 3 managed to make it safely through the night of 1-2 August, which coincided with the gap in German contact. *Wetaskiwin* never did rejoin but made her way to St John's. In the afternoon of the second, *Agassiz*, which had not sailed originally with the group, joined from Newfoundland, and command passed to her captain, Lieutenant Commander B. Johnston, RCNR. In the early hours of the day both Johnston and the commodore were informed by British and American authorities that U-boats were once again in contact. The prospects for ON 115, now guarded by only four corvettes, looked grim in an area where, but for foul weather, which thwarted attempts by Canadian and USN aircraft to affect the battle from the first to the third of August, the escort might have expected air support.

In the early afternoon of 2 August lookouts aboard *Agassiz* sighted a U-boat off the port quarter of the convoy, and *Agassiz*, in company with *Galt*, gave pursuit. Forty minutes later, with only *Sackville* and *Louisburg* in the screen, the commodore altered course to bring the convoy closer to the destroyers *Witch* (RN) and *Hamilton*, sent to reinforce C 3 following the departure of *Skeena* and *Saguenay*. By 1730Z the two destroyers were in sight, and within an hour both were busy attacking a U-boat put down by gunfire from *Hamilton*. Nothing came of either of the contacts pursued on the second, and at dusk the escort – now a scratch team – was assembled around ON 115 in screening formation NE 6: one escort off each bow, one on each beam, and one in each quarter.

All was quiet until one hour before midnight, when *Sackville* reported an asdic contact on the port bow. As *Hamilton* turned to assist, *Sackville* attacked, but the contact was not considered worth pursuing. The search was quickly abandoned, and the two escorts returned to the convoy. *Sackville* later reported that there was some confusion over which position she was now expected to fill. Shortly after this dislocation of the screen the commodore reported a U-boat within the convoy. Moments later *Lochkatrine* (41) and *G.S. Waldon* (52) were torpedoed. Neither ship sank quickly, but both soon lost way and began to fall out of station. The commodore immediately ordered two emergency turns to starboard (to course 330 degrees), while the escort conducted Operation Raspberry.

As *Sackville* made her way back to ON 115 following the completion of Raspberry, she came upon the two damaged ships, from which *Agassiz* and *Hamilton* were taking survivors. Lieutenant A.H. Easton, RCNR, *Sackville*'s commander, decided to screen the rescue work and was rewarded for his consideration forty minutes later by a radar contact. Course was altered to investigate, and the blip soon resolved itself into a U-boat. In the wild action which followed, *Sackville*'s attempts to ram were frustrated, but the corvette managed to lay a very accurate depth-charge pattern over the U-boat as it submerged. The accuracy of the latter remained unknown to Easton for some time, and he felt profound disappointment at having failed in his ramming attempt. He had just brought *Sackville* back on to a course to begin an asdic search when the torpedo officer, Sub-Lieutenant N.H. Chapman, RCNVR, arrived on the bridge in a breathless state. 'We are wasting ammunition now, Sir,' Chapman reported. *Sackville*'s depth charges had blown the U-boat clear out of the water, and she was plainly seen by the crew, breaching like a great whale, with a third of her hull pointing skywards at an angle of forty-five degrees. As the submarine hung momentarily, suspended by her momentum, a depth charge exploded under her keel and she then plunged into the sea, surrounded by a huge column of water. Chapman concluded, 'she will never rise again,' but U43 eventually made port in France. Easton's subsequent attempts to establish asdic contact failed, and although *Sackville* obtained permission to remain in the area to search for debris, no further contact was made.

Heavy fog closed in around *Sackville* by 0430Z, but her SWIC radar continued to work and she soon gained a second radar contact. Initially no precise bearing was evident, although the target clearly lay ahead. As the corvette closed slowly, a U-boat was spotted directly abeam, lying still and fully buoyant on the surface. Easton ordered a course to ram, but before *Sackville* could do so, the U-boat plunged to safety. One inaccurate depth-charge attack was made on the swirl before the corvette turned to undertake a deliberate search. However, once again a U-boat so near at hand eluded the hunter. No asdic contact was ever established, and *Sackville*, frustrated for the second time in just a few short hours, set course to rejoin ON 115.

While *Sackville* pursued what must have appeared to be phantoms and while other escorts were busy with rescue work, U553 penetrated the now defenceless convoy and torpedoed *Belgian Soldier* (94). She, too, remained afloat and drifted in the wake of ON 115. *Sackville*, her trip to the convoy now interrupted by a decision to screen *Agassiz* as she towed the damaged *G.S. Waldon*, came upon *Belgian Soldier* as she drifted behind the advancing columns. A boarding party removed the ship's confidential books and the one survivor who had not already abandoned ship; then *Sackville* returned to her screening duties, leaving the fate of the Belgian ship undecided.

Heavy fog persisted through the day, making the work of both escorts and U-boats difficult. Fortunately, things remained quiet around the convoy, now protected by two destroyers and two corvettes. The salvage operations of *Agassiz* continued without incident until at 1502Z *Sackville*, two miles ahead of *G.S. Waldon* and her tow, obtained a contact by hydrophone. (Asdic was frequently used as a passive listening device, by which it was possible to detect a U-boat and obtain a bearing.) Course was altered to intercept; action stations were sounded, and the radar, which had been resting, was started up. Subsequent changes in course to close the target were effected by radar, which was able to locate and track a faint echo to starboard. This soon manifested itself as yet another U-boat, on a slightly closing, almost parallel course. Once again the U-boat outmanoeuvred *Sackville* as she tried to ram. Caught in the midst of a turn to the wrong direction, Easton wisely held his course, allowing the main armament to depress sufficiently to engage the U-boat – which was less than a ship's length away. The first round from the 4-inch struck the base of the conning tower and erupted in a bright yellow flame. The second passed just over as the U-boat submerged. *Agassiz* slipped her tow to assist, but attempts by both corvettes to regain a firm asdic contact were once again unsuccessful.

German operations against ON 115 were finally terminated in the fog of the Grand Banks on 3 August. Three ships had been torpedoed, two of which sank (one as the result of a second attack). In exchange, one U-boat was known destroyed, and *Sackville* had damaged two. Wallace was understandably pleased with the outcome of C 3's operations, particularly those before he was forced to leave the scene. He considered that the sweeps and the extended screens had kept the U-boats at bay, thus preventing the horror of night attacks. However, he also cautioned that extended sweeps would become increasingly less effective as the days grew shorter. Although C 3 had made good use of MF bearings, none of the ships in the escort group had been equipped with HF/DF, and this capacity 'was sorely missed.' Wallace also felt that the 'large and evasive turns did much to confuse the enemy.'[5]

Dyer's comments on the battle echoed those of his SOE, particularly with respect to the need for HF/DF. What Captain (D), Newfoundland, and even Murray thought of C 3's *defence* of ON 115 remains unclear. Evidently they considered it well done, for both limited their remarks to the successful destruction of U558 and *Sackville*'s brushes with three submarines. One might have expected some comment on Easton's complaint that German successes on the night of 2–3 August stemmed from

poor co-ordination and teamwork in a group by then composed of individual units. Easton very strongly criticized the new Senior Officer, Lieutenant Commander C.H. Holmes, RN, of *Witch*, for not making known
his intentions. In fact, it was not clear to Easton who the SOE in the last
phase of the battle really had been. 'It would seem to have been most
unfortunate,' Easton wrote in his report, 'that the senior officer [that is,
Wallace] ... was absent at the critical time as far as the members of his
own group were concerned.' The remnants of C 3 'were left rather on a
limb,' and for this reason the conduct of the escort was not as effective
as it might have been.[6]

In the euphoria of *Skeena*'s and *Wetaskiwin*'s dispatch of *U558*, Easton's was the only Canadian voice of dissent. Admiral Brainard saw both
ON 113 and ON 115 as examples of effective use of destroyer sweeps and
now wanted the slow Coast Guard cutters in A 3 replaced or at least
augmented by USN destroyers.[7] But the real hue and cry over ON 115
came from across the Atlantic.[8] Western Approaches officers were upset
about the number and size of the course alterations and about Wallace's
use of destroyer sweeps. They were advised that the whole matter was
to be placed before the Admiralty and that minutes should be framed
accordingly. The DCOS (Operations) Captain R.W. Ravenhill, RN, described as 'reckless' the expenditure of fuel by destroyers on sweeps and
as a result of 'the convoy zig zagging across the ocean with 90° alterations
of course.' His sentiments were echoed by others, especially the A/S
officer, Commander Howard-Johnston. The latter was particularly acid
in his assessment of Wallace's performance:

This is an example of reckless expenditure of fuel and disregard of the object
which must always include 'timely arrival.' The timely arrival was ignored to
an exceptional degree (eventually) reducing the protection given by the escorts.
The success achieved against the enemy in destroying a U-boat should not be
allowed to cover up this basic failure.

Before the convoy had reached 12 degrees West the *Saguenay* was tearing
off at midday to run down MF/DF bearings to a depth of 30 miles astern. I find
in this story the ignorance of inexperienced officers who think that they are being
offensive by acting in a reckless manner and without real consideration of their
obligation to protect the convoy throughout the period it is entrusted to them.

Clearly someone had read Easton's report.

Wallace at least understood the limits imposed on C 3 by its lack of
HF/DF, and in its absence had been forced to use his destroyers on frequent

but poorly directed sweeps. While there is no debating Wallace's zeal for such sweeps, his real shortcomings were a misplaced faith in the utility of MF/DF intelligence – an error which so clearly annoyed Howard-Johnston – and want of modern equipment. Some WA Staff officers noted that C 3 had serious equipment deficiencies. The convoy officer wanted HF/DF-fitted rescue ships assigned to convoys where the escort was without such equipment, and the signals officer wanted to 'rub in HF/DF for the Canadians.' The pressing need for modern radar in Canadian escorts was also noted. The radar officer concluded bluntly 'that *Sackville*'s two [sic] U-boats would have been a gift if she had been fitted with RDF type 271,' and he wanted all the Canadian sets replaced immediately. However, since most of the equipment shortfalls in the RCN had been acted upon by the Naval Staff by the time these assessments were made in Liverpool, none of these remarks emerged as formal recommendations to the RCN.

Actually, while the report on ON 113 and ON 115 was being prepared, the Admiralty lodged a complaint with American authorities, through the British Admiralty Delegation (BAD) in Washington, concerning the use of drastic course alterations in mid-ocean. 'In general,' the Admiralty's instructions to BAD read, 'the shortest route to safe waters is the soundest policy and by safe waters is meant those where additional air and / or surface escort can be provided.'⁹ This fundamental axiom was transgressed in the case of ON 113 by the USN's convoy authorities and in the case of ON 115 by Wallace and the convoy commodore. Ironically, ON 115 was in technically safe waters when it lost ships to the combined efforts of Pirate and Wolf.

Attempts by the RCAF's Eastern Air Command (EAC) and USN aircraft to locate and support ON 115 were frustrated by bad weather and fog. The persistence of poor flying conditions off Newfoundland rendered air cover in the Western Atlantic much less effective than that provided on the other side by Coastal Command. Not only could packs continue attacks well within technically safe waters, but in the absence of air cover U-boats could shadow eastbound convoys from very close to Newfoundland. The early and sustained contact with eastbound convoys meant a long and bitter passage through the air gap. Further, as with the RCN, the RCAF's A/S and escort tactics and equipment lagged behind those of their British counterparts in 1942. Officers at Western Approaches appreciated these problems, particularly those of weather. 'It is in fact quite surprising,' Commander Howard-Johnston wrote following ON 115, 'the amount of flying that the Americans and Canadians manage to do in spite of the appalling conditions ... They were prepared to, and actually did, set out under conditions which would be regarded as quite impossible elsewhere.'[10]

With the battle for ON 115 a pattern of attacks on westbound convoys dating back to early May was evident, while other tentative patterns of enemy action were emerging. The apparent German preference for ON convoys and the renewal of pack attacks were noted by RCN officers. Prentice had covered many westbound convoys during his training cruises and saw in them a unique opportunity to modify existing escort tactics in order to destroy U-boats. The Germans, Prentice believed, studied each convoy battle in great detail and were exploiting the weakness of standard escort screening patterns. Recent losses, he felt, came primarily from the weakly defended quarters or from a second wave of attackers after the escort had been drawn astern of the convoy. To overcome the limitations of a fixed and predictable defence, Prentice wanted the escorts to sweep irregularly in sectors around the perimeter of the convoy. An unpredictable and mobile screen might discourage attacks. But Prentice was only partly interested in perfecting defence; what he really wanted was to trap attackers in the wake of the convoy by redisposing the screen in strength in the quarter and stern positions. Basing his analysis on the speed of a surfaced U-boat, the time it took for an escort group to react, and the advance of the convoy, Prentice prepared diagrams outlining the most likely areas for illumination, sweeps, and asdic searches behind the convoy immediately following an attack. He even wanted the escort's destroyers positioned well astern in order to catch an attacker emerging from the convoy 'with his head over his shoulder.'

Prentice's suggestions and diagrams were submitted to Captain (D), Newfoundland, on 1 August. They represented a fascinating glimpse of one man's perception of the tactical situation in mid-1942, but they were much too tentative to adopt. Aggressive patrolling in sector screens would come with time, as would better use of illuminants. In the meantime, leaving the front of the convoy unguarded to trap U-boats astern simply invited disaster, especially as the size of U-boat packs increased. Prentice was on much firmer ground with his concern about the disruptive effects that the first attacker had on the escort's ability to defend convoys from a second wave. But his ideas on defence of convoys (other than by destroying U-boats) were never fully developed. Not surprisingly, Captain Mainguy dismissed Prentice's schemes summarily. 'I think *Chambly* credits the Hun with too much intelligence,' Mainguy minuted, 'and the average Corvette CO with much too much.' Captain (D) rejected this attempt at tactical sophistication because it seemed to him unlikely that the Germans on the scene had a clear picture of a night battle, when 'very often the escorts themselves do not know if it's Christmas or Easter.'[11]

Mainguy's somewhat trite dismissal of an attempt to come to grips with the escorts' problems was not only a sign of resignation to a certain level of inefficiency within the corvette fleet, but it also pointed to a serious deficiency in the RCN itself. What the navy needed was an establishment, similar to the WA Tactical Training Unit at Liverpool, where new ideas could be worked out. By the summer of 1942 just such a unit was in the embryo stage at Halifax, but so far its efforts had been directed into essential training areas. In the absence of some central authority (Murray's command at St John's was still a separate entity) local Captains (D) ruled the scene, and they were generally much too busy with administrative details.

Prentice's case was also weakened by a frank admission that the future of U-boat tactics along the main trade routes was far from certain. He speculated that, 'perhaps when the real attack comes,' after defensive measures along the U.S. east coast had made conditions there 'too unhealthy for the U-boat, the methods employed will be entirely different.'[12] Indeed, even as Prentice wrote these words, another convoy battle, which was to break the pattern observed between May and July, was shaping up off Newfoundland.

On 2 August, the day ON 115 was attacked east of Cape Race, group C 1 assumed the escort of SC 94, thirty-six ships heavily laden with war supplies for Britain. The escort had undergone few changes since its last brush with the enemy in early June. *Chilliwack* and *Orillia* had joined immediately following the battle of ONS 100, and *Primrose* (RN) had replaced the French corvette *Aconit* on the return to the UK. One further addition was the destroyer *St Croix*, also assigned to C 1 after the battle with group Hecht in early June. But when C 1 sailed to escort SC 94, *St Croix* was detached for A/S exercises in Conception Bay. This left C 1 with a technically acceptable strength of seven escorts: one destroyer (*Assiniboine*) and six corvettes (in addition to the three already mentioned, *Battleford*, *Dianthus* [RN], and *Nasturtium* [RN]), all under the command of Lieutenant Commander A. Ayer, RNR, the captain of *Primrose*.

The poor weather which had prevented aircraft from intervening successfully in the battle for ON 115 also affected SC 94. On 3 August an RCAF Digby from Gander located the convoy by radar in heavy fog, but with the ceiling down to sea level the aircraft could do nothing except report SC 94's position and head home. Bad weather and heavy fog kept aircraft grounded at both Gander and Argentia until 5 August, and even on that date the only air support available was half an hour provided by a Canso from Botwood in the morning. In the meantime BdU brought the battle for ON 115 to an end and sent the U-boats northeastwards with the intention of laying a patrol line in advance of the next eastbound convoy. Before the line could even be properly formed, *U593*, at the very northern end, reported SC 94, and the chase was on.[13]

The ships sighted by *U593* were actually only a portion of the main convoy; they had misinterpreted a course alteration in heavy fog on the third and were striving to rejoin the main body. *U593* attacked immediately after passing her sighting report on the fifth and successfully torpedoed the *Spar* at 1649z. *Orillia* and *Nasturtium*, escorting the errant section, each depth charged asdic contacts, and *U593* and *U595* (also in contact) were driven off as a result. But the Germans did not lose contact, despite a sweep in the area by *Assiniboine*. The convoy was reunited by 2130z, with all the escort present except the destroyer. The sweep by *Assiniboine* revealed nothing save for the sobering knowledge that smoke from SC 94 was clearly visible thirty miles away.

On 6 August SC 94 sailed through intermittent fog patches as it made its way eastwards. Attempts by the RCAF to support C 1 continued to suffer from the low ceiling, and the airmen contented themselves with flying sweeps along the convoy's anticipated line of advance. Below them the escorts of C 1 could have used help, for they were busy with several U-boat contacts, some of which were made or pursued with the aid of radar. Of the actions on the sixth *Assiniboine*'s proved successful, when she rammed and sank *U210* in a wild running fight through fog banks. For nearly an hour *Assiniboine* and her prey played cat and mouse in the patchy fog around SC 94. Finally the range closed, and a fierce gun duel developed. C.P. Van der Hagen, one of *Assiniboine*'s gunnery-control ratings, recalled watching the action from his perch atop the bridge, unable to assist the main guns because *U210* was too close. 'The Old Man said "We're going to attempt to ram,"' Van der Hagen remembers, and 'vaguely you could see this little dark thing in the fog, and he was running.'[14] In fact the captain of *U210* had no choice, since *Assiniboine* was too close to allow him to steady course long enough to dive. Instead, her captain could be seen calmly stooping to pass helm instructions through the hatch as *U210* struggled to escape. Finally, the range closed, and at about two hundred yards the U-boat's guns opened fire, followed immediately by intense fire from *Assiniboine*. For most of the time the destroyer was too close to permit her main guns to fire, while her machine gunners swept *U210*'s crewmen from her deck as they tried to man the

U-boat's main gun. None the less, *U210*'s 40-millimetre secondary armament soon riddled the destroyer's bridge with gaping holes and ignited a gasoline fire amidships. Eventually *Assiniboine* was able to get off a round from one of her 4.7-inch guns, striking the conning tower and killing *U210*'s captain. A short time after, Stubbs brought the U-boat under *Assiniboine*'s bows, ramming her twice. Meanwhile, *Dianthus*, who had heard the battle raging in the mist but was unable to locate it, arrived to find *Assiniboine* fire-blackened, shrouded in smoke, and riddled with holes, standing by *U210* as she made her last dive.

Still smouldering, her bows buckled and leaking and her crew busy attending to the wounded, *Assiniboine* turned for home. *Dianthus* set course for sc 94, now thirty miles away. Although much delayed by U-boat sightings and asdic contacts, the corvette eventually rejoined the depleted screen around sc 94 early on the seventh.

While *Assiniboine* and *Dianthus* were engaged with U-boats well astern of the convoy, sc 94's remaining corvettes were also busy chasing U-boats as they darted in and out of the patchy fog. *Orillia* attacked a good contact (a U-boat which she had forced to dive) at 2120z, but bad drill ruined her chances, and the depth charges served only to put the corvette's asdic temporarily out of action. Moments later, however, she reported a periscope – as had many other ships with the convoy. Because of the fog *Primrose*, who tried to come to *Orillia*'s aid, was unable to locate the scene of the action. Meanwhile *Nasturtium* located an attacker with her 271 radar at 2200 yards and drove it off. The balance of the night and the whole of 7 August passed uneventfully. A combination of good luck, aggressive pursuit, and an inexperienced enemy kept the pack at bay. But for the fog, effective use of aircraft might well have ended the battle even before it had begun.

No further U-boat contacts were reported until the early hours of 8 August, when *Battleford* attacked an underwater contact. Counter-attacks on underwater targets by *Orillia* and *Nasturtium* followed, with the latter once again using her radar (in the last hours of darkness) to prevent the penetration of the screen by a surfaced U-boat. This latter contact was driven off and pursued at length by *Nasturtium*, but to no avail.

The first three nights of the battle therefore passed rather well for C 1. German attacks had not been on a large scale, had not been persistent, nor indeed had any, with the exception of the sinking of *Spar* in the early going, been successful. However, the enemy soon upset this quietude – and the character of the whole apparent pattern of convoy battles – by launching two almost simultaneous submerged attacks in broad daylight. The first came at 1325Z on the eighth, while *Dianthus* and *Nasturtium* were still detached after the night's action and while the rest of the escort was disposed in DE 4: one directly ahead, one on each beam, and one directly astern. Without closing to within the convoy, *U176* and *U379* each fired salvos of torpedoes from positions ahead. In a matter of minutes five ships, including most of the fifth column, were hit: *Trehata* (51), the commodore's ship, *Kelso* (52), *Kaimoku* (73), *Anneburg* (64), and *Mount Kaisson* (53). Reaction of the escort was well controlled by Ayre, the Senior Officer, but produced no results other than screening the rescue of survivors. This in itself was work enough, but explosions from *Kaimoku* just after she sank convinced the crews of three other ships that they too had been torpedoed. *Empire Moonbeam* (31), *Empire Antelope* (71), and *Radchurch* (84) were all abandoned in great haste. All but the latter were subsequently reboarded and rejoined SC 94. The crew of *Radchurch* refused to go back aboard and the ship fell astern, where she was finally sunk by *U176*. With the unfortunate loss of that perfectly able ship the toll from SC 94 reached seven.

Further sightings of U-boats were made during the day on the eighth as no less than eighteen attempted to operate against the convoy. Their number was reduced by one in the last hours of daylight when *Dianthus* followed *Assiniboine*'s example by ramming and sinking *U379*, which she had blown to the surface with several very accurate depth-charge attacks. As in the previous ramming incident, damage to the escort (which had five attempts at *U379* before she was successful) rendered her non-operational, and *Dianthus* took position 54 in the ranks of the convoy. With the escort reduced to five corvettes it was fortunate that the destroyer *Broke* (RN) arrived on the scene early the same evening. Her commander, Lieutenant Commander A.F.C. Layard, RN, took over as SOE.

The rest of the night of 8 August was not without incident, as both U-boats and torpedo tracks were seen. But no attacks were pressed home, and no counter-attacks by the escort were successful. The next day SC 94, now just within range of Coastal Command, received four hours of continuous air support, while the close escort was bolstered by the arrival of the Polish destroyer *Blyskawica*. With the addition of two WA destroyers HF/DF was finally available to the escort, and at least one successful HF/DF-directed sweep, by *Primrose* and *Battleford*, took place on the tenth. While the latter were away and while *Blyskawica* was temporarily out of touch owing to a faulty gyro-compass, SC 94 suffered its second double, nearly simultaneous submerged daylight attack. At 1023Z *U438* and *U660*, both firing from positions ahead, hit four ships: *Condylis* (33, which was hit, turned 140° to starboard, and was hit again), *Empire Reindeer* (61), *Oregon* (52), and *Cape Race* (62). Again the escort swept astern of the convoy as it passed over the firing positions, but again no trace of the attackers could be found. These proved to be, in any event, the U-boats' parting shots. From the afternoon of the tenth onwards SC 94 received almost continuous air coverage, and the escort was further reinforced. Pursuit of the convoy in the face of these mounting odds was futile, and the pack was called off on the eleventh. No further ships were lost: the count stood at eleven.

The post mortem of SC 94 was by far the mildest of recent convoy battles. The conduct of the escort under RN Senior Officers was not found to be wanting to staffs on either side of the Atlantic. None the less, Ayre's use of his corvettes to pursue contacts at length in the wake of the convoy, and the resultant reduced screen, constituted an invitation to disaster and might have drawn criticism. This undoubtedly would have been the case had group Steinbrink and the U-boats sent to assist it been able to mass ahead of SC 94 and launch large-scale night attacks. That they did not was the result of the escort's good fortune and the poor visibility which plagued German operations. Much more disconcerting than the would-have-beens of the battle was the German use of apparently simultaneous submerged daylight attacks from ahead of the convoy. Admittedly, losses to these attacks came when the escort screen was reduced – such as on the tenth, when only half of the escort was present. But even with all the escort present the problem admitted of no solution, since it was nearly impossible to provide a complete asdic barrier for large mercantile convoys. Any German adoption of such tactics on a large scale promised to make things extremely difficult for the Allies in the mid-ocean. For the moment the U-boats' good fortune in launching almost simultaneous attacks introduced an element of uncertainty into the tactical situation.

The novelty of SC 94 clearly tempered any harsh criticism of the escort. *Blyskawica*'s complaint of a faulty gyro-compass and her loss of the convoy for a day speak volumes for the success of Canadian escorts in managing without this equipment at all. The only stern comments to arise from the battle actually came from naval engineers in Britain and Canada who despaired that, with all their modern weaponry, escorts were still reduced to bludgeoning the enemy to death with their bows. Indeed, the temporary loss of *Assiniboine* (she did not return to duty until January 1943) placed a heavy burden on Murray's already overworked and inadequate destroyers.

But on the whole even the British were happy to trade eleven ships in a novel battle for two confirmed U-boat kills. They considered, and their opinion was shared by American authorities, that the outcome was favourable in light of the weakness of the escort and its poor state of equipment. None of the original escorts carried HF/DF, and only one, *Nasturtium*, had 271 radar. This meant that it was difficult for the Senior Officer to orchestrate sweeps designed to break up the pack, particularly after *Assiniboine* was forced to leave. The absence of 271 was cited as a crucial factor, although *Nasturtium*'s successful use of her set on the night of 7–8 August may well have prevented the opening up of the battle which usually followed a successful night attack. As the American commander at Londonderry observed, 'anti-submarine radar sets of the nature of type 271 are essential for proper night protection of slow trade convoys.' He went on to add that 'the type SW1C and SW2C [the improved SW1C] ... cannot fulfill the function of detecting a U-boat trimmed down at close range, and are therefore useless for this purpose.'[15] The British concurred with the American assessment, and this was confirmed when the battle of ON 115 was reviewed a few weeks later. For all intents and purposes the Canadians were fighting without radar.

The Germans were particularly pleased with the outcome of the battle for SC 94, despite the loss of two U-boats. All but one of the U-boat commanders were new COs, and their score of eleven ships sunk 'against heavy opposition seemed to give promise for future operations.'[16] The Germans even went so far as to report publicly over radio on the battle, noting that it was especially important because of the youth and inexperience of the U-boat captains.

Having been carried along to the edges of the Eastern Atlantic in the battle for SC 94, the U-boats of group Steinbrink were reformed into group 'Lohs,' of eleven submarines, and placed astride the main convoy route six hundred miles west of the North Channel. On 13 August BDienst, the German radio-monitoring service, obtained the position of a convoy by radio, but before Lohs could intercept, the pack was drawn off by SC 95, which passed inadvertently through the middle of the German patrol line on the fourteenth. According to German accounts, the 'manoeuvres of the screen' provided by A 3 (USS *Schenck*, USCG *Spencer*, the corvettes *Bittersweet*, *Collingwood*, *Mayflower*, *Trillium*, *Snowflake* [RN], and *Wallflower* [RN]) kept the attackers from determining the course and speed of SC 95, but in fact the German operation was confused because the Germans were expecting an ON convoy. Only three U-boats were able to attack, sinking one ship, before SC 95 slipped into range of effective air cover.[17] BdU then once again reformed the group farther to westward on the seventeenth, in anticipation of the next ON convoy. Adjustments to the group's position led them first southwards and then, on the twenty-second, due north. The latter movement actually drew Lohs away from ONS 122, which cleared the southern tip of the patrol line unnoticed. However, while Lohs drew away to northward, *U135*, sailing independently, happened upon ONS 122 by sheer chance and was able to provide accurate details of position, course, and speed. Lohs was ordered to intercept.

The battle for ONS 122 marks at least one significant departure from the pattern of convoy battles during the first seven months of 1942.[18] To date all of these had been C- or A-group battles. In fact, until August no B group of MOEF had suffered from sustained German pressure, and none had yet fought a major convoy battle in 1942. Ironically, the first B group to feel the weight of German attack was very largely Norwegian. Only the sole B 6 destroyer, HMS *Viscount*, was a British ship, and she was well appointed with the latest equipment: 271 radar, HF/DF, and the new A/S mortar 'hedgehog.' *Viscount*'s captain, Lieutenant Commander J.V. Waterhouse, was the group's Senior Officer, but the balance was made up of Norwegian corvettes: *Acanthus*, *Eglantine*, *Montbretia*, and *Potentilla*. Their crews, like those of their Canadian counterparts, were all reservists, but there the similarity ended. The Norwegian navy was small and very professional throughout the war. Its reservists were deep-sea sailors in their own right, well trained for war even in peacetime, and all on active duty since 1939.[19] The corvette nucleus of B 6 was of long standing by August, having formed the bulk of the USN's A 4 earlier in the year (it still retained its USN task-unit designation, 24.1.4). All of the escorts were equipped with 271 radar, which they were able to maintain in running order.

From the time of the first U-boat contact until the pursuit was abandoned by the Germans on 26 August, B 6 busied itself with pushing the enemy aside and forcing a safe passage for ONS 122. It is clear from the Senior Officer's report of proceedings that his regard for the safe and timely arrival of the convoy governed his actions. On the first day of contact *Viscount*, in order to conserve fuel, refused to engage in a long stern chase with a U-boat. Instead, Waterhouse consistently used corvettes to pursue HF/DF bearings in order simply to put the U-boats down (one of the Norwegian corvettes could make nineteen knots and was considered a fast ship). On 23 August, and particularly during the following night, the Senior Officer used *Viscount* more aggressively, putting down and attacking all U-boats known to be around the convoy. This kept both *Viscount* and *Potentilla* away from ONS 122 for the entire night – the one instance when the screen was reduced for any length of time. It was just as well for the four remaining corvettes that no attack developed.

Numerous U-boats were pursued and attacked during the day on the twenty-fourth. None of these counter-attacks produced successful results, in large part because Waterhouse was reluctant to devote a great deal of time to individual hunts. By dusk on the twenty-fourth all of B 6 was back in station around ONS 122, braced for action because, as the Senior Officer later reported, 'the situation on this night was somewhat grim.' And it was, for nine U-boats were known to be in contact (the SOE estimated seven), only four of which could be accounted for by the escort. Avoidance of the remaining U-boats was considered impossible. Accordingly, course was altered at 2300Z, as instructed by American convoy authorities, to 267 degrees, although this was expected to carry the convoy on to waiting U-boats. In view of the likely failure of evasive action, Waterhouse hoped that 'the new course would bring [the convoy] closer to air support and reinforcement.' At the time of the course change the sky was overcast; visibility was down to seven thousand yards, and there were patchy squalls. Otherwise the sea conditions were calm – good weather for 271 radar.

Sixty minutes after ONS 122 assumed its new course, *U605* penetrated the screen on the heavily defended starboard side and torpedoed *Katvaldis* (91) and *Sheaf Mount* (94). The escort immediately conducted Operation Raspberry, which revealed nothing. But shortly thereafter *Viscount* obtained a radar contact on a U-boat and gave chase. The U-boat eventually submerged, only to suffer heavy and accurate depth charging. *Viscount*'s pursuit was soon interrupted by the torpedoing of *Trolla* (71) and *Empire Breeze* (41) by *U176* and *U438* respectively as these boats penetrated the convoy almost simultaneously from directly ahead. The escort was still too dispersed from the original Operation Raspberry to effect any concerted action following the second attack. However, numerous radar contacts by the escorts were pursued and counter-attacks made on asdic contacts until dawn on the twenty-fifth.

Although nine U-boats were still in contact with ONS 122 at daybreak on 25 August, they soon lost touch as the convoy entered heavy fog. With this fortunate disappearance, operations against ONS 122 ended, and no further losses were suffered. Four ships had been lost in exchange for two heavily damaged U-boats.

Staff response to ONS 122 was, to say the least, enthusiastic. Both

British and American officers emphasized the success of sweeps directed by the HF/DF sets of *Viscount* and the rescue ship with the convoy, *Stockport*. These not only produced four U-boat sightings but had been accurate enough to confirm shore estimates of German activity near the convoy. Equally important in wresting the initiative from Lohs was B 6's 271 radar. No less than thirteen radar contacts had been made on U-boats closing to attack, and all of these led to immediate counter-attacks. What success the U-boats achieved was attributed to a numerically weak escort. The British were disappointed that thirteen close-range contacts were not transformed into a number of U-boat kills. This short-coming was put down to some lack of training in the group and the tendency to use too small a depth-charge pattern during first counter-attacks. Otherwise, B 6's performance was considered by Captain (D), Liverpool, to have been almost brilliant.

The high professionalism displayed by the Norwegians, who were in their first battle, drew praise from all quarters. 'It was a pleasure to see (and hear) the Norwegians going into action,' Waterhouse wrote in his report. 'Raspberry went like clockwork and whenever, during the night, the cry of "Tally-ho" was raised on the scram, I had only to check the bearings.' Thus, although it was their first battle, the 'training ... coupled with intensive intercommunication exercises, resulted in perfect coop-eration and prompt understanding' among the members of B 6.

The high incidence of U-boat contacts within lethal distance during the battle for ONS 122 augured well for the future. Whether the battle would have swung sharply against ONS 122 had it not found the safety of fog while still some distance from air cover is debatable. What is clear is that without good group discipline, HF/DF and especially 271 radar, B 6 could not have prevented losses in the last night of action. Moreover, had B 6 been forced to fight without modern equipment, its profession-alism would have been severely tested and the initiative would have gone to the attacking pack. The contrast between the success of B 6 and the struggling C groups did not go unnoticed by the RCN. The battle of ONS 122 could easily have been a disaster. For both B 6 and the Canadians, however, the worst was yet to come.

ONS 122 was not the last MOEF-escorted convoy attacked as August drew to a close. For the first time in 1942 the Germans had sufficient U-boats in the mid-ocean towards the end of August to establish two patrol lines – one at either edge of the air gap. The eastern group, 'Vorwärts,' was newly formed and contained a greater leavening of ex-perienced captains. But in its first contact Vorwärts was unable to mount a sustained offensive because the convoy which it intercepted was east-bound and very near effective air support. The convoy, SC 97, fifty-eight ships escorted by C 2 – *Broadway* (RN) and *Burnham* (RN), Lieutenant Commander T. Taylor, RN, Senior Officer, both Town-class destroyers, and the corvettes *Brandon*, *Dauphin*, *Drumheller*, and *Morden* – was also intercepted near the northern tip of the patrol line, which made rapid concentration against it all but impossible. Because of the convoy's proximity to air support the shadowing U-boat, *U609*, was ordered to attack at once. At 0804Z on the thirty-first she torpedoed two ships from a submerged position, taking the escort completely by surprise. In calm seas it was a simple matter to save the entire crew of the stricken SS *Bronxville*, but the majority of the men on *Capira* were not so fortunate. Torpedoed well forward, *Capira*'s bows quickly filled with water, raising the ship into a vertical position. Just sixteen of her fifty-four crewmen survived the final plunge. That night Taylor and his escorts kept six U-boats at bay. Only two fired torpedoes, none of which found any targets. The issue was decided on 1 September, when USN Catalina aircraft arrived from Iceland to begin what became almost continuous air support over the next three days. One U-boat, *U756*, was sunk by American aircraft on the first, and Vorwärts gave up the chase the next day.[20]

With the loss of two ships from SC 97 the C groups' record over July and August of at least balancing losses with U-boat kills came to an end. The battles of ON 113, ON 115, and SC 94 had been fairly equal contests. Despite the frequent angry comments of British officers, of which the RCN knew nothing, the Canadians had every reason to be happy with the recent accomplishments of their escorts in MOEF – three U-boats in less than one month. The battle had been rejoined, and the RCN seemed to be equal to the test. There were also successes on other fronts, most notably *Oakville*'s sinking of *U94* (and capture of Oberleutenant Ites) in the Caribbean, where the corvette was operating as part of the USN's Eastern Sea Frontier forces.[21]

Yet despite this string of victories, not everyone felt that all was right with the RCN's escort fleet. Mainguy, as Captain (D), Newfoundland, had confessed a lack of confidence in his escorts' abilities. This sentiment was held much more strongly by British staffs, whose concern over the RCN also included the ability of Murray and his staff. The roots of Canadian shortcomings in the mid-ocean extended deeply into every facet of the service. One British escort commander with WLEF confided in September that the RCN's problems were largely organizational. The jury-rigged structure of the early days of expansion was no longer adequate

to cope with the larger navy. Commander J.M. Rowland, RN, CO of HMS
Walker, who became Captain (D), Newfoundland, in early 1943, concluded 'that the stage has now been reached where maximum possible
effort with the forces available to us is not being directed against our
chief menace – the U-boats.'[22]

Rowland was not the only RN officer to comment critically on the
attention paid to the navy's A/S responsibilities in the late summer of
1942. Late in August Commander P.W. Burnett, RN, of the RN's A/S
school HMS *Osprey*, tabled his report on the RCN's A/S training before the
Naval Staff in Ottawa. Burnett had completed a brief tour of Canadian
establishments and was able to report that Canadian training now par-
alleled that of the RN. The real problem was that the schools were un-
derattended.[23] In short, A/S was unpopular in an A/S navy. Considering
that specialization in ASW was not yet integral – or even useful – in career
advancement, Burnett's findings were unremarkable. But Burnett seemed
surprised to find the RCN fighting one kind of war and preparing for
another. As Rowland surmised, the navy was still busy building and had
not yet begun to focus on the problems and issues arising from its wartime
experiences.

Evidence to support Burnett's and Rowland's contentions is not hard
to find. In 1942 it was commonly believed that specialization in A/S was
a sure ticket to a shore posting or – worse still – bouncing from bunk to
bunk in the fleet spreading A/S expertise. There was truth in the persistent
wardroom gripe. By the fall of 1942 more than half of the forty-two
A/S-qualified officers were ashore. The small number qualified is notable
and was a direct result of the need to keep men at sea. No RCNR officer
had qualified for A/S from either the short or long course by the end of
1942, although these men still made up the great majority of escort
commanders. During the first years of the war A/S training was limited
almost exclusively to young RCNVR officers, who were able to fit the
short course into their training programs. No reservist had yet qualified
from the long course. Perhaps more disturbing than this veneer of qualified
personnel was their distribution. Of the forty-two A/S qualified officers
in the RCN in the fall of 1942, only three were serving in the mid-ocean.[24]

The need for training extended beyond the theory and function of asdic
and depth charges. RCN escort commanders needed instruction in group
co-operation. Some instruction was available in Londonderry during layovers. But because C groups were not based there, the stay in 'Derry
was shorter than that in St John's. This meant that a large portion of time
was still spent in a port which offered little except recreation. Prentice

maintained his instructional duties at St John's through July and August, though this became an increasingly questionable assignment. At the end of August *Chambly* was reassigned to operations and Prentice to command C 1, and the scheme died. The official reasons given for ending it were the primacy of operational needs and the increasing value of training programs in Canada. Moreover, it could be argued, as it was later on, that MOEF access to Londonderry put its escort personnel ahead of those of WLEF and the rest of the RCN in any event. Certainly, Murray made no known protest over the termination of his training group, perhaps because he, too, realized that it had never developed in a meaningful fashion.[25]

Finally, despite the lessons of recent convoy battles the Naval Staff was still undecided on a number of issues concerning equipment in early August.[26] Gyro-compasses were approved for new construction on the tenth, though the Staff gave no consideration to the needs of ships already in operation. At the same meeting the Staff was unable to agree on 271 radar for *Saguenay* and *Skeena* because fitting it in the most efficient place, atop the bridge, entailed removal of the ships' range-finders. This would restrict the usefulness of the ships in a conventional role, making escort destroyers of them and reducing the navy's offensive capabilities. The matter was referred to the Admiralty for clarification of British policy, and left unresolved. The issue of HF/DF was also discussed at the 10 August meeting. The value of this equipment had already been demonstrated in a number of convoy battles, and even the RCAF knew of its importance. Yet the Canadian Staff remained unconvinced. It was noted that *Restigouche* was already fitted, but the Staff 'recommended that the fitting of this gear be deferred until it has been given an adequate trial.' Apparently no one on the Staff had read the report of proceedings from ONS 102.

Staff irresolution changed somewhat towards the end of the month, although a sense of uncertainty still lingered in the minutes. By the end of August the latest asdic, type 145, with depth-determination ability and suitable for use with the new A/S mortar hedgehog, and its attendant modifications were approved in principle for sixty-nine corvettes already in commission. Conversion, however, could not begin before the spring of 1943 and even then would take an estimated two years to complete. Radar for River-class destroyers, including *Saguenay* and *Skeena*, was finally approved, with fitting to take place in the UK. The issue of HF/DF continued to confound the Staff. They were finally convinced of its merits by Captain F.J. Wylie, RN, a member of the Admiralty's Signals Division who was on a visit to North America. Wylie reported to the Canadian

Naval Staff on the subject on 31 August. Yet despite Wylie's success in persuading the Staff that HF/DF was essential, the knowledge he brought imparted no sense of urgency to plans to outfit the fleet. Wylie in fact advised that the new HF/DF set, FH4, which recorded bearings automatically and displayed them on a cathode-ray tube, was a great improvement over the FH3 type, as fitted in *Restigouche*. Unfortunately, the newer set would not be ready in large numbers for another five months. Clearly it would be inadvisable to fit obsolete equipment. The Canadian director of Signals Division, Commander G.A. Worth, recommended that one destroyer per group be fitted with FH3 pending the availability of FH4, at which time the whole issue was to be reviewed. Although the director of Operations, Commander H.N. Lay, interjected to note that both HF/DF and MF/DF had been of great assistance in recent battles, the Staff agreed to Worth's proposal that HF/DF be limited to one set per group (which followed British practice) – for the time being and, naturally, subject to financial approval.[27]

The inability of the Naval Staff to react quicky and decisively to rapid technological and tactical developments directly affected the course of events at sea. In large part the Staff's indecision stemmed from a failure in the navy's structure, as Captain Rowland pointed out. Through 1942 not only Murray but Jones as well complained repeatedly about the quality of their escorts, facilities, equipment, and their overextended responsibilities. In the absence of a proper mechanism, such as the Admiralty's Anti-Submarine Warfare Division, for the handling of crucial technical and operational matters, requests and complaints from the coast all received the same, largely ad hoc, treatment. Sorting out the wheat from the chaff would have allowed the Naval Staff to establish an order of priority for the endless stream of demands emanating from operational authorities.

In fairness it must be said that blame for the inadequacy of Naval Staff administrative decisions does not rest solely with NSHQ. In sharp contrast to the British practice of preparing detailed comments on reports of proceedings, those forwarded from RCN operational commands to NSHQ all too frequently were accompanied by a minute sheet with the briefest possible comment – 'Submitted.' It is not surprising that, lacking guidance from operational commands, the Naval Staff vacillated over what we now know were key issues. Certainly British authorities at Western Approaches were often sharply critical of both Murray's and Mainguy's handling of reports, in terms of judgments when these were expressed but also in terms of their rather casual handling of the whole business of minuting and forwarding reports. Eventually the Naval Staff threw the ball back into the court of FONF and COAC, where it belonged, signalling to all senior commands in November,

It is of great assistance to Naval Service Headquarters in deciding whether suggestions put forward from sea can be and should be acted upon, if Operational and Administrative authorities will remark on these points. It is also of great assistance if these authorities will clear up any doubtful points in the Report, as they are probably more 'au fait' with the situation than Naval Service Headquarters may be.[28]

The distressing aspect of this belated complaint is that it arose not from the travails of MOEF but from recent heavy losses in the Gulf of St Lawrence, where RCN performance was politically more sensitive. It is not too much to suppose that the Naval Staff considered anything which transpired east of Newfoundland to be a British responsibility.

NSHQ would also have benefited greatly from direct access to the analysis of convoy battles by British and American authorities. These were circulated to RCN operational commands, but NSHQ was not on the original distribution lists. It was up to FONF and COAC to forward these reports to Ottawa. As a result, convoy analyses, which took considerable time to produce, were slow to reach the Naval Staff. The Allies could also have made NSHQ's job easier by conducting an effective liaison with the RCN's service headquarters. Frequently the only direct contact the RCN had with Admiralty officials – such as Wylie – was when these men, who invariably came to North America to visit Washington, made fleeting weekend visits to Ottawa as something of an afterthought.[29] Obtaining information on the development of new equipment, for example, was often difficult and always time consuming.

But if the British attitude towards the RCN was bad, that of the USN was even worse. Canada's fully independent status within a redefined empire was a murky concept, poorly understood by Americans. Further, in appearance and practice the RCN was virtually indistinguishable from the RN. Not surprisingly, then, Canada and the RCN came under 'British Empire and Colonies' in the USN's filing manual. Americans preferred to deal with Commonwealth naval issues through the British Admiralty Delegation in Washington. The presence of a Canadian naval attaché who professed to represent the views of an independent service only confused the situation. The USN at least considered the Canadians a British 'problem.'

The Naval Staff's position with respect to developments in MOEF was therefore not enviable. Moreover, the focus of RCN operations now lay between New York and Newfoundland. Despite this, MOEF remained the navy's most prestigious commitment, its original contribution to the larger war, and the closest thing the RCN had to participation in a decisive theatre. Further, from the RCN perspective its MOEF escorts had done very well through July and August 1942. Despite their outdated equipment, Canadian escorts had scored three of MOEF's four U-boat kills over the period – a record which more than balanced losses from Canadian-escorted convoys. And if the eleven ships lost from the novel battle of SC 94 were not counted against them, the RCN's balance sheet was enviable.

Official commentary on the battles of July and August gave little indication of British dissatisfaction with some apparently basic flaws in C-group operations. Nor was there any indication of British lack of faith in the ability of senior RCN officers. Unfortunately, the fall of 1942 brought a rapid intensification of the mid-ocean battle, an increased importance to the main transatlantic convoy routes, and a sharp decline in the fortunes of Canadian escorts. The combination of all these factors added tremendous weight to lingering British doubts about the capability of the RCN.

Two of Newfoundland's most important Captains (D), J.M. Rowland and E.R. Mainguy, share a drink in the Crowsnest Club, St John's, in 1944. The club, which still exists, was founded by Mainguy two years previously.

OPPOSITE

top Ottawa I, lying in Lough Foyle sometime in early 1942, not long before her tragic loss while escorting ON 127

bottom Regina, a revised corvette, seen off Halifax in June 1942. The improved sheer and flare of her bows and the extended foc'sle show clearly. *Regina* was one of the TORCH corvettes.

The end of *Saguenay*'s operational career. She is shown limping into St John's after damage suffered while escorting SC 109.

Restigouche in June 1942. Her HF/DF antenna is atop the short mast near the stern, with the 286 radar atop the foremast.

HMS *Churchill*, a well-equipped RN Town-class destroyer assigned to group C 4 in December 1942

The fate of Western Support Force: HMS *Mansfield* alongside at St John's,
30 January 1943

Captain H.N. Lay (right), director of Operations, and Commander P.M. Bliss, RN, staff officer (A/S), seen here in March 1943, after the successful campaign to establish a separate Canadian theatre in the Northwest Atlantic

OPPOSITE

One of the ablest of RCN staff officers, Captain H.G. DeWolf, seen here when serving as director of Plans in 1942

OPPOSITE

top Sinking a disabled merchant ship. Depth charges (and their carriers) from *Shediac* fall around the ss *Vestfold* in January 1943.

bottom Five WLEF Town-class destroyers and a gaggle of smaller escorts berthed at jetties 4 and 5, Halifax, probably in the spring of 1943. Just beyond the ships and partly obscured by smoke is Halifax shipyards, where the RCN's new Tribal-class destroyers were under construction.

The Allied Anti-Submarine Survey Board leaving Ottawa, 10 May 1943. Left to right, Group Captain P.F. Canning, RAF; Rear Admiral J.L. Kauffman, USN; Rear Admiral J.M. Mansfield, RN; and two unidentified officers

Trillium, with 167 survivors from ONS 166 aboard, about to receive medical officers and supplies from *Spencer* during a lull in the battle

OPPOSITE

Despite the addition of modern equipment, most RCN corvettes remained unchanged structurally until 1944. This is *Arvida* as seen from *Ottawa II* in mid-1943. She retains her short foc'sle, outdated bridge, and mast before the wheelhouse but has modern radar and a heavy secondary armament. The 'barber-pole' funnel band, originally adopted by C 3 in 1942, was pinched by C 5 in 1943.

Battleford in the spring of 1943. She now carries 271 radar and 20-millimetre oerlikon guns on her bridge.

First of the second generation of River-class destroyers, *Ottawa II*, in May 1943. She carries HF/DF aft and 271 radar atop the bridge, and one forward gun has been removed to fit hedgehog.

The original Flower-class corvette in its final form. This is *Shediac*, seen off the west coast after her modernization in 1944. The cluster of hedgehog bombs can be seen just forward of the bridge.

The wave of the future: *Swansea*, the RCN's second frigate

Hedgehog, seen here aboard *Moose Jaw* after her modernization in 1944

Angus L. Macdonald and Winston Churchill outside 10 Downing Street, London, July 1942. On the left is Rear Admiral P.W. Nelles (in civilian clothes) and Captain F.L. Houghton, RCN, secretary of the Chiefs of Staff Committee.

6

The Disquiet Grows

It is a waste of time trying to go into what happened. Captain (D)
Newfoundland has congratulated them on their effort personally.
It seems to me a complete muddle. *Amherst* seems to think that
operation Raspberry consists of steaming up and down the columns. I note that *Arvida* opened fire on him – serve him right!

Captain Ravenhill, RN, of ON 127

The convoy battles of August signalled the full-scale resumption of the
German campaign in the mid-ocean. With Allied countermeasures in the
Western Atlantic now in good order, the main trade routes once again
became the most cost-effective area for U-boat operations. 'For every
U-boat that the enemy can operate in, say, the Caribbean,' Admiral Pound
wrote in July in anticipation of the renewal of convoy battles, 'he can
operate three in the Western Approaches to the United Kingdom.' Moreover, given that Dönitz would now have to face convoyed trade wherever
he turned in the North Atlantic, he had to attack shipping where it could
be assailed by 'four or five times the strength' available in distant waters.[1]
   British concern over the prospects for the future stemmed not only
from the U-boats' likely switch of forces to the now highly vulnerable
North Atlantic routes, but also from the rapidly growing U-boat fleet
itself. By the summer of 1942 the products of Germany's first wartime
building program were pouring forth at a rate of nearly twenty U-boats
per month. British ability to read the ciphers of the Baltic and North Sea
German naval commands allowed them to keep close track of the progress
of new U-boats and of the rate of their deployment to operations. The
intelligence they obtained thereby gave clear cause for concern. The
simple number of U-boats at sea on any given day was increasing, from

an average of twenty-two in January to eighty-six by August, reducing the potential for successful evasive routing of convoys. At a time when British intelligence was unable to read the ciphers of North Atlantic U-boats, the prospect of the mid-ocean filling up with U-boats, among which convoys could only be safely routed by very precise intelligence, was worrisome, to say the least.[2] In the absence of decisively effective routing, the close-escort screen became crucial to the delicate balance between sustainable and unsustainable shipping losses. As early as August it was clear to the Germans and the Allies alike that the confrontation in the mid-Atlantic air gap would soon escalate rapidly. Further, as 1942 drew to a close, yet more pressure was added to MOEF's responsibilities as the Allied landings in North Africa disrupted normal trade patterns and the flow of imports into Britain.

Although from the Allied perspective the outlook for German success over the short term was good, the Germans watched the development of Allied countermeasures with growing concern. The gathering strength and efficiency of escort forces through the spring and summer was noted anxiously by BdU. Recent victories in the mid-ocean had been bought with German losses. Surface escorts were improving their efficiency, and there was evidence of better co-operation with aircraft. Worse, for the Germans, was the discovery of land-based aircraft eight hundred miles from shore – three hundred miles farther than in 1941 – the result of the deployment of 120 Squadron to Iceland with new very-long-range (VLR) 'Liberator' bombers.[3]

Despite these developments Dönitz was by no means despondent. BdU believed that Allied adherence to the great-circle route in mid-1942 resulted from a shortage of shipping. This augured well for the future, and Dönitz was prepared to press home the battle ruthlessly. In July, as the inshore defensive system of the Western Hemisphere reduced the returns on distant operations, Dönitz braced the German people for the coming crisis. In a public statement he warned of higher casualties in the months ahead, a point which the Allies took as a 'tip straight from the horse's mouth.'[4]

Unfortunately for the Allies, a substantially higher casualty rate in the U-boat fleet was not in the offing in late 1942, and the exchange rate between Allied shipping losses and U-boats destroyed continued to favour the Germans heavily. Through the last months of 1942 U-boats exacted a punishing toll from North Atlantic shipping as the number of submarines committed to the air gap rose inexorably. By early September the use of two patrol lines was established, and their number and the size of packs increased as the year wore on.

Operating two or more patrol lines gave the Germans great flexibility in the mid-ocean and, of course, a higher interception rate. Although hampered by heavy gales throughout most of the fall, the two-group system did get off to a promising start. One of the groups, Vorwärts, of thirteen U-boats, had a brief encounter with sc 97 in late August before being reformed on 4 September. For the next five days Vorwärts lay astride the great-circle route like a huge drift net, waiting to enmesh the next ON convoy. That target was sighted briefly on the seventh, resulting in a slight redeployment of Vorwärts to the south. The move sufficed to prevent the convoy from clearing the southern end of the patrol line, and on the ninth firm contact was made with ON 127. The convoy was technically a fast one, though as with other westbound convoys most of its ships were travelling in ballast. Against prevailing westerlies this condition usually made the distinction between fast and slow ON convoys academic. But summer weather prevailed for ON 127, and in the absence of prolonged alterations in course the convoy made good time throughout its passage.

Once again this latest MOEF convoy to fall afoul of a waiting pack was escorted by a Canadian group, this time C 4. With the exception of the RN corvette *Celandine*, herself a member of C 4 since June, the group was wholly RCN. The destroyer *Ottawa* was also a long-standing member. Her captain, Acting Lieutenant Commander C.A. Rutherford, RCN, was on only his third trip in command, although as the previous captain of *St Francis* Rutherford was not new to either C 4 or the mid-ocean. The group's other destroyer was the venerable old four-stacker *St Croix*, with Acting Lieutenant Commander A.H. 'Dobby' Dobson, RCNR, in command. Dobson was another veteran and also Senior Officer of C 4 since reassignment from C 2 prior to the group's previous convoy (sc 96). Of the other escorts, *Amherst*, *Arvida*, and *Sherbrooke* had all served with C 4 since June. The captain of the latter, however, had only taken over in July. Thus, despite some movement of personnel C 4 was not a scratch team. It had a minimum of two months' and three crossings' experience as a unit, and this accounted for some cohesion. None the less, it is clear that the firm hand of a determined and long-established Senior Officer was missing from the group's performance with ON 127.

The escort sailed from Lough Foyle on 5 September and joined its convoy just before noon on the same day. Aside from a brief period of air cover on the sixth, the next five days passed without note. Unknown to either the escort or the commodore, U-boat pack Vorwärts lay in wait just beyond the range of land-based aircraft. The first warning of U-boat contact received by ON 127 and its escort was the torpedoing of *Elizabeth van Belgie* (12), *F.J. Wolfe* (22), and *Svene* (32) at 1430Z on the tenth in a single submerged attack by *U96*. *F.J. Wolfe* eventually made it safely to St John's, but the other two ships sank. The U-boat's successful penetration of the screen must have come as some surprise to Dobson. No doubt aware of recent German success in daylight attacks (SC 94 and SC 97), Dobson had arranged his escort to effect the best possible asdic barrier. Having neither discouraged nor prevented the attack, he immediately ordered the two destroyers and *Celandine* to sweep through the convoy in hopes of finding the assailant in ON 127's wake. *Sherbrooke* meanwhile was instructed to stand by the stricken vessels. In the brief hunt which followed, *St Croix* attacked a doubtful underwater contact, but sweeps by the three escorts failed to turn up any promising contacts, and *U96* made good her escape. While the hunt continued, Dobson ordered *Sherbrooke* to sink the freighter *Svene*, which was too heavily damaged to proceed, while the crippled tanker *F.J. Wolfe* struggled to regain her position in the convoy. Only the fate of *Elizabeth van Belgie* remained to be determined; finally, *Sherbrooke* was instructed to send her to the bottom as well.

With the evident failure of the post-attack sweep Dobson sent *Celandine* back to the convoy and *Ottawa* to a position well astern of ON 127, 'in order to prevent the submarine from surfacing and following the convoy.' Dobson then took *St Croix* to the port side of the convoy to make inquiries about the attack, leaving the close-screening duties to *Amherst*, *Arvida*, and *Celandine*. By 1913Z *St Croix* was back in station ahead of ON 127, at which time she made an underwater contact one thousand yards ahead of the centre columns. Before the destroyer could investigate, the convoy swept over *U659*, and two minutes later *Empire Oil* (43) was struck on her starboard side, then a few minutes later on her port side. The tanker was later sunk by *U584* astern of the convoy.

In the action which followed, various underwater contacts were pursued by *St Croix*, *Ottawa*, and *Celandine* in the wake of the convoy, but none of these were profitable. Once again the RN corvette was ordered back to the convoy while the destroyers lingered to prevent pursuit by the enemy. On the way back to ON 127 *Celandine* obtained a promising contact, which she hunted at length, eventually forcing Dobson to order her to abandon this latest search and return to ON 127 to take charge of its defence. In the meantime *St Croix* and *Ottawa*, who had removed the survivors from *Empire Oil*, had also set course for the convoy. Unfortunately, neither destroyer was able to rejoin before *Celandine* signalled, at 2225Z, that *Marit II* (82) had been torpedoed (by *U404*). Fortunately, *Marit II* was able to make harbour with the convoy. Still some distance from the scene, Dobson could do nothing, nor could he help an hour later when more illuminants were seen over ON 127. These latest heralded *U218*'s successful torpedoing of *Fjordaas* (23), also damaged but able to proceed.

Following *U218*'s attack the escort took effective action against a series of attempts to penetrate the screen. Between 2355Z and 0200Z on the eleventh *St Croix* detected one U-boat by radar and drove it off; *Arvida* depth charged the swirl left by a U-boat following a visual contact; *Amherst* attacked an asdic contact off the convoy's port bow, and *Ottawa* engaged a similar target off the starboard side. By 0200Z all was again quiet. C 4 was closed up in position NE 5 (one ahead, one on either bow, and one in each quarter), having done a creditable job of forestalling the latest attacks. Immediate prospects, however, were not good, because of the failure of all the group's radar, including *Celandine*'s 271. *Sherbrooke*, meanwhile, was still well astern, 'sinking torpedoed ships.' The night's action ended with a brief but promising surface engagement between *Celandine* and a U-boat.

The early daylight hours of 11 September passed relatively quietly, with only *Ottawa* finding a submerged target worthy of attack. In the early forenoon Dobson finally took *St Croix* to visibility distance ahead of ON 127 and was rewarded with a U-boat sighting. While the Senior Officer was busy six miles away, *U584* eluded the screen and in yet another submerged daylight attack torpedoed *Hindanger* (11). Rutherford, now acting SOE, ordered an emergency turn to port, which the convoy held for the next five hours. During this course alteration ON 127 sighted its second VLR aircraft from 120 Squadron, Iceland, the only air support ON 127 could expect in the depth of the mid-ocean gap. As ON 127 set off on its new course, Dobson ordered *Amherst* to sink the *Hindanger*, while the destroyer turned to rejoin the convoy. *St Croix* was delayed, however, by her investigation of a radar contact and did not regain position in the screen until 0100Z. With *Amherst* still absent following her destruction of *Hindanger* and with *Sherbrooke* still twenty-five miles astern of ON 127, the close escort was now down to *Ottawa*, *Arvida*, and *Celandine*. Not surprisingly, they were unable to prevent *U211* from torpedoing *Hektoria* (42) and *Empire Moonbeam* (31) almost simulta-

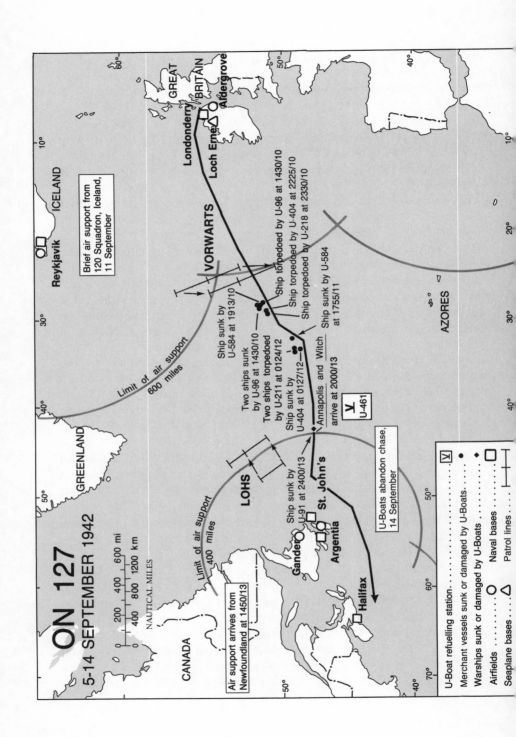

ON 127
5–14 SEPTEMBER 1942

CANADA

GREENLAND

ICELAND

GREAT BRITAIN

Reykjavik

Halifax

St. John's

Gander

Argentia

Londonderry

Loch Erne

Aldergrove

VORWARTS

LOHS

AZORES

Brief air support from 120 Squadron, Iceland, 11 September

Limit of air support 600 miles

Limit of air support 400 miles

Air support arrives from Newfoundland at 1450/13

U-Boats abandon chase, 14 September

Ship sunk by U-91 at 2400/13

Two ships sunk by U-96 at 1430/10
Two ships torpedoed by U-211 at 0124/12
Ship sunk by U-404 at 0127/12
Annapolis and Witch arrive at 2000/13

U-461

Ship sunk by U-584 at 1913/10

Ship sunk by U-584 at 1755/11

Ship torpedoed by U-96 at 1430/10
Ship torpedoed by U-404 at 2225/10
Ship torpedoed by U-218 at 2330/10

NAUTICAL MILES
0   200   400   600 mi
0   400   800   1200 km

60°
50°
40°
10°   0°   10°   20°   30°   40°   50°   60°   70°

U-Boat refuelling station	⋯⋯ ☑
Merchant vessels sunk or damaged by U-Boats	●
Warships sunk or damaged by U-Boats	◆
Airfields	○
Seaplane bases	△
Naval bases	□
Patrol lines	├─┤

neously. Both ships were later sunk by *U608*. Operation Raspberry revealed nothing, and *Arvida* was ordered to stand by the stricken ships. While thus engaged *Arvida* also picked up survivors from *Daghild* (64), hit at 0127Z. Dobson's report claims that one further ship was torpedoed before the night was over, but this is not confirmed by German sources. In the interim *Celandine* attacked two U-boats lurking in the flotsam astern of ON 127. Both escaped without serious damage.

At dawn on 12 September Dobson arranged his four remaining escorts forward of ON 127 to guard against further submerged attacks. It was a most inadequate asdic barrier, and C 4 was fortunate that no such attacks were attempted. In part, failure to press home with more submerged attacks may have stemmed from the excellent visibility prevalent on the twelfth, which allowed C 4 to push off U-boats sighted as much as seven miles away. Yet despite the presence of U-boats and excellent visibility, Dobson made no use of his destroyers on wide-ranging sweeps on either beam of ON 127. Caught on the horns of an insoluble dilemma, he kept the escorts close, pushed back U-boats that ventured near, and tried to maintain the screen around the convoy. Dobson's adherence to a defence role was probably effective. Only two attempts were made to attack ON 127 on the following night, both unsuccessful – indeed, both unknown to the escort at the time. For C 4, then, the third night of the battle passed quietly.

The first air support from Newfoundland arrived over ON 127 on the thirteenth, and it was instrumental in driving most of the remaining shadowers off. At dusk C 4 was reinforced by the RCN Town-class destroyer *Annapolis* and the RN destroyer *Witch*, both WLEF escorts. None the less, Vorwarts had some parting shots left. Just minutes after midnight *U91* torpedoed *Ottawa*, who had been investigating radar contacts ahead of the convoy. *St Croix* raced to her assistance and arrived to find *Ottawa* stopped and down somewhat, but otherwise on an even keel and not badly damaged. But as *St Croix* swept up ahead of the damaged ship, *Ottawa* was hit again and sank quickly, with heavy loss of life (including Rutherford, who passed his lifebelt to a rating). One more successful attack was made on the convoy before the weight of Newfoundland-based air power ended the battle on the fourteenth. The final score was impressive: seven ships and the destroyer *Ottawa* sunk and four other merchantmen damaged. In exchange, one U-boat was damaged, although of this the Allies were by no means certain at the time. In addition, ON 127 gained the dubious distinction of being the only convoy during 1942–3 against which all the U-boats engaged were able to fire torpedoes – the price of early interception, lack of air cover, and a poorly equipped escort group.

Dobson's conduct of the defence of ON 127 drew little official criticism from British and American staffs. Both Western Approaches Staff and Admiral Brainard, Commander, Task Force Twenty-four, believed that the 'escorts were active and took lively countermeasures against attacking U-boats.' However, they also felt that Dobson had conducted his escort too tamely. CTF-24 noted that only one sweep was made by *St Croix* when 'a greater use of the destroyers in sweeping at visibility distance during daylight might have beneficial.' Moreover, the Americans felt that such action would have justified a reduction in the close screen ahead of the convoy. As Admiral Brainard noted, the inability of five or even more ships to provide an effective asdic barrier made Dobson's concentration on underwater defence during the day questionable. (It should be noted, however, that establishing an effective radar barrier at night with a similar number of 271-equipped escorts was a very different matter.)

Again the Canadian staffs, perhaps shocked by the loss of service lives and one of the navy's most modern and powerful destroyers and faced with the worst disaster of the year thus far, made little comment on the conduct of the escort – at least in writing. That Mainguy offered his personal congratulations to C 4 upon its arrival in St John's indicates that the RCN considered the job well done. Indeed, Murray blamed the heavy losses directly on the lack of 271 radar in the group.[6] The dearth of comment on the complete failure of the group's radar (with the exception of that aboard *Celandine*, all outdated) is mute testimony to contemporary opinion of the early sets.

But while all agreed that C 4 had fought well without HF/DF, 271 radar, and air support and that the outcome could have been much worse, the conduct of the escort once again drew acid comments from officers in Liverpool. Commander Howard-Johnston was particularly savage in his internal minutes about ON 127. 'There is an unnecessary waste of escorts' efforts to sink damaged ''freighters,'' ' he wrote: 'At 0200Z *Sherbrooke* has managed to get 25 miles astern of the convoy in order to sink torpedoed ships. At 1928 on the same day *Amherst* is detached to sink torpedoed ships. What is *St. Croix*'s idea, what is his meaning [illegible]?? He is helping to reduce our tonnage by weakening the escort and completing the enemy's work.' The official submission to the Admiralty regarding ON 127 and the conduct of its escort was more discreet but summed up the gist of the British complaint by noting laconically, 'It is the enemy's purpose to sink our tonnage.'

Captain Ravenhill, the WA Operations officer, shared these concerns for Dobson's performance, but once again his consternation also extended to the RCN Staff at St John's. Pointing to a critical weakness in the Canadian struggle for efficiency, Ravenhill minuted a scathing comment on FONF and his Captain (D). They 'never make any attempt to collect the reports on one convoy and forward them under one covering letter with remarks,' he commented, a criticism that he shared with NSHQ. In sum Ravenhill strongly believed that 'neither FONF or Captain (D) have the remotest idea of what is expected of them.' The situation was, as Ravenhill described it, a 'complete muddle.'[7]

Eventually, lack of faith in the C groups' higher command and administrative officers cast the burden of action on to the British, or so they believed. In fact, the British took action to improve the efficiency of C groups shortly after the caustic comments noted above were pencilled in mid-November. In the meantime, RCN reaction to ON 127 took two forms: replacing *Ottawa* and fitting its escorts with 271 radar.

Within two days of the destroyer's loss NSHQ signalled the Admiralty requesting assistance in finding more destroyers or, as a substitute, frigates, for both MOEF and WLEF.[8] For the moment the RCN asked only that this problem be given 'consideration' – although with *Ottawa* lost and *Assiniboine* and *St Laurent* in refit there were only three modern destroyers in the four C groups. As an interim measure NSHQ wanted to commission two RN frigates, nearing completion in Canada, into the RCN. Frigates were on order for the Canadian navy from domestic yards, but the ten building to British accounts, which had been ordered sooner, were much further advanced. Indeed, the navy had even delayed in launching its frigate program because of a desire not to disrupt British shipbuilding projects which brought in both money and, more importantly, expertise.[9]

The acquisition of frigates for MOEF would, in 1942, have been of marginal value. Unlike destroyers, they lacked a high turn of speed, essential if a group was to provide its own strike component. Frigates did have a much greater radius of action, and this would have permitted using them more aggressively throughout convoy battles without fear of reducing the escort by the dispatch of ships to refuel. They were also suitable for Senior Officers' ships and would have made a welcome addition to any group. But they were not a substitute for destroyers. Frigates were analogous to the American Coast Guard cutters in A 3, whose poor tactical performance in July had led to complaints from CTF-24 and a request for their replacement by destroyers.

The need for destroyers was inescapable. Yet aside from the Town class, which the navy had accepted with understandable reluctance, the RCN had made no attempt to secure destroyers other than fleet-class Tribals since 1939. Tribals were, to say the least, ill-suited for A/S escort. At the same time, the RCN was reluctant to convert the River class fully to escort work because that would limit their role. It was not until 1 October 1942 – three years after the war began – on the direct advice of the Admiralty and the strong endorsement of the V/CNS (Commodore H.E. Reid, RCN, who was about to replace Murray as FONF) that the Naval Staff approved the removal of range-finders from River-class destroyers in order to fit modern A/S radar. Five days later the Naval Board agreed in principle that priority in the acquisition of destroyers should now be given to escorts, not Tribals.[10] The Naval Board determined that the fleet was fourteen destroyers short of its minimum requirements. The ships were needed immediately, and Canadian industry was no more capable of mass-producing escort destroyers in 1942 than it had been of producing Tribals in 1939. It was a long-term problem which admitted of no immediate solution.

The issue of radar for the fleet was more manageable and confronted the Naval Staff from two rather disparate sources. On 16 September, the day after C 4 secured alongside at St John's, Murray sent a strongly worded request to NSHQ asking that MOEF escorts be given priority for fitting of 271 radar. In addition, he wanted NSHQ to give shipyards in Britain carte blanche to install the sets on Canadian escorts forthwith. MOEF escorts, Murray observed, were in a bind. The only RCN base with supplies of 271 radar and with the necessary facilities for fitting was Halifax, where MOEF escorts hardly, if ever, called. Canadian escorts had access to several UK ports capable of fitting the radar quickly, but NSHQ's standing order against all unauthorized additions or alterations to Canadian warships prevented MOEF from taking advantage of fleeting gaps in British repair work. If NSHQ still felt any anxiety over the value of 271 radar, Murray set out to chase it away. He stated bluntly that 271 radar was essential for night operations. Drawing on recent experiences of B 6 and C 4, Murray noted that German attacks on ON 122 and ON 127 were 'similar in scale,' and the 'more successful outcome of [the] former is attributed to the fact that all ships in escort [B 6] had type 271 and one destroyer and rescue ship had HF/DF.'[11] The Naval Staff concurred with Murray's recommendations, and starting in October MOEF ships were given permission to fit with 271 radar when and wherever they could.

A far more serious problem was growing American concern over the standard of 'material maintenance and readiness' of the Canadian fleet, as exemplified by the apparently high incidence of breakdown. Perhaps inspired by the recent complete failure of an entire group's radar (that of C 4, during its defence of ON 127), Admiral Brainard on 21 September submitted a memo to FONF (now Captain Mainguy, in an acting capacity pending the arrival of Commodore Reid) dealing with Canadian maintenance standards and procedures. The memo, which the American admiral intended as constructive criticism, contended that the RCN was at present incapable of keeping a sufficiently high proportion of its escorts at sea and that 'every ship-day-out-of-service improves the enemy's chances against the convoys.' Canadian maintenance standards were, Brainard wrote, 'appreciably below the standards demanded of experienced regulars,' and this reduced the operational size of the fleet to a 'dangerous and unacceptable figure.' This situation existed for three reasons: the inexperience of personnel, the overextension of those who were qualified, and poor administration of existing maintenance standards. Brainard wanted a systematic and responsible engineering establishment developed in every ship, led by an experienced and qualified officer with the aid of similarly skilled ratings. To facilitate such a scheme Brainard offered the RCN the loan of USN engineer officers.[12]

Brainard's memo was received in the spirit in which it was submitted, and Mainguy advised acceptance of the offer. But the RCN was well aware of its problems and had already undertaken remedial action along the lines put forth by the American admiral. There was no escaping the fact that maintenance standards were not professionally acceptable, and this was admitted by all concerned. The RCN was now faced with repairing the damage done by its very rapid expansion. But Brainard had cited the latter as the source of Canadian woes in such a way as to imply that the RCN had made a bad choice of priorities earlier on. Such criticism, coming from the admiral who had benefited most from RCN expansion, was sufficient to result in Canadian rejection of both the meaningful criticisms and the offer of assistance. 'With the plea from all sides for more and more escorts,' Murray commented in response to the memo, 'ships have been sent to sea as soon as officers could be trained to handle them, and maintenance has taken a second place in the training programme of Executive Officers.' All agreed that the situation was now well in hand and would be cured with time. The American offer of assistance was never seriously considered, if for no other reason than that the more senior USN engineer officers would have embarrassed the command structure of whichever ships they were posted to.[13]

While the RCN dismissed this American 'tampering' in its domestic affairs, it also admitted that the impact of jamming three years of expansion into less than two and engaging in increasingly demanding operational duties at the same time was serious. Maintenance, like proper operational training and modernization of the fleet, was a casualty of frantic growth. In some measure the problem of maintenance rested with the shipyards, overseers, and acceptance staffs, all of whom allowed mechanically suspect ships to commission – a symptom of the forced pace of expansion. The problem was compounded by the low level of experience and training of engineering personnel. Men could be quickly trained to operate equipment, but proper maintenance was much more demanding. Not surprisingly, escort commanders came to rely on dockyards for maintenance of the most rudimentary kind, even in late 1942. The supervising naval engineer, Maritimes, Engineer Captain F.H. Jefferson, RCN, when considering Brainard's comments, complained that the executive branch was 'inclined to leave as much maintenance work as possible to be dealt with during periods of refit.' Such a practice also led to protracted refits, further compounding the problem. To this was added the current practice of submitting all outstanding defects on the same list, without arrangements by priority. This practice, too, Jefferson alleged, was the fault of executive officers who did not consider 'what is essential for the seagoing and fighting efficiency of the ship, but how much can be entered as a defect to be dealt with by Dockyard or Contractor.'[14] Clearly, the headlong plunge into expansion had created a monster which would take some time to tame.

But it is, of course, unfair to rest the weight of this burden on the independent-minded and overworked captains of the corvette fleet. The whole maintenance and repair establishment of the east coast was in need of overhaul in late 1942. Captain (D), Newfoundland, was still not responsible for additions and alterations to Canadian escorts operating with MOEF.[15] C groups were thus caught in a bureaucratic nightmare – as Captain Rowland so aptly pointed out. Resolving the problems of fleet maintenance – the very foundation of operational efficiency – was one of the most difficult battles the RCN ever fought.

In view of developments discussed in the next chapter it is important to note Brainard's dissatisfaction with the state of the RCN. Others shared his belief. Yet at a time when the fleet had serious maintenance problems and desparately needed new equipment and refits, the RCN continued to take on new responsibilities. In August, when things were admittedly going well on all fronts (at least for the RCN), Nelles was asked by the First Sea Lord to make a number of escorts available for 'an operation of some importance.' Further details of TORCH, the landings in North Africa, were available by late in the month. No firm request with respect to numbers was made of the RCN; it was simply asked to do what it could. By stripping the west coast of all its corvettes, replacing seven corvettes in WLEF with Bangors, and withdrawing all corvettes from the Gulf Escort Force, the RCN scraped together seventeen (one of which was actually RN).[16] The first six sailed for Britain on 10 September and were the only ones involved in the initial assaults. The other eleven sailed as extra escorts for transatlantic convoys during October and November.

Before proceeding to duty with TORCH, all the RCN corvettes were re-equipped with a heavier secondary armament and 271 radar (some in Canada prior to leaving). Thus in the fall of 1942 the navy's best-equipped corvettes were operating in the Eastern Atlantic. It is also noteworthy that six of the nine revised corvettes (with modifications included to make them better ocean escorts) then in commission were sent to TORCH. Two others were serving with the USN in the Caribbean, leaving only *La Malbaie* under 'Canadian' command, appropriately enough with MOEF. This assignment of the more modern corvettes did not go unnoticed by RCN officers in MOEF.[17]

The tendency to send the best to serve with other navies is understandable, although there is no firm proof that it was NSHQ's intention. The deployment of the four original corvettes that had by 1942 been partially modernized (extended foc's'le and improved bridges) suggests that the RCN took no cognizance of these factors when assigning ships, since here again only one was committed to MOEF. But perhaps the most disturbing aspect of the decision to send such a large number of escorts to TORCH was the impact this had on fleet flexibility. A total of seventeen corvettes was just one short of the number needed – admittedly, from all sources, not just RCN – to bolster MOEF at the onset of winter. By mid-September Murray was already complaining about his inability to meet refit schedules because of the need to keep up the strength of operational groups.[18] The effect on WLEF and Gulf Force was no less profound. Moreover, WLEF was about to be stretched even further in mid-September, when the British and the Americans – with Canadian concurrence – agreed to shift the assembly point for all North Atlantic convoys from Nova Scotia to New York. They also agreed that WESTOMP should be moved further eastward in order to increase the tactical flexibility of MOEF groups.[19] WLEF was thus drawn in two directions.

Halifax-based escorts now assumed a heavy responsibility for large ocean convoys for fully one-third of their passage. To cover the area between New York and WESTOMP it was necessary to restructure WLEF into two relays since neither the Bangors nor the Town-class destroyers had the endurance to complete the whole trip. The small WLEF groups changed off Halifax. Depending on the timing of cycles, Halifax was now to be either bereft of escorts or choked with them. At a time when every escort was badly needed, the image of large numbers of warships lying alongside at Halifax, apparently idle, further injured the RCN's already tattered reputation with the British,[20] who, it must be admitted, remained remarkably ignorant of WLEF for some time to come. With these last commitments the RCN was finally stretched to the breaking point, and it was not long before the first cracks began to appear.

In the mid-ocean, September proved to be a month of largely Canadian battles. SC 99, escorted by C 1 (*St Francis* and the corvettes *Battleford*, *Chambly*, *Chilliwack*, *Eyebright*, *Napanee*, *Orillia*, and *Rosthern*), was sighted on the thirteenth and was pursued without success by five U-boats. The pack formed ahead of SC 99 was fortuitously drawn off by ON 129. The escort of the latter convoy, C 2 (two RN destroyers, *Burnham* and *Winchelsea*, and the corvettes *Drumheller*, *Dauphin*, *Morden*, and *Polyanthus* [RN]), disrupted German attempts to mass around the convoy. Both SC 99 and ON 129 escaped without loss in part because they had been intercepted by the extremities of U-boat patrol lines, which made it difficult for the Germans to effect a good concentration.[21]

By the time the U-boat patrol line was reformed, the British-escorted HX 206 (B 1) was well clear of the area. The next convoy, SC 100, was not so lucky.[22] Fortunately, it did have a large escort (A 3: USCG cutters *Campbell* and *Spencer*, Captain P.R. Heineman, USCG, Senior Officer, the corvettes *Bittersweet*, *Mayflower*, *Trillium*, and *Rosthern*, and the TORCH corvettes on passage *Lunenburg*, *Nasturtium* [RN], and *Weyburn*), was fairly close to British air cover when detected, and the convoy itself was quite small (only twenty-four ships). The escort kept the pack at bay for four days (18–21 September) through a combination of tight screening and offensive sweeps. One ship was lost on the twentieth to a submerged attack by U596, but a mounting gale scattered both the convoy and the pack as the battle progressed. One further ship was lost as SC 100 sailed in ragged order, and two stragglers were damaged. Coastal Command aircraft ended the battle on the twenty-fifth.

Throughout its week of contact with the enemy A 3 was spared sustained pressure from twenty U-boats sent to attack. This was due to deteriorating weather and to a well-conducted escort. However, SC 100 was also spared some pressure by the interception of RB 1, a special convoy of Hudson River steamers which the Germans mistook for troop-ships. Fortunately, the steamers' speed prevented groups 'Lohs' and 'Pfeil' from effecting an overwhelming concentration, but two ships and the RN destroyer *Veteran* were sunk.

The gale which scattered SC 100 and the scramble to attack RB 1 left three U-boat packs strewn throughout the mid-ocean. BdU was therefore unable to co-ordinate attacks on ON 131, the next convoy intercepted. None the less, ON 131's escort, C 3 (Wallace as Senior Officer in *Saguenay*, with *Skeena* and the corvettes *Agassiz*, *Anemone* [RN], *Galt*, *Sackville*, and *Wetaskiwin*), was busy with U-boat contacts, and Wallace was able to direct destroyer sweeps with the HF/DF set carried by the commodore's ship, SS *Cairnesk*. Only one of the fifteen U-boats in pursuit of ON 131, *U617*, was able to gain firm contact, and her attack suffered from torpedo defects (premature detonation).[23]

The abandonment of operations against ON 131 on 30 September brought to an end a very busy and disappointing month for the Germans. Aside from the battle of ON 127, from which they could reasonably have ex-pected greater success, attempts to mount heavy concentrations against a series of favourably placed convoys had come to naught. Two more frustrating weeks followed in early October in which only one convoy, HX 209, was intercepted. Even then, this British-escorted convoy was discovered just as it entered the range of effective air cover and was intercepted by only the northern tip of group 'Luchs.' Neither of these conditions allowed for an effective concentration, and the U-boats were hampered once again by gales. Increasingly oppressive air support forced the abandonment of operations against HX 209 on 4 October; then, before the members of Luchs could clear the area, Coastal Command destroyed two U-boats, one on the fifth and the other the following day.

It was not until the second week of October that BdU was able to operate against a convoy favourably placed before its patrol lines. On the night of the eleventh ON 136, escorted by B 3, passed through the middle of group 'Panther.' Eight U-boats, designated group 'Leopard,' were told off to pursue and attack, while the gap in Panther was filled by new arrivals. In heavy weather, attempts by Leopard to press attacks home failed, and *U597* was lost to a VLR Liberator of 120 Squadron operating in support of B 3 on the twelfth. After this incident Leopard reported sighting only stragglers and independents. BdU therefore redi-rected them against an eastbound convoy reported by group 'Wotan' to be just entering the air gap on the eleventh.[24]

Wotan had lain in wait for SC 104 for two days while, unknown to the

Germans, the convoy edged its way around to the north of the U-boat line.²⁵ A chance sighting of an escort by *U258*, the northernmost member of Wotan, revealed that the convoy was slipping away to the east. Redeployment of the pack to intercept SC 104 was delayed for a day owing to a distraction towards ON 135 (A 3), so that on the twelfth only one submarine, *U221*, under command of Lieutenant Commander Trojer, was in touch with the eastbound convoy. Unfortunately for the well-equipped escort of SC 104, B 6 (*Fame*, Commander S. Heathcote, RN, Senior Officer, and *Viscount* with the Norwegian corvettes *Acanthus*, *Eglantine*, *Montbretia*, and *Potentilla*), this one skilful hunter proved more than a match.

Dreadful weather characterized the first phase of the battle for SC 104, and it was under such difficult conditions that Trojer was able to press home his attacks. His first approach, at 0425Z on the thirteenth, disabled *Fargesten* (102), but in the howling wind and crashing seas the escort remained unaware of *U221*'s attack. It was only after Trojer's second attack at 0508Z, which sent *Senta* (104) and *Ashworth* (105) quickly to the bottom, that *Fargesten* was found astern of SC 104. Despite B 6's futile efforts to locate him, Trojer made good his escape.

U221 maintained contact with SC 104 during the following day and homed four other U-boats on to the convoy. B 6, using its HF/DF sets, was able to detect each newcomer and force him off. But at the end of the day Trojer, presumably homing on MF, was still in contact, while three of the escort, *Viscount* and the corvettes *Eglantine* and *Potentilla*, were all well astern of SC 104 as a result of their HF/DF pursuits. *U221* therefore had little difficulty penetrating the convoy after sunset on the thirteenth. At 2215Z *Susana* (93) was hit and sank abruptly, and fifteen minutes later *Southern Express* (95) was hit while straggling. The convoy's small escort took no action following *U221*'s attack, but Trojer's U-boat was nearly rammed by *Viscount* as the destroyer came upon the intrepid submariner astern of SC 104. Frustrated by heavy seas, *Viscount* had to content herself with putting *U221* down, and then set course for the convoy.

Bad weather prevented the escort from detecting a series of attacks which followed later the same night. *U607* sank *Nellie* (13) after slipping past *Acanthus* on the port side at 2335Z. Several hours later *U661* penetrated the screen on the starboard side and sank *Kikolnia Matovik* (102). Finally, at 0230Z *U618* torpedoed *Empire Mersey* (101). Following the last attack B 6 conducted Operation Raspberry, but two of the three escorts which participated found nothing. *Fame* obtained an asdic contact and, while pursuing it, a promising radar contact. The radar contact revealed itself to be a U-boat, upon which *Fame* poured down a heavy fire from her main armament. The U-boat was forced to submerge, but the destroyer was unable to locate her prey by asdic.

Daylight on the fourteenth ended the first phase of the battle, and it had not gone well for B 6. During the day HF/DF-directed sweeps drove off three of the four shadowers, which helped keep things quiet around SC 104 in the early hours of darkness. More importantly, on the night of 14–15 October B 6 was favoured by better weather and a much reduced sea. The first U-boat to close, *U619*, was detected by *Viscount*'s radar, rammed, and sunk. Six further attempts by U-boats to attack the convoy were foiled by 271 radar in the early hours of 15 October. Daylight once again brought HF/DF-directed sweeps and cover by 120 Squadron Liberators. The latter sighted three shadowers and drove them off. The night of 15–16 October passed almost without incident.

The morning of the sixteenth brought a relay of air cover, while *Fame* uncovered an attempt by *U353* to launch a submerged attack. In two skilful depth-charge attacks *Fame* blew the U-boat to the surface and then sank it by ramming. *Fame*, like *Viscount* the day before, was forced into an early retirement as a result of damage she had sustained. The four remaining Norwegian corvettes, under Lieutenant Commander C.A. Monsen, RNorN, in *Potentilla*, had a relatively quiet last night while in contact with group Wotan. *U571* was detected by radar and damaged by gunfire in the only attempt to penetrate the screen. The Germans abandoned operations against SC 104 on the seventeenth because of the growing effectiveness of air support and the interception of a favourably placed westbound convoy, ON 137.

Despite the loss of eight ships the British considered the battle of SC 104 a heartening success. It marked the first time in two months that the escort had forced the pack to pay for its actions. Indeed, in the last comparable action, SC 94 (eleven ships lost in exchange for two U-boats), the balance sheet had been much the same. In SC 104's case the loss of eight ships could be explained by the bad weather of the early phase of the battle, which had rendered detection equipment inoperative. 'Such circumstances are no fault of the escort,' the Admiralty's analysis concluded, 'and set an extremely difficult problem admitting of no complete solution as things are at present, against a determined enemy.' Trojer in *U221* was nothing if not determined. But Trojer's second attack and those of *U607* and *U661* were greatly facilitated by the reduction of the escort by half in order to pursue contacts astern of the convoy and in support of rescue operations on the fourteenth. This was a serious error of judgment on the part of the Senior Officer, Commander Heathcote, and it is not too partisan to suppose that British authorities would have been less charitable with a Canadian officer. In fairness to Heathcote, his group's score of two U-boats and the many successful actions in preventing the penetration of the convoy lifted the battle for SC 104 from a potential disaster to a victory. In that achievement B 6 was very fortunate to have been so well equipped and blessed by moderating weather. Otherwise, the German success of the first night would undoubtedly have been repeated, and the dislocation of the escort which would inevitably have followed could have led to much heavier losses.

SC 104 demonstrated that good equipment under the right conditions, with a proper balance between destroyers and corvettes in a group, gave MOEF an edge over attacking packs, provided that the escort was not asked to fight alone for too long. The first night of the battle indicated clearly what could befall an escort operating without benefit of 271 radar (in this instance, due to heavy seas). Comments on the battle from contemporary authorities and post-war analysts agree that fairer weather on 15–16 October allowed B 6 to retrieve the initiative with the benefit of the modern equipment of its ships. Radar was not only vital in defence; it was also instrumental in *Viscount*'s destruction of *U619*. Further, the Norwegians once again displayed the professionalism evident in the battle for ONS 122, and 'it was probably their lack of speed alone which prevented them achieving some tangible results.'

The positive kill of two U-boats did much to shape British opinion of B 6's performance, as did the group's rally after the first night. The British assessment of the conduct of the escort as a whole – the role of weather, modern equipment, and the early judgments of the SOE – contrasts sharply with their jaundiced view of C groups. Yet the apparent poor professionalism of Canadian escort groups stemmed in large part from their lack of good tactical intelligence. In the quickening pace of mid-ocean battles such data were only available through modern equipment.

The pack which dogged SC 104 across the Atlantic was redirected, along with Panther (twelve U-boats), to ON 137, escorted by C 4 (*Restigouche*, fitted with HF/DF, *St Croix*, the corvettes *Amherst*, *Arvida*, and *Celandine* [RN], and the rescue ship HMS *Bury*, also fitted with HF/DF).[26] The convoy was intercepted, as anticipated, on 16 October, but attempts to concentrate upon it were frustrated by bad weather. Pursuit of ON 137 by Panther and Wotan was finally given up on the nineteenth.

BdU then turned its attention to the next convoy, located by BDienst. The convoy, ON 138, escorted by B 2, was never firmly contacted by the group ('Puma') sent to intercept it on 16 October. B 2's Senior Officer, Captain Donald Macintyre, RN, CO of the destroyer *Hesperus*, was credited with having driven the pack off by 'aggressive action' and good use of HF/DF. However, it is evident that no attempt was made by BdU to force the issue around ON 138, although it was shadowed – by accident – on the 24–25 October. In fact, German attention was drawn away from ON 138 almost immediately, as ON 139 was discovered coming up astern. Initially this convoy was very well placed for a large concentration, but its position was not firmly established until 22 October. By then only the shadower, *U443*, was in position to attack, which he did on the night of 22–23 October. The escort, C 2 (*Broadway* [RN], *Sherwood* [RN], and *Winchelsea* [RN], all Town-class destroyers, and the corvettes *Drumheller*, *Morden*, *Pictou*, *Polyanthus* [RN], and *Primrose* [RN]), was unable to prevent the loss of two ships in what was a totally unexpected attack. The group's Senior Officer, Lieutenant Commander E.H. Chavasse, RN (*Broadway*), later received a commendation for his efforts in defence of ON 139, but the U-boats directed to attack Chavasse's convoy were too far astern to effect a concentration. The chase was abandoned on the twenty-fifth when it was found that the pack had shadowed the wrong convoy (probably ONS 138).

While the U-boats from the muddled operations against ON 138 and ON 139 made their way northwards to regroup, Puma swept westwards in search of yet another ON convoy. BdU was therefore pleasantly surprised when, on the twenty-sixth, *U436* in the middle of the patrol line reported an eastbound convoy. Not only was this convoy, HX 212, well placed for a concentrated assault, but the presence of heavy seas in the area was 'regarded as difficult for the enemy's surface and submerged detection devices and favourable to our U-boats.'[27] The Germans would have been even more encouraged had they known that the escort, A 3 (the destroyer USS *Badger*, the cutter *Campbell*, the corvettes *Dianthus* [RN], *Rosthern*, and *Trillium*, and the RCN TORCH corvettes *Alberni*, *Summerside*, and *Ville de Quebec*, on passage to the UK), still lacked modern equipment.

Commander Lewis, USCG, the Senior Officer in *Campbell*, was aware that his convoy was entering troubled waters. He therefore adopted a two-phase screen: six of the escort were arranged in conventional fashion close to HX 212 and two in advanced screening positions on either beam of the convoy at visibility distance. With only one escort fitted with 271 radar (*Summerside*, apparently before she left Halifax for passage to Britain), Lewis's situation, despite his numerically large escort, was not enviable, and the Germans were able to make good use of the heavy seas. The first attack came at 2110Z on the twenty-seventh, when, without notice, *U436* torpedoed three ships in quick succession – *Sourabaya* (12), *Guerney Newlin* (21), and *Frontenac* (23). A 3 carried out the USN version of Raspberry, Operation 'Zombie,' with no tangible results. However, just after the action died down, *Summerside* obtained a radar contact at six thousand yards. Investigation revealed a U-boat, but by the time the corvette reached its position, even the swirl of the U-boat's dive was lost in the tossing sea.

By the time of the second attack at 0345Z on the twenty-eighth the close screen of HX 212 had been re-established as *Rosthern* and *Trillium* moved in from their distant positions to replace *Alberni* and *Summerside*, who were now astern tending to the wreckage of the first sinkings. The first victim of the second attack was *Cosmos* (22), torpedoed on her starboard side by *U606*. As she fell astern, *Barrenhim* (14) dropped back to rescue the crew while *Rosthern* screened. Tragically, both merchant ships were later lost as they straggled in the wake of HX 212. Sweeps by the escort produced nothing, and the rest of the night passed quietly. Some of the pressure on HX 212 was relieved the next day when a Liberator from 120 Squadron arrived in support, forcing off five U-boats as they attempted to gain a march on the convoy in preparation for a night assault. As night fell on the twenty-eighth, Lewis, mindful of the successful penetration of his close screen the previous night, arranged all his escorts in a protective barrier around the convoy. Yet once again heavy weather favoured the enemy, and two more ships, *Pan New York* (42) and *Bic Island* (24), were lost to unseen assailants. Effective air support on the twenty-ninth – made possible in part by HX 212's high speed – brought the battle to an end. Seven ships, the entire second column and two stragglers, were lost. No retribution was exacted from the enemy.

It was fortunate for A 3 that HX 212 was a fast convoy and that its routing carried it north, where the air gap narrowed like a funnel. These conditions contrived to keep the battle short and thereby reduced losses. Rough weather worked just as the Germans had hoped – indeed, better: it rendered the escort's only effective substitute for 271 radar, the human eye, equally ineffective. The performance of the numerically large group was, moreover, disappointing. This was attributed to the rather large size of the convoy and the bad weather, which aggravated the problems of keeping stations. The real disappointment, however, was the absence of continuous air support. Although HX 212 had received perhaps more than its share of effective land-based air cover while in the air gap, Lewis had reason to complain: HX 212 had been promised an auxiliary aircraft carrier as part of its escort.

The first auxiliary carrier to provide air escort for convoys had been HMS *Audacity*. Formerly the German steamer *Hannover*, she was intercepted in March 1940 off the Dominican Republic by the British cruiser *Dunedin* and was salvaged with help from *Assiniboine*. Converted to an auxiliary aircraft carrier, her success on the UK-Gibraltar route was immediate. But for *Audacity*'s untimely loss while escorting HG 76 in December 1941, she would have made a contribution to safe and timely arrival of shipping out of all proportion to her size and cost. By October 1942 there were only four escort carriers operational in the Atlantic. One, HMS *Avenger*, had already sailed with a Russian convoy, and the Admiralty hoped to use the others in the mid-Atlantic. Unfortunately, all of these vital escorts were swallowed up in the TORCH landings, and MOEF had to make do for another six months.[28] A similar fate awaited the first official support group of 1942, Escort Group 20. It managed to provide reinforcement for only SC 100, SC 102, and ONS 132 in September before being shifted to the TORCH operations.[29] Here again it was not until the spring of 1943 that the obvious – and intended – remedies to the problem of small, close screens in charge of huge convoys were finally applied with decisive results.

MOEF, and particularly the struggling Canadians, could well have used the resources swallowed up by TORCH. Although the battle in the mid-ocean was still going reasonably well by late October, German inability to concentrate effectively against a convoy had been as much the result of Allied good luck as it was of successful countermeasures. It was inevitable that that luck would change, as it did in the last week of October. BDienst was able to intercept and decrypt a series of signals pertaining to an eastbound convoy, and BdU received early confirmation of its position, course, and speed from *U522* on the twenty-ninth, while the convoy was still westward of Cape Race.

The convoy *U522* reported was SC 107, forty-two ships escorted by C 4.[30] The group was not unusual, although it had suffered perhaps more than its fair share of misfortune, such as the battle for ON 127. By the end of October several changes in composition had been necessary, in part because of the loss of *Ottawa*. Just prior to SC 107, *St Croix* went to refit, leaving *Restigouche* (HF/DF) the only destroyer in the group since the RCN was unable to provide even a temporary replacement. Lieutenant

Commander D.W. Piers, RCN, now became the Senior Officer. Although a very young man and a very junior officer, Piers had been SOE on seven previous occasions and had yet to lose a ship. He was also an experienced escort commander, having been on convoy duty since September 1939. There were two other personality changes in C 4 prior to SC 107. The captain of *Amherst* was relieved – forcibly – immediately after ON 127, and the commanding officer of *Arvida* had left as well, though for no untoward reason. In the absence of Dobson and Rutherford and in the presence of two new corvette captains and a new Senior Officer, C 4 was not a well-settled and -prepared group. Its two other escorts, *Celandine* and *Sherbrooke*, were unchanged, and the group received the assistance of two TORCH corvettes for the passage, *Algoma* and *Moose Jaw*. The convoy's rescue ship, *Stockport*, was fitted with HF/DF, although with only one destroyer Piers could not make good use of his two sets. Finally, only *Restigouche* and *Celandine* were fitted with 271 radar, but the latter's set was broken down for most of the battle (1–5 November).

At once HF/DF proved to be a vital element in C 4's valiant attempt to defend SC 107. From the first sighting report of the convoy on 29 October to the end of the battle seven days later, HF/DF operators in *Restigouche* and *Stockport* intercepted and plotted every U-boat HF transmission as the Germans sought to concentrate on the convoy. During the first day of the battle Piers was able to force the shadowers off, but his task was insurmountable. Group 'Veilchen,' of seventeen U-boats, lay across SC 107's path even before *U552*'s first sighting report. On the thirtieth BdU ordered Veilchen to close its ranks and move westwards in anticipation of the convoy. Despite a fortunate coincidence in which *U658*, the U-boat holding the position in the line through which SC 107 had to pass, was sunk by RCAF Hudson aircraft, Veilchen obtained firm contact with the convoy on 1 November.

The convoy's steadfast adherence to its original course and the German interception and decryption of its routing signal made BdU's work easy. From noon on 1 November until morning of the following day no less than twenty-five HF transmissions were DF'd by *Stockport* and *Restigouche*. With only one destroyer it was impossible to pursue all of these, but the early attempts by Veilchen to press home attacks were frustrated before sunset on the first. With many bearings still uninvestigated Piers could take little comfort from the apparent success of his early sweeps, or from the reports that two of his group were now without the use of their radar. Darkness brought the expected panoply of events.

During the night *U402* and *U522* attacked SC 107 repeatedly. The first blows fell on the starboard side around midnight, when *U402* penetrated through *Arvida*'s section of the screen (her radar was one of the sets out of service) and torpedoed *Empire Sunrise*. As the stricken freighter fell astern, *U381*, firing from a mere eighteen hundred yards, narrowly missed *Restigouche*. The destroyer was saved only by a routine course alteration as she came to the end of one leg of her zigzag just as the torpedoes reached her position. In the meantime, the torpedoing of the *Empire Sunrise* had the typical effect of opening the convoy to further attacks. Von Forstner, the intrepid commander of *U402*, was twice able to enter SC 107 through gaps left by *Celandine*'s detachment to screen *Stockport*, sinking three more ships and damaging a fourth, which, like *Empire Sunrise*, fell astern, only to be hit again and sunk by another member of Veilchen. *U402*'s score was nearly matched on the first night by *U522*, which also made two attacks – almost simultaneous with those of *U402* – sinking two ships and picking a third from the convoy (later sunk by *U521*).

The loss of eight ships in a single night was a heavy blow, but more of the same was yet to come. Heavy weather on the second nearly ended the battle, as only *U522* was able to maintain contact. However, the seas which threatened Veilchen's operations also prevented C 4 from taking effective action against the lone shadower. The escort, now reinforced by *Moose Jaw*, was also incapable of keeping *U522* from adding injury to insult by launching a successful daylight attack and adding a ninth victim to the score-sheet. After this and in deteriorating weather, contact with SC 107 was briefly lost. This lapse in enemy contact gave SC 107 and the escort, reinforced again before the end of the day by *Vanessa*, a British destroyer switched from HX 213 (B 2), a quiet second night.

But when visibility improved on 3 November, nine U-boats regained contact with SC 107, still clinging to its original line of advance. Once again many HF/DF bearings were obtained, and *Vanessa* and *Celandine* were able to locate and attack six of the shadowers as a result. Four U-boats received damage, but Veilchen hung on. At mid-day *U521* sank another ship in a skilful daylight attack. Piers later reported that escorts near the convoy were successful in driving off shadowers in the period after *U521*'s attack, but he was mistaken. The only promising actions took place well astern of SC 107 as *Celandine* endeavoured to rejoin. An evasive turn to port at dusk also failed to shake Veilchen and actually carried the convoy on to *U89*. The latter slipped into the convoy from ahead between *Vanessa* and *Moose Jaw*, two escorts unfamiliar with each

180 North Atlantic Run

other, and sank *Jeypore*, the commodore's ship. Once again the escort's search for the first assailant opened the convoy to further attacks, and *U132* was able to slip in unseen and sink three more ships.

By morning on the fourth the rescue ship *Stockport* and the USN tugs *Pessacus* and *Uncas*, which had also taken up this onerous task, were heavily laden with survivors (more than three hundred on *Stockport* alone). They were therefore detached to Iceland in company with a tanker under escort by *Arvida* and *Celandine* (both of which were short of fuel). The reduction of the escort was to be only temporary, as three powerful American ships, the destroyers *Leary* and *Schenck* and the cutter *Ingham*, were en route from Hvalfjordhur and joined later in the day. Before they arrived, however, *U89* claimed one last victim from SC 107 in a daylight attack. The following night passed quietly, and the next day the seven remaining shadowers were driven off by VLR aircraft from 120 Squadron, directed on occasion by HF/DF bearings supplied by *Restigouche*. In the face of growing pressure BdU finally abandoned operations against SC 107 on the sixth, well satisfied with the results.

SC 107 was the disaster which Murray had long feared, and reaction to it proved crucial to the navy's role in the next phase of the mid-ocean battle. In the meantime, two confrontations following in the wake of SC 107 must be mentioned. The precipitate departure of virtually all available U-boats to waters off North Africa after the TORCH landings in early November reduced the number operational in the air gap to nine. They were soon reinforced by six new submarines redirected from northern waters in order to take advantage of an anticipated reduction in escort strength as a result of TORCH (which, of course, had already occurred). Nine of these U-boats ('Kreuz-otter') located ONS 144 on 15 November as the convoy passed through the centre of their patrol line. The escort, B 6, was particularly weak since both of its destroyers were still under repair after ramming U-boats in the battle for SC 104. ONS 144 was escorted by five corvettes, the four Norwegian members of the group and HMS *Vervain*.[31] Fortunately, all were equipped with 271 radar, and the rescue ship *Perth* carried HF/DF. Despite the escort's small size (the convoy too was very small), its lack of destroyers, and five days of contact with the enemy, ONS 144 lost only six ships and the corvette *Montbretia* (*Potentilla* was credited after the war with sinking *U184* on 20 November). Attacking U-boats were kept at bay by B 6's efficient radar screen and by a reluctance on the part of the attackers to close to short range (seven torpedoes were known to have exploded at the end of their runs). Through it all the Senior Officer, Lieutenant Commander Monsen, RNorN, kept a tight rein on his escort, concentrating on maintaining the radar barrier.

The combination of good radar, aggressive and well co-ordinated team-work and good leadership drew plaudits from all concerned. Captain (D), Liverpool, considered it a 'magnificent performance' by B 6, marred only by the high incidence of lost underwater contacts, which 'was due to the small amount of training ... recently owing to quick turn 'rounds.' C-in-C, WA, and his staff concurred with this assessment. The captain of the Norwegian corvette *Rose* pin-pointed the key to B 6's triumph in his report. '*Rose* came from a long refit a couple of months ago [September],' he wrote, 'and I like to add that I do not believe all these good attacks could have been made without all the improvements we got during that refit.' It is also noteworthy that *Rose* had been given a full month to work up following her refit – more than even new commissions in the RCN could expect.

The battles of SC 107 and ONS 144 illustrate the significance of HF/DF and 271 radar. Unless the escort through its use of HF/DF drove the shadowers off, 271 radar was essential to the prevention of losses at night. P.M.S. Blackett, the famous British scientist who spent much of the war engaged in operational research on ASW, described the battles of late 1942 as unstable equilibriums.[32] Gaining and maintaining the initiative at the outset was crucial to success or failure for either side. It took only one successful attack to tip the equilibrium in favour of the pack, particularly if the escorts were ill prepared. But the corollary was also true. Teamwork and good leadership needed good equipment in order to obtain the necessary tactical information. As Blackett surmised, a well-equipped team could hold its own in the air gap in late 1942.

Without good tactical information as provided by HF/DF and 271 radar, Canadian escorts could not perform up to the standards set by B groups. RCN officers understood the Canadian dilemma and the frustration of fighting blind. To know with certainty that U-boats were lurking on the fringes of the convoy and yet lack the means to deal with them was galling. C groups desperately needed the means to strike at the enemy and wrest the initiative from him at the outset. A temporary solution to this problem was finally developed by Lieutenant Commander K.L. Dyer, captain of *Skeena*, in the fall of 1942. Dyer invented a new escort tactic called 'Major Hoople,' intended to expose U-boats as they closed to attack.[33] Basing his analysis on the intelligence available to him as the Senior Officer and in light of the prevailing moon, sea, and visibility conditions, Dyer estimated the likely moment when U-boats would begin their approach to firing positions. The escorts, having been exercised in the procedure and prepared by a cautionary signal, were then ordered to illuminate the threatened side of the convoy upon receipt of the code words 'Major Hoople.' Deciding when and if to order Major Hoople was a heady responsibility, for it might needlessly expose the convoy's position. Further, even with the pack pressing in, illuminants fired too early would allow the attackers sufficient time to regroup for another try at a much less predictable time. Too late and the night sky would be lit by pyrotechnics of an uglier kind.

Major Hoople was first used by C 3 in the defence of SC 109 in November 1942 and was considered successful, but words of praise for Dyer's new invention were laced with words of caution. As Admiral Brainard, CTF-24, commented, Dyer could have achieved the same results – if not better ones – with similar sweeps by escorts equipped with 271 radar. Eventually, the acquisition of modern equipment eliminated the need for such gambler's tactics as Major Hoople, though it was absorbed into the Atlantic Convoy Instructions as Operation 'Pineapple' and continued to find favour in poorly equipped WLEF groups of the RCN.[34]

At the time it was believed that use of Major Hoople and Dyer's conduct of C 3 had preserved SC 109 from serious attack, but it is now clear that BdU did not press its contact with the convoy.[35] Instead the quasi battle for SC 109 was the dénouement for the C groups. Early in the passage *Saguenay* was permanently disabled when, following a collision with a ship in the convoy, her stern was blown off by her own charges. The RCN was now down to four modern destroyers, but with *Assiniboine* still under repair there was not enough for even one per C group. Resignation to tactics such as Major Hoople, however innovative, illustrated graphically just how far the RCN had fallen behind the pace of the battle.

The RCN had begun to move on many crucial issues by the fall of 1942, partly as a result of its experiences with MOEF. Modern radar, HF/DF, and more destroyers were all essential to success in the mid-ocean. But the impetus for action on material matters and on broader issues – such as those alluded to by Captain Rowland – also came from events closer to home. U-boat attacks within sight of the Canadian coast, particularly those in July, when *U132* torpedoed three ships off Cape Chat, Quebec, brought strong public pressure on the RCN. The same was true of the second U-boat campaign in the Gulf of St Lawrence, later in the summer.[36] In late August and early September twelve ships and two escorts were lost in the gulf, most in the mouth of the St Lawrence River. Further losses followed in October, when two ships were sunk at anchor off Wabana, Newfoundland, and 137 people perished in the sinking of the Nova Scotia–to–Newfoundland ferry *Caribou*.

Not surprisingly, the navy stated in November that the Northwest Atlantic had finally become 'an anti-U-boat war zone of great strategic importance.'[37] After three long years of hostilities the war had finally washed up on the shores of Canada, and the RCN was engaged on all fronts. Now reconciled to fighting a major – and strategically important – campaign at home, the navy and the RCAF earnestly began to rationalize the command structure, establishments, duties, and support facilities for the 'new' theatre. The navy had actually begun its restructuring in September, when the first major changes in east-coast appointments in over a year were settled. Murray went to Halifax as COAC on 18 September, replacing Jones, who became the new vice-chief of the Naval Staff. The new FONF, Commodore H.E. Reid, formerly the VCNS, held his new post at his old rank. FONF was not yet subordinate to COAC, but Murray was now the ranking RCN officer on the Atlantic coast. Other changes in Captains (D) at Halifax and St John's followed before the end of the year. Mainguy went to Ottawa as the new director of Naval Personnel, simply trading posts with Captain H.T.W. Grant. Finally, Prentice was appointed Murray's Captain (D) at Halifax in December.

Apart from the resolution of interservice rivalries, the consolidation of Canadian naval and air forces in the Northwest Atlantic faced another serious impediment. Although Canadian services took domestic, political, and public heat for losses off Canada and Newfoundland, Canada ostensibly was still not responsible for operations beyond the three-mile territorial limit. That remained CTF-24's task. It is against this backdrop of a nascent battle for consolidation, improved efficiency, and operational control of the Northwest Atlantic that the crisis of Canada's mid-ocean battle was set.

The balanced outcome of C-group battles of the summer had not carried forth into the fall. From early September until mid-November four MOEF-escorted convoys were heavily attacked. Those protected by B 6, SC 104 and ONS 144, fared better than ON 127 and SC 107, escorted by C 4. Indeed, B 6 suffered the only B-group losses, thirteen ships, and claimed MOEF's only U-boat kills, two known, of the period. In contrast, twenty-two ships were lost in C 4's two battles alone, while C 2 and A 3 lost another six. Against this the Canadians and Americans could claim no U-boat kills. At the best of times this imbalanced score-sheet would be cause for concern. But by November 1942 the consequences of heavy shipping losses earlier in the year, with the added demands of TORCH, put enormous pressure on C-in-C, WA, to see ships safely through. With the mid-ocean slowly filling up with U-boats, this was increasingly harder to do. It was imperative, therefore, that MOEF escorts defend their convoys adequately, and better yet that they reduce the number of U-boats in the process.

7

The Reckoning

I appreciate the grand contribution of the Royal Canadian Navy
to the Battle of the Atlantic, but the expansion of the RCN has
created a training problem which must take some time to solve.
Churchill to Mackenzie King, 17 December 1942

The last months of 1942 and the first months of 1943 were the turning
point of the war. As Canadian escorts struggled to bring SC 107 safely
to port, the German campaign in Russia was finally checked at Stalingrad.
At the same time, in the far-away Solomon Islands, the battle to breach
– or to hold – the perimeter of Japan's new empire reached its peak on
Guadalcanal. In the west, too, the Axis tide was ebbing, beginning at El
Alamein in October. On 8 November Allied forces landed in Algeria and
Morocco in the largest amphibious assault yet undertaken. The success
of all these operations depended ultimately on secure communications.
Those in North Africa and, eventually, Western Europe depended in
particular on victory in the Battle of the Atlantic, a battle still undecided
but rapidly escalating to a climax.

Yet despite its importance, the crucial Atlantic battle could not quickly
be brought to a successful conclusion. The TORCH landings drew off much
needed escort forces, and indeed the impact of TORCH on the merchant
shipping situation was very nearly catastrophic. The mustering of sufficient escorts to cover the landings and the buildup stripped the South
Atlantic of small warships, forcing the temporary abandonment of the
Sierra Leone (SL) series of convoys. The elimination of convoy in the
Southern Atlantic gave the Germans their greatest-ever score in that theatre: twenty ships of 148,142 tons in October alone.[1] In addition, the
stoppage of the SL convoys forced all trade bound for Britain to take a

circuitous route through the interlocking convoy system of the Western Hemisphere. In consequence, the main North Atlantic convoys became, by November, the only link between Britain and the rest of the free world. Further, convoy routing remained imprecise. Although the Allies had had some success at slipping convoys around the edges of U-boat patrol lines, routing without the aid of special intelligence was never reliable – certainly, it could never be decisive. Moreover, with the increasing size of the U-boat fleet the likelihood of consistently effective routing grew increasingly remote. Although few MOEF sailors can have given these problems much thought, the onerous responsibility now placed on MOEF was painfully evident to senior British officials.

Reduction of trade links to a single heavily embattled route slowed the flow of imports into Britain. This in itself was cause for concern. But Britain remained an arsenal and base for overseas operations, the strategic centre of those offensive campaigns which most needed to be maintained. The TORCH landings added to this burden since the UK was the primary staging area for the assault and the buildup. Though much of this was to be shared by the Americans, who instituted direct U.S. – Mediterranean convoys in December, British planners underestimated the drain on resources that North African operations would become. The War Office predicted that an average of sixty-six ships per month would be needed to support TORCH during the first four months. In fact, the average proved to be 106 ships per month, with a proportionately higher outflow of war supplies. A sharp decline in imports as a result of dislocating shipping was therefore compounded by a higher than expected dispatch of goods – notably oil – to Africa. The effects of this accelerating disparity between supply and demand were felt in Britain by the end of November. British industry began to draw on reserves at a rate which threatened to curtail essential war work. A cut-back in industry spelt unemployment and possible domestic morale problems. It could also mean a curtailment of operations in other theatres. In addition to these problems there was a very real danger of a collapse in the morale of the merchant marine if the heavy losses in the North and South Atlantic and on the Russian route were not checked. Churchill was particularly distressed by the impact of losses on the morale of merchant seamen by November 1942 and made his concern known to the Admiralty in no uncertain terms. Thus, the outlook for Britain by early December was gloomy. The import and shipping crises were extremely delicate, immensely complex, and potentially disastrous. They would, moreover, clearly be compounded by any further losses at sea.[2]

A measure of growing British concern over the events in the mid-ocean was the convening of Churchill's special Anti–U-boat Warfare Committee on 4 November. The committee included senior political and service officials, technical specialists, and scientists. At its initial meeting the First Sea Lord revealed the sobering news that U-boats were being destroyed at only one-third their rate of construction. The second session, on the tenth, dealt at length with the shipping losses from submarines in the North Atlantic, which was now 'the real danger.' The committee continued to meet weekly over the next six months, until the crisis was past, and was instrumental in bringing together the forces needed to defeat U-boat packs in the Atlantic.[3]

A further indicator of British concern for the security of the North Atlantic trade lanes was the replacement of Admiral Sir Percy Noble by a new C-in-C, Western Approaches, Admiral Sir Max Horton, in mid-November. Noble's quiet and gentlemanly manner no longer suited the requirements of his office. His tireless efforts to improve all aspects of his command were, however, just about to bear fruit when Horton was appointed. Horton was a man of contrasting character. As an accomplished submariner Horton was believed to be a match for Dönitz in the increasingly complex, chess-like battles of evasion, interception, reinforcement, and counter-attack now current in the mid-ocean. In some measure Horton's appointment brought new earnestness to Western Approaches simply by virtue of the change in command, since a certain lethargy accumulates naturally in any organization over time. But it is also clear that Horton had instructions to sweep the old order out completely, a task greatly eased by his own business-like and very professional manner. Despite the remarkable differences in the characters of the two commanders and the evident effect Horton's dynamism had on Western Approaches, much of what the new C-in-C was able to achieve over the next few months was possible only because of the solid foundations left by Noble. Indeed, Horton reaped much of what Noble had so laboriously sown. But perhaps more importantly, Horton assumed command at a time when the insecurity of the North Atlantic threatened the Allied war effort and demanded the undivided attention of senior officers and officials on both sides of the Atlantic.

Not surprisingly, Horton's new broom soon caught up with the Canadians, but the brief interim was filled with major developments in the building crises in the mid-ocean and in the RCN. Persistent difficulties in providing effective air support for convoys in the Western Atlantic and recent German success in the western portion of the air gap (roughly

35–45° W) were unacceptable to the British. Indeed, the apparent inadequacy of Newfoundland-based air support was highlighted by the early interception of sc 107 and the resultant bitter and costly battle. The British preferred to handle this problem by basing Coastal Command squadrons on RCAF bases in Newfoundland. The Canadians welcomed the British offer of help yet insisted that air operations in the Western Atlantic should remain an RCAF responsibility.[4]

The British were not without alternatives. In fact, even as Churchill attempted to rectify the issue of air support, the RN acted to ensure increased surface support in the same area. On 18 November the Admiralty proposed to the USN (with a repeat to NSHQ) that a support force of destroyers be formed to assist convoys in the western portion of the air gap. The Admiralty recommended that all destroyers from WLEF be reassigned to this task, formed into groups of three, and shifted to St John's. The new Western Support Force (WSF) was to augment the regular MOEF group between WESTOMP and roughly 35° W. The reduction of WLEF strength such a transfer entailed was considered acceptable by the British in view of 'the much reduced threat to these convoys in the area west of Cape Race where provision of air cover is easier.'[5] There is no indication that either the Admiralty or the USN sought the opinion of the RCN with respect to the threat in WLEF's area, or indeed regarding the consequences of moving a large force of destroyers from a command in which the Canadians were responsible for the maintenance of groups and group strength.

The USN agreed to the Admiralty's proposal and five days later instructed C-in-C, Atlantic Fleet, to implement the scheme 'as soon as practicable.' Admiral Brainard, CTF-24, was given the go-ahead and on the twenty-fifth officially established WSF by withdrawing all the destroyers from WLEF and reassigning them to St John's. Although NSHQ was privy to the initial discussions of the scheme, Brainard acted without consulting the RCN. By virtue of his overall command of escort forces in the Western Atlantic he was entitled to take whatever action he deemed necessary. But the RCN was responsible for the availability of escorts and their maintenance at Halifax and St John's, both of which were affected by the transfer.

In the event WSF, despite its well-equipped ships, proved to be a dismal failure. The heavy weather of December and January, which kept U-boat activity low, also reduced WSF's aging destroyers to hulks. By Christmas Day only four of the twelve destroyers assigned to WSF were operational, and this figure was no better two months later. Indeed, by February

Brainard was forced to admit that the combination of breakdowns, bad weather, and short endurance of the ships made it a 'distinct probability that Western Support Force as constituted may not be able to meet projected commitments.'[6] In part the poor performance of WSF was due to immediate and successful RCN attempts to have its Town-class destroyers reassigned to WLEF. Despite this, the absence of twelve other destroyers from WLEF posed serious problems and led the RCN to request formally the release of six corvettes on loan to the USN's Commander Eastern Sea Frontier.[7] This marked the first attempt by the RCN to stem the flow of escorts away from its primary responsibilities or to have those lent for other duties repatriated to bolster Canadian escort groups. As such, the controversy over WSF heralded a new era of consolidation of the navy's war effort, consistent with the November declaration that the Northwest Atlantic was a major theatre of war.

The row over WSF was only one of a series of incidents in late 1942 which drove a wedge between the British and the Canadians and forced the RCN to act as the independent service it had always claimed to be. Concurrent with the WSF clash, a dispute arose between the RCN and the USN over the promulgation of intelligence from the Canadian shore-based DF network to RCN escorts operating in the Northwest Atlantic. The USN objected to this practice because dissemination of intelligence in the Western Atlantic was its responsibility. The British Admiralty Delegation in Washington sided with the Americans, putting the RCN in an impossible position. Compliance with the Allied request would mean that the Canadian navy would be unable to transmit useful and immediate tactical intelligence to RCN ships operating virtually within sight of Canada. With this a campaign to oust CTF-24 from his position and replace him with an RCN officer was begun by NSHQ.[8]

There were other incidents which fuelled the Canadians' desire to run their own show free from British and American tampering. Specifically, there was the performance of C groups, and British and American concern that something should be done about it. The tenor of private British reaction to Canadian convoy battles in late 1942 has already been traced in detail. In the case of SC 107 even official criticism of the conduct of the escort was strongly worded. Piers himself was not censured, but the British were upset that responsibility for a large convoy and the conduct of an unconsolidated escort group was entrusted to such a junior officer. Further, the senior American officer at Londonderry, Captain H.T. Thébaud, Commander Task Group 24.7 (CTG 24.7), made his long-standing views officially known. As one senior Admiralty staff officer minuted, 'CTG

24.7 again emphasises the need of the C groups for training which C-in-C, w.a., is continually advocating.'[9]

The problem, as the British perceived it, went beyond the escort of sc 107, and by the end of November Horton had the scientific data to make the British case. Horton's proof came in the form of a study prepared by P.M.S. Blackett, then engaged in operational research for Western Approaches. Blackett set out to quantify the intangibles of convoy battles and produced a report entitled 'A Quantitative Estimate of the Importance of Training, Leadership and Efficiency of Escort Groups in the Convoy Battles.'[10] His analysis was based on the relationship between losses and the number of days a convoy / escort group was shadowed by U-boats. The results were arranged in 'order of merit of efficiency' (no mention has been found of which groups were actually in which designation) and divided into two major classes. The first-class escorts were shown to have lost 20 ships over 181 U-boat days, and the second-class escorts 78 ships over 175 U-boat days. Had the second-class escorts been as efficient as those of the first class, Blackett concluded, actual losses would have been 38 ships. The disparity in escort-group quality therefore cost the Allies 60 ships. Moreover, Blackett considered this estimate conservative 'since the more efficient groups undoubtably succeed in reducing by tactical evasion the number of days U-boats are in contact with a convoy.'

In the absence of Blackett's working papers it is impossible to verify his data thoroughly, and the accuracy of the number of U-boat days that convoys were shadowed must be suspect since he did not have access to German records. In any event, the accuracy of Blackett's report and its conclusions is an academic problem, not one which concerned Horton and his staff to any great extent. Whether or not they knew that C groups were in fact being intercepted at almost twice the rate of B groups – the result of sheer luck – in the latter half of 1942 is unknown. This by itself increased the likelihood of heavier losses and pitched convoy battles. Nor is there any indication that Blackett considered the speed of convoys. The arrangements made with the usn in August 1941 whereby the rcn escorted slow convoys carried through into 1942. By the last half of the year the rcn still escorted the bulk of sc convoys (including A 3, seventeen in all, as compared to seven for the B groups). In exchange, C groups were given the higher proportion of nominally fast westbound convoys (nineteen for the C's and A 3, nine for the B groups), but again, the distinction between fast and slow westbound convoys was a debatable one. Slow convoys, it must be noted, spent 29 per cent longer a time at sea than fast ones, and this too had an effect on escort performance.

While these considerations leave Blackett's 'Quantitative Estimates' open to doubt now, in November 1942 his report provided some hard scientific evidence to show that low levels of efficiency were having a drastic effect on the loss rate of Allied shipping. It also confirmed the long-standing British belief in the imeptitude of the wartime RCN.

Not surprisingly, then, one of Horton's first official chores was to prepare a strongly worded memo for the Admiralty, stressing the need for proper training. The memo, submitted on 5 December, observed that recent heavy losses were due to lack of resourceful leadership, of training in groups, and of proper equipment. Horton warned that the heavy losses would continue until all three of these conditions were rectified. In the absence of any substantial reinforcement of his command, Horton's immediate objective was therefore to 'raise the standards of the less efficient groups to the level of the most efficient ones.'[11] Improved training was on the minds of the Anti–U-boat Warfare Committee as well; they had also agreed on 2 December that this offered the best chance for more U-boat kills.[12]

The RCN was not privy to C-in-C, WA's mounting concern for the efficiency of C groups, a concern which reached a peak in late November, when the reports of ON 127 and SC 107 arrived at Western Approaches almost simultaneously. Indeed, the whole budding affair posed a rather difficult problem for the British. Commonwealth navies – and nations – were stubbornly proud and enjoyed a curious independence from the parent service. For Commonwealth governments and services both, the war offered a unique opportunity to transform military and industrial effort into international recognition and prestige. For the larger nations this internal struggle was a bone of much contention, and it must frequently have seemed that Commonwealth countries found the Germans a convenience in a family battle. The truth of this condition is easy to overstate, but the condition itself is not so easy to understand. Suffice it to say that Dominion sensibilities were easily injured. They would suffer being ignored or even pandered to for the sake of the common cause. But criticism was received either as a reprimand from the imperial parent or as meddling in the affairs of a sovereign state. Disguising the pill which the RCN was now to swallow was no easy assignment.

In some measure the problem of Canadian efficiency, which by early December concerned the British government as well as naval authorities, was eased by Canadian admissions of difficulty. Shortly after the battle of SC 107 Nelles wrote to Vice-Admiral E.L.S. King, who was just stepping down as ACNS (Trade), discussing the looming crisis in the

Atlantic and the RCN's training problems. King's reply, sent on 6 December, advised Nelles of the import crisis, particularly the shortage of oil. He warned that measures of a 'fairly drastic' nature, directed at dealing with these crises, would soon be transmitted to the Canadians. However, the general mood of King's letter was conciliatory. 'The bedrock of the whole matter, of course,' King wrote, 'is the shortage of escorts.'[13] This much was true, and perhaps King was trying to soften the blow of the drastic measures of which he warned. But perhaps more important was King's comment that he had 'put forth a powerful plea to the 2nd Sea Lord for sympathetic consideration' of the RCN's training problems. He made no reference to MOEF, and the implication of King's letter is that the concern he shared with Nelles was for the fleet training program as a whole, not simply that of C groups.

Just what Nelles was able to glean from King's obscure warning remains a mystery. Yet by the first week of December Nelles had other reasons for feeling uneasy about the RCN commitment to MOEF. On 3 December NSHQ received, via the naval member of the Canadian Staff in Washington, a copy of a signal transmitted by Thébaud to Brainard (with repeats to C-in-C, WA, and COMINCH but not to any RCN authority) dealing with the efficiency of C groups. How Vice-Admiral V.G. Brodeur in Washington obtained the signal is unknown, though conceivably the leak was a contrived one. The signal was certainly blunt. 'British authorities and I are concerned,' Thébaud commented, 'with the current state of readiness of Canadian groups since Londonderry can fit only 2 types (271) [at a time].' The observation on equipment was not so remarkable as what followed when Thébaud returned to a persistent American theme: 'general maintenance and repairs are assuming such proportions that essential sea training is interfered with.' Thébaud also claimed that group cohesion suffered from 'constantly changing escort commanders and ships within the group.' The American captain wanted senior officers and escorts together as much as possible, especially during layovers in the UK, where Canadian groups were prone to dispersal.[14]

Thébaud's signal echoed many of Brainard's concerns from the previous September, and so the criticisms came as 'more of the same' to the RCN. None the less, NSHQ was disturbed by the Allies' lack of faith in C groups, their reasons for this, and the secrecy of the signal. The latter – that is, the failure to include NSHQ as an addressee – added fuel to the Canadian campaign to remove CTF-24 from the scene and get on with the consolidation of Canadian responsibilities. Claims of C-group inefficiency were serious enough for a copy of the signal to be forwarded to Commodore Reid at St John's for his comments. Reid replied that Thébaud's assertions were inflated. Changes to C groups were kept to a minimum and had been 'certainly no more frequent in RCN groups than in "B" groups.' Canadian groups were kept together whenever possible, including during layovers in the UK. Reid mentioned that dispersal of C groups upon arrival in Britain was only undertaken to secure repairs or to fit radar (which was a frequent occurence in late 1942). Although he did not mention it, it was also common practice for the RN membership of C groups to sail to ports other than Londonderry in order that British servicemen might be granted home leave. Reports from Operations, Personnel, and the chief of Naval Engineering and Construction all confirmed Reid's conclusion that the signal contained nothing new. On 7 December the VCNS, G.C. Jones, declared the matter 'clarified' and laid to rest.[15] The most lasting effect of the intercepted message was to arouse RCN suspicion of British and American motives and to firm Canadian resolve to secure a permanent presence for the RCN in the North Atlantic by putting an RCN officer in CTF-24's stead.

As Brainard's contentions had been three months before, Thébaud's were easily dismissed by the RCN as ill founded. Indeed, short of recalling all of the escorts on loan to the RN and USN – a process just beginning – the navy had taken what action it could on matters of efficiency in light of existing operational commitments and the limits of Canadian resources. The most pressing need, aside from modern equipment, was for a large infusion of escort destroyers capable of working in the mid-ocean. Further, with the dispatch of RN destroyers to WSF, WLEF was now seriously short of both escorts in general and destroyers in particular. Although the British were unconcerned about the strength of WLEF groups and tended to think of WLEF as comparable to their own totally inshore Eastern LEF, which parted with convoys within sight of Ireland, the RCN was painfully aware that the stretch between New York and Newfoundland was open water all the way. The threat to convoys while under WLEF protection was substantial, if for no other reason than that WLEF groups were much too small to effect any defence. The British were correct in their assessment that any protracted threat to the convoy lanes west of Cape Race could be handled by superior local air power. But this was cold comfort to officers who preferred to prevent the development of any serious U-boat campaign through effective initial defence. The weakness of WLEF, its potential for exploitation by the enemy, and the RCN's desire to secure this theatre would linger on through 1943.

The combined shortfalls of destroyers in MOEF and WLEF amounted to fourteen ships, seven for each. The only possible source of such a large number on short notice was Britain. On 5 December a formal request was therefore made of the British government by the Canadian prime minister for the sale of fourteen destroyers to Canada, to be manned by and commissioned into the RCN.[16] This in itself was further admission of Canadian difficulties. The reaction of the British was much delayed and eventually brought their opinion of Canadian expansion into sharp focus.

Almost as if to prove Horton's point about the importance of training, leadership, equipment, and air support, a major battle developed in the second week of December which demonstrated the successful application of all these elements. The convoy HX 217, escorted by the ubiquitous B 6 (*Fame*, with Commander Heathcote as Senior Officer, the Polish destroyer *Burza*, the corvettes *Eglantine*, *Potentilla*, *Rose*, and *Vervain* [RN], and initially *Montgomery* of Western Support Force, was located on 6 December by *U524*, which was monitoring the escort's radio-telephone traffic.[17] Four U-boats were drawn on to HX 217 by late afternoon but were distracted after dark by a ruse staged by *Montgomery*, who fired starshell well away from the convoy. The next day HX 217 was in the middle of the air gap with five U-boats in contact, but Liberator H, of 120 Squadron, operating eight hundred miles from her Icelandic base, drove them all off. Despite the aircraft's efforts, by dusk five U-boats were back in touch with the convoy. Attacks during the night were repeatedly detected by B 6's radar and asdic (used as hydrophones). One ship, *Empire Spencer* (101), bound for the Mersey with a cargo of aviation gas, was sunk. A relay of Liberators arrived at dawn, again driving off the shadowing U-boats but not totally breaking German contact with the convoy. Further attempts to press home attacks during the night of 8–9 December were largely frustrated by the Norwegian corvettes, although *U553* sent the *Charles L.D.* (33) to the bottom with all hands.

Even though by 9 December HX 217 was well within range of other shore-based aircraft, bad weather prevented air support. It also reduced the effectiveness of asdic and radar, and U-boats were able to work ahead of the convoy. On the tenth Heathcote reported heavy attacks all through the night, but B 6 intercepted every attempt to penetrate the screen. Massive air support arrived on the tenth, including six Hudsons of 269 Squadron, Fortresses from 220 Squadron, and USN Catalinas. None the less, B 6 had one busy night left, and it was not until late on the eleventh that BdU finally abandoned the chase.

The Germans later noted that the escort's pursuit of U-boat contacts was not outstanding, but they missed the whole point of Heathcote's superb defence of HX 217. As the Admiralty assessment observed, '*Fame* was the master.' Intelligence provided by the shipborne HF/DF sets allowed Heathcote to anticipate attacks and to adjust his screen accordingly, while the 271 radars of B 6 provided a tight barrier. The escort also undertook no prolonged pursuit of U-boat contacts, contenting itself with putting the enemy down and returning to the convoy. It was, perhaps, the best example of *defence* of a convoy in the entire war. The tale might have been different had Liberator H not disrupted the pack on 7 December as it assembled around HX 217 in the middle of the air gap, or the 'Black Pit.' Certainly, air power was instrumental in limiting German success and accounted for the only U-boat kill of the operation, *U611* on the eleventh. The speed of the convoy and its routing were also crucial, since HX 217 was able to transit the air gap in about thirty-six hours.

This latest triumph of B 6 was soon to be set against yet another Canadian disaster. In the meantime, by the second week in December Canadian problems and Anglo-American suggestions for improving the oil situation were clear to Churchill and the Admiralty. The British prime minister therefore instructed the Admiralty to prepare proposals for dealing with the issue of RCN escorts in MOEF and also with the import crisis. According to Vice-Admiral E.L.S. King's letter to Nelles, the Naval Staff already had some idea of how it wanted to handle both, but producing an acceptable final draft took several days. Thus it was not until 15 December that A.V. Alexander, First Lord of the Admiralty, placed the RN's proposals before Churchill.

Of primary concern was the oil crisis. Alexander's memo advised that the current disparity between usage and imports was 250,000 tons per month. If the erosion of reserves was not immediately arrested, stocks of all petroleum products would be down to twelve weeks' normal expenditure by the end of February. This, the First Lord noted, would curtail all movement of oil-fired ships – including those of the RN. Britain was now feeling the pinch of heavy tanker losses earlier in the year. Given the inability of the Admiralty or the Ministry of War Transport to increase the number of tankers allocated to Britain's oil trade, Alexander proposed to make more efficient use of those available. He recommended the establishment of direct convoy links between Britain and the Dutch West Indies. Sailing tankers directly from Aruba instead of sending them through the interlocking convoy system of the Western Hemisphere would permit each ship to make five round trips per year instead of the four then being made. Convoys of forty tankers sailing at twenty-day intervals were expected to provide the UK with an additional 100,000 tons of fuel per month, still less than half of the current shortfall but clearly a start. The escorts needed for these long-range convoys could be obtained from among the sloops of Western Approaches Command then assigned to TORCH. Their place in the UK-to-Gibraltar convoys would be taken by escorts drawn from MOEF. The cycle of North Atlantic convoys could be opened from eight to ten days to allow for the reduction of MOEF groups.

Not surprisingly, the four MOEF groups which Alexander proposed to have transferred to the Eastern Atlantic were Canadian, or largely so. The British considered A 3 part of the efficiency problem as well but did not include the British escorts interspersed among the C groups. As a result, the four groups which Alexander wanted transferred were A 3 and three C groups, constituting the entire Canadian contribution to MOEF. The British escorts of Canadian formations were to be retained in MOEF and reformed into a new group, a plan hardly consistent with the aims of Horton's campaign for group permanence. Conceivably the British felt the situation warranted such major alterations. Certainly Alexander did not mince words when dealing with the reasons for this transfer. 'Recent heavy losses,' the memo read, 'in trans-Atlantic convoys have shown that the Canadian and American groups are not nearly so well trained ... as British groups.' It was decided, therefore, to run MOEF with eight B groups while the Canadians and Americans were transferred from CTF-24 to C-in-C, WA, to be 'given really thorough training.' Some of the RCN corvettes already assigned to TORCH were to be used to bolster the C groups. Further, the availability of continuous air cover on the UK-Gibraltar route would, in the early stages of the training program, 'offset the inexperience of the Canadian groups.' The replacement of faster sloops with MOEF escorts necessitated a two-knot reduction in the speed of TORCH convoys. 'In view, however, of the paramount importance of bringing the Canadian groups up to standard,' the memo concluded, 'it is considered that this disadvantage should be accepted.'[18]

The British were clearly concerned about the security of any RCN-escorted convoy. This was perhaps justified, though the Canadians could hardly be described as inexperienced. The wording of the last sentence quoted suggests a sense of urgency which may have stemmed from the suspicion that the RCN would not readily agree to any protracted withdrawal from MOEF, as proved to be the case. In any event, Churchill accepted Alexander's proposals, and the British turned immediately to the matter of obtaining American support for the establishment of a new convoy route, the reallocation of escorts, and the diversion of tankers. Copies of Churchill's signals to Roosevelt outlining the proposals and a request for Canadian compliance were sent to Mackenzie King late in the day on 17 December – King's birthday. Churchill's telegram summarized the proposals as set forth by Alexander and then tactfully, but firmly, put forth the reasons for the British request for the withdrawal of the RCN from MOEF:

A careful analysis of attacks on our transatlantic convoys has clearly shown that in those cases where heavy losses have occurred lack of training of the escorts, both individually and as a team, has largely been responsible for these disasters.

I appreciate the grand contribution of the Royal Canadian Navy to the Battle of the Atlantic, but the expansion of the RCN has created a training problem which must take some time to solve.[19]

The shortage of escorts may have been a common problem, but its effects were not uniformly felt. The strength of British reaction to the navy's too-rapid expansion is best exemplified by their hesitant response to the Canadian request for destroyers. Officials in the British prime minister's office were engaged in drafting a reply to Mackenzie King's telegram of 5 December when a copy of Alexander's proposals was passed to them. Having considered the nature of Churchill's 17 December telegram to the Canadian prime minister and in view of the Canadian government's request for a large number of destroyers, the PMO official dealing with the matter confessed to an Admiralty colleague that it 'would be difficult to send an interim reply without risk of prejudicing the Canadian reply on the tanker escorts or explaining the relation of the two questions.'[20] For the time being it was better to say nothing, which was precisely what the PMO did. Clearly, a large addition to the RCN would only have compounded the problem as the British saw it.

British concern for Canadian reaction was justified. Although outwardly the Naval Staff received the proposals with good grace, Nelles at least greeted the news with shock and disbelief, a mood which soon changed to anger – as one RN officer at NSHQ discovered, much to his chagrin. Captain E.S. Brand, RN, the director of Trade at Ottawa, had many contacts within his own service at home. Brand felt he might be able to mitigate the British proposals and strode bravely into Nelles's office to offer his services. There he was informed in no uncertain terms to 'keep to hell out of it!' Discretion being the better part of valour, Brand withdrew to do what he could.[21]

Nelles's resentment was understandable. Although the RCN had responded unreservedly to every demand, notably by operating the very important WLEF, Canadian interest remained focused on the mid-Atlantic: on convoy battles and U-boat packs. The RCN had been part of mid-ocean A/S escort since its inception. Now after stretching and scrimping for the common cause the Canadians were being asked to remove their escorts from the decisive theatre of the Battle of the Atlantic because the British believed they were inefficient. Moreover, the blame for recent convoy disasters was being laid squarely on the RCN. This was not in the spirit of load sharing that NSHQ had come to expect.

The charge that heavy losses in the mid-ocean were mainly due to poor training in Canadian escorts and groups was ill received at NSHQ. Nelles sought to challenge the charge, and soon various reports relating to the readiness of the RCN were circulated in Ottawa. These included a report on the extent of fitting of modern radars to Canadian escorts; an analysis of experience in terms of years of service in comparable RCN and RN escorts; a study of the feasibility of the Admiralty's proposed changes to convoy and escort arrangements; a summary of the impact of the proposals on the Canadian case for an independent RCN command in the Northwest Atlantic; and an assessment of the validity of the Admiralty's claim that training was a significant factor in recent losses.[22] While NSHQ prepared its case against the British proposals, the matter was brought before the War Committee of the Canadian cabinet, which had to approve such large-scale transfers. The committee discussed the issue on 24 December but deferred it for further study.[23]

One of the most important of the memos submitted dealt with the Admiralty's theory about the role of training compared to that of equipment. The memo, passed to Nelles by his director of Operations, Captain H.N. Lay, was actually the work of Lieutenant Commander P.M. Bliss, the staff officer, A/S. Bliss was another RN officer on loan to the RCN and a veteran of the RN's A/S establishment, HMS *Osprey*. What made his opinion doubly important was that he had just recently been posted to NSHQ from St John's, where he had served as port A/S officer. In the latter post Bliss had worked constantly with MOEF escorts, and even with Prentice's ill-fated training group. His memo noted that the RCN had always recognized the need for more and better training, as evidenced by the establishment of Prentice's group in April 1942. Unfortunately, Bliss observed, increased operational commitments had wrought havoc with training schemes in Newfoundland. Despite this, C groups had had access to training facilities in Londonderry for nearly a year, and Bliss considered it 'ridiculous to say that lack of training alone can account for these losses.' Rather, the new SO (A/S) believed, the difference between success and failure in the mid-ocean lay with equipment. 'I cannot help feeling,' Bliss wrote, 'that when C. groups are brought up technically to B groups a very great increase in efficiency will result without reference whatever to training and experience.'[24]

Bliss's qualifications gave weight to his opinion, particularly since they offered a plausible response to the Admiralty's allegations. But Nelles also solicited views from east-coast commanders. Reid in St John's felt that losses were due to weak destroyer complements in C groups as well as to outdated equipment. He did admit, however, that poor training played a role in the poor showing of the RCN. So too did 'recent extensive changes in so of groups,' which was something of a switch from his contention just two weeks earlier that these changes were not exceptional. Finally, it is significant that Reid warned of the erosion of Canada's position in Newfoundland – and Reid's new command – if the transfer went ahead. Worse still, Reid commented with some alarm, 'we may lose control of our own ships for good' as a result.[25]

Murray's comments on the matter expressed a great deal more confidence and yield considerable insight into the character of the man himself. Murray was 'loath to believe that convoys escorted by C groups have fared worse than those convoyed by B or A groups.' To Murray the Admiralty's disappointment in the state of Canadian training seemed odd, given that the Canadian groups 'have not been without success in destruction of submarines' – which was not the issue. Murray went on to shed himself of all responsibility for the apparent poor performance of C groups. Like Reid, Murray cited weak destroyer complements as a cause of Canadian problems. He noted that this was not an RCN failing but reflected the unreliability of the RN destroyers assigned to Canadian groups. Since September 1941, the reliability of RN destroyers 'has left much to be desired and their breakdowns cannot be ascribed to any lack of Canadian repair facilities.' As for Canadian maintenance standards and the effect of this on group permanence, Murray laid the blame squarely on NSHQ. 'Owing to the small numbers available for each group and necessary reshuffling on each occasion of weather damage,' permanence of composition was unattainable. While the latter was a contributory factor, Murray reiterated his contention that the lack of destroyers for high-speed sweeps was the nub of the issue and that this shortcoming was due to the 'failure of the RN destroyers nominally attached.' As for the ability of the RN to manage the task alone, with only eight groups 'which can be relied upon not to break down,' Murray felt that the RN should be given the opportunity.[26]

From someone who had continually been at loggerheads with NSHQ over the issue of fleet efficiency, Murray's I-told-you-so attitude was understandable. But he was not yet finished with NSHQ. By December 1942 he was once again united with Chummy Prentice, now in Halifax as Captain (D). Obviously prompted by the fierce storm raging in Ottawa over having been brought to book by the Admiralty, Prentice submitted a memo outlining yet another training scheme to Murray on 23 December. As with the previous attempts, this latest also dealt with the need for group training. 'Even ships with considerable experience in convoy work,' Prentice wrote, 'are often extremely difficult to handle as a group.'[27] Once again Murray endorsed Prentice's plans and sent them off with a covering letter. Clearly not willing to miss an opportunity to needle NSHQ over its handling of expansion, Murray noted perfunctorily that 'progressive training of new construction and of other ships after major changes in complement' had been in progress at Halifax before the receipt of the Admiralty's proposals. The nest of pirates Murray had complained of a year before was now working for him.[28]

Murray's prophecy that the reputation of the RCN in this war would rest with mid-ocean operations had come to pass. The Naval Staff in Ottawa was now scrambling to demonstrate that the RCN had the ability to assume responsibility for the Northwest Atlantic. Murray's view from Halifax was not as jaundiced as it might have been. He evidently decided that the time for recrimination was past, that the requirement now was for professional solidarity to overcome the embarrassment in which the navy found itself.

Captain H.N. Lay, the director of Operations, was in Halifax to discuss the issue of command relations in the Northwest Atlantic (among other things) when news of the British proposals broke. Lay reported that Murray fully supported the campaign to oust Brainard. However, a prerequisite of independence was capability. As Lay reported, the secret to successful ASW was good initial and ongoing training and the provision of modern equipment. Lay recommended that the RCN adopt a 'very hard and fast' rule that no ship should go to sea unless thoroughly trained. Further, he supported the idea of a training group, which he recommended be put 'into effect forthwith and without any regard to the reaction of the Admiralty or the USN ... This,' Lay confided to his CNS, 'is probably our best answer to the Admiralty's criticism of badly trained Canadian ships and escort groups, which is undoubtedly true.'[29]

By Christmas Eve 1942 the RCN's position on the Admiralty's proposals and the reasons for Canadian convoy disasters was still unclear. The plausibility of the new arrangements for MOEF was accepted; it could function satisfactorily with only eight groups. But sorting out the apparently conflicting views of Bliss and Lay, and the obvious truths of both, was not easy. For the moment, however, the Canadians had time to organize their case, for it was the Americans who took exception to the new escort and oil arrangements proposed by the British.

The Americans had been aware of the British desire to find escorts for tanker convoys since the end of November[30] and so were well prepared for Alexander's proposals when they finally arrived. In his initial response Roosevelt questioned the need for special convoys, and even the existence of an oil crisis in Britain. Indeed, the president pointed out that the UK enjoyed much greater reserves of petroleum than 'other combatant areas' such as Australia, Greenland, Noumea, and even Newfoundland.[31] His absurd comparison of Britain with other advanced bases of operations may have been valid from the American perspective, but it did nothing to enhance Anglo-American relations. Churchill, in one of his now-famous 'pray' memos, despaired of this American slight to what he termed 'the heart of the whole resistance to the enemy.'[32]

Quite apart from the issue of oil, Admiral King was not prepared to relinquish his 'partial control' over the C groups and allow the Admiralty a free hand in disposing of them until the whole issue of escort employment had been thoroughly discussed.[33] The Admiralty had already allowed for this contingency. Horton's chief of staff, Commodore Jack Mansfield, a clear thinker with a strong personality and cheerful disposition, was due to arrive in Washington on Christmas Day to present the British case. The Admiralty informed NSHQ of this and asked if Mansfield should visit Ottawa too. Nelles responded several days later – presumably after the uproar at NSHQ had subsided – accepting the offer. The knowledge that a senior British officer was being sent to Washington to discuss the operational deployment of the RCN was injury enough, but to have Ottawa added to his itinerary almost as an afterthought can have done little to mollify RCN suspicions and resentment. It was, moreover, typical of British handling of the kindergarten.[34]

Before Mansfield could visit Ottawa, he had to reach an agreement with the Americans. The ultimate irony, of the RN and the USN bargaining over the operational deployment of the RCN, had come to pass. It was this embarrassing circumstance which the RCN was now resolved to rectify, and during the ensuing conference in Washington (convened to discuss the matter) the case for and of Canadian independence was made forcefully. RCN representatives to the three-day event (29–31 December) included Rear Admiral Brodeur, the naval member of the Canadian Staff in Washington, Commander J.G. Mackinley, RCNVR, NSHQ's liaison officer with the USN's trade sections, and the director of Plans of the RCN, Captain H.G. DeWolf. DeWolf, who was described by a colleague as a 'remarkable guy' with a clear mind and an instinctive knowledge of what was right, was the only non-Washington-based RCN officer present.[35] British representatives included Mansfield and three officers from the British Admiralty Delegation in Washington, among them Rear Admiral Patterson, head of the BAD. The large USN delegation was led by Rear Admiral P.N.L. Bellinger of Admiral King's staff, who chaired the conference, and included Brainard, who flew in from Argentia, four other USN admirals, and nine non-flag-rank officers.

The conference opened with an address by Admiral Bellinger, who briefed the officers on the telegrams exchanged by Roosevelt and Churchill. Mansfield then presented the British position, and there followed a general discussion of the proposed changes. In the afternoon the conference broke down into two subcommittees, one to assess the escort situation and the other to deal with trade matters. Commander Mackinley took his seat in the latter. Brodeur, the RCN's most senior representative, was not assigned to either (with the exception of Brainard, none of the officers involved in the detailed discussion was of flag rank). The RCN member of the escort subcommittee, Captain DeWolf, was not yet in attendance, owing to a snowstorm which delayed his train. DeWolf missed the whole first day of the conference, and discussion in the escort subcommittee proceeded without Canadian input.

The escort committee noted the absence of an RCN member – went, in fact, to great pains to emphasize that absence in its report. No record of the discussions of either committee was made, only of their recommendations. The escort subcommittee recommended that the four C groups of MOEF be transferred in accordance with the British proposals. It appears that A 3 at no time entered into the deliberations, although it had been included in the original British scheme. Why the lone American group disappeared from the scene is unknown. Conceivably the USN simply said no, or the RN was reluctant to confront the Americans, or the British decided to maintain what permanence there was in existing groups. In any event, the British contention of poor training in A 3 was very weak. Its senior officers, Heineman and Lewis, had put enormous effort into co-ordinating A 3's operations and ensuring that individual escorts were well prepared as well. Despite this, its record was almost identical to those of the most blooded of Canadian groups, C 1 and C 4. So too was its equipment. Whatever the case made for A 3 in Washington, its subsequent failure to defend ONS 166 and the heavy losses which resulted from this battle in February 1943 would substantiate Bliss's contention that equipment was a vital factor. But in December 1942 it was decided that the token American force would remain with MOEF. The recommendation that the four C groups would go intact was at least in keeping with the stated official objectives of the transfer and patently less victimizing of the RCN.

DeWolf arrived the next day, as the conference met to hear and discuss the recommendations of the subcommittees. His belated presence was noted, and the chairman made it clear to DeWolf that all papers relating to the previous day's sessions were readily available to him. The conference then turned to the 'item in which the RCN is most directly interested,' the report of the escort committee. Item two, which recommended the transfer, was read, after which DeWolf presented the RCN's views. He told those assembled that the first consideration they must all bear in mind was that only the Canadian government had the authority to make transfers on the scale being discussed. Before the government would agree to such a redisposition, it would require assurance 'that the groups in question would in due course return to the North Atlantic convoys, which were looked upon as a permanent and principal Canadian commitment.' DeWolf also advised that no permanent dispersal of Canadian forces could be recommended until both WLEF and MOEF were brought up to strength. Despite the political tone of his remarks, DeWolf's comments amounted to a qualified acceptance of the proposals. Mansfield then spoke to DeWolf's remarks, saying that the transfer was only part of a concerted training drive in Western Approaches. 'The Canadian Groups were selected to get first benefit,' Mansfield said, coating the pill somewhat, 'as they were on the whole less experienced than British Groups.' The transfer had also been recommended, Mansfield explained, 'because the next few months in the North Atlantic will, under the proposed cycle, be a critical period and will severely test the eight groups remaining.'[36]

As a reason for removing the C groups of MOEF, Mansfield's last is something of a riddle. The cycle was only going to be tight and presumably a severe test *because* MOEF was being reduced to eight groups, a situation which would not have developed if the Canadians had been left in. It is only possible to speculate on what motives, other than the desire to see that C groups were properly trained – and equipped, as will be evident in the next chapter – were behind the proposal to eliminate *both* the Americans *and* the Canadians from MOEF. The pending crisis in the mid-ocean clearly influenced the hopes and fears of Horton, the Admiralty, and other senior officers. They knew only too well that the battle in the mid-ocean was building to a climax at a time when the decisive potential of 'special intelligence' was unavailable to convoy routing authorities. It is also noteworthy that by transferring A 3 and the C groups out of MOEF and leaving only B groups, Horton would have been able to extend his de facto control as far west as Newfoundland, a long-standing British objective. Under the terms of the proposals put forth by Alexander, that could have been effected without forcing the issue of CTF-24's role or even outwardly embarrassing his position. The time-limit on the transfer agreed to by Mansfield would seem to disqualify these motives. However, NSHQ was already putting heavy pressure on the USN to pull CTF-24 out. All the RN needed to do was encourage a settlement of command relations in the Northwestern Atlantic – to everyone's benefit – and make sure that the primacy of its claim to operations east of WESTOMP was recognized.

The offer of a time-limit to the transfer was all that the RCN needed to sell the idea to the cabinet. Mansfield believed that a period of three to four months would be enough to complete the retraining of the groups. He also agreed, after prompting by Brodeur, that the limiting of their use to the UK-Gibraltar route and the time-limit could be made part of any agreement. DeWolf then advised the conference that the recommendation of the escort subcommittee should stand.

Having accepted that the four C groups should be withdrawn from MOEF, DeWolf then had to convince his colleagues in Ottawa. Fortunately for the very able director of Plans, this proved no crisis of conscience. His memo to Nelles on the feasibility of the Admiralty's proposals, submitted a week before the Washington conference, recommended that the RN scheme be fully supported by the RCN. 'The war is in a crucial stage,' DeWolf wrote; 'unless we have a better solution to offer we should place no obstacle in the way of the one proposed.'[37]

While others admitted that there were definitely serious problems, DeWolf was the only senior officer to advocate acceptance in the days immediately following receipt of the Admiralty proposals. By Christmas Nelles, too, may have been reconciled to the transfer, but by the time DeWolf left for Washington the CNS was preoccupied by the larger implications of the removal of Canadian forces from MOEF and their transfer to the RN. His thoughts were outlined in a memo prepared for the minister in the week between Christmas and New Year, which Nelles then withheld pending DeWolf's return from Washington. It is clear that the matter of efficiency in MOEF had quickly become a question of RCN operational control over its own ships and thereby, of service independence. The first two pages of Nelles's memo dealt solely with the mechanics of the transfer and the possible repercussions of having the main portion of the fleet serving overseas under RN command (which of course is what the RCN had striven to achieve in the early days of the war). The Admiralty proposals Nelles viewed as part of a larger conspiracy, as 'the third, but most serious attempt on the part of the Admiralty to get operational control of our ships.' Only at the very bottom of page two did Nelles address the issue of efficiency as it was affected by training. The CNS danced around this problem without making any concrete statement. Indeed, he even managed to turn Canadian redeployment to the UK-Gibraltar route into a Canadian victory. 'The ships will have the same, or greater submarine menace,' Nelles wrote, 'plus that from enemy air forces. Thus it may be a hotter spot.' Presumably this reading of the war was intended for ministerial consumption and was not a reflection of Nelles's understanding of operational conditions in the two theatres. Nelles concluded with a long quote from Vice-Admiral E.L.S. King's letter of 6 December that stressed the general shortage of escorts as the root of all current troubles.[38]

For Nelles at least, the issue of fleet efficiency had quickly become enmeshed in the struggle for an independent Canadian presence in the Northwest Atlantic. As a result, his first memo to Macdonald on the situation of the Canadians in MOEF was less than honest. If Nelles ever seriously believed that the Eastern Atlantic was more dangerous than the mid-ocean, he was soon given stark evidence to the contrary. Even as he prepared the first memo to Macdonald, C 1 was engaged in the last of a long string of Canadian convoy disasters stretching back to September 1941. This last battle demonstrated all that was wrong – allegedly or otherwise – with C groups in late 1942. C 1 had undergone a number of changes since its previous major battle around SC 94 in August. Despite this a steady cadre had, until very recently, formed the backbone of the group, the corvettes *Battleford*, *Chambly*, *Chilliwack*, *Eyebright*, and *Napanee*. *Chambly* finally went to refit in late November, and *Eyebright* was forced to return to St John's in early December, while on passage with SC 110, because of defects. Thus as C 1 assembled in Londonderry in advance of ONS 154, two of its stalwarts were absent. The nominal strength of the group remained up to standard, however, since *Kenogami* and *Shediac* had been added from WLEF in November. The most serious aspects of the group's development were the frequent changes in senior officers and problems with destroyers. With the temporary loss of *Assiniboine* in August, Stubbs was no longer in charge. The post of SOE was filled for one convoy (ONS 123) by the CO of HMS *Broke* before Prentice was called into service for two months. When Lieutenant Commander Guy Windeyer, the former CO of the corvette *Wetaskiwin*, took command of the destroyer *St Laurent* (which completed refit at the end of September), Prentice went to Halifax as Murray's Captain (D), and Windeyer took over C 1. The shortage of suitable officers and suitable ships had delayed the reappointment of a permanent Senior Officer for the group. Windeyer was by no means inexperienced, but the passage to the UK with SC 110 in early December was the first in his new post.

Upon its arrival in the UK following SC 110, C 1 immediately dispersed, as the Canadian corvettes went to fit the last portions of their 271 radars and *St Laurent* went to have her HF/DF installed. The group gradually reassembled in Lough Foyle in time to undertake a scheduled group exercise and in plenty of time for Windeyer to convene a pre-sailing conference to familiarize his captains with his intentions. The training exercise was subsequently cancelled when the submarine broke down and the weather turned foul. Despite this additional time to hand, Windeyer did not call his officers together. The reason given in his report of proceedings for not assembling C 1's captains – that there were no boats available other than those carried by the escorts themselves – was not surprisingly found to be totally inadequate.

C 1 (*St Laurent, Battleford, Chilliwack, Kenogami, Napanee*, and *Shediac*) sailed to join ONS 154 on 19 December.[39] *St Laurent* departed without her HF/DF officer, which was not as serious as it might have been, since her set was not calibrated before sailing. Far more serious for the outcome of the forthcoming battle was the absence of C 1's second destroyer, HMS *Burwell*. She missed sailing with ONS 154 owing to defects which could not be repaired during the short layover. The lack of a second destroyer meant that offensive sweeps, made possible by the HF/DF of the rescue ship *Toward* and the special-service ship HMS *Fidelity*, fell to a lone destroyer. As the Senior Officer's ship and the only fast escort available to C 1, *St Laurent* had to use her fuel judiciously. Finally, what bearings Windeyer did receive from *Toward* were not considered fully trustworthy because she was not equipped with gyro-compasses.

The defence of ONS 154 was complicated by other factors, none of which reflected on the RCN or its officers. Although the group was completely outfitted with 271 radar, operators were still unfamiliar with the equipment. In addition, the routing of ONS 154 left more than a little to be desired. To give the escorts and merchantmen a break from the vile weather of high latitudes and to permit ships bound for the South Atlantic to break off earlier, ONS 154 was directed towards the Azores. As a result, the convoy crossed the air gap at the widest possible point. Progress was also delayed by the tail-end of a hurricane. Further, British cryptanalysts had only just broken the German's Atlantic cipher for U-boats as C 1 sailed, and it was some time before all the U-boats could be accurately plotted. For ONS 154 the imprecise intelligence of the black-out days still obtained. Its routing carried the convoy just to the south of two U-boat packs, 'Spitz' and 'Ungestüm' – twenty U-boats in all – but not far enough to avoid detection. On 26 December the southern tip of Spitz reported ONS 154, and BdU ordered the U-boats to attack.

Until 28 December the battle for ONS 154 was a draw, although no one believed so at the time. On the night of the twenty-sixth, in poor visibility, drizzle, and heavy spray, U356 made two passes through the convoy, sinking Empire Union (121), Melrose Abbey (101), and King Edward (81) and leaving Soekaboemi (114) adrift with a gaping hole in her stern. St Laurent engaged what was possibly U356 at 0330Z, drenching the U-boat in oerlikon (20-millimetre) fire and rounds from her 4.7-inch gun. At least one shell was thought to have struck the U-boat, and as it dived a shallow pattern of charges was laid over the swirl. St Laurent gained a good asdic contact on her target and delivered a ten-charge attack. Windeyer later reported that eleven detonations were heard, 'the last being delayed and intense.' As the destroyer closed for another attack, the target appeared stopped and a large oil slick was observed. Ten further charges were dropped before St Laurent made her way back to ONS 154. Windeyer was optimistic, but only after the war was it learned for certain that U356 had perished sometime during the night of 26–27 December at the hands of C 1.

St Laurent located another interloper at 0615Z and drove him off with gunfire. The Germans then lost contact with ONS 154 for most of the next thirty hours. Only U225 got a glimpse of the convoy on the twenty-seventh, torpedoing Scottish Heather as she refuelled Chilliwack astern of the convoy. The tanker was not seriously damaged – she merely exchanged sea water for fuel oil – and was able to return safely to the Clyde. Chilliwack, with '100 tons of fuel and many grey hairs,' went back to her escort duties. During the day HF/DF operators aboard Toward and Fidelity intercepted many U-boat transmissions astern of the convoy, but firm contact with ONS 154 was not re-established until the morning of the twenty-eighth. None the less, during the night contact was made with the shadowing pack, when at 0137Z *Chilliwack* hit one interloper with a round from her 4-inch gun and then depth charged the submerged U-boat, producing an 'enormous' underwater explosion.

U260 was the first to regain contact on the twenty-eighth, and twelve other U-boats were homed on to the convoy during the day. The pending assault was watched anxiously by both shore and escort staffs. Horton had already ordered the destroyers *Milne* and *Meteor* diverted from a TORCH convoy, but they did not arrive until the next day. Meanwhile, in the late afternoon of the twenty-eighth Windeyer was finally able to persuade *Fidelity*'s captain to launch one of her two float-planes in an attempt to break up the pack. Although *St Laurent* laid an oil slick to calm the sea, the aircraft struck the destroyer's wake and crashed. While the destroyer stopped to rescue the pilot and observer, far away on the starboard side of the convoy the onslaught began.

At 1920Z HMCS *Battleford*'s lookouts spotted an 'object on the surface outlined against a break in the cloud on the Western horizon.' She altered course to investigate, gained a radar contact, and then immediately four U-boats, neatly arranged in line abreast about a mile apart, were seen heading for ONS 154. The nearest soon dived, and the second was lost from sight, remaining only a radar echo. Lieutenant F.A. Beck, RCNVR, the escort's captain, elected to pursue the third and fourth U-boats, which he engaged with the corvette's 4-inch gun while alternately illuminating the scene with starshell. The U-boats were seen to exchange signals by light and then departed in opposite directions. The shock of gunfire soon disabled *Battleford*'s radar, and her lookouts lost sight of the fleeing enemy. Reluctantly Beck turned for ONS 154; unknown to him, the convoy had altered course just after dusk, and he was unable to find it again until the next morning. Beck later expressed himself 'unspeakably sorry' about his failure to relocate the convoy in its hour of need, but the fault was Windeyer's for neglecting to make his intentions known to the escort.

The Germans had no problem finding ONS 154. Beginning at 2005Z the 'convoy was attacked apparently from all directions simultaneously.' Although it seemed that the whole U-boat fleet was loose within the convoy, only five U-boats accounted for the damage. *U591* struck first, disabling *Norse King* (112), followed by *U225*'s destruction of *Melmore Head* (113) and torpedoing of *Ville de Rouen* (102). As the stricken ships wallowed astern of ONS 154, *U260* sank *Empire Wagtail* (111) and *U406* put holes in *Baron Cochrane* (12), *Lynton Grange* (22), and *Zarian* (13) on the other side of the convoy. The fleet of derelicts was then added to by *U225*, on its second pass hitting *President Francqui* (62) and the commodore's ship *Empire Shackleton* (61). Within two hours nine ships were plucked from ONS 154, producing a scene of chaos.

Lieutenant Stuart Henderson, the commanding officer of *Napanee*, wrote later that the scene 'resembled a holocaust': 'All ships appeared to be firing snowflakes, and tracers crisscrossed in all directions, escorts firing starshells. The sea was dotted with lights from boats and rafts, and two burning wrecks which had hauled out to starboard helped the illumination.' 'At one stage of the attack,' *Shediac*'s captain, Lieutenant J.E. Clayton, RCNR, commented later, 'torpedoes were so numerous in the convoy ... that the officer of the watch remarked, "there goes ours now, sir," ... as if next week's groceries were being delivered.'

Kenogami, *Napanee*, and *St Laurent* all reported sighting and attacking U-boats, the destroyer at one point coming close enough to ram. Windeyer wisely decided not to risk damage to his one fast escort, and the U-boat escaped. Action continued around ONS 154 until midnight, when 'suddenly all was quiet.'

For all practical purposes the battle for ONS 154 was over on the morning of 29 December although no one could have known it then. The U-boats spent the small hours of the morning and the rest of the day picking through the flotsam astern of the convoy, sinking wrecks. During the twenty-ninth they could be heard by the HF/DF operators of *Toward* and *Fidelity* (herself straggling, with engine trouble), and Windeyer suspected they were planning the next night's attack. In mid-afternoon *Milne* and *Meteor* arrived and drove off three shadowers. The night of 29–30 December passed without incident, at least for the convoy. *Fidelity*, now well astern of the main body, was repeatedly attacked during the day and finally succumbed to *U435* in the afternoon: 334 crewmen perished with her.

With many U-boats still lurking around ONS 154 Windeyer grew more anxious as the thirtieth wore on. *Milne*, *Meteor*, *Shediac*, and *Battleford* all departed for the Azores in the afternoon in order to seek fuel. It appeared to Windeyer that 'tonight would see our final carving, with only four escorts to take the bowling.' He advised the steamers *Calgary* and *Adrastus*, fast ships with civilian passengers aboard, to use their judgment about whether or not to stay with the convoy. They held on, and miraculously no further attacks developed. *Fame* joined on the thirty-first and conduct of the escort passed to Heathcote. Windeyer, exhausted by the ordeal and now seeing torpedoes at every turn, was put to bed. The battle had cost the Allies fourteen ships and 486 lives. In exchange, one U-boat was thought to have been damaged.

ONS 154 was a disaster of the first order. Despite the escort's obvious handicaps, better group training and the steady hand of able leadership would have reduced losses. They would also have resulted in more tangible damage to the enemy. All agreed that the individual escorts performed well, but they never worked as a team. On the whole, reaction to ONS 154 was muted by events which followed in January. However, the RCN did find some support for its position on C-group efficiency in it. The failure of *Burwell* to meet her commitment to C 1 and the impact of her absence on the battle were evidence of precisely the problem Murray had complained of earlier. His sentiment was shared by the staff at St John's, as an angry comment pencilled by Captain R.E.S. Bidwell on the convoy's report demonstrated. 'How about giving us a few decent destroyers in the C groups, Maxie [Horton],' Bidwell asked rhetorically, 'instead of the discarded sweepings you're giving us now?' Reid, the new FONF, shared this sentiment and raised the matter in his formal report. He was also upset about the routing assigned to ONS 154, which carried it towards a 'large concentration of U-boats ... through which, it appeared from our plots, they would have to pass.'

Naturally, the battle for ONS 154 was followed closely in Britain, where the fate of *Fidelity* was watched anxiously, and in Ottawa, where the battle held wider implications. Its outcome undermined any hopes Nelles had of challenging the British. Mansfield and DeWolf arrived in Ottawa on 2 January, doubtless well prepared to present and defend the conference's decisions. In the afternoon Mansfield met unofficially with the Naval Staff, and the gist of that meeting was transmitted to Macdonald in Nelles's second memo on the affair. According to the CNS, Mansfield admitted that the general shortage of escorts was to blame for the current problems in the mid-ocean. The only alternative immediately available, Nelles advised, was to improve the 'killing efficiency' of all the groups, 'not only the Canadians as was originally thought.' To facilitate this ongoing scheme, Mansfield explained, a new group-training unit was being established at Londonderry. The broadening scope of the British plans, which was by no means evident at the outset but was at least in keeping with Horton's stated objectives, made the Admiralty's proposals more palatable to the RCN. It also lifted the burden of failure in the mid-ocean from the RCN, a point which was made very plain to Macdonald. Nelles therefore recommended acceptance. The RCN would not only re-

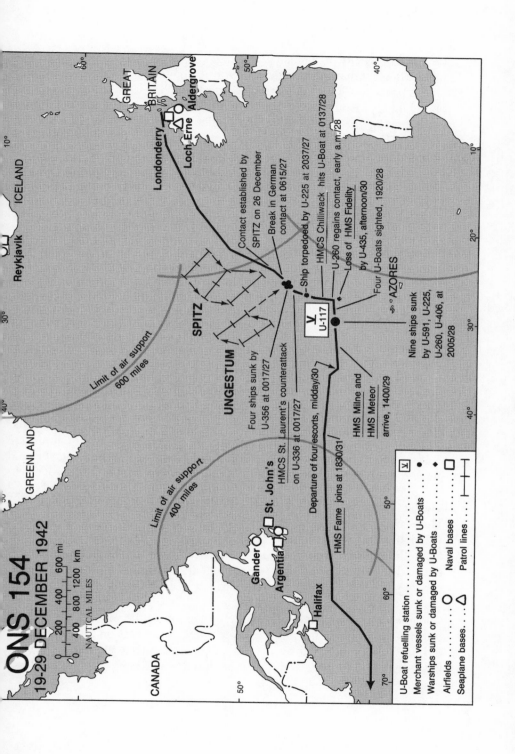

ONS 154
19-29 DECEMBER 1942

Scale:
0 200 400 600 mi
0 400 800 1200 km
NAUTICAL MILES

CANADA

GREENLAND

ICELAND

Reykjavik

GREAT
BRITAIN

Londonderry
Loch Erne Aldergrove

Limit of air support
600 miles

Limit of air support
400 miles

Gander
St. John's
Argentia
Halifax

SPITZ

UNGESTUM

AZORES

U-117

Contact established by
SPITZ on 26 December

Break in German
contact at 0615/27

Ship torpedoed by U-225 at 2037/27

HMCS Chilliwack hits U-Boat at 0137/28

U-260 regains contact, early a.m./28

Loss of HMS Fidelity
by U-435, afternoon/30

Four U-Boats sighted, 1920/28

Four ships sunk by
U-356 at 0017/27

HMCS St. Laurent's counterattack
on U-336 at 0017/27

Departure of four escorts, midday/30

HMS Milne and
HMS Meteor
arrive, 1400/29

HMS Fame joins at 1830/31

Nine ships sunk
by U-591, U-225,
U-260, U-406, at
2005/28

U-Boat refuelling station . . . . [V]
Merchant vessels sunk or damaged by U-Boats . . . . . . ●
Warships sunk or damaged by U-Boats . . . . . . ◆
Airfields . . . . ○   Naval bases . . . . . . □
Seaplane bases . . . . . △   Patrol lines . . . . . . ├──┤

ceive the 'benefit of intensive training,' Nelles wrote, 'but we also establish the fact that we consider the North Atlantic our operational area.'[40]

The proposals were again considered by the War Committee of cabinet on 6 January. Both Nelles and DeWolf, who were in attendance, spoke in support of the British plan, and Nelles's memos to Macdonald were tabled. The War Committee readily agreed, and Nelles signalled acceptance to the First Sea Lord the next day, subject to three conditions. First, Canadian escorts were to be returned to MOEF 'as soon as they have reached a satisfactory state of efficiency and, in any case, not later than May 1943.' Second, the RN was not to reduce its commitment to WLEF. And third, the TORCH corvettes were to be sent home as quickly as possible. Having faced the dual horror of being brought to book for performing badly and of risking the loss of the battle for recognition and independence in the Northwest Atlantic, the RCN clearly felt it had salvaged a strategic victory from a tactical defeat. And so it had. The strength of the RCN's attachment to MOEF is best exemplified by the following passage from Nelles's signal to Pound:

It has been our policy to build up Canadian escort forces for the specific purpose of protecting North Atlantic trade convoys in addition to our coastal communications. Public interest in the Canadian Navy is centered on the part it has taken in this task, which is without question one of the highest and enduring priority [sic] upon which the outcome of the war depends. We are satisfied that the Canadian Navy can serve no higher purpose than to continue to share this task, which we have come to look upon as a natural responsibility for Canada ...

It is our desire, therefore, to concentrate all Canadian escort vessels for this purpose to which end the above conditions ... are necessary.[41]

The RCN was now resolved to do better by catering to its own needs. There were, in fact, few alternatives.

On 9 January Mackenzie King sent virtually the same telegram to Churchill, and the course of Canadian participation in the mid-ocean over the next four months was set.[42] Undoubtedly the British reaction was one of relief. A very awkward situation had been brought off, for all the British knew, without serious difficulty. Churchill's acknowledgment of Canadian acceptance tactfully omitted mention of the real reason for the transfer (included in the original drafts were comments on efficiency and training) and concluded by saying, 'This is another real good turn you have done us.'[43] Officers at NSHQ, having driven the navy at a merciless pace only to be called up short by those who had sought and received their help, might well have wondered who had turned whom.

In noting the Canadians' passing from the mid-Atlantic, the Admiralty's *Monthly Anti-Submarine Report* for January 1943 generously (and accurately) observed, 'The Canadians have had to bear the brunt of the U-Boat attack in the North Atlantic for the last six months, that is to say, of about half of the German U-Boats operating at sea.' That the RCN's small ships, manned almost exclusively by reservists, 'put up a good show is immensely to their credit.' For the RCN the most active and important phase of its participation in the Battle of the Atlantic was over. The RN's director of Anti-Submarine put his finger on the real reason for the transfer when he wrote in early January: '80% of all ships torpedoed in Trans-Atlantic convoys in the last two months were hit while being escorted by Canadian groups.'[44] In the final analysis, that was all that mattered.

8

The View from the Sidelines

This is the end of a chapter. Soon – but oh, make haste! – the vast resources of the United States will be hurled into the North Atlantic to turn the tide ... But until that happy day – and long after ... remember the Canadian corvettes – those far flung, storm tossed little ships on which the German Führer had never looked and yet which have, since 1940, stood between him and the conquest of the world.

Lieutenant P. Evans, RCNVR, CO, HMCS *Trillium*, February 1943

Evans was right. For the Canadian corvettes and for the RCN, early 1943 was the end of a chapter. Now there were no new theatres into which it was sufficient to pour untrained men and ill-prepared escorts. It is remarkable that Evans sensed this fundamental change, more so that he wrote it down.[1] But he may well have known from his frequent contacts with Americans that the U.S. would produce nearly four hundred destroyer escorts (roughly equivalent to RCN and RN frigates) in 1943 alone – all purpose-built and all modern. Yet it was the British who determined the outcome in the mid-ocean in early 1943, and they did it largely with existing forces. The Canadians of MOEF watched the battle being won by their colleagues. For them and for the RCN as a whole it was a traumatic experience.

Changing the direction of three years' effort was not easy. Policies which seemed useful at the outset of expansion had to be reconsidered in light of the need to consolidate. By early 1943, with the navy's shore establishments well manned and the initial shipbuilding programs completed, the manning policy was modified. Heavy drafting from existing crews was now limited to ships in refit and even then was restricted to a few key ratings and perhaps half of the officers. Such changes in personnel were easily handled by the new minimum work-up periods – fourteen days for a ship from refit.[2] Similarly, the navy's training programs were working well, as indeed they had been in August 1942, when Commander Burnett reported on them. The only critical shortage was, as it had always been, a shortage of training submarines.[3]

The future looked promising, but in January 1943 the immediate situation for Canadian MOEF escorts was still unacceptable. Although regularly only a few hundred miles from Canada, St John's–based sailors still seldom got home. Partly because of the problem of distance the RCN did not grant boiler-cleaning leave to its personnel in Newfoundland, and regular extended leave was granted only during prolonged refits. Because of the hectic pace of operations in 1942, the latter form of leave had been infrequent and the morale of the men suffered. The problem was exacerbated by the contrasting situation of RN MOEF escorts. They regularly returned to Britain, and even with only a few days' leave British crewmen could easily get home. RCN authorities were well aware of the problem but could find no quick solution.[4] The idea of rotating WLEF and MOEF groups was considered, but differences in group size and composition conspired against it. Similarly, in the interests of group permanence it was impossible to rotate individual ships.[5] Until the RCN was able to develop an orderly refit program, MOEF would remain trapped in an endless cycle of operations. The effect of this on operational efficiency cannot be measured, but it cannot have been good.

Far more serious were the material and institutional limitations to the attainment of operational efficiency. Facilities at St John's were overcrowded, short on storage space and repair personnel, and unable to keep up with essential repair work. Indeed, it was not until March 1943 – nearly two full years after the establishment of NEF – that it was decided to develop a full support facility for Newfoundland-based Canadian escorts. More extensive support was actually available at the American base in Londonderry, which by 1942 functioned almost exclusively in aid of the RCN. Indeed, during 1942–3 the overwhelming majority of the work undertaken by Naval Operational Base, Londonderry, was on HMC ships.[6] But Londonderry had no Canadian staff and certainly no co-ordinated scheme for dealing with the RCN's outstanding material problems. Canadian escorts in the mid-ocean still lacked access to a fully equipped and properly staffed establishment devoted entirely to their support. Moreover, the entire fleet was not much better off. WLEF escorts too had been driven hard, and their list of accumulated defects was no shorter than that of the C groups. Repairing the neglect of 1942 was, by itself, sufficient to clog the navy's refit facilities for a year. But efficiency required more than maximum performance from existing equipment. The escort fleet needed to be modernized. For the corvettes this meant not only extensive structural changes (modification of the bridge and lengthening of the foc'sle) but also a complete rewiring with the low-power circuits needed to operate gyro-compasses and, in turn, hedgehog. NSHQ had authorized the upgrading of the corvette fleet's type 123A asdics to type 123D in December as an interim measure. All that this entailed was the provision of an additional magnetic compass on the forward portion of the bridge so that the captain would not have to peer through the window of the compass-house to check bearings during an action. No further modernization was possible until the ships were rewired, and this alone necessitated a long refit.

In fairness to the Naval Staff, the impetus for full modernization simply did not exist before December 1942. Up to that point the crucial need had not been modern escorts but escorts of any type. When planning for modernization finally went ahead in earnest in early 1943, it was evident that the infrastructure erected to produce ships could not be quickly adapted to their maintenance. The navy's own new fleet bases at Shelburne, Sydney, and Bay Bulls were still many months away from operation, and the facilities at both Halifax and St John's were past saturation. The yards from which many of the escorts originated lay far inland, beyond the system of locks through which a fitted-out corvette could not pass. The RCN therefore had to fall back on local yards in the Maritime provinces.

The small shipyards of Atlantic Canada had suffered from neglect before the war and from inconsistent business during it. Their key problem lay in the shortage of skilled manpower. Both the navy and the government were alive to the need to maintain a body of skilled shipfitters, machinists, and electricians from the outset. The decision to build Tribal-class destroyers in Halifax was made largely to hold workmen over slack periods in essential work.[7] It was also clear to the navy in early 1942 that the reserve of skilled manpower outside the Halifax area was in danger. In fact, it would have been much better on this count too if the proper proportion of escorts had been refitted in 1942. But the problem was compounded by other factors. After two decades of depression, Maritime shipyards of the late 1930's were populated by an aging work-force. On the eve of the war a new apprenticeship program was instituted, taking in young men who were, by 1942, of prime military age. With new yards to man, the navy eyed these men eagerly, but the army also had need of them, particularly of those who were eligible for active service abroad.

The issue of recruiting marine machinists was first aired in May 1942, when the RCN insisted that its needs were as pressing as those of the army. Yet when the navy began to plan the refit and modernization of the fleet in early 1943, many yards reported an inability to take on work – or to complete it to satisfaction – because of call-ups to the army. They admitted that many of these call-ups had been deferred because the men in question were doing essential war work, but the six-month deferrals served only to keep the 'men in a state of uncertainty and did not encourage them to put forth their best efforts.' As the spokesman for Thompson Brothers of Liverpool, NS, went on to say, 'we are constantly in fear that this policy of postponements will be changed, and we will find ourselves minus half of our machine-shop staff and many skilled workers.' Thompson's had the good fortune of being a year-round port. The Sydney Foundry and Machine Works reported that it was unable to forecast what work it would be capable of because it was unable to keep skilled personnel through the winter months – a problem which could be overcome by laying up a corvette for modernization through the freeze-up. It was not until June 1943 that the RCN finally secured the maintenance of a skilled manpower pool in small shipyards.[8] The problem of finding skilled men to undertake repair work was further complicated by construction of Tribal-class destroyers at Halifax. The first ship was laid down in September 1942, and by the following January the supervising naval engineer, Maritimes, was already complaining that the push to launch the ship had absorbed surplus manpower. This, he pointed out, was quite the reverse of the original intention.[9]

Finding space to modernize ships in foreign yards initially proved easier. In February the Admiralty agreed to take six RCN corvettes in hand during 1943. This eased the burden on Canadian establishments and ensured that the bulk of the work would be completed in about a year. The RCN also considered American yards and watched RN attempts to gain access to them in early 1943 very closely. From the correspondence between senior British and American officials passed to the RCN by the British Admiralty maintenance representative in Washington it was clear that, as a matter of policy, no wholesale modernization of any warship was being entertained by American authorities, and the Americans expected others to be similarly restrained. The Americans wanted modernization done piecemeal, with only work of a major nature undertaken by yards. The piecemeal scheme was rejected by FONF for his escorts because their layover periods were once again much too short. The scheme was also rejected by Murray's staff in Halifax, largely because under the existing conditions the RCN was totally dependent upon refits to effect all repairs.[10]

The problems of modernization gained enormous importance during 1943 as the character of the war at sea changed. But in January they were still somewhat remote from MOEF, where the day-to-day problems of maintaining group strengths were most pressing. Naturally this was a function of good maintenance, of keeping escorts running. In the second winter of mid-Atlantic operations this was still a difficult problem. It was, moreover, compounded by serious delays in obtaining reliefs for ships long overdue for refits. In late 1942 Commodore Reid complained to Murray that the three-month period required to refit ships from his command in Nova Scotia was intolerable and placed an unacceptable strain on those next in line for work. Murray eventually felt compelled to write a letter of apology to Reid, citing work slow-downs over wage differences in the private yards as the underlying cause of the delays. The situation was, as Murray described it, 'rather explosive' and meant that RCN MOEF escorts could expect little immediate relief from Canadian sources.[11]

Ironically, St John's–based escorts were within just a few hours' steaming of a well-equipped and underworked escort base at Argentia. Reid was obviously aware that Argentia had potential and in February sent one of his engineer officers, Lieutenant (Engineer) E.N. Clarke, to investigate. Clarke found fourteen berths capable of handling corvettes and three cranes ranging in strength from three to twenty-five tons, and discovered that the repair ship alongside, the USS *Prairie*, could 'undertake approximately 50% more work than she averages at present.' Moreover, Clarke also learned that the Americans had already done major alterations to British corvettes, including the resiting of masts and modernizing of bridges.[12]

Canadian interest in Argentia was, of course, not new, and use of the facilities had been extended to the RCN in late 1941. For a brief period in the spring of 1942 St John's–based RCN escorts had made frequent use of the base,[13] but with the establishment of MOEF and the replacement of American escorts in the Western Atlantic by British, Argentia became the western terminus of B groups. Its use by RCN escorts was thereby ended. The RN maintained a small staff to oversee the handling of its escorts (in contrast to the Canadian practice at Londonderry), and they jealously guarded access to the American base. The 'Instructions and

Orders for HM and HMC Ships in Argentia' issued by the RN Maintenance Office in February 1943 stated emphatically: 'It is clearly understood that the repair and store facilities are primarily for the ships of B groups. Ships based at St. John's should only require assistance in an Emergency.'[14] Much to its credit the RN had better support facilities on both sides of the Atlantic than C groups did. It was a lesson the RCN had not yet learned. A year after the absorption of NEF into the MOEF its successors were still very much between a rock and a hard place.

Reid's concern for the improvement of his refit and repair arrangements was understandable, and sound maintenance was the basis of efficiency. But success in the mid-ocean also required destroyers for the C groups. While the issue of the C groups' transfer to C-in-C, WA, was being resolved, the British had sat on the Canadian request of 5 December 1942 that the RCN be allowed to acquire fourteen escort destroyers. Not all senior RN officers were opposed to the idea, and the RN's director of Trade, Captain B.B. Schofield, for one wanted the Canadian request met in order to strengthen the Canadian groups of MOEF. But the British stalled, and it was only when the RCN proposed assigning its new Tribals, soon to be commissioned from British yards, to MOEF that action was forthcoming. The RN Naval Staff regarded the employment of Tribal-class destroyers in A/S escort as a great waste of resources. Moreover, they desperately wanted the new destroyers to serve with the Home Fleet. Consequently the Admiralty was forced into making the RCN an offer of escort destroyers on 21 January. The RCN could have its choice of some new American-built British destroyer escorts (BDEs) or refitted D&I-class RN destroyers, roughly similar to the RCN's River class. To the Admiralty's surprise, the RCN chose the latter, in part because they were more compatible with the ships already in Canadian service and in part because the older destroyers were faster and more powerful than the BDEs. When the final details were ironed out, the British generously presented the RCN with a gift of six destroyers, all thoroughly overhauled for escort duty – just enough to meet the RCN's needs in MOEF.[15]

The first of the second generation of River-class destroyers, *Ottawa II*, was not commissioned until the end of March and was not operational until May. In the meantime the shortage of destroyers in C groups was rectified by an infusion of RN escorts. Outwardly this had the much-needed effect of bringing the C groups up to strength. But it also allowed Horton to place the C groups under RN senior officers. The new SOES – Lieutenant Commander C.E. Bridgman, C 1; Commander R.C. Medley, C 3; and Commander A.M. Mackillop, C 4 (C 2 remained under Lieutenant Commander Chavasse, RN) – were well-qualified and experienced Western Approaches veterans.[16] Indeed, it would have been inconsistent with Horton's stated objectives not to place the C groups under what he considered more able and more permanent leadership. NSHQ later professed its hope that these men would be replaced by suitable Canadian officers as they became available. But in early 1943 the RCN was prepared to leave well enough alone and even asked for more experienced RN senior officers to assist with the integration of the second-generation River-class destroyers.[17]

Further temporary steps were taken to ensure the safe conduct of C-group operations immediately prior to the training program. The first group to leave St John's in the new year, C 1, was still suffering the effects of ONS 154 and needed stiffening. Windeyer had been relieved of his command for reasons of health, and his ship, *St Laurent*, was in Halifax for repairs. Commander Dobson, in *St Croix*, was hurriedly dispatched following the completion of refitting, but the actual conduct of the escort rested with two British destroyers, *Vansittart* (formerly of B 1) and *Chesterfield* (formerly of B 7). Both RN destroyers were attached to C 1 for one passage only. The final precaution was assignment to a fast convoy, HX 222. In fact, through January and February 1943 C groups escorted as many HX convoys as they had in the last six months of 1942.[18] This alone would have kept losses and the potential for losses down considerably. A strong escort, high speed, and the better routing now available combined for a rather safe passage. U-boat group 'Jaguar,' northeast of Newfoundland, was deployed against HX 222 and SC 117 (B 3), but operations were disrupted by wireless interference. HX 222 lost only one ship and SC 117 a straggler before Jaguar, which was unable to gain firm contact with either convoy, was given the slip.[19] C 1 secured alongside at Londonderry on 22 January. It would be over two months before the group made another North Atlantic crossing.

Although for the next few weeks the activities of individual escorts varied, C 1 (*St Croix, Battleford, Chilliwack, Kenogami, Napanee*, and *Shediac*, later joined in the UK by *St Laurent*) set a pattern which the other groups followed. The activities of *Kenogami*, for example, are indicative of the C groups' experience and are worth relating in some detail.[20]

Immediately upon arrival in 'Derry long leave was granted to half the ship's company. Those remaining aboard then began a week of cleaning, painting, and routine harbour duties. *Kenogami* did not require dockyard attention, but others did. They were taken in hand as space allowed, and new equipment, principally 271 radar and oerlikon guns, was fitted whenever possible. Following the return of the liberty men, *Kenogami*'s crew spent the rest of the week completing the work already under way. Sunday, 31 January was observed as a day of rest, but on 2 February, after nearly two weeks alongside, intensive training began. For a week various parties were landed from *Kenogami* to attend Londonderry's shore training facilities. Depth-charge crews went to the D/C driller; lookouts visited the night lookout trainer; machine-gun and 20-millimetre crews used the A/A dome teacher (escorts which had just fitted 20-millimetre guns sent their personnel there repeatedly); boarding parties exercised on a mockup of a U-boat conning tower; the 4-inch gun crew laboured on a similar piece under the gaze of an RN instructor; asdic and radar operators attended their respective simulators; and the bridge personnel were exercised as a unit. In all cases the officers and men trained together. Every warlike function of the escort was put through its paces.

As the week of harbour training drew to a close, *Kenogami* prepared for sea. On 11 February she proceeded down Lough Foyle to the escort anchorage off the Irish village of Moville. There the corvette refuelled from the duty oiler and was joined by *St Croix*. The next day the two escorts put to sea for exercises, which included A/S, towing, and manoeuvring in company. Both then refuelled once again prior to sailing eastwards on the thirteenth.

Kenogami and *St Croix* arrived at their destination within hours. As far as can be determined, all of C 1 was assembled at HMS *Western Isles* (commonly known by its geographic name, Tobermory) on 13 February. This otherwise placid Scottish port was, of course, the RN's escort work-up base and the preserve of Commodore G. Stephenson, 'the Terror of Tobermory.' Stephenson paid his customary visit to the escorts as they arrived, a visit which usually instilled a desire to do well. C 1's first full day in Stephenson's lair crewmen spent ashore, doing much the same things that they had just done in Londonderry. The rest of the six-day stay alternated between sea time, working individually or in company and frequently with a tame submarine, or exercising in harbour. Both aspects of training were supervised by the staff of *Western Isles* or by personnel from the training ship HMS *Philante*. The latter was just on her way to form a key element in Londonderry's operational-training establishment. Her presence in Ireland eliminated the need to send the other C groups to Tobermory – a small mercy for which many Canadian sailors might justifiably have been thankful. The training program ended with a night firing exercise, following which C 1 set course for Lough Foyle.

Kenogami and her consorts were back alongside at 'Derry on 21 February and spent the next week in routine harbour duties and preparation for sea. On the twenty-seventh the group sailed to escort KMS 10, bound for North Africa. The passage of this convoy proved to be the most interesting of those of the six TORCH convoys escorted by C groups. It was located by German aircraft west of Oporto on 5 March, and three U-boats were sent to attack. *U107* was driven off by the escort; *U445* made contact but was unable to attack; only *U410* managed to bring success to the operation. She penetrated the screen and sank one ship, and later a straggler. C 1 balanced the score by sinking *U87*, a U-boat which technically was not part of the operation against KMS 10.[21] It was the only wholly RCN U-boat kill in this phase of the war. C 1's return trip with KMS 9 and those of the other C groups were not noteworthy.

While C 1 underwent its period of recuperation, re-equipment, and training, a great deal transpired in the mid-ocean. December and January were, with the exception of HX 217 and ONS 154, generally quiet months. The combination of severe weather and good intelligence kept the incidence of interception down, and MOEF was reduced to battling its old enemy – the Atlantic itself. Convoys were scattered by the endless gales, escorts driven to the brink of catastrophe by repeatedly sailing to the very extreme limits of fuel capacity, and of course all suffered weather damage. The RN destroyer *Roxborough* of Western Support Force had her captain and first lieutenant killed when a heavy sea smashed the ship's bridge. As in the previous winter MOEF was in danger of being blown apart by the weather.[22]

This situation was not aided by the increasing size of BdU's commitment to the mid-ocean or by the withdrawal of the C groups. The Germans too watched the interception rate of Allied convoys decline in early 1943 and put enormous effort into cracking the Allied ciphers. Their efforts soon paid off, but not before HX 224, escorted by C 4 (*Churchill* [RN], *Restigouche*, *Amherst*, *Brandon*, *Celandine* [RN], *Collingwood*, and *Sherbrooke*), was intercepted by chance. Foul weather and the convoy's distance from any formed U-boat line prevented BdU from staging an operation against HX 224. *U456*, the first U-boat to sight the convoy, kept 'exemplary contact' for three days and sank two ships from it in the process.[23] The most significant development from the battle for HX 224 was the intelligence gained by BdU from a survivor that SC 118 was due to pass through the same area in two days. The indiscretion of that Allied sailor cost many of his colleagues their lives.

With SC 118 the exceptional run of luck enjoyed by B groups since the renewal of mid-ocean pack attacks in the summer of 1942 came to an end. What Clausewitz called the friction of war now came to visit with a vengeance, and SC 118 was just the first of an exceptionally bitter series of battles. Its escort, B 2, was large but not well established. Indeed, MOEF was already feeling the combined effects of bad weather and the reduction of the force to nine groups (with the transfer of the C groups) by February. It is also clear that operational authorities were trying to meet the increasing size of U-boat packs by providing convoys with a larger escort. For a number of reasons, then, B 2 was not the epitome of Western Approaches groups. The regular Senior Officer, Captain D. Macintyre, was away while his destroyer *Hesperus* was refitted. The interim SOE, Commander F.B. Proudfoot, was new to the job and to his ship, *Vanessa* (HF/DF). *Hesperus* was replaced by *Vimy* (RN) just prior to the last westbound passage, and an additional destroyer, *Beverley*, formerly of B 4, had also just been assigned to B 2. None of these older destroyers was equipped with HF/DF. However, HF/DF was fitted in the rescue ship *Toward* and in the U.S. cutter *Bibb*, which joined the escort for SC 118. At the outset B 2 also had its long-standing corvette members, *Campanula* and *Mignonette* (Free French), as well as two other Free French corvettes, *Aconit*, formerly of B 4, and *Lobelia*, from B 3. Finally, B 2 was reinforced on the second day of the battle by the U.S. destroyers *Babbitt* and *Schenck* and the cutter *Ingham*.[24]

In view of the recent criticism of C groups, the make-up and performance of B 2 in the battle of SC 118 was tragic irony. The group managed to salvage its reputation by sinking two U-boats – something which might have been expected from so large and powerful a group – but it proved incapable of preventing heavy losses. The first phase of the battle went well enough. *U187* was sunk on 4 February by *Beverley* and *Vimy* after it was located by HF/DF, and on the following night five shadowers were driven off. On the fifth the pack managed to sink two ships, one from the convoy and one straggler, but with the help of heavy USN reinforcement B 2 forced off the last shadower before nightfall. Air cover on the third day helped push the pack off again, though the Germans never lost contact. By sunset on 6 February five U-boats were once again in touch with SC 118. The first three attempts to penetrate the screen were foiled by the escort, but in the small hours of the next morning *U402*, commanded by Baron von Forstner, sank six ships, including the rescue ship *Toward*, in two attacks. B 2 obtained no immediate retribution from the pack for its success, though the escort rallied during daylight on the seventh and once again drove the pack off. Von Forstner hung on, however, and although he was chased away once by *Bibb* and *U624* was destroyed by Coastal Command near the convoy, *U402* remained to fight another day. On the night of 7–8 February *U402* penetrated B 2's defence, and von Forstner sank his seventh and final ship from SC 118.

The loss of eleven ships from such a heavily defended convoy was a hard blow for the RN. Indeed, both sides considered it perhaps the hardest-fought convoy battle of the war.[25] To the British the performance of the escort drove home the need for training, teamwork, and good leadership. It also illustrated the fundamental weakness in the current organization of mid-ocean escort. 'Although this is very terrible,' Horton confided to a colleague in the aftermath of SC 118, 'it is all lending weight to my arguments, and I believe I shall get Cabinet approval for forming Support Groups.'[26] The example of SC 118 and Horton's persistence probably helped influence the British cabinet, but the cabinet was already well aware of the potential impact of increasing resources committed to the mid-ocean. The Anti–U-boat Warfare Committee was, by January, deeply involved in finding ways of improving the shipping situation and the American buildup (Operation 'Bolero') in the UK. In early February P.M.S. Blackett produced a report indicating that losses could be cut by 25 per cent by increasing the size of escort groups from six to nine ships, and by a phenomenal 64 per cent through effective mid-ocean air support.[27] Not surprisingly, Horton received permission to restructure his escort forces to permit the rapid and heavy reinforcement of threatened convoys. In early March each Western Approaches group was reduced in strength by one escort (frigate, sloop, or destroyer), which provided sixteen ships to form four support groups. In addition, one half-flotilla of Home Fleet destroyers was released to Western Approaches to form a fifth support group.[28]

The battle for SC 118 also demonstrated the need for effective air support in the mid-ocean, a need painfully evident from previous battles. Blackett's figures on the savings in shipping likely from proper VLR aircraft coverage of the mid-Atlantic were astonishing. Moreover, he also demonstrated to the Anti–U-boat Warfare Committee that more VLR aircraft would bring a much improved score of U-boat kills, which in turn meant still lower shipping losses. Despite the strength of Blackett's case, the Admiralty (not to mention the Air Ministry, Bomber Command, and the Americans) believed for some time yet that it could not afford to reduce its heavy air offensive in the Bay of Biscay or to abandon the bombing of German bases by the RAF. The number of VLR aircraft operating in the North Atlantic in February was only eighteen, and no substantial increase was made until after the crisis of March.[29]

Perhaps the most important new lesson of the battle for SC 118 was the need to provide night air patrols around convoys in the mid-ocean, something not forthcoming until the fall of 1943. Otherwise the story of SC 118 held nothing new. Everything the Anti–U-boat Warfare Committee now agreed was essential to winning the battle in the mid-ocean – and reducing the loss rate of shipping so that broad strategic plans could go ahead – had long been on Horton's predecessor's list of requirements. To what extent Admiral Noble's earlier attempts to establish support groups and obtain effective air cover were undermined by news of 'yet another Canadian disaster' must remain conjecture. It is difficult to believe that affirmative action would have been so long delayed (TORCH notwithstanding) had ON 127, SC 107, and ONS 154 been B-group battles. In the event, the unfortunate passage of SC 118 made the efforts of C groups in late 1942 look much more respectable.

B-group operations were not without success in February. B 6's venerable old destroyers *Viscount* and *Fame* were back, their damage suffered in defence of SC 104 now repaired. While SC 118 staggered under heavy attack in another part of the Atlantic, B 6 detected by HF/DF the first two U-boats to make contact with their convoy, ON 165. Both were promptly sunk: *U69* by *Viscount* and *U201* by *Fame*.[30] But dreadful weather conditions, which had kept the interception rate in January mercifully low, continued through February and most of March. This spelt trouble for MOEF. The battle for SC 118 had signalled the beginning of the climax of the Battle of the Atlantic. For just as the Allies were now set upon forcing the issue by the infusion of sea and air resources, the Germans too realized that a decisive confrontation was at hand. The decline in the interception rate through January, despite the presence of approximately sixty U-boats in the air gap, was also painfully evident to BdU. With four patrol lines now in station, the inability to inflict repeated defeats on Allied convoys was exasperating. In an effort to improve the situation BDienst launched an attack on the British naval cipher number three, the so-called convoy cipher. Although it handled largely routine trade-organization traffic, the convoy cipher was also used to issue the Admiralty's daily U-boat–position report. By February BDienst's efforts were rewarded, and for the next five months the Germans were able to read the Admiralty's estimates of U-boat positions almost daily.[31] Knowing what the enemy used to base his movements on allowed BdU to anticipate routing with devastating results.

There was, finally, perhaps a more likely reason to believe that a decisive confrontation between escorts and U-boats was at hand in early 1943. Until the end of 1942 the German navy had always attempted to maintain a balanced threat to the Allied sea lanes. Though with the loss of the *Bismarck* the burden of trade interdiction had fallen to BdU, the German navy remained a conventional fleet-in-being. Its powerful surface units operating principally out of Norway not only represented a real threat to shipping in northern waters, but they drew off a very considerable Allied naval and air force which might have been used elsewhere. When, at the end of December 1942, a powerful German squadron composed of a pocket battleship, a heavy cruiser, and six destroyers was driven away from a Murmansk convoy by a much weaker RN force, Adolf Hitler finally lost all patience with the fleet-in-being concept and surface-raider strategy. He fired Grand Admiral Raeder, chief of the German navy and staunch proponent of the balanced fleet, and ordered all major surface units struck from the navy lists. Admiral Dönitz was appointed to succeed Raeder, with the task of dismembering the surface fleet and directing a new, totally U-boat–oriented war on Allied shipping. Dönitz was able to salvage most of the fleet's major combatants, but his new post brought increased prestige and importance to the U-boat arm. With the reins of power now firmly in his own hands, Dönitz launched a new offensive in the Atlantic.[32]

The first convoy to suffer from the combination of huge U-boat packs and excellent German intelligence was ONS 166, a convoy of forty-nine ships escorted by A 3.[33] Despite having had a number of escorts move through the group in recent months, A 3 retained a core which had been together since the previous August: the U.S. cutters *Spencer* (HF/DF) and *Campbell* (HF/DF) and the Canadian corvettes *Rosthern* and *Trillium* (both equipped with 271 radar). Of the others *Dauphin* (271) and *Dianthus* (RN, 271) were members of good standing making their fourth and sixth passages, respectively, with ONS 166. Only *Chilliwack*, returning to Canada to refit, was a transient. A 3 was thus well established and, apart from its lack of destroyers, well equipped. The group was also well led. Commander Heineman and his stand-in, Commander Lewis, had always put great effort into co-ordinating the group during layovers. Indeed, perhaps because A 3 was a mixed group, the senior officers always went to considerable pains to ensure that each escort's responsibilities were clearly laid out in operational orders issued in advance of each sailing. Yet despite this effort, ONS 166 lost fourteen ships in a six-day battle with eighteen U-boats.

As in earlier instances when a pack made firm contact in poor weather, the group's modern equipment was of little help. Six of the seven successful U-boat attacks were made without previous detection. With no escorts bearing down on them, the U-boats' aim was good, and losses were high. Moreover, the early loss of the rescue ship *Stockport* (HF/DF) had the usual disruptive effect on a small escort, since several of its members were employed in rescue work. None the less, A 3 performed to everyone's satisfaction, in part because of the terrible weather experienced. Further, not only did *Campbell* sink *U606* (by ramming), but a high level of professionalism was displayed by the other members of the group. Only when the group was down to four escorts, following the detachment of *Campbell* to port and two corvettes to pursue U-boat contacts, did heavy losses ensue. Heineman's combination of slow cutters, of which he complained after ONS 166, and corvettes had responded well to his continuous efforts. The defence of ONS 166 snatched qualified success from the jaws of defeat. The British seem to have considered the final outcome rather 'a bit of bad luck.' It is likely that similar efforts at co-ordination and teamwork within C groups in late 1942 would have been equally effective, at least in mitigating criticism. It was here that the lack of continuity of senior officers in C groups hurt the RCN.

By February 1943, if not sooner, MOEF alone was clearly no match for the enemy that now haunted its territory. Groups were too small; U-boat packs were too large, and interception of convoys was becoming more frequent. But before MOEF's weaknesses could be made good, several further bitter battles marked by even heavier losses followed in the wake of ONS 166. C groups were spared this calamity as they went in rotation to train. C 4 was the second group to arrive for training, coming alongside at 'Derry on 5 February. Its previous convoy, HX 224, had been one of six attacked during the month, but speed and the small concentration of U-boats directed against it kept losses down to two ships.

The training regime for C 4 was virtually identical to that of C 1 except that sea exercises were all conducted off Northern Ireland by *Philante* and her officers. Both C 4 and C 2, which arrived on the fifteenth after escorting HX 225 safely across, spent about a month in and around Londonderry doing maintenance, fitting new equipment, and, of course, training. C 4 sailed on 1 March to escort KMS 10B to Africa, and C 2 followed two weeks later with KMS 11. Neither the outward nor the return passage of either group was subject to enemy action.

The last group to arrive for training was C 3. Its late arrival may have owed something to its record, the best of the C groups'. But by the time

C 3 commenced its program it bore little resemblance to the group which had fought the battles of ON 115, ON 131, and SC 109. *Saguenay* was permanently disabled and awaiting disposal; *Skeena*, *Agassiz*, *Galt*, *Sackville*, and *Wetaskiwin* all went to refit – as a unit – after ONS 152 in December, evidence of NSHQ's new zeal for group permanence. The new C 3 of early 1943 showed some interesting and innovative consideration for the needs of MOEF groups. *Bittersweet* and *Eyebright* were two of the RCN's 'British' corvettes, with extended foc'sles and relatively modern bridges, and had been equipped with 271 radar for some time. *La Malbaie* was a revised corvette (RPV), part of the second construction program, which took into account the lessons of deep-sea operations. Although she was not up to date in the latest equipment, *La Malbaie* was the only Canadian RPV with MOEF, and she was soon fitted with 271 radar. Only the old RN four-stacker *Burnham*, fresh from refit in November when she joined to replace *Saguenay*, was a holdover from 1942. *Assiniboine* joined briefly in January to replace *Skeena*. She made one passage with the group, then went to Halifax to have some defects attended to. While making an independent passage to the UK to rejoin C 3, *Assiniboine* had a chance encounter with a lone U-boat and so damaged herself in a missed ramming that the ill-starred destroyer was out of service for another six months. Her place in C 3 was taken by the British frigate *Jed*. Thus the group which secured alongside at 'Derry at the end of February represented a new era in Canadian MOEF operations.

It was ironic that just as the conditions of the transfer were being fully met and all the C groups were busy training, plans were well under way for their immediate return to mid-ocean. The impetus for their return came from two sources. Even as the transfer was being discussed by the Canadian cabinet on 6 January, Admiral A. Andrews, USN, commander of the Eastern Sea Frontier, petitioned COMINCH in Washington to increase the flow of strategic goods to Britain by sailing more convoys. Andrews's proposition was really a workable solution to Britain's import crisis, though it took no account of the apparent need to upgrade the Canadian groups.[34] The British Anti–U-boat Warfare Committee dealt with the same issue on 6 January. The Admiralty advised that only by reducing losses by 25 per cent and shortening the cycle for North Atlantic convoys from ten to eight days would it be possible to meet the import quotas set for 1943.[35] By the end of January it was clear that the scheduled buildup of American forces in Britain, Operation Bolero, was threatened unless the flow of goods to Britain in the first half of 1943 was increased from the current projections. Thus on 2 February the Admiralty advised NSHQ of its intention to return C 3 and C 4 to MOEF, an estimation revised three days later to include C 1 and C 2 as well.[36]

Another reason for the British change of heart was the exceptional severity of the winter weather. By February, after nearly three full months of operations, Western Support Force had yet to field a complete unit of three ships, and at any one time only four of its twelve escorts were operational. The effect on MOEF was no less profound. By the second month of 1943 the scheduled five-day layover for escorts in Newfoundland was down to less than forty-eight hours on occasion.[37] Of course, all of this had been suffered by many of the same escorts in the previous winter. Yet no mid-Atlantic escort labouring through the winter of 1941–2 had been faced with the burden of extremely long and very bitter convoy battles. Murray had said that the RN should be given the chance to run MOEF in winter with only nine groups, and his belief that it could not be done proved correct. To ease the strain on MOEF and to increase the flow of imports, the Admiralty now wanted C 3 back on the main trade routes by 11 March and the others by early April, when the convoy cycles were to be stepped up.

The suggestion that the C groups should return to the mid-ocean – if not to RCN 'command' – was only part of the enormous reorganization of convoy and escort arrangements in the offing. The RN had never abandoned its desire to reassert C-in-C, WA's authority over convoy operations in the North Atlantic. Ideally, they wanted a 'Supreme Commander in Chief for Strategic Control of All Anti–U-boat Resources in the Atlantic Ocean.'[38] In this they were not completely alone. Despite the fact that the USN represented the single greatest obstacle to the appointment of a supreme commander, Captain Thébaud, USN, at Londonderry urged COMINCH as early as November 1942 to endorse the idea.[39]

As the battle in the mid-ocean intensified, the weaknesses of the existing command structure became glaringly evident. While the Germans exercised continuity of command over convoy battles (indeed, over the whole U-boat campaign), Allied command still changed hands at roughly 35° W – the middle of the air gap. It was this fundamental weakness which the British had complained about and sought to change a year before, when the U-boats were elsewhere. Not only was it inherently inefficient to change the overall responsibility for a battle in mid-course, but British and American directing staffs also had very different opinions of how a convoy under attack should be handled (such as in the battle of ON 113, when somewhat conflicting route alterations were ordered). Confusion held serious consequences for life and property, for the entire war effort as well. These pressures alone were enough to force a re-evaluation of the North Atlantic command structure. But the USN was now under very considerable pressure from the RCN (as the British well knew) to sort out command relationships west of WESTOMP, where there were no less than nine independent commands.

The Canadian campaign to oust CTF-24 and replace him with an RCN officer had already begun in earnest in November 1942. In December Nelles had written personally to Admiral King requesting a high-level conference to discuss the matter. King agreed to the conference but refused to specify a date. The Americans were worried about the principle of unified command, which they felt included promulgation of intelligence and diversion of shipping. They obviously lacked confidence in the RCN's ability in the two latter tasks.

The events of December – 'yet another attempt to get control of our ships' – clearly fired Canadian resolve to see CTF-24 out. Indeed, in January the RCN sought to make Brainard's position untenable by doing just what King had feared, introducing yet another authority to the North-western Atlantic. After an attempt by CTF-24 to shuffle RCN escorts within his command, Brainard was informed by NSHQ that all such transfers must first be cleared by Ottawa, including those between escort groups. Such obstructionism finally made an impression on Admiral King, who instructed CTF-24 to comply with the Canadian request and then informed NSHQ (on 2 February) of his intention to convene a conference on command issues in Washington on 1 March.[40]

In the meantime the RCN strengthened its position by informing Admiral King on 6 February of the navy's intention to establish a Canadian C-in-C in the Northwest Atlantic to handle escort and convoy operations. With respect to MOEF the most important step was the relegation of the St John's establishment to a subcommand of COAC, Halifax, on the twenty-second. For nearly two years these independent commands had vied for resources, manpower, and attention, to the detriment of MOEF and of the navy as a whole. They might well have been reconciled earlier, but so long as the war swirled and eddied around them the relative importance of the two bases was never clear. For the first year of the expansion fleet's activities St John's was the foremost operational base. It was only when the enormous significance of Halifax as a support base and admin-istrative centre was once again matched by its importance as an operational base that the ascendancy of one over the other was clear. This change was exemplified by Murray's appointment to Halifax as COAC in late 1942 and his replacement in Newfoundland by an officer of less senior rank,

Commodore Reid. The subordination of FONF to COAC also made CTF-24's position even more incongruous, since Reid would have to serve two masters.

The Atlantic Convoy Conference convened in Washington as planned, with senior representatives from all the Allied services involved in the Atlantic battle. As in the previous December, the RCN was represented by Admiral Brodeur and Captain DeWolf, but there were others as well. Among these were Captain Lay, the director of Operations and principal author of the RCN's campaign for autonomy, Captain E.S. Brand, the director of Trade Divison, NSHQ, and Murray's chief of staff, Captain W.B. Creery. The USN was represented by thirty-five officers, led by Admiral King. Admiral Sir Percy Noble, now the head of the British Admiralty Delegation in Washington, led the British, who included the VCNS, Vice-Admiral Sir H. Moore, and now Rear Admiral J. Mansfield. After an initial flap over the failure of the USN to include discussion of command relations in the Northwest Atlantic on the original agenda, the conference got down to business. Opening remarks were made by Admiral King, following which there were preliminary discussions of a general nature. The first session of the conference concluded with the designation of five committes: Command Relations (Canadian representative, Admiral Brodeur), Convoy and Escort (Brand, DeWolf, and Lay), Air Support (Air Vice-Marshal Anderson, RCAF), Training and Material Readiness of Operations Escorts and Groups (Creery), and Communications and Operational Intelligence (Commander De Marbois, RCN, Deputy director of Signals Division, NSHQ.)

The Convoy and Escort Committee was the first to be heard by the conference as a whole on 3 March. It basically recommended that the Admiralty's proposals for increasing the flow of trade to Britain be adopted. The cycle for fast convoys was to be stepped up to five days and that for slow convoys to eight. To handle the increased traffic MOEF was to be strengthened to fourteen groups by the return of the four C groups from the Eastern Atlantic and the employment of the two RN groups designated for the tanker convoys (A 3 was not considered, since it was expected to be disbanded). The USN agreed to take over responsibility for the direct movement of tankers to the UK, thus freeing the two B groups. The increased convoy cycle meant that WLEF too needed strengthening, and it was recommended that all RCN escorts on loan to other theatres be returned immediately to permit this. The recommendations of the Convoy and Escort Committee, which were accepted, thus put the whole of the North Atlantic trade routes into the hands of the Commonwealth navies.[41]

The issue of command relations was much more difficult to resolve. In large part this was because it involved possible trade-offs of world-wide strategic responsibilities. Perhaps not least because of the RCN's persistence and irascibility, the USN was prepared to withdraw Admiral Brainard. But American naval authorities were reluctant to yield too much to the British, and their fears were justifiable. Captain B.B. Schofield, the RN's DTD, for one, wanted any new Canadian zone placed directly under C-in-C, WA, which would have stretched British control to the shores of Maine. Yet this, Schofield mused in a memo on the subject prepared in February, 'would be asking more than the Americans would be prepared to swallow in one bite.'[42] In lieu of this and in lieu of a single supreme commander, the British were satisfied with a joint RN-USN Allied Anti-Submarine Survey Board struck to review and make recommendations on the co-ordination of A/S measures throughout the Atlantic.[43] The AA/SSB was formed at Washington and included as its principal members Rear Admirals Mansfield, RN, and Kauffman, USN. It was also given air representation.

With respect to the actual arrangement of responsibilities, the RN was well prepared to settle for command and control of convoy operations east of Newfoundland, leaving the new Canadian zone under the USN. But the Americans had no interest in overseeing Canadian operations, much less participating in RCN-directed activities, without a USN officer in a responsible position. No one questioned the strength or validity of the Canadian claim for control of its escort forces, but the RCN did not have the balanced fleet needed to assume strategic responsibility for its zone. In effect, either the USN or the RN had to take the Canadian zone under its wing. Although agreement on the shape of these responsibilities was reached by 8 March, the RN at least was not happy with letting the Canadians manage on their own. They wanted more USN input, but the Americans would not be pressured into propping up the new Canadian zone. Admiral Moore, reporting to the First Sea Lord on the ninth, stated that to pursue the matter was unwise. The Americans, he wrote, threatened 'to step out and leave it to us to deal with the Canadians.'[44] They would not participate actively in the Canadian zone under an RCN officer, nor would the USN permit its promised carrier support groups to operate west of WESTOMP. The danger of being saddled with the Canadians was evidently sufficient intimidation, and the command agreements remained unaltered.

Probably the only intimation the RCN got that the USN was less than enthusiastic about the new Canadian zone came when King suggested that Murray be appointed to CTF-24 during the transition period in order to learn the job and that Brainard be appointed a permanent adviser to the new C-in-C, Canadian Northwest Atlantic. Not surprisingly, the RCN declined the offer, noting rather caustically that Bristol (the original CTF-24) had learned his job from Murray in the first place.[45]

The findings of the Communications and Intelligence Committee were crucial to the decisions reached on command relations at Washington. The RCN already had experience in diverting shipping, and its naval-control-of-shipping organization was second to none. Ottawa had been an integral part of the Commonwealth's global NSC and naval intelligence system since before the war. As part of this responsibility the RCN had built an effective shore-based DF network in Canada and Newfoundland. The conference concluded, therefore, that the Canadians could handle the prerequisites of command and control, with some expansion of communications, in the proposed theatre. It was the efficiency of the RCN in these non-operational areas, coupled with its large commitment of forces, which made the Canadian Northwest Atlantic possible. Further, the new theatre was roughly equal to that mapped out by the RN before the conference as a suitable Canadian responsibility.[46] The British, too, it will be recalled, had a long-standing desire to see CTF-24 removed and as early as May 1942 had considered offering command of some portion of the Northwest Atlantic to the RCN as a means of putting pressure on the USN from another source. There is no evidence of a combined Commonwealth campaign, but the two royal navies sought the same goal. For the RCN the Canadian Northwest Atlantic was a dream come true and the only distinctly Canadian theatre of war.

The Americans agreed to withdraw CTF-24 and gave up participation in MOEF. They retained responsibility for a number of very small routes, such as convoys to U.S. air bases in the far north, and for strategic direction of the Western Atlantic. Canadian convoy operations and the new theatre therefore were still under the protective wing of the U.S. Atlantic Fleet. The USN also undertook to provide support groups for the main trade routes, using some of their growing number of escort carriers. Further to the south the USN concentrated on developing the U.S.-to-Mediterranean convoys. The great irony of these changes is that command of St John's–based escorts now passed from Admiral Brainard, USN, to Admiral Horton, RN. Commodore Reid at St John's retained responsibility for the availability of C groups and their escorts, but his function was increasingly that of support as actual control of the ships gravitated to Halifax and Liverpool.

The Training and Material Readiness Committee agreed that the training programs in all three navies were satisfactory, although it was noted that more effort was required to produce enough good engineers. Operational training for ships in commission and the need for special attention to group training were also stressed. The committee recommended that the USN system of separate senior officers be adopted to provide the continuity in leadership crucial to good group training. Lastly, the committee noted that material readiness was also a function of good training. With the exception of the suggestion of separate SOES, none of the committee's recommendations was new. However, they were an important affirmation of policies in which all the navies believed but had, on many occasions, been forced to push aside. For the RCN especially, the recommendations of the Training and Material Readiness Committee cleared the way for it to excuse itself from any future demands for escorts in the interests of efficiency.[47]

The Atlantic Convoy Conference was a watershed in Canadian and RCN history. In the simplest sense it represented a recognition of Canada's special interest in the North Atlantic and a delegation of responsibility commensurate with the nation's commitment. It also provided the RCN with a much-needed and firm base upon which to consolidate and from which to dispatch with confidence aid to other theatres. The psychological effects of the conference on the RCN were at least as great as the material benefits. The impact of all this on C groups was slow to develop, and in the long term the effects of consolidation at home were intertwined with the powerful influence of operating directly under C-in-C, WA. However, of far greater importance to the escorts of MOEF was the profound change which the imminent infusion of forces was to have on the future of convoy battles.

One of the most important decisions reached at Washington was the decision to base VLR Liberator aircraft (to be operated by the RCAF) in Newfoundland and Labrador to help close the air gap.[48] The redirection of these aircraft from Pacific theatres was a major coup for the British and Canadians. But the reconciliation of this and other conflicting views at Washington owed something to events at sea. Even as the delegates discussed the future shape of the Allied campaign, their fortunes in the mid-ocean reached rock-bottom. Indeed, things were so bad in the first weeks of March that the Admiralty actually considered the abandonment of convoy – a serious consideration, since there was no viable alternative. Recent German success against the convoy cipher was partly to blame. But this would never have forced the issue so quickly had it not been for the introduction of a new rotor for Atlantic U-boat cipher machines on 1 March. For the next twenty-two days the Allies were without special intelligence.[49] While British cryptanalysts worked feverishly to crack the new permutations, BdU intercepted all of the transatlantic convoys sailed. Only the sheer physical limitations of the U-boat fleet kept them from annihilating convoy after convoy. As things turned out, fully 20 per cent of all the ships that sailed in trade convoys on the North Atlantic in the first weeks of March failed to arrive. Both the interception and the loss rates were the highest of the war. Without the ability to route convoys around the huge packs now operating in the air gap, confrontation was unavoidable.

In early March battle followed on battle. A 3, only just finished with the frightful passage of ONS 166, turned eastward again in the last week of February with SC 121.[50] Heavy gales shattered the convoy's formation and the escort's frail detection equipment – which, in any event, was rendered virtually useless by the weather. Even with strong reinforcements on the third (cutters *Bibb* and *Ingham* and the destroyer *Babbitt*) and fourth (the RN corvettes *Campion* and *Mallow*) days of the battle, A 3 (*Spencer*, the U.S. destroyer *Greer*, corvettes *Rosthern*, *Trillium*, and *Dianthus* [RN]) could not prevent the twenty-seven U-boats sent to attack from sinking thirteen ships without loss to themselves. The tragedy of SC 121 brought A 3's losses in two successive convoys to twenty-seven merchantships. HX 228, following close behind SC 121, was also beset by attackers. In more moderate weather its escort, B 3, fared better, losing only four ships and the destroyer *Harvester*. However, in a remarkable example of coincidence, good fortune, and professionalism, the Free French corvette *Aconit* sank two U-boats: *U444*, which *Harvester* had rammed just prior to being torpedoed, and *U432*, the U-boat which had sunk the destroyer.

The next two eastbound convoys suffered as badly. HX 229, escorted by B 4, lost thirteen ships in two days when it was preyed upon by thirty-eight U-boats in the mid-Atlantic. In a simultaneous battle SC 122 lost eight ships. Eventually HX 229 and SC 122 were merged to provide their escorts with marginally less frontage to cover, but only the overwhelming power of Coastal Command was able to terminate the battle. The total losses from both convoys: twenty-one ships.[51]

With the exception of *Rosthern* and *Trillium* with A 3, and *Sherbrooke*, temporarily attached to B 4 during the battle for HX 229, the string of disasters owed nothing to Canadian involvement. Undoubtedly C groups, even at their best, could not have done better, and certainly, given the physical limitations of the U-boats, the Canadians could not have done worse. However, at the height of the battle for HX 229 and SC 122 there was a Canadian-escorted convoy in the mid-ocean – ON 172, escorted by C 3 (*Burnham* [RN], *Jed* [RN], *Bittersweet*, *Eyebright*, *La Malbaie*, and *Mayflower*) and reinforced by the returning TORCH corvettes *Port Arthur*, *Summerside*, and *Woodstock*. The combination of RCN corvettes was exceptional: three were RPVs; three were partially modernized RN escorts on loan, and even *Rosthern* and *Summerside* – the only members of the original RCN construction program present – were well equipped. It is, perhaps, not accidental that the lone C group operating in the mid-ocean at the very crisis of the defensive battle embodied most of the improvements to the original Flower-class corvette design intended to make that class proper deep-sea escorts. Fortunately, C 3's large and unconsolidated membership was untested. ON 172 was mercifully routed well to the north of the embattled British convoys HX 229 and SC 122. It arrived without loss.

On 22 March the staff at Bletchley Park broke the new German rotor settings and re-established the vitally important supply of special intelligence. The key to Allied success in the next two months was the combination of this excellent intelligence, which permitted not only avoidance of the enemy but also concentration upon him, the presence of powerful air and sea reinforcements, and better weather. As the C groups prepared for their return to MOEF, the five escort support groups became operational, one of them built around the escort carrier *Biter* (RN).[52] Their task was simple and their effect on MOEF's duties profound. Directed by operational commands to a threatened convoy and, once there, by their own modern equipment, support groups formed the outer ring of the convoy's defence. They pushed the U-boats back and pursued U-boat contacts at length. More importantly, in late March the Admiralty cancelled its air offensive in the Bay of Biscay and switched all of its long-range and VLR aircraft to the mid-ocean. By April there were forty-one VLR Liberators operating in support of MOEF.[53]

The Allied offensive in the mid-Atlantic coincided with a sharp decline in the morale of U-boat crews. In part this was because the large number of U-boats now in service were operating with captains inexperienced in command. Moreover, these new captains went to sea at a time when Allied countermeasures, built soundly on a growing body of experience, were making the U-boat's existence precarious. The battles of late February and early March were all fiercely contested. U-boats which pressed home attacks were given very rough treatment by better-equipped and more-professional escorts. Indeed, despite the heavy losses of shipping, February 1943 was the most successful month to date in the anti–U-boat war: nineteen U-boats destroyed. The score for March was four less, but fifteen confirmed kills was encouraging news to the Allies. Moreover, by the end of March it was clear from deciphered signals that the morale of U-boat crews was shaky. It was fortunate for the Allies that resources were immediately to hand to give the German's weakening resolve a fatal push.[54]

Allied convoy and escort operations were also blessed with moderating weather as March drew to a close. The winter of 1942–3 had been the worst since the outbreak of war. Between 1 October and 18 February there were well over one hundred days in which gales of force seven or greater were reported in the North Atlantic. The impact on convoy battles was significant. Heavy weather not only made it hard for convoys to keep good order, but again it adversely affected the efficiency of asdic and radar, and reduced air support. U-boat operations, in contrast, were much less affected, since successful attacks were usually aided by all but the worst of weather. Not surprisingly, then, the First Sea Lord, in making his assessment of the outlook for the Allied mid-ocean offensive in the spring of 1943, cited 'improving weather' as the first crucial factor.[55]

Thus as C groups resumed their mid-ocean duties in late March and early April, the operational environment was vastly different from that which they had left. But while the British went on the offensive, the Canadian restoration to MOEF did not constitute a return to normal operational status. Only the cycle for slow convoys increased in April (not March, as the British had originally hoped), and as a result the cycle for C groups remained comparatively slack. During long layovers in Londonderry the training program continued under the direction of the shore establisment and *Philante*. It was not until May, when the cycle for fast convoys was stepped up, that C groups once again shouldered their fair share of MOEF's burden.

Despite the fact that the battle in the mid-ocean was in its most important phase, the month of April was singularly unspectacular for the RCN. Though over the next two months the U-boat campaign was beaten and enormous losses inflicted upon the enemy, few Canadian escorts gained sight of a U-boat. With frequently very precise intelligence available and support groups to screen them from nearby concentrations, convoys and their close escorts generally avoided confrontations. Only two Canadian-escorted convoys were remotely threatened in April. SC 127 and its escort, C 1 (*St Laurent, St Croix, Itchen* [RN], *Agassiz,*

Napanee, and *Woodstock*), were simply routed around the pack sent to intercept them. Another convoy, HX 235 escorted by C 4, slipped gingerly between two packs, screened from the nearest by a support group.

And yet MOEF was fighting battles, some of the most important of the war. On the night of 11–12 April HX 232, escorted by B 3, was attacked by two members of group 'Luche,' the pack directed to intercept. Three ships were picked from the convoy – without retribution – before a combined sea and air escort drove off all the remaining shadowers during the twelfth. A 3's last convoy, HX 233, was also attacked in the mid-ocean. But in the calmer waters of southern latitudes A 3 was able to prevent the eight U-boats detailed to operate against the convoy from seizing the initiative. Only four U-boats actually attacked, sinking one ship. But *Spencer* balanced the score by destroying *U175*. Relief, in the form of the Third Support Group, ended the battle less than forty-eight hours after it had begun.

Towards the end of April much more serious battles, one of which was decisive, raged around a series of westbound convoys. Attempts by BdU to concentrate around ONS 3 (the slow-westbound series was renumbered at the end of March, following ON 171) and ON 178, then around ONS 4 and ON 179, were thwarted by the Allies' new skill and confidence and by very bad weather. The latter condition, and accurate location of U-boat patrol lines through decryption of U-boat signals, had made the successful avoidance of a very large U-boat concentration possible. But for about a week starting on 26 April the Allies suffered a gap in the flow of special intelligence, and U-boat plotting authorities in Canada and Britain gradually lost track of the enemy's exact positions. The next convoy to be intercepted, ONS 5, was therefore not as lucky as its immediate predecessors had been.[56]

ONS 5, escorted by B 7, Commander Peter Gretton, RN, Senior Officer, was detected by group 'Star' while still far to the north of the main U-boat concentration. The convoy actually skirted the tip of Star, and the pack was unable to effect a concerted attack. Meanwhile, to the southwest, in an area through which ONS 5 had to pass, BdU was directing another group, 'Fink,' in vain towards SC 128 (escorted by EG 40 [RN]). Having given Star the slip in heavy weather, ONS 5 ran into Fink on 4 May. Fink was temporarily facing the wrong direction, but it was very well placed to concentrate on ONS 5. Moreover, yet another pack, 'Amsel,' lay farther to the southwest and was also in an excellent position to intercept. Eleven of Amsel's U-boats were therefore detailed to join Fink's twenty-nine in a massive attack on ONS 5.

By 4 May ONS 5 was still disorganized and split up as a result of its earlier experience with bad weather. Over the next two days Amsel and Fink pressed home their attacks against an excellent but overwhelmed defence. Eleven ships had been lost by the sixth, with the prospect of many more to come. Yet just as it seemed that ONS 5 was to be annihilated, the battle, which in any event was rapidly running out of sea room, was beset by fog. In otherwise calm weather the modern radar of B 7 and the First Support Group was able to locate the plethora of U-boats now groping aimlessly in search of the convoy. On the night of 6–7 May the escort depth charged fifteen known U-boat contacts, rammed and damaged two, forced four others to beat a hasty retreat on the surface, and sank no less than four. In little more than a single night's action the mystique of the U-boat pack had been shattered.

Although back in the mainstream of MOEF operations by May, the C groups continued to play a small role in the unfolding drama because they were part of a close-escort force. In the meantime, the command arrangements agreed to at Washington went into effect. On 30 April Brainard struck his flag and Task Force Twenty-four was abolished. Immediately thereafter the Canadian Northwest Atlantic came into being, and Murray assumed the post of C-in-C. With the USN departure, A 3 was dissolved, and the remaining American escorts in the North Atlantic turned their attention to support of U.S. bases in the Arctic. The nucleus of A 3 formed around a new leader, *Ottawa II*, and became C 5. By the end of April all the escorts which had been on loan to the RN and USN were back in Canada. These escorts provided the RCN with much-needed leverage with which to modernize and repair the fleet and to participate in the new offensive phase of the war. One manifestation of the navy's desire to partake in the latter was the formation of the Canadian Support Group. Unfortunately, it did not become operational until June, by which time the crisis was over.[57] The composition of the group was noteworthy, however, as it included escorts which were all equipped for sinking U-boats: two RN frigates, *Nene* and *Tweed* (the former was transferred to the RCN in 1944), recently commissioned, and five corvettes – *Calgary*, *Edmundston*, and *Prescott*, all modernized; *Camrose*, partially modernized (no hedgehog); and *Lunenburg*, the only short-foc'sle corvette of the group.

In May 1943, then, the Allies had the U-boats on the run and were in hot pursuit. The offensive in the mid-ocean was greatly aided in that month by the final elimination of the air gap when RCAF VLR aircraft based in Newfoundland became operational. The pace set in April (when eighteen U-boats were destroyed) was quickened as support groups, British escorts, and air power dominated the action. This was the case in the battle for HX 237, the closest that C groups came to a convoy battle during the crisis months.[58] C 2, still largely British in complement (*Broadway* [RN], *Lagan* [RN], *Chambly*, *Drumheller*, *Morden*, and *Primrose* [RN]), punched HX 237 through an exceptionally well-directed U-boat concentration with the aid of HMS *Biter* and her aircraft. During the battle *Drumheller* participated, along with a Sunderland of 423 RCAF Squadron and *Lagan*, in the destruction of *U456*. *Drumheller*'s one-third of a kill was the only RCN contribution to the great carnage then being inflicted upon Germany's U-boat fleet. A week later C I (*Burnham* [RN], *Skeena*, and the corvettes *Bittersweet*, *Eyebright*, *La Malbaie*, *Mayflower*, and *Pictou*), escorting HX 238, slipped past a U-boat concentration with the help of special intelligence and the newly arrived USN Sixth Support Group, built around the small carrier *Bogue*.

The presence of *carrier* support groups with both of these C-group battles may have been coincidental. Yet through May and June C groups received a higher proportion of carrier-based air cover than their B counterparts. Further, in each case where a C group received aid from either form of support group, the help arrived in advance of enemy contact and lingered until after the last U-boat was well astern. In contrast, B groups only received help once the battle was joined.[59] The assignment of forces may have reflected a continued lack of confidence in the C groups. But what is more plausible, given the stage of the war, is the other side of the same coin – a tremendous confidence in the ability of British escorts.

Whatever the case, by May the C groups had finished their stint under C-in-C, WA, and were returned to the RCN. Ironically, this now meant little, except from an administrative point of view, since C groups came under Horton's command when engaged in operations. Further, it was not long after the return of the C groups to Canadian control that the battle in the mid-ocean reached its finale. In attacks on two British convoys in the third week of the month the Germans suffered their final humiliation. HX 239, escorted by B 3, and SC 130, escorted by B 7 and covered at stages by the First, Fourth (HMS *Archer*, carrier), and Sixth (USS *Bogue*) support groups, passed through a large U-boat concentration totally without loss, while the combined sea and air escort destroyed eight U-boats. ON 184, escorted by C I, passed through the same area shielded by the Sixth Support Group, also without losses. U-boat losses on this scale without any gain whatsoever were clearly unsustainable. The same was true for the whole month of May, when forty-seven U-boats were sunk.

As the wounded packs moved westwards to intercept two C-group convoys on 24 May (ONS 8, C 4, and HX 240, C 5), Dönitz withdrew his forces from the main trade routes. The climax of the Battle of the Atlantic had passed.

9

Summer of Discontent

The PM gave an account of his trip to Washington. Generally he
appears to be dissatisfied with the recognition that is being given
Canada's war effort and Canada's place by both Mr. Churchill
and Mr. Roosevelt.

Angus L. Macdonald, diary entry, 26 May 1943

My impression is that the failure to equip these ships with modern
material is keenly felt by all their officers and widely discussed,
and is tending to discourage them.

Lieutenant J. George, Historical Records Officer, RCN,
London, June 1943

'There was no period in the war,' wrote Mackenzie King's private secretary many years later, 'when the war itself seemed so remote from
Canada as the first six months of 1943.'[1] While Allied fortunes in the
Battle of the Atlantic went from near catastrophe to signal victory, Canada
was war-weary and restless. Her mood prevailed even after the escorts'
triumph in the Atlantic was made public in June and Canadian troops
landed in Sicily in July. Disquiet on the home front was matched by
frustration in the fleet over the navy's poor showing in the recent defeat
of the U-boat packs. As a result, 1943 brought a battle of memos, reports,
and often acrimonious debate within the navy and between the navy and
the government.

Few – if indeed any – seagoing officers had been happy with the state
of equipment in the expansion fleet prior to 1943. In the earliest days the
overwhelming concern was the provision of rudimentary naval and marine
equipment – signal lamps, duffle coats, and secondary armament in any

form, to name but a few commodities in short supply. When these matters had been attended to, more complex equipment shortfalls remained. By early 1942 Murray was complaining about the need for 271 radar and, in mid-year, HF/DF. These requests were not ignored by NSHQ, but lacking persuasive information, even from Murray, the Staff was slow to react. Further, for senior planners the problem in 1942 was lack of quantity, not quality. There simply were not enough escorts, a refrain which persisted until the spring of 1943.

The action of the U-boats confirmed the opinion of NSHQ that the prime need in the Atlantic was for more escorts. So long as the U-boats had new, unguarded theatres into which they could move when pushed, the combination of convoy and indifferently prepared escorts was adequate for the needs of trade defence. That had been the lesson of the first unrestricted U-boat campaign on trade, in 1917, and it was the lesson of the first three years of the Second World War. Submariners displayed an understandable preference for unprotected trade whenever the choice was available. Even an incompetent escort complicated the attacker's task, and this was particularly so when he was operating three thousand miles from home across seas totally dominated by hostile forces. Under such conditions even slight damage to a submarine could prove fatal. Further, until the easy theatres ceased to exist, there was no purpose in challenging the Allied escort system directly. Unlike the Allied navies, which sought victory through destruction of opposing enemy fleets, the submarine service of the Kriegsmarine was directed at the merchant marine, which it sought to destroy. Only when Allied countermeasures became truly efficient in the spring of 1943 was Dönitz forced to modify this guiding strategy and adopt one meant to prevent the redeployment of Allied resources to other theatres.[2]

Throughout 1942 the RCN strove to close off the weak points in the Allied defensive system which gave Dönitz's war on tonnage its great successes. Many of these weak points only became apparent – or important – after serious attacks were already under way. The small and overworked Canadian Naval Staff was reduced to reacting to one emergency after another, leaving short- and medium-term planning of the war at sea to the larger navies. What planning was undertaken by the RCN before November 1942 pertained to the very long-term consequences of these events – the need for a balanced fleet.[3]

It was only as the battle in the mid-ocean and in waters off Canada and Newfoundland was finally joined that the quantitative impetus of Canadian escort operations gradually gave way to an equal need for quality. Admittedly, there had always been a need for quality in defence, but the enemy was too numerous by late 1942, and defences were being swamped. The insistence of the British on quality had already made their home waters untenable for large U-boat operations. The problem now was to extend effective ASW westwards into the mid-ocean and the Western Atlantic. The establishment of the Anti–U–Boat Warfare Committee and Noble's replacement by Horton were indicators of British resolve to settle the U-boat issue. The C groups were among Horton's first 'victims.' But while it was possible to upgrade the training level and basic equipment of a few escorts, reorienting the whole RCN was no easy matter. NSHQ had to alter a jury-rigged organization, erected primarily to produce men and ships, into a responsive, well-integrated, well-supported and -supplied, efficiency-oriented A/S service – and to do so almost overnight. It could not be done.

Convoy battles of late 1942 made it clear to the Naval Staff that the state of the fleet was inadequate, and this was driven home by the British in December. It is also significant to note that the 'crisis' of late 1942 arose from the navy's demonstrable inability to *defend* convoys rather than from shortcomings in conventional fleet operations. The keys to proper defence were fairly accessible: modern radar, HF/DF, better operational training, more destroyers, steady group compositions, and able leadership. Rectification of these shortcomings was either completed or well in hand when the character of convoy battles altered fundamentally. By the spring of 1943 C groups were well prepared to fight and win the battles of 1942, but the war had once again gained a march. The old concepts and standards of MOEF were swept aside by the introduction of support groups and the closing of the air gap. Since the RCN possessed no support groups during the crucial months of April and May, Canadian escorts laboured in purely defensive roles. Moreover, the transfer of C groups to Western Approaches for training kept Canadian MOEF escorts busy with other duties through most of the crisis.

Thus, many of the reasons for the RCN's small role in the offensive against the U-boat were not readily apparent to those at sea. One RCN officer later recalled that he and his fellow officers believed that the period of intensive training and re-equipment with heavier secondary armament and modern radar was undertaken to prepare them for the more serious task of escorting TORCH troop convoys.[4] But while Canadian officers had to speculate on the significance of their role, the magnitude of the RN's success against the U-boats was common knowledge in the wardrooms and mess-decks of Canadian warships. Lieutenant J. George, the Historical Records Officer based in London and quoted at the head of this chapter, found the mood of the officers in Canadian MOEF escorts sombre in the spring of 1943. RCN officers serving in the mid-ocean, George observed, felt let down by the Naval Staff and blamed them for the debilitating manning policy, bad equipment, neglect, and generally poor staff work. The languishing state of modernization of Canadian escorts and the dispatch of better-equipped long-foc'sle corvettes to TORCH in the fall of 1942 were both 'keenly felt.' Moreover, the Canadian officers noted that even when a C group was successful, as C 2, for example, had been with HX 237 in May, the well-equipped RN members walked off with all the laurels.[5]

In some measure the discontent fomenting in the C groups was a direct result of their prolonged exposure to Western Approaches personnel and establishments during the transfer period. Nowhere is the impact of this exposure more evident than in the report submitted to Captain (D), Newfoundland, by Acting Lieutenant Commander D.W. Piers, RCN, CO of the destroyer *Restigouche*, on 1 June 1943. Piers's 'Comments on the Operation and Performance of HMC Ships, Establishments and Personnel in the Battle of the Atlantic' was a detailed summary of C-group complaints, many of them of long standing. Piers described the Canadian component of MOEF as a poor second cousin to both the RCN and the RN. Both the B groups and the whole of WLEF had better access to major centres, regular leave, proper support facilities, and reliable mail service. For all these reasons morale in C groups was low. More importantly, Piers made it plain that Western Approaches Staff were not pleased with the general state of the RCN's contribution to the mid-ocean either. Piers described the British as 'enthusiastic' about the accomplishments of the RCN but disturbed by the lack of modern equipment. 'It is a blunt statement of fact,' Piers wrote, 'that RCN ships are outdated in the matter of A/S equipment by 12 to 18 months, compared to RN.' Moreover, not only Horton but also 'Commodore [(D)] Londonderry and his staff realize that Canadian personnel are not getting the chance they deserve, due to lack of modern equipment.'[6] Although NSHQ could not know it, Piers's mention of Commodore G.W.G. Simpson's displeasure at the state of equipment in Canadian MOEF ships was a portent of the commodore's involvement in the confrontation over the equipping of the fleet which erupted in the fall.

Piers's report went on to comment on other sources of inefficiency such as poor initial training for reservist officers, short work-up periods for escorts, and the manning policy. Many of these, Piers confessed, 'have undoubtedly been corrected already.' Indeed, it is likely that none of the points raised in Piers's report, not even those concerning the state of equipment, caused NSHQ much anxiety. But the officers of MOEF – and Western Approaches – were not the only ones concerned about the RCN's apparent inability to destroy submarines on a scale in proportion to its size.

In May Murray in Halifax reported that the Canadian zone as constituted by the Atlantic Convoy Conference had one of the poorest records of U-boats destroyed of any theatre in the world. During 1942 only one U-boat had been destroyed by surface escorts in exchange for the loss of 112 merchant ships. In sharp contrast, the global ratio of U-boats destroyed to ships lost was one to 10.3. Had the RCN been pulling its weight in the offensive against the enemy, the RCN's score of U-boats in the Canadian zone should have been at least ten, or the extent of losses to shipping much lower and the ratio between the two more in line with the world average. Murray believed that BdU studied such figures as well and would inevitably launch a major campaign in the Canadian zone.[7] To forestall this, he and Prentice altered the doctrine of WLEF to one of offensive escort. In a memorandum on tactical doctrine Prentice exhorted WLEF to conduct operations on the basis of what 'will give you the greatest chance of a kill ... rather than in terms of the safety of the convoy.'[8] What made WLEF's offensive against the U-boats so remarkable was that it actually began at the end of March 1943, simultaneous with the beginning of the British offensive in the mid-ocean. Fortunately, WLEF's freedom from large and sustained attacks allowed it to modify its doctrine without introducing changes to the escort arrangements, without an influx of reinforcements, and, more importantly, without risking serious losses to shipping. MOEF was never so lucky.

While WLEF and, somewhat later, the Canadian Support Group attempted to carry the war to the enemy, east-coast establishments joined in the clamour to bring swift change to the state of the fleet. Among the memos generated on this subject in the spring of 1943, two warrant discussion here because of their later importance in the debate over the performance of NSHQ. The staff at St John's were more acutely aware of the disparities between RCN and RN escorts in MOEF than was any other Canadian establishment. They were also more sensitive to the effect that this disparity had on the success, or lack of it, of RCN operations. It was also significant that in the spring of 1943 Captain H.T.W. Grant, who had succeeded Mainguy as Captain (D), Newfoundland, in late 1942, was in turn replaced by Captain J.M. Rowland, RN. Rowland's displeasure with the conduct of the navy has already been mentioned, and he was clearly not prepared to suffer the neglected state of his MOEF ships. On 1 May Rowland petitioned FONF to obtain priority for the fitting of MOEF with all the latest equipment, 'at whatever cost.' He outlined the changes needed to upgrade radar and asdic, and returned repeatedly to the need to modernize without reference to cost. 'This,' Rowland noted, referring to the financial burden attendant on new equipment, 'should not matter as being so much less than the losses being suffered in the mid-Atlantic.' The new Captain (D) wanted his ships put on an equal footing with the RN so that they could have 'equal chances of proving themselves.'[9]

The tone of Rowland's memo was characteristic of a seagoing officer, impatient with and lacking in understanding of NSHQ. Commodore Reid, as vice-chief of the Naval Staff until the end of October 1942, had actually been part of the establishment against which Rowland now vented his displeasure. But clearly, as Flag Officer, Newfoundland, Reid shared Rowland's concern for the state of Canadian escorts. Reid endorsed the memo with a strongly worded covering letter and passed both on to NSHQ on 13 May. In the letter FONF charged that 'there have been numerous cases where delay in obtaining the necessary authority has resulted in ships missing good opportunities to fit this vitally necessary gear.' Reid wanted a blanket clearance granted to Commodore Simpson to fit the RCN with the latest equipment. His letter concluded by noting that the disparity in equipment between the RCN and the RN left the Canadians in 'the unacceptable position of having to fight modern war with outdated equipment.'[10]

Not surprisingly, the staff at St John's were not alone in their quest for greater efficiency. Like Rowland, the senior officers at Halifax had only just assumed their posts in early 1943, and they, too, were displeased with the state of the fleet. Six of these senior officers, including Rowland, met in Halifax in late June to discuss 'maintaining and improving efficiency' and passed their conclusions and recommendations on to Murray. Their complaints centred around the manning policy, the lack of proper work-ups, and the lingering effects of 'operational emergencies in 1942.' The group's submission, forwarded to Admiral Murray by Captain R.E.S. Bidwell, his chief of staff, noted that all of the officers present agreed with the policy of 1942 whereby emphasis was laid on keeping ships at sea and escort groups up to strength. 'So far we have managed not to fail in any of our commitments,' the six concluded, 'but possibly this has been at the expense of efficiency.' This mild reflection upon their predecessor's policies was then followed by recommendations for re-dressing the situation. Most of the officers desired a fundamental alteration in the manning policy, which they saw as a major impediment to attaining efficiency. The officers wanted the RCN to adopt the American practice of commissioning each new ship with a totally new crew, working it up to operational status, and thereafter leaving it largely unmolested. Such a policy would maintain the efficiency of operational escorts, a goal believed to be more important than catering 'to the needs of new con-struction which may not even be operational this year.'[11]

The only dissenter from the group of senior east-coast officers was Captain (D), Halifax. Prentice quite rightly felt that the time to worry about the manning policy was past. In a minute appended to Bidwell's report explaining his position, Prentice stated that the scale of drafting from operational escorts was now small and limited almost exclusively to ships undergoing prolonged refits. The return of efficient ships from refits and the commitment of efficient new construction to operations could, in Prentice's estimation, be achieved by adhering to proper work-ups for both. Moreover, Prentice felt that the RCN was now well enough developed to support both efficiency in operations and further expansion, a view which contrasted sharply with that of his colleagues. Murray passed both views on to NSHQ at the end of June.[12]

Reaction to Rowland's and Bidwell's memos at NSHQ was subdued. Signals Division was asked to comment on the allegations of serious delays in fitting new radars and found ample evidence to show that the situation was well in hand. Rowland's contention that the version of 271 radar with which his ships were currently fitted was now out of date found little sympathy at NSHQ, especially with the director of Signals Division, Commander G.A. Worth. 'Sam' Worth was one of the RCN's genuine characters and something of a legend. A skilled communications expert, he had left the navy in the early thirties and, according to popular belief, had thrown in his lot with Nova Scotia rum-runners and even developed a sophisticated signal and code system for 'operations' off the New England coast. A gruff and brusque character, Worth – like most of his contemporaries – was ill suited to staff work. He noted in response to this latest request for better equipment that Reid was prone to 'flying off on his typewriter' without first checking the real story. While NSHQ pondered what to do with more of the same, Reid petitioned NSHQ on 30 June for action on his requests. It was not until 20 July that the secretary of the Naval Board replied. At that time Reid was informed that the Naval Staff concurred with his desire to have MOEF fitted with all the latest, but advised that radar and HF/DF policy was under constant review in both Canada and Britain.[13]

The two-month delay in responding to what Reid apparently considered an urgent request was unfortunate – though the fact that Rowland's memo sat on Reid's desk for nearly two weeks before it was sent to Ottawa suggests that the Naval Staff was not alone in its tardy handling of allegedly urgent matters. NSHQ perhaps also delayed responding to Bidwell's memo because the Naval Staff felt as Prentice did on the matter of the manning policy. The delay occurred in part because of disagreement over the latest complaints from the coast, in part because NSHQ was in the midst of a major restructuring. When headquarters moved into its new building at Cartier Square in November 1942, a new Directorate of Organization had been formed to look into the structure of NSHQ and its various departments. Considerable thought and planning was given over to making NSHQ more efficient during the early months of 1943. On 23 April Captain Wallace B. Creery was appointed to the new post of assistant CNS, and on 1 June he was placed in charge of four key staffs: Operations, Plans, Trade, and the newly formed Directorate of Warfare and Training (DWT). The latter was created 'primarily for the purpose of establishing the standards of fighting efficiency of RCN ships and maintaining them.'[14] Formation of the DWT was a crucial step in the struggle for efficiency since the RCN had hitherto lacked a co-ordinating body for such matters. It is, however, significant that the DWT saw both Rowland and Bidwell's memos, which also caused delay in the official replies.

Before turning to look at other sources of discontent, we should note that the Directorate of Organization also recommended action in mid-June on the morass of delayed refits and insufficient facilities. These were to be handed over to a commodore superintendent of refits. The problem itself was 'so urgent and of such vital importance that time does not permit of a full investigation of all the factors contributing to it.' The new commodore, G. Hibbard, and his establishment were ready to go by early October.[15]

It was bad enough for the RCN that its hard running in 1942 had brought a sour reward in early 1943: no glory at a time of great Allied triumph and no sense of a job well done. And it was enough that the navy had struggled to redeem the situation only to find its path littered by the flotsam of earlier years. But the RCN was not allowed the privilege of solving its own problems internally. Indeed, even as it strove to catch up on the neglected refits of 1942, to commission the latest flood of new construction from the St Lawrence River, to establish the Canadian Northwest Atlantic, to carry on operations and plan the modernization of the fleet, the RCN came under the critical gaze of the Allied Anti-Submarine Survey Board. The board had been formed at the Atlantic Convoy Conference as a substitute for a supreme commander, Atlantic. Its two principal members, Rear Admiral J.M. Mansfield, RN (formerly chief of staff to C-in-C, WA) and Rear Admiral J.L. Kauffman, USN, (formerly commander, Caribbean Sea Frontier), were charged with co-ordinating the Allied A/S effort in the Atlantic. In its eight months of existence the Mansfield-Kauffman board toured all the major North Atlantic establishments, including air bases, beginning in Britain on the first of April. Visits to Canadian facilities began on 7 May in Ottawa, moving three days later to Halifax and ending up in Newfoundland from the twelfth to the fourteenth.

The board's report on its visit to Canada was divided into three main segments: operations, training, and maintenance. Comments and recommendations respecting operations focused on problems associated with the proper co-ordination of air and sea forces within the new Canadian zone. The report advised 'most strongly that full operational efficiency cannot be realized until this is done.' The air member of the board, Group Captain P.F. Canning, RAF, was, in reports made directly to his superiors in Britain, more candid about the depth of this problem. 'We were disappointed in the Canadian setup,' Canning wrote to Air Marshal Slessor, and 'made it quite clear that the RCN and RCAF must get together immediately.'[16] As for training, the board found little to comment on critically, and there is no evidence in the board members' confidential memoranda to British senior officers indicating that their private opinions differed from those expressed in the report. The gravest shortcoming of Canadian training continued to be the shortage of training submarines, a problem noted at the Atlantic Convoy Conference to be general.

The issue of maintenance, which included modernization of the fleet, was the most pressing and controversial. The Mansfield-Kauffman board was actually ill disposed to the Canadian situation well before it left for Canada. The problems of Canadian maintenance had dominated discussion of the general subject during a meeting with Horton at Western Approaches headquarters on 14 April. Horton told the board that he had received complaints from convoy commodores 'of the very large numbers of Canadian warships that appeared to be idle in Canadian harbours at one time.'[17] Admiral Kauffman mentioned that he had already spoken with Admiral Brainard, CTF-24, about the matter and proposed to take it up with Captain Bidwell (Murray's COS) shortly. It was noted that the

RCN's current policy was to refit whole escort groups as units, since the rapidity of the navy's expansion had created maintenance difficulties on a large scale. When the board met in Londonderry six days later to discuss training, the issue of Canadian maintenance came up again. The feeling was that the RCN granted too-frequent leave and that this interfered with training. Those attending the meeting wanted to restrict leaves to long refit periods, and Kauffman noted that this might (somehow) have a good effect on morale in Canada and would 'help the Board in bringing pressure to bear on the Canadians on the question of maintenance.'[18]

During the board's visit to Canada and Newfoundland it found the RCN eager to discuss its maintenance problems, not least perhaps because the board itself was interested in the matter. In Ottawa a special session on maintenance was held at which a representative of Engineer Rear Admiral G.L. Stephens, the chief of Naval Engineering and Construction (who was in Britain), presented NSHQ's estimation of the problems. Discussions with the staffs at Halifax and St John's along similar lines also absorbed much of the board's time. In its final report to Nelles the board's comments and recommendations on maintenance were extensive. The RCN's own maintenance facilities at St John's and Halifax were found to have long since 'passed the saturation point,' while the small Maritimes yards were inefficient to the point of forcing naval facilities to make major repairs to escorts just released from refit. The proportion of escorts due for refit was 'unacceptably high,' and new construction and merchant shipping took up 'a very large number of available shipyard mechanics and to a certain extent [had] priority.' The board concluded that escorts must be given priority in maintenance over all else, that six thousand men were needed immediately to fill out the staffs of Maritime shipyards, that a floating drydock was needed in St John's for the exclusive use of escorts, and that new construction should be halted or curtailed until the existing fleet was in good shape. It is noteworthy that many of these suggestions, including another that would have given UK authorities carte blanche to fit RCN escorts with the latest equipment, found their way to NSHQ in submissions from east-coast staffs after the visit of the board. Admiral Stephens also fully supported the findings of the board and made his views (which included a desire for British assistance) clear to the First Sea Lord Admiral Sir Dudley Pound, before leaving Britain.[19]

In all the discussions that Mansfield and Kauffman had with RCN officers, the latter stressed that the management of shipyards and resources 'rests in civilian hands.'[20] That was true enough, since the first organization of Canadian shipyards had been undertaken to provide maintenance for merchant shipping. In November 1940 a controller for Ship Repairs (later extended to include Salvage) had been appointed to oversee work to civilian accounts, and his organization was well established by the time the RCN developed a pressing need for the same resources.[21] Breaking into the system was difficult and indeed may not even have been contemplated in view of the ongoing development of naval bases at Sydney, Shelburne, and Bay Bulls. But in early 1943 the need was urgent, and the RCN was found without good plans for coping with the situation. On at least one occasion Mansfield confronted the complainants with their own culpability in the apparent failure of planning. After listening to the Halifax staff grumble over their inability to obtain priority in the allocation of resources for the navy, Mansfield agreed that it was indeed a matter of government policy but 'doubted whether the case had really been represented to them as a long term policy.'[22] This was the only hint at the board's dissatisfaction with the RCN's planning to emerge in the formal minutes. However, Mansfield was more candid when he reported to Admiral Pound. 'The Board,' Mansfield wrote, 'was undoubtedly shocked with conditions as they found them on visiting Canada.'[23]

Both Mansfield and Group Captain Canning made their confidential reports upon returning to Britain in early July. During the same month Mansfield also visited his colleagues at Western Approaches, where undoubtedly the refit situation in Canada was discussed (there were no formal meetings of the board in July and thus no minutes). It was not surprising, therefore, that towards the end of the month Commodore Simpson took an extraordinary step to clear the apparent log-jams at NSHQ.

In July Captain W. Strange, RCN, the assistant director of Naval Intelligence at NSHQ, took passage to Britain in HMS *Duncan*, the captain of which, Commander P.W. Gretton, was one of Britain's most able escort commanders. During their many discussions Gretton expressed his admiration for the RCN and also his sadness that the effort was so crippled by the lack of modern equipment. Strange had heard rumblings of this from Canadian officers and was persuaded by Gretton to discuss the matter with Simpson, who, as Commodore (D), was responsible for the operational efficiency of all WA escorts. When Strange met the commodore, he perfunctorily protested that equipment lay outside the responsibility of an intelligence officer, but Simpson insisted on being heard. According to Strange's later recollection, Simpson claimed that he had put the matter of the poor equipment of Canadian escorts to a number of senior RCN officers, but to no avail. Simpson expressed his belief that something 'quite unorthodox' was now needed. In the words of C.P. Stacey, the official historian of defence policy, Strange thereupon 'became convinced that existing communications channels and organization were ineffective, and that he had a duty to see that the information reached the Canadian Naval Minister.'[24]

Strange took his return passage to Canada in the destroyer *Assiniboine*. Her captain, Commander K.F. Adams, RCN, had only just gone back to sea and had obviously been surprised at the situation RCN escorts were now in. Adams helped Strange prepare a confidential memorandum for the minister, Mr A.L. Macdonald, on the subject of equipment and then produced his own, which he passed through the proper channels (Captain [D], Newfoundland) on 9 August. Although Adams's memo later gained notoriety as a statement of the condition of the fleet in the summer of 1943, it was Strange's which garnered credit for attracting Macdonald's attention to the efficiency of the fleet. This interpretation is, however, only partly true.

Macdonald was sensitive to the performance of the fleet for more practical political reasons in August 1943. The war had never seemed more remote to Canadians. From the perspective of the Canadian public, their forces had not, with the two tragic exceptions of Hong Kong and Dieppe, seen action, although the nation had been at war for nearly four years. Canadian industry, it is true, had accomplished a great deal, but its successes bordered on profiteering and did not constitute the type of war effort with which Canadians readily identified. By late 1942 pressure was building on the government to commit the Canadian army to an active theatre. Of all the Dominions, Canada's role in actual fighting had been the least, and with the Allies advancing on all fronts the shoddy edifices of fascism might collapse at any moment. 'If the war ended now,' Colonel Ralston, the minister of Defence confided to the War Cabinet in December 1942, 'we would have to hang our heads in shame.'[25]

Early 1943 complicated the government's domestic political position by bringing a surge of war-weariness and labour unrest. Canadians were bitter about wage and price controls and vented their anger on the government. Mackenzie King and his party attempted to assuage resentment by focusing public attention on the achievements of the Liberal government and by committing Canadian forces to the landings in Sicily. In both cases the prime minister sought to strengthen his domestic position by securing more recognition of Canadian efforts in the pronouncements of American and British leaders, who quite naturally monopolized the media. As Macdonald noted in his diary, Mackenzie King expressed his 'dissatisfaction with the recognition ... given Canada's war effort' internationally following his return from the Trident Conference, convened in Washington from 12 to 25 May 1943 to discuss the higher direction of the war.[26] He was also upset at the initial press releases on the Sicilian landings, which spoke only of an Anglo-American assault. Fortunately, Mackenzie King was able to get those releases altered before publication, but it was clear that the battle for recognition was just beginning.

The most obvious example of the government's attempts to improve its domestic image was its sponsoring of the Quebec Conference of top-level British, American, and, of course, Canadian leaders and staffs in August 1943. Mackenzie King managed to find a place in most of the publicity photographs, and in terms of selling the Canadian prime minister as an important third party in the Anglo-American axis, the conference was a success. But for the Liberal party, that triumph of image was dimmed by flagging fortunes at the polls. On 4 August the Liberal government of Ontario was swept from office, its ranks decimated by an angry electorate (a defeat from which it has never recovered). Five days later – the day Churchill arrived in Halifax – four federal by-elections all went heavily against the government. On the eve of the Quebec Conference the Liberal party's popularity had reached a new low.

Not surprisingly, when Churchill met with the Canadian War Cabinet at the Château Frontenac in Quebec City on 11 August, the government was looking for support. Mackenzie King immediately took the British prime minister to task for the Sicilian slight. Churchill was also assailed for the recent announcement that all U-boat sinkings would be reported to the public on the tenth of each month by Roosevelt and himself. As Macdonald confided to his diary and as was apparently made clear to Churchill, 'such policies embarrassed us in Parliament.' Churchill explained that the Sicilian incident was his fault and was caused by his having too much to do and differences in time zones. It was a plausible excuse in the handling of one, highly secret major operation. But Mackenzie King was also after recognition of Canadian contributions of long standing, efforts which involved no concern for timing and little for the secrecy of broad details. The huge contribution of the RCN to the Battle of the Atlantic was an excellent example, and Mackenzie King immediately confronted Churchill with the fact that Canada was doing about 40 per cent of the escort work in the North Atlantic. Churchill replied laconically, 'I didn't know it was 40 per cent,' and then proceeded to thank Canada in general for all that it had done.[27]

Churchill was clearly ignorant of the RCN's contribution, but it is inconceivable that he could have been so had the RCN sunk 40 per cent of the U-boats recently destroyed. For Churchill was an avid 'Hun-basher,' and his interest in the Battle of the Atlantic, even from the time he was First Lord at the outset of the war, was primarily in how many U-boats were sunk. His remarkable confession of ignorance must have come as a great surprise and disappointment to the War Cabinet. Not only had the RCN not made an impression at home; it had not made one abroad either. Thus, at Quebec in August 1943 the performance of the navy and fortunes of the government became inseparably linked. Perhaps this one meeting with Churchill would have been sufficient to turn Macdonald on to NSHQ in search of answers. But there were other important persons at Quebec with whom Macdonald probably spoke on naval matters, among them Admiral Sir Dudley Pound, who had seen Mansfield's report on the state of Canadian maintenance.

By all accounts the first hard evidence of the reason for the fleet's poor showing reached Macdonald on 20 August (while he was still at Quebec), when Strange's memo arrived. The latter contained some basic statistics on the extent of fitting of certain pieces of modern equipment in the RCN as compared to the RN. Concentrating on gyro-compasses and hedgehog as a measure of the level to which an escort had been modernized, Strange noted that whereas only five corvettes in the RN were without this equipment, only two Canadian corvettes had yet been fitted. Lack of this equipment 'prevented our ships from making a good showing,' and because of this they were relegated to minor roles. The next day Macdonald ordered Nelles, the CNS, to report on 'the completeness of our Anti-Submarine equipment as compared to similar equipment on U.K. vessels on the North Atlantic run [MOEF],' with particular attention to asdic, radar, gyros, and hedgehog. In the same memo the minister also asked for information on RCN discipline in Britain, the state of the navy's representation in Londonderry, and what had become of a suggestion that officers be given better access to their superiors when offering ideas for innovations. Macdonald instructed Nelles to spare no effort in completing his report on these matters, including calling upon FONF, C-in-C, CNA, and Commodore Simpson.[28]

There is no indication that Nelles went as far afield in search of information as Macdonald had suggested. He received reports from various NSHQ offices and by 1 September had prepared a response to Macdonald's request. In the interim, the navy's planning of fleet modernization was thrown into disarray by the Admiralty's announcement on 28 August of its intention not to take any more RCN corvettes in hand for modernization.[29] Two had been completed since February in British yards, and one was in hand. The reason given was a sudden increase in the need for refits to RN ships, which admittedly had been driven hard in early 1943. The Admiralty's withdrawal left NSHQ and its modernization schedules out on a limb and accentuated the mishandling of maintenance planning by the RCN. Whether or not this decision was part of a larger plan to shake up NSHQ is a mystery. It was, however, entirely consistent with the displeasure expressed by the Mansfield-Kauffman board and with Commodore Simpson's belief that the time for 'unorthodox' action had arrived. In any event, British withdrawal from the modernization program forced NSHQ to recast its plans many months after the issue was first given top priority and made NSHQ's inability to plan appear all the worse – a fact which did not go unnoticed by its detractors.

While the Naval Staff scrambled to find berths for the corvettes which the RN could not (or would not) modernize, Nelles's memo on equipment was placed before Macdonald.[30] The CNS's response dealt with the minister's request for information in a general way. No direct comparisons, such as that advanced by Strange, of RN and RCN equipment in MOEF were made. Rather, Nelles concentrated on the state of the RCN as a whole, its policy on different pieces of equipment (asdic, gyros, hedgehog, radar, and armament) and the current RN policy – not the state of issue to the British fleet. Conceivably Macdonald would have received more specific information from Nelles had he made the contents of Strange's memo evident. However, the fact was that Nelles failed to meet Macdonald's unequivocal request for a comparison of equipment *as issued* to forces in MOEF. Nelles later confessed that the information necessary for such a comparison was unavailable at NSHQ, which was not only an indictment of the Naval Staff but also an inadequate excuse in light of the minister's specific instructions that no effort be spared to obtain detailed information from operational authorities. Macdonald suspected a cover-up and was thereafter suspicious of anything Nelles said on the matter. Further, the minister dispatched his executive assistant, Mr J.J. Connolly, to Britain on a fact-finding mission. Captain Strange wrote letters of introduction for Connolly addressed to the important personages of Western Approaches, and Nelles unwittingly made Connolly's travel arrangements.

Not surprisingly, Connolly was well received in Britain and even stayed with Commodore Simpson while in Londonderry. His host 'talked at length on many occasions ... on the comparative lack of efficiency of RCN ships'[31] and made sure that Connolly met all the responsible officers of his staff. According to Connolly's later report to the Naval Staff,

'British and American officers at 'Derry expressed great concern at the relative fighting efficiency of the Canadian Escort Craft as a whole, due to lack of modern fighting equipment.' When Connolly met Horton he found (apparently with some astonishment) that the C-in-C, WA's views 'coincided exactly with those of Commodore (D).'

Connolly returned to Ottawa in late October with confirmation of the poor state of the fleet's equipment and a British promise to once again take some corvettes in hand for modernization. The first intimation which Nelles got of the nature of his mission was the receipt, from Connolly on 10 November, of an anonymous British memo dealing with the modernization of the RCN. The memo had been given to Connolly during his visit to the Admiralty and was, to say the least, highly critical of NSHQ. Adopting the criticism of Canadian persistence in new construction (101 frigates, 26 Algerine minesweepers, and 38 corvettes currently 'under construction') at a time when the operational fleet was desperately in need of repair work – a theme first aired by the Mansfield-Kauffman board and subsequently impressed on Connolly by Horton – the memo accused the Naval Staff of incompetence. It criticized the organization of the staff and made the remarkable assertion that 'the modernization of Canadian corvettes is an extremely simple matter.' All that the chief of Naval Engineering apparently had to do was decide which ships to work on, and then get on with the job. The inability of the Canadian Naval Staff to 'make forecasts and decisions is a nuisance here and upsetting to the personnel of the ships concerned.' The memo then made reference to the latest refit program for the RCN, dated 30 September, paragraph two of which was deemed 'typical': 'As the whole question of extended foc'sles and fitting hedgehog in RCN corvettes is at present under review, it is not possible to state at this moment which ships will be taken in for these alterations and additions.' 'A very remarkable admission,' the memo concluded, 'in the fifth year of the war.'[32]

The severity of the charges contained in the anonymous memo caused considerable consternation at NSHQ. Commander Griffiths, RCN, the new director of Operations, commented simply that 'the man is Mad!' What could be done was being done. Rear Admiral Jones, the VCNS, rather typically considered it constructive criticism, noting that it had been more important in 1942 to keep ships at sea – an honest statement from a former COAC. Rear Admiral Stephens, chief of Naval Engineering and Construction, whose staff bore the brunt of the criticism, was particularly upset by the memo's contents. The RCN, he said, was behind for many reasons, not the least of which was having 'taken on more than our fair share of providing ships for escort duty ... It is obvious that while we have been keeping our ships running and providing escorts, Admiralty have kept their ships home and modernized them.' The memo, Stephens charged, displayed a complete lack of understanding of the bind in which the RCN now found itself. As an example Stephens noted that the need to review modernization policy and planning in September stemmed from the British decision in August to withdraw. The CNEC now wanted modernization given absolute priority, even ahead of operations, leaving the Admiralty to find whatever escorts were needed.[33]

On 15 November Connolly finally went before the Naval Staff to present his findings. After noting the nature of his visit, the discussions he had had with Horton, Simpson, and their staffs, and the bare fact that Canadian corvettes were only 15–20 per cent modernized, Connolly made some recommendations. Most of these dealt with improving communications and liaison with the RN. Rear Admiral Stephens pointed out that most of the points raised by Connolly were well known to the Naval Staff and that 'action had already been taken to remedy them.' However, it was clear from Connolly's remarks that technical liaison between the RCN and the RN needed enormous expansion. Indeed, until mid-1943 there had been only one technical-liaison officer on staff in London, and the work was simply too much for one man. Further, the Admiralty's distribution of technical data and drawings, even to its Technical Mission in Washington, was never very good. If the RCN wanted the latest information, it would have to seek it out. As a result of these conclusions a separate meeting of senior naval and civilian technical experts was held at NSHQ on 16 November, at which time the necessary increases in technical staff were agreed to.[34] The planned increases went ahead in December, and by January 1944 proper technical liaison was in place.

Action on technical liaison did not divert the minister from pursuing his inquiry into the reasons for the failure to keep the fleet up to date. He instructed Nelles to produce all the reports available at NSHQ dealing with equipment matters. According to Connolly this request got lost in the shuffle of further staff reorganizations, and eventually Connolly himself was forced to search the files.[35] What the executive assistant produced for the minister were the memos from Rowland and Bidwell of the previous spring and their related correspondence, which of course had not been promptly dealt with. Macdonald compiled the summary of complaints from these, a summary of Strange's memo (for which he gave no source), and the reports produced by Connolly upon his return from

Britain, added his comments on what he thought it all meant, and passed it on personally to Nelles, asking for his remarks.

Macdonald's 'Memorandum on the State of Equipment on RCN Ships' concluded with eight 'Comments' which contained serious charges of inefficiency on the part of the Naval Staff.[36] First, he believed, and quite rightly, that the memos of Rowland and Bidwell had not been dealt with promptly or (which is less justifiable) with 'the careful attention ... which their importance demanded.' Second, Macdonald expressed his displeasure with Nelles's memo of 1 September and with the supporting memo from Jones which explained why the fitting of the fleet was behind. The minister did not want explanations, and he would not accept that the development of weapons in the UK could mean that the RCN was denied 'a proportionate share.' Third, Macdonald contended that more could have been done to obtain better equipment from the British 'had we pressed for it.' He charged NSHQ with being 'lackadaisical' and placed the blame for the lack of impetus squarely on headquarters. This line of criticism was pursued further in the fourth comment, wherein the minister accused NSHQ of a serious lack of 'energy and capacity.' In his fifth comment Macdonald lamented that he had had to learn of the poor state of the fleet from outside sources. Sixth, he accused some officers at NSHQ with being overly impressed with the sheer size of the navy. 'The price of this,' he added, 'was the fact that of the last one hundred and fifty subs destroyed not one has definitely been destroyed by a Canadian ship of War.' In his seventh comment, a carry-over from the previous point, Macdonald observed that simply sending ships to sea was not enough; they 'must be competent to deal with the submarines ... If the British did not realize this and insist upon the best equipment possible for ships and planes, the success which they enjoyed in the summer months would not have been possible.' Finally, in the last comment Macdonald chastised Nelles for not seeking political help to secure better equipment for the navy. Had Macdonald failed at the ministerial level, he would have been prepared to take it to Churchill through Mackenzie King. Failing satisfaction at the prime-ministerial level, the minister 'would have recommended that our ships be withdrawn from the North Atlantic run.'

Although Macdonald had raised some telling points, much of what he wrote was preposterous, and it is remarkable that Nelles kept his equanimity. But he did, at least for a while. And while the CNS pondered Macdonald's eight comments, the minister prodded him again, this time with Commander Adams's memo. The latter stated that the poor state of equipment among the Canadian members of group C I, of which Adams was Senior Officer, meant that the RN ships of the group had to be used as its strike forces.[37] This, the minister wrote to Nelles, probably answered the question 'Why over a period of nine months has the Canadian Navy had such comparatively little success in dealing with submarines?'[38] Macdonald confessed his awareness of the defensive purpose of the convoy system but added he believed that the navy had failed in its primary task of protecting all ships from the enemy by destroying submarines. Again he wanted to know why he had not been shown the Adams memo, charged NSHQ with lack of a sense of urgency and with excessive adherence to red tape, and alleged that his inquiries into the state of equipment had been met by 'explanation and delay.'

Nelles protested his previous ignorance of the Adams memo but the next day (26 November) presented part of NSHQ's case to the minister by forwarding the memos on modernization prepared at the CNS's request by the CNEC, CNES, VCNS, and DOD, with a promise of his own to follow.[39] The staff's memos supported the view that what could be done had been done, and this position was reinforced by Nelles's own memo on the following day. In a long and carefully worded discussion of the hows and whys of equipment procurement, Nelles outlined the history of the problem, extending back to a time even before the war. The CNS professed himself 'baffled' at Macdonald's lack of knowledge of the 'state of affairs practically from the time you took office.'[40] Moreover, Nelles claimed to have taken 'particular care' to keep his minister informed. 'Time and again at the Naval Council and Board,' Nelles wrote, 'I have heard the Chief of Naval Engineering and Construction inform you that we could not get on with the work "because we have no plans" – no plans ... from the Admiralty of any kind until they are dragged out of them some six months or longer after they are in use in the U.K.' The rest of the memo described, in very restrained language, the steps taken by NSHQ from the outset to keep abreast of new developments and adapt staffs to cope with changing situations.

Macdonald was out of the country in late November, and it is not known when he received Nelles's nine-page memo, nor is it clear whether he made any written reply. However, there were any number of ways the minister could have made his displeasure with the latest 'explanations' known to the CNS. Indeed, Macdonald would have been quite justified in demanding more from the CNS, since Nelles had not even mentioned the eight comments raised in the minister's memo of 20 November. It was, in fact, the second time that Nelles had avoided the issues with which Macdonald had specifically requested he deal. In any event, Nelles's equanimity was completely shattered by 4 December, the day he prepared a 'continuation' of his memo of 27 November – yet another nine pages.

Quite apart from what Macdonald might have said, there was good cause for the CNS's loss of composure in the first week of December: a direct confrontation with his nemesis, Commodore Simpson. The commodore or, according to his later account, a member of his staff sent an indiscreet signal to NSHQ concerning a request by the RCN to remove one of the inefficient new Canadian 10-centimetre radar sets (RXU) from an RCN corvette in 'Derry. Commodore (D), Londonderry, replied that they would remove the set, adding, 'The happy day when no more RXU sets will be fitted to Canadian ships is looked forward to in hopeful anticipation.' Nelles was livid over this impertinence, and it could not have come from a worse source or at a worse time. He sent an immediate signal putting Simpson, a 'junior officer,' in his place, and followed this with a protest to the Deputy First Sea Lord. As a result Simpson was officially censured by Horton, and an order was issued whereby no criticism could be made by Western Approaches establishments without prior clearance by the C-in-C.[41]

Catching his main detractor in an indiscretion may have been all Nelles needed to warm to the crisis at hand. But he also received strong support for his position from Captain A.R. Pressey, the new director of Warfare and Training, who studied the docket upon which Macdonald had based much of his criticism. Pressey concluded, in a letter to Nelles on 2 December, that 'what would appear at first sight to be incriminating evidence of the existence of ineffectual administration at NSHQ is not the case once the whole story is knitted together.'[42] Buttressed by such support from his staff and having squared accounts with Simpson, Nelles produced his 'continuation' on 4 December. Again the memo was long, but its style and tone show clearly that the CNS had had enough.[43] Indeed, it is a wonder that Macdonald even got past the first page, though his pencilled copy shows that he did. What was also clear from Nelles's second memo and from the minister's written reply was that the issues had now become lost in a barrage of charges and countercharges. And yet Nelles's memo of 4 December presents NSHQ's position very well. Rowland's and Bidwell's memos were placed in context and problems of measuring efficiency through a straight comparison of equipment explained. As for the minister's comments, Nelles tackled them one at a time.

Nelles admitted that the handling of Rowland's and Bidwell's memos was not prompt, but claimed that they had been dealt with adequately.

Moreover, the matter of future manning policy was still under investigation. So too was the matter of equipment comparisons, which had been Macdonald's second point. As for the third, that more could have been done to acquire modern equipment, Nelles was unconvinced. The CNS pointed out quite rightly that the Battle of the Atlantic in 1942 was 'a very serious business and continued so until the spring of 1943.' Moreover, modern equipment was in short supply and the fastest way to get it to sea was to fit it at source – that is, through the RN. Nelles had nothing to say about the minister's allegation in comment four that NSHQ lacked 'energy and capacity' but had plenty to say about the next comment, concerning the minister's recourse to outside sources of information. Nelles stood by his contentions in the first memo, that Macdonald had been part of the scene for years and had said nothing, and then he expressed surprise that the minister became 'aware' of the problem through outsiders. The British in particular, Nelles claimed, did not have 'the slightest conception of our difficulties in Canada.' As for comment six, that NSHQ was too intent upon size and therefore had not been able to claim any of the 150 U-boats recently sunk, Nelles countered commendably. Until the spring of 1943, he wrote, 'anything that could kill a submarine was essential.' Fortunately, that situation was now altered, but there was no point in withdrawing the fleet from operations for a wholesale modernization. Certainly there was no merit whatsoever in withdrawing more ships than the repair facilities could handle, and in the meantime the navy had to carry on with essential operations and training. As for the RCN's failure to contribute to the 150 subs sunk in August, September, and October, Nelles noted that this was the whole total from all causes for an area stretching from the Indian Ocean to Iceland. In MOEF's zone only 18 had been destroyed, and of these only 8 fell to surface escorts. Thus the RCN got none out of 8, not out of 150. The suggestion in comment seven, that the RN was prescient enough to modernize its ships and, by implication, that the RCN was not, sounded a bitter note and struck at the core of resentment which many senior officers then felt towards the RN. Nelles commented tersely that the British had worked on the principle of fleet modernization 'to the detriment of the RCN.'

The CNS's handling of Macdonald's last comment, that the navy should have sought political help and failing its success should have withdrawn from operations, was much weaker than it could have been. In fact, Nelles confessed that 'we did not think of recommending that you take the matter up with the First Sea Lord of the Admiralty or that the matter be dealt with by Prime Minister to Prime Minister.' He added that even if the RCN had secured a large proportion of modern equipment in this fashion, it would then have been necessary to obtain a priority in the use of repair facilities. 'At the time,' Nelles continued, 'we considered the situation so serious that we did not think the U.K. could or would be willing to allow our ships priority.' This case looked painfully weak by 1943, and even more so by virtue of the fact that the staff had not even tried political action. But Nelles could have gained a strong purchase on Macdonald's position had he tackled the absurdity of removing RCN escorts from operations in 1942 simply because the British would not share equipment. Moreover, he might have noted that RCN escorts were withdrawn from MOEF for reasons of efficiency in early 1943 and operations in the mid-ocean nearly collapsed because the remaining escorts were overworked. How the minister could have justified the abandonment of operational commitments at a time when the mere presence of escorts was the key to the convoy system was never explained, nor indeed did Nelles take him to task on it. Confrontation over this point was averted by Nelles's confession that the Staff did not even think of political action. In Macdonald's defence it should be noted, however, that the British had moved on their own to improve the efficiency of C groups in December 1942 and might well have been amenable to an upgrading of the Canadian contribution to MOEF much earlier had the idea been advanced by NSHQ.

Macdonald's reply, dated 10 December, to both of Nelles's memos took sharp objection to the suggestion that the minister was in any way responsible for the state of the fleet or that his ignorance of the problems was somehow self-inflicted.[44] 'The intimation here seems to be,' Macdonald wrote, 'that if there is something wrong with our ships, it is my fault as much as anybody else's.' The inability of the Naval Staff to provide the minister with detailed comparisons of equipment in British and Canadian ships operating in the escort force indicated a serious failing on the part of Staff:

The great questions are 'were our ships putting to sea inadequately equipped as compared to British ships, and were they doing so over an unduly long period of time?'

The answer to both questions, in my considered judgement, must be a definite and unequivocal 'Yes.' Your memoranda and the supporting documents do not disprove these facts. Therefore, I must ask you to indicate who is to blame for these conditions.

Macdonald went on to charge that he, the forces at sea, and the Canadian people (not to mention the government) had been let down by NSHQ. He reiterated his claim that the RCN could have been withdrawn to 'Canadian coastal waters' if the British had not agreed to modernize 'a fair share of our corvettes ... in British yards if that were necessary.' In concluding Macdonald dismissed the notion of Staff infallibility: he wanted to know what portion of it had been 'inefficient' and warned that the 'chips must fall where they like.'

Macdonald made it clear that he would have his pound of flesh, and Nelles undoubtedly sensed from where it was likely to come. In his own defence Nelles launched an investigation into staff arrangements at home and abroad. The investigation revealed the need for yet more changes and undermined Nelles's position.[45] In consequence Nelles was relieved of his duties as CNS in early January 1944 and sent to London to serve as senior Canadian naval officer. The man who had, in the words of a colleague, 'taken the job of CNS in 1933 when it wasn't much'[46] was cast out, carrying with him the sins of omission from the turbulent days of early wartime growth. Ironically, the new CNS was Vice-Admiral G.C. Jones, the man who, as COAC in 1941–2, had benefited most, when the focus was on building up home establishments and escort forces, from the navy's concentration on quantity.

The historical problem of right or wrong remains, and it may never be resolved to everyone's satisfaction. Connolly later described the equipment crisis as a cover-up by Nelles and his director of Signals Division, Commander G.A. Worth.[47] Initially, at least, this seems improbable, and the notion of a cover-up was to a considerable extent a self-fulfilling prophecy. The latter was certainly the case after Connolly's return from Britain, when the Naval Staff was faced with what the executive assistant called 'a skeleton in the closet.' The problem with the skeleton, which the Naval Staff understood very well but the civilian administrators refused to countenance, was that it was very much a fabrication of 1943. Admittedly, by November the remains were sufficiently decomposed to give off a very foul odour, but that was more the result of the heat under which it had been stored than its length of time in storage. The key was the absolutely fundamental change in the character of the Battle of the Atlantic in the spring of 1943, which rendered most of the RCN obsolete virtually overnight.

It is significant that Macdonald's interest in the performance of the navy developed after a period of serious domestic political discontent and after the battle in the mid-ocean had been won by the British. Not surprisingly, Macdonald's papers – which aside from an extensive file on the equipment crisis of late 1943 contain virtually nothing on the development of the RCN, its problems, and goals – reveal him as first and foremost a politician. Much as did Mackenzie King, Macdonald believed that the very future and ultimate success of the Allied war effort depended upon the preservation of Canada's Liberal government. In addition to party and constituency work in this cause, Macdonald also devoted considerable effort to the reindustrialization of Nova Scotia. Naval matters may have dominated the minister's day-to-day affairs, but they never dominated the man.

The crisis of December 1942 had been specifically concerned with the efficiency of the navy, and yet the minister seems to have taken no interest other than to see that the recommendation to accept the transfer proposals was passed by the War Cabinet. The issue then, of course, had been training, but Nelles had advised his minister that the state of equipment was also not good: 'This is especially so in the matter of RDF and certain wireless equipment (the Air "Asdic"). The most modern equipment is simply not available, it is being installed as quickly as it does become available.'[48] Though this was by no means an unequivocal statement, it is clear that Macdonald had been kept generally informed about the state of issue of modern equipment and its availability. It is also noteworthy that the minister's knowledge of equipment was such that Nelles had to describe HF/DF as 'the Air "Asdic" ' even at this late date.

When Macdonald finally did confront Nelles over the state of equipment in the fleet, he focused on two pieces, gyro-compasses and hedgehog. Neither of these had been mentioned by Nelles in December 1942 because they were not essential elements in the defensive phase of the war. Gyro-compasses admittedly would have made a profound impact on the fleet's efficiency from the outset; they would have meant more-accurate navigation, more-accurate depth-charge attacks, better co-ordination between escorts, and the like. All of these would have improved the overall image of the fleet, and the ripple effect in other areas, such as confidence, would have been enormous. Gyros would also therefore have given the RCN the chance of a better score of U-boat kills, but in 1942 gyros alone would not have kept losses to shipping down. In convoy battles from that period the key pieces of equipment were 271 radar, HF/DF, and more destroyers – all shortages rectified by the spring of 1943. But by then the vital weapon of the new offensive phase was hedgehog. In defence of NSHQ, hedgehog had been in use for a year by the summer of 1943, and it was still not a proven weapon. Although its theoretical advantages over depth charges were well understood, hedgehog suffered serious teething troubles and a consequent unpopularity at sea. Moreover, because the hedgehog bombs were contact-fused, the equipment offered no psychological advantages. Even depth charges that missed shook the morale of U-boat crews and bolstered that of merchant seamen and naval personnel. Escort captains were so reluctant to use hedgehog in early 1943 that the RN was forced to issue an order instructing captains to report why they did *not* use the weapon on an underwater contact, if that was the case.[49] Further, scientists were already working on a more powerful and more deadly ahead-throwing weapon than hedgehog, the 'Squid.' This three-tube mortar fired very heavy, hydrostatically detonated bombs whose depth setting and firing time were handled automatically by the new type 145 asdic. For a while, then, the future of hedgehog was undecided, and it was only later, after testing, that the Squid was found to be too heavy for Flower-class corvettes.

NSHQ experienced similar problems with other types of equipment. Rowland's complaint, for example, that the mark of 271 radar fitted to his ships was outdated was true enough. But it did not follow that it was inadequate for the task involved. For this reason Captain (D), Newfoundland's memo was not exceptional, nor indeed was Bidwell's. The same can, unfortunately, be said for the time taken to handle them, which in itself was a poor reflection on NSHQ. However, Nelles was quite right to go on to question Macdonald's sources. Both the RN in general and many senior British officers were remarkably ignorant of the RCN. As late as January 1943 the Admiralty's director of Trade, Captain Schofield, confessed that 'we have very little knowledge of the workings of Canadian escorts who form a large proportion of the available escort forces.'[50] In March Horton explained his dissatisfaction with the Canadians' maintenance organization on the basis of complaints from convoy commodores, and in April the Canadian liaison officer aboard *Philante* reported that the ignorance of the RCN in the RN went very deep indeed.[51] By the summer of 1943 there were only two bright spots in the darkness which cloaked British knowledge of the RCN, Commodore Simpson and the Mansfield-Kauffman board. Simpson and other staff officers at Western Approaches had been aware of serious equipment problems within the RCN at least since ON 113 in July 1942. Moreover, the staff at Western Approaches had had a prolonged exposure to C groups in early 1943, and this had included exposure to the many grouses current in wardrooms. Still, while there is no reason to doubt that Canadian officers serving in MOEF understood just what their ships needed, there is good reason to be suspicious of their understanding of the situation in Canada. And since MOEF officers had borne the brunt of heavy enemy action in 1942, then watched the British inflict a resounding defeat on their old enemies in early 1943, their opinion of NSHQ was predictably anything but balanced.

The Mansfield-Kauffman board, however, presents a very different problem. Their professional abilities allowed them to get quickly to the root of a problem, as evidenced by Mansfield's pointed question about refit planning. The board's conclusions and recommendations were both sound, but it is debatable if they were qualified expert witnesses on the state of the RCN, the reasons for its existence, and how it could be rapidly changed. The anonymous memo from the Admiralty probably owed a great deal to Mansfield, and it was rejected by one senior RCN officer as madness. Yet despite the displeasure of British operational staffs and executive officers over the handling of maintenance in the RCN, it came as a pleasant surprise to the commodore superintendent, Halifax, to learn during his visit to Britain in the late fall of 1943 not only that the RN's director of Dockyards, Vice-Admiral A.G. Talbot, had 'a very complete knowledge of the problems that the RCN had been up against' but that the Canadians had accomplished more than he had expected.[52] Finally, one of the complaints raised by both the Canadians of MOEF and British authorities was the length of time it took for new equipment to make its appearance in the RCN escorts of MOEF. It is doubtful if even senior RN officers really understood that sending modern equipment to Canada meant that it was still a very long way from Newfoundland, and thus from Canadian ships operating in the mid-Atlantic.

The irony of the remoteness of St John's from Canada and the operations of escorts based there is that the Canadians of MOEF were more closely connected with Western Approaches Command and the RN than with NSHQ. Halifax was the closest MOEF ever got to a Canadian 'establishment,' and trips there were infrequent even at the best of times. Ottawa was light-years away. On the other hand, C groups regularly visited the very heart of Western Approaches Command, which was itself an absolutely vital part of the RN, with easy and direct access to the Admiralty. Further, Western Approaches Command had a long-standing interest in standardizing the tactics, doctrine, equipment, and procedures of MOEF and in unifying command of escort operations east of Newfoundland. As early as January 1942 the RN expressed its interest in eliminating U.S. involvement in MOEF, 'in order to preserve the continuity of both British and Canadian group training and operations.'[53] Shortcomings in training were made good during the transfer of C groups in early 1943. Continuity of operational control was settled at the Washington Conference of March. The 'campaign' to upgrade equipment in C groups was entirely consistent with these other developments.

The controversy thus resolves itself into two crucial issues: the inability of the RCN to bring outdated escorts and modern equipment together fast enough in the spring of 1943, and the inadequate arrangements for technical liaison with the RN. On both counts the Naval Staff can properly be blamed for poor planning. Of the two, the failure to arrange for sufficient refit and repair facilities and to settle priority of manpower and resources for the fleet was the more fundamental. Facilities on the east coast had only just been able to cope with the demand in the winter of 1941–2. The Staff should have been able to forecast the increased need with the growth of the fleet and with the decision of the Naval Staff in July 1942 to go ahead with modernization. Yet the small yards upon which so much depended in 1943 were unprepared even for the influx of routine refits. The British decision to participate in the modernization program took some of the heat off, just as their withdrawal made a bad situation intolerable. In the end the U.S. took up the slack and modernized nineteen RCN corvettes in American yards and one at NOB Londonderry. The British, despite Connolly's apparent triumph, modernized none after the three completed by August 1943.

The failure to develop a proper technical-liaison staff (and to provide C groups with a proper staff in 'Derry) was no less excusable, but certainly easier to understand. Although the RN and the RCN were separate services, in practice officers moved around almost as though they belonged to one navy. Even in 1942 it would have seemed a waste of manpower to provide an RCN support staff in Londonderry. For regular RCN officers the establishments of the RN were as much home as were Halifax or Esquimalt. It took considerable time for the RCN to realize that its own best interests were better served by its own representatives, even when dealing with the RN (or, it might be said, especially when dealing with the RN).

Both of these fundamental errors proved serious. They contributed to unacceptably low levels of efficiency at sea and, in turn, to loss of life and property. They also caused the greatest upheaval NSHQ would ever know. The burden of guilt was borne by Nelles, and he retired at the end of 1944 a tired and bitter man. In his defence it is sufficient to say that these errors stand small beside the overall significance of Canada's naval contribution to the Battle of the Atlantic. As Nelles had recognized by 1943, without the RCN there might not have been efficient escorts in anyone's navy.

Epilogue

Happy is the convoy with no history.

Anonymous

With one notable exception (the battle of ONS 18 and ON 202) the focus of the war at sea shifted away from the main trade routes in the last two years of the war. Yet, as in the latter half of 1942, convoy operations in the mid-Atlantic after May 1943 were tremendously significant for the RCN. Within little more than a year from the time when there were no C groups in the mid-ocean, the whole North Atlantic route – from New York to the North Channel – was an exclusively Canadian operation. Although the route was now a milk run, it was dominated by the RCN, and that was the navy's crowning achievement and just reward. For while it was denied a primary role in the victory of May 1943, the RCN's selfless – and sometimes thankless – performances earlier had been a decisive contribution to that victory.

The momentum generated by the Allied mid-ocean offensive in the spring of 1943 was quickly redirected to the Bay of Biscay following the collapse of the U-boat pack campaign. The Allies' aim was not only to continue large-scale destruction of U-boats but also to punish them in their bases and on passage through the bay to operational areas. The latter, it was hoped, would help reduce the frequency and length of German operational cruises.[1]

The British had begun to plan the new Bay of Biscay offensive in late March 1943, when they proposed to reduce the strength of MOEF from fourteen to eleven groups, sending three to work in the bay. These changes, which eventually saw MOEF reduced to nine groups and included adjustments to convoy cycles and routing practices, went into effect in June.

Not surprisingly, it was the better-equipped and more effective B groups which were transferred to the scene of action. The Americans, too, joined in the offensive, using three support groups built around the escort carriers *Bogue*, *Core*, and *Santee*, to smash U-boat operations in the area between the Azores and Portugal. In the summer months the ships and aircraft of these USN groups not only destroyed sixteen U-boats, but their score included most of Germany's limited number of 'milch cows,' the supply U-boats so essential to pack operations over the previous year. American carrier support groups continued to operate in the North Atlantic with devastating effectiveness for the rest of the war. Their success at this form of ASW dwarfed efforts by the RCN to destroy U-boats over the same period.[2]

German attempts to counter the Allied offensive and to re-establish their position on the main trade routes were hampered by the limitations of their diesel-electric U-boats and the slow development of effective anti-escort measures. The real solution, as Dönitz realized, was the production of a true submarine, one capable of circumventing Allied mastery of the air and surface of the sea by operating totally submerged. Development of such U-boats, the types XXI and XXIII, was pushed after May 1943. Only the small inshore type XXIII saw action in appreciable numbers by the end of the war. There were, however, over a hundred of the large ocean-going type XXIs in various stages of work-up by 10 May 1945, although only two made operational cruises.

The advent of the type XXI on the sea lanes would have brought another crisis in the Battle of the Atlantic. It was designed from the outset to operate exclusively underwater. The type XXI could dive deeper (by one hundred metres), stay down longer (several days at economical speed), and attack from a fully submerged position using an impressive array of sophisticated torpedoes and targeting systems.[3] Effective countermeasures for the XXI were under development by the Allies by the close of the war, but the new U-boat presented an awesome challenge. The Allied escort fleets – even the frigates and destroyer escorts – were built to handle the older diesel-electric submarines. Their margin of speed over the type XXI (seventeen knots submerged, for a short period) was very small, even in ideal conditions. Moreover, the hull-mounted asdics of escort vessels were gradually rendered inoperable as speed increased beyond the optimum twelve-knot search speed. A frigate might be able to keep up to a submerged type XXI if sea conditions were good, but the noise generated would have made it all but impossible to track the target. For the Allies, the crisis-that-never-was was a very close-run thing.

Unfortunately for Dönitz the type XXI was still on the drawing-board in the summer of 1943, and he was faced with a difficult choice. The older type VII and IX U-boats were now obsolete and were being destroyed in very large numbers. Dönitz considered withdrawing them completely pending the development of new weapons and the arrival of the true submarines. But after consultation with his senior officers Dönitz decided he must keep up pressure on the Allies if possible.[4] In some measure, the potential of U-boats to inflict damage or seriously dislocate Allied plans was restored in 1944–5, when the older submarines were equipped with snorkels. Although not able to operate in packs, snorkel-equipped U-boats enjoyed considerable success inshore, laying mines and attacking convoys in the approaches to harbours. As a result, support groups previously used to guard shipping on the high seas were used in the last year of the war to push convoys through the dangerous entrances to assembly ports. This represented, in fact, a reversion to pre-war concepts of submarine warfare. But until the arrival of more modern submarines, the Germans fought nothing more than a desperate holding action and at a horrendous cost.

By mid-1943, then, the roles of the earlier years had been reversed. It was the Germans who now scrambled to sustain the war in an increasingly hostile environment. The odds were truly against them, not least because the products of American industry were finally coming forth in impressive numbers – 379 destroyer escorts in 1943 alone.[5] In addition, there were the frigates and improved corvettes coming from Commonwealth yards. The strength of Allied escort forces doubled in a year and, equally important, most of the new ships were built to hunt and kill submarines wherever they were to be found. The impact of escort production and the defeat of the U-boat packs was such that most massive building programs, including those of the RCN, were sharply curtailed by the end of 1943. For example, only 78 of the 300 destroyer escorts ordered by the RN and only 70 of the 167 frigates ordered in Canada were ever delivered.[6]

Concurrent with the tremendous growth in the escort fleet came subtle changes in the convoy-escort system which led to the more efficient use of ships. One of these was the decision in the spring of 1943 to adopt a fixed convoy route for the North Atlantic.[7] The Americans, of course, had always advocated this, and it was a temporary by-product of the reduction of mid-Atlantic A/S escorts to a single force (MOEF) in February 1942. In the spring of 1943 USN operational scientists did an exhaustive study of the fixed-route concept, arguing that it offered the best chance of freeing escorts for killing U-boats while drawing the enemy to objectives which could then be supported with overwhelming force. Not all RN officers agreed that the potential trade-offs were favourable, but the issue eventually resolved itself. With so many U-boats in the Atlantic, effective evasion became virtually impossible in any event. Further, with the defeat of the U-boat packs there was a natural gravitation towards the great-circle route. What the USN had seen as the means of obtaining victory therefore became one of its benefits.[8]

Adoption of the great-circle route also helped ease pressure on shipping, as did the sharp decline in losses, increased American production, and, later in the year, the reopening of the Mediterranean to convoyed shipping. The general improvement in the shipping situation, including the commissioning of ever more modern merchantmen, eventually led to the de facto elimination of slow convoys in 1944. This trend was already evident in 1943, as merchant navies gained the sophistication of auxiliary naval services. The very character of convoys was altered as sunken ships were replaced by new, more reliable, and faster ships. The general improvement in merchant navies made the escorts' task easier.

Further economy in the use of escorts came from the adoption of larger, less frequent convoys. Although Professor Blackett was unable to sell his theories completely in 1943, the trend towards single, larger concentrations of shipping was also already evident. In June the Admiralty altered the cycles of convoys slightly so that fast and slow ones reached the mid-ocean danger area within supporting distance of one another.[9] Blackett's research had revealed, and it was gradually accepted, that a given number of U-boats could only do so much damage. Six ships, for example, might be lost from each of two forty-ship convoys to the same pack. But the U-boats could still sink only six ships from one eighty-ship convoy. The proportion and number of real losses therefore declined with larger, less frequent convoys. However, the idea caught on slowly, and it was not until the spring of 1944 that the average size of transatlantic convoys reached sixty ships.[10]

The concept of mutual support was accepted in 1943 and played a major role in MOEF's last important battle. But the real effort in the summer of 1943 was put into getting as many ships as possible into the Bay of Biscay offensive. The result was a further reduction of MOEF in August, when the average size of groups was dropped from seven or eight to six. The surplus was transferred to the Eastern Atlantic; it included enough escorts to form the first far-ranging RCN support group, EG 9: the Town-class destroyers *St Croix* and *St Francis*, the RN frigate *Itchen*, and the corvettes *Chambly*, *Morden*, and *Sackville*. A third Canadian support group, comprising four short-range Towns, was also formed in August to work with what was now known as the Western Escort Force (the RCN having dropped the pejorative word *local* from the title of its Halifax-based force).[11] EG 9's first action in its first incarnation was destined to be its last, and it gained the dubious distinction of being the only support group destroyed by U-boats.

The destruction of EG 9 owed nothing to its make-up or efficiency. It was simply caught in a German attempt to renew the mid-Atlantic campaign on shipping by blasting a way through defences with acoustic torpedoes. By 16 September 1943, group 'Leuthen,' of twenty U-boats, had managed to elude Allied patrols off their bases and was formed into a line awaiting the next ON convoy, expected on the twentieth. One of the patrol line was sunk on the nineteenth by an RCAF Liberator, while the two convoys in danger, ONS 18, escorted by B 3, and ON 202, escorted by C 2 (*Gatineau*, one of the second-generation River-class destroyers under Commander P. Burnett, RN, now on loan to the RCN and Senior Officer, two RN frigates, *Icarus* and *Lagan*, and the corvettes *Drumheller*, *Kamloops*, and *Polyanthus* [RN]), were routed northwards.[12] Discovery of Leuthen on the day it formed also led to the dispatch of EG 9 to support the two convoys. In addition, ON 202 also had with it a new form of escort, the merchant aircraft carrier *Empire MacAlpine*: a large bulk carrier fitted with a small flight-deck from stem to stern and three aircraft. The aircraft, usually aged Swordfish biplanes, were not high-performance craft, but they were reliable and were large enough to carry surface-warning radar.

EG 9 arrived in the vicinity of ONS 18 and ON 202 (which were only about thirty miles apart) just as the convoys came afoul of Leuthen. Indeed, on the night of 19–20 September the U-boats had launched a mild attack in which two ships were sunk and *Lagan* had her stern blown off by an acoustic torpedo. When EG 9 joined on the morning of the twentieth the two convoys made an effective junction in order to combine the escorts in defence of a single objective. The escort, now under Commander M.J. Evans, RN, in *Keppel*, was able to frustrate attacks directed at the convoy during the following night. But astern, where the U-boat contacts were pursued, a fierce battle developed. During its course the venerable old destroyer *St Croix* was struck twice by acoustic torpedoes and sunk, carrying down with her Dobson and most of her crew as well. The British corvette *Polyanthus* was also lost to acoustic torpedoes. Her survivors and those of *St Croix* were picked up by *Itchen*.

Fog shrouded the convoy for most of 21 September, but the ships were none the less able to attain good order, with ONS 18 taking station to starboard of ON 202. The following night the large escort was able to keep the U-boats at bay, while *Keppel* rammed and sank *U229*. Dawn on the twenty-second saw the air 'filled with Liberators' of the RCAF; yet they were unable to force Leuthen off. The following night, with the convoy rearranged in echelon, four more ships were lost. So too was *Itchen*, another victim of an acoustic torpedo, with all the survivors of *St Croix* and *Polyanthus* aboard. Only three men from the combined ships' companies (one of them a rating from *St Croix*) were recovered.

Increased air support and preparations among the escort for the next round filled the day on the twenty-third, but BdU had given up the chase. The U-boats claimed twelve escorts destroyed and a great many ships lost, but the truth was quite different. Three escorts were sunk, one heavily damaged, and six merchantmen lost. Countermeasures for the acoustic torpedo, the appearance of which came as no surprise, were quickly developed. Towed noise-makers, such as the British 'Foxer' and the Canadian 'anti-torpedo,' or CAT, gear, were in service within weeks.

Group Leuthen attempted to renew attacks on a series of convoys but was frustrated, largely by superior Allied air power. In one of these operations, around SC 143 in early October, an aircraft equipped with a Leigh light stayed with the convoy after dark, marking yet another milestone in ASW.

The loss of *St Croix* and *Itchen* was a heavy blow to EG 9 and resulted in the temporary disbanding of the group. The blow could have been much worse, since both *Chambly* and *Morden* had had acoustic torpedoes blown up by the wash of their propellers. The hiatus in the group's existence was destined to be short lived, but its allocation to a British command in the first instance illustrates that the navy felt secure and that consolidation of the Canadian Northwest Atlantic had been achieved. Indeed, not only did ships flow to the RN once again, but skilled men too continued to be loaned to the parent service.

The RCN had its basic-training establishments in good order by mid-1943, and with delays in the completion of its frigates and the prospect of massive cut-backs in the escort building programs the navy once again faced a surplus of manpower. The manpower surplus coincided with a resurgence in planning for the post-war navy, following the victory of May. These threads came together at the Quebec Conference in August. Through a conspiracy with the British, the RCN managed to have the government accept the Canadian manning and commissioning of two cruisers, two additional fleet-class destroyers, and two flotillas of landing craft. The additions to the fleet actually came in the form of a request from the British prime minister, and Mackenzie King later regretted his moment of weakness. But he seemed unwilling to check the navy's impetus, and in 1944 the RCN took over manning of two escort carriers while plans went ahead to acquire light Fleet-class carriers and a naval air arm.[13]

In many ways the professional navy took only a brief pause between November 1942 and August 1943 before it returned once again to its long-cherished schemes. In the event, the interval proved sufficient to set the escort fleet on a sound footing. Moreover, consolidation of the escort fleet now left the navy free to deal with its primary task, the defence of Canada, a role which had been left in default. Further, it followed logically from the establishment of the Canadian Northwest Atlantic that the new theatre would never be truly independent until it was removed from under the protective wing of the American battle-fleet. It was, therefore, inevitable that the RCN would at least attempt to complete its plans for a large conventional fleet. Mackenzie King, who had encouraged an independent role for the RCN and whose government had introduced pre-war plans for a large conventional fleet, now despaired of the navy's ventures into new and ever more costly tasks. In some ways he was caught in a trap of his own construction. Unlike the army, the growth of which was largely the result of public pressure, the navy was very much a product of the government. The fulfilment of the RCN as a service was therefore consistent with the broader aims of Mackenzie King and his cabinet.

After the battle for ONS 18 / ON 202, operations in the mid-Atlantic remained quiet for the rest of the war, while the RCN commitment to MOEF and other areas continued to expand. By the end of 1943 there were four Canadian support groups operational: Western Escort Force's W 10, a reconstituted EG 9, the newly formed EG 6, and C 2, released from MOEF for support purposes.[14] By March 1944 both EG 6 and EG 9 were made up entirely of RCN frigates. Escorts of this class had also begun to make an impression in MOEF and WEF by the spring of 1944, when there were thirty-three in commission. Their arrival in large numbers brought the relegation of the surviving Town-class destroyers to training duties.[15]

As the first major wave of new construction since 1941, the frigates presented almost as much of a training problem as the earlier, much less sophisticated corvettes had. The increasing complexity of combined air and surface anti-submarine warfare and the reversion of U-boats to submerged tactics brought an endless array of new challenges. Modern ASW demanded proper and thorough work-ups, but weather conditions off Nova Scotia did not always permit the conduct of training exercises. Work-ups in the winter of 1943–4 were once again disrupted by bitter winter weather, forcing the RCN to shift its training area to Bermuda in early 1944. A major reorganization of Captain (D), Halifax's training responsibilities followed, culminating in the establishment of a proper work-up base at St Georges, Bermuda, in August 1944 under Captain K.F. Adams. HMCS *Somers Isles* was a direct – and successful – attempt to imitate the RN's escort training base at Tobermory, HMS *Western Isles* – but it had taken five hard years of war to establish. Ironically, one of the victims of the struggle to set up *Somers Isles* was Captain Prentice, who, as Captain (D), Halifax, had preferred to keep all training centred on himself. His opposition to the restructuring of training responsibilities led to a posting overseas in May 1944 to command the Eleventh Support Group. Fittingly enough, Prentice ended the war in command of *Somers Isles* and charged with preparing Canadian frigates for the war in the Pacific.

In addition to the frigates, there were other changes in C groups in late 1943 and early 1944. Many of the old stalwarts from 1942 – the original corvettes of the first construction program, which had held the line – were in refit or assigned to less arduous tasks. C groups were now dominated by modernized and later-model corvettes and by the new frigates. The new lists of group compositions are filled with the strange names of ships which would never be associated with the classic confrontation between U-boat and escort – *Atholl, Giffard, Frontenac, Norsyd, Wentworth*.[16] They too held the line, but their greatest enemies were now boredom and the relentless North Atlantic itself. Fortunately, their real test, the type XXI U-boat, never materialized.

The North Atlantic convoy and escort arrangements underwent further substantial change in the months before the landings in Normandy. The old series of slow convoys, the SC and ONS, were finally abandoned at the end of March 1944, and a substantial increase in the size of convoys was adopted. Other changes in the escort arrangements intended to free warships for the landings were agreed to in the spring. All of the Canadian destroyers in MOEF were withdrawn to form two support groups, the Eleventh (commanded by now Captain J.D. Prentice) and the Twelfth (Commander A.M. McKillop, RN), and all B groups were withdrawn as well, while C 2 was reassigned to MOEF from its support role. The result was a totally RCN MOEF and a virtually 100 per cent RCN escort of convoys along the main transatlantic route.[17] Admittedly, losses in the area were now very small, and so too was the threat. But for the RCN it was a remarkable achievement and shows just how far the service had come since 1942.

Not surprisingly, it was these late-war accomplishments – the size and scope of escort operations, Prentice's success with the Eleventh Support Group in the Channel, Canadian Tribal-class destroyer operations off occupied France, the participation of the cruiser HMCS *Uganda*, under Captain Mainguy, in the Okinawa campaign, the peak strength of ninety-six thousand all ranks (more than fifty times the size of the pre-war professional service) reached in December 1944[18] – which captured the imagination of the professional navy and Canada's post-war historians. The last two years of the war witnessed the fulfilment of the navy's long-term ambition to have a large conventional fleet. In the interim, however, it had built a very different kind of navy and fought a very different kind of war.

The significance of the RCN's contribution to the Battle of the Atlantic lay in its successful efforts to hold the line until the Allies could assume the offensive. There can be no doubt that the fleet was inefficient prior to 1943 and that this inefficiency can be measured in lost lives and ships. However, one can only speculate on the number of lives and ships saved simply because the RCN somehow found the escorts necessary to establish convoy routes and support operations – regardless of the consequences in the fleet.

The other side of the same issue is the effect which an efficient RCN might have had on the course of events in 1942–3. Assuming that the same number of escorts had been available for operations, a Canadian navy at the top of its form could not have changed the shape of the campaign. The bulk of the RCN was simply not engaged. Those segments that were (MOEF) lost more ships than their British counterparts but not enough to affect the world-wide shipping crisis. Further, C groups claimed their share, four of nine, of MOEF U-boat kills in late 1942.

The convoy battles of early 1943 illustrated that neither were B groups any longer capable of handling the U-boats alone. The decisive element of Allied victory was the diversion of large-scale air and surface forces to the mid-Atlantic at the end of March. Air power was crucial, claiming twenty of the fifty-two U-boats sunk around convoys between Newfoundland and Ireland in the first five months of 1943. Of the remaining thirty-two kills, nineteen went to warships of the RN, principally the support groups, which destroyed eleven. Royal Navy MOEF escorts sank eight U-boats, but five of these kills occurred while the escorts were operating in conjunction with support groups. Only three U-boats were sunk by RN MOEF escorts working alone in early 1943 (one additional kill was shared with the Free French Navy). Against this, the RCN claimed one-third of one kill, obtained while C 2 was working with a support group (and *Shediac*'s destruction of *U87* off Portugal, which does not figure in these calculations). Given that the RCN lacked the resources to establish long-range support groups and given the small role of close escorts per se, regardless of their efficiency, in the final defeat of the U-boats the RCN's potential for affecting the outcome was minimal.[19]

When peace finally came the escort fleet, much of which was simply worn out, was scrapped. A small reserve of frigates was retained against any new crisis and to train reservists, but the navy ran down very quickly to the hard core of 'fleet' units. The men, too – the VRs and the NRs – quickly returned to peacetime pursuits, leaving a small but highly experienced cadre of professional naval men behind. Many of the officers who featured in this story – H.G. DeWolf, H.T.W. Grant, J.C. Hibbard, K.L. Dyer, E.R. Mainguy, H.F. Pullen, H.S. Rayner – rose to flag rank after the war, and three of them, DeWolf, Grant, and Mainguy, became CNS. Vice-Admiral Nelles, as mentioned, retired from the RCN in January 1945 and a day later was promoted to full admiral. His wartime efforts were recognized in the king's New Year's honours list of January 1946, when Nelles was made a commander of the Order of Bath. Rear Admiral Murray suffered an ignoble fate. Held largely responsible for the breakdown in discipline during the infamous VE Day riots in Halifax, Murray was relieved of his command in August 1945 and a month later left for voluntary exile in Britain. His post as C-in-C, Canadian Northwest Atlantic, was held briefly by Vice-Admiral Jones, who continued on as CNS until his untimely death in February 1946. Captain James Douglas 'Chummy' Prentice, RCN, took his second – and final – retirement from naval life in March 1946.

The postwar RCN, as an institution, shunned the bitter experiences of the escort fleet. Indeed, the post-war navy saw no merit whatsoever in any detailed analysis of its wartime convoy operations. The poor performance of the fleet in the early years and the overall low score of U-boat kills by 1945 were painfully evident to those who had served. They understood only too well that the RCN had engaged primarily in close-escort duties and had therefore not had an opportunity to obtain a kill rate proportionate to the navy's size. They also understood the obvious lessons of the war – poor training, inexperience, and lack of modern equipment – and were content to leave well enough alone. In any event, the post-war navy returned to its intended role, the defence of Canada, a role built around the traditional naval weapon, guns, and the fighter-bomber aircraft of the new naval air arm. Indeed, if there was one paramount anti-submarine lesson to be drawn from the Second World War, it was the need for integrated naval air power, and this was taken to heart by the post-war RCN.

In the difficult years which followed, the RCN's guns found few targets – mostly North Korean trains – and its attack aircraft found none. Eventually the cold war drew Canada back into an alliance remarkably similar to that of the war years, and into a similar role – one suited to a small nation with limited resources. In 1951 a new HMCS *St Laurent* was commissioned into the RCN, the first anti-submarine destroyer designed and built in Canada. Over the next two decades many more *St Laurents*, and variations on the basic design, were built, and many of the significant innovations in anti-submarine warfare – variable-depth sonar and the marriage of ASW helicopters to small ships – were made by the RCN. In time, the balanced-fleet concept gave way to specialization in ASW. What Nelles had derisively called the 'stepping stones,' the corvettes, had truly laid the foundations of the modern Royal Canadian Navy.

APPENDIX 1

A Selective Summary of Principal Staff Appointments and the Officers Who Held Them 1941–3

ROYAL CANADIAN NAVY

Naval Service Headquarters

† denotes members of Naval Board
* denotes members of Naval Staff
° denotes members of Naval Staff after reorganization of June 1943

Minister of Defence for the Naval Service
    Honourable Angus L. Macdonald   July 40–Apr 45
Chief of the Naval Staff†*°
    Vice-Admiral P.W. Nelles   1934–Jan 44
    Vice-Admiral G.C. Jones   Jan 44–1945
Vice-Chief of the Naval Staff (Deputy CNS until Jan 41)†*°
    Captain L.W. Murray   Sept 39–Oct 40
    Captain H.E. Reid   Oct 40–Oct 42
    Rear Admiral G.C. Jones   Oct 42–Jan 44
Assistant Chief of the Naval Staff (est June 43)°
    Commander W.B. Creery   June 43–Dec 44
Chief of Naval Personnel†*
    Captain H.T.W. Grant   Sept 40–Oct 42
    Captain E.R. Mainguy   Oct 42–Sept 44
Chief of Naval Equipment and Supply (Technical Division until Jan 42)†
    Engineer Commander J.F. Bell   Oct 40–Feb 41
    Captain G.M. Hibbard   Feb 41–Oct 43
    Captain E. Johnstone   Oct 43–Dec 44

Chief of Naval Engineering and Construction (est Jan 42)†
    Engineer Rear Admiral
    G.L. Stephens   Jan 42–1945
Naval Secretary / Secretary of the Naval Board†
    Paymaster Captain M.J.R.O.
    Cossette   1935–Jan 42
    Paymaster Commander
    R.A. Pennington   Jan 42–June 43
    Paymaster Commander
    J. Jeffrey   June 43–1945
Director of Operations Division*°
    Captain L.W. Murray   Sept 39–June 40
    Commander R.E.S. Bidwell   June 40–June 41
    Captain H.N. Lay   June 41–Apr 43
    Captain W.B. Creery   Apr 43–June 43
    Commander G.F. Griffiths   June 43–Dec 44
Director of Trade Division (Naval Intelligence and Trade until July 42)*°
    Captain E.R. Brand   July 39–1945
Director of Plans Division (Plans and Signals until Jan 42)*°
    Commander F.L. Houghton   July 39–June 42
    Captain H.G. DeWolf   June 42–Aug 43
    Captain G.R. Miles   Aug 43–Dec 44
Director of Signal Division (est Jan 42)*
    Commander G.A. Worth   Jan 42–1945
Director of Naval Intelligence Division (est July 42)*°
    Lieutenant C.H. Little   July 42–1945
Director of Warfare and Training Division (est June 43; post not filled until
Dec 43; run by Deputy DWT, Captain H. McMaster, June 43–Dec 43)°
    Captain K.F. Adams   Dec 43–Aug 44

Halifax

Commanding Officer, Atlantic Coast
    Captain H.E. Reid   Oct 38–Sept 40
    Rear Admiral G.C. Jones   Sept 40–Sept 42
    Rear Admiral L.W. Murray   Sept 42–Apr 43
C-in-C, Canadian Northwest Atlantic
    Rear Admiral L.W. Murray   Apr 43–1945
Chief of Staff to C-in-C, CNA
    Captain R.E.S. Bidwell   Apr 43–Apr 44

Captain (D)

Captain E.R. Mainguy	June 41–Nov 41
Captain G.R. Miles	Nov 41–Sept 42
Captain J.D. Prentice	Sept 42–May 44

Newfoundland

Commodore Commanding, Newfoundland

Commodore L.W. Murray	May 41–Dec 41

Flag Officer, Newfoundland

Rear Admiral L.W. Murray	Dec 41–Sept 42
Captain E.R. Mainguy	Sept 42–Oct 42
Commodore H.E. Reid	Oct 42–Oct 43
Commodore C.R.H. Taylor	Oct 43–1945

Chief of Staff

Commander R.E.S. Bidwell	July 41–Apr 43
Captain F.L. Houghton	Apr 43–Sept 43
Captain G.A.M.V. Harrison, RN	Sept 43–Dec 44

Captain (D)

Captain E.B.K. Stevens, RN	June 41–Nov 41
Captain E.R. Mainguy	Nov 41–Oct 42
Captain H.T.W. Grant	Oct 42–Apr 43
Captain J.M. Rowland, RN	Apr 43–Dec 44

UNITED STATES NAVY

Chief of Naval Operations (later COMINCH)

Admiral H.R. Stark	to Mar 43
Admiral E.J. King	from Mar 43

Commander, Task Force Twenty-four (previously Commander, Support Force, and CTF-4)

Vice-Admiral A.L. Bristol	Mar 41–Apr 42
Vice-Admiral R.M. Brainard	Apr 42–Apr 43

ROYAL NAVY

Western Approaches Command

C-in-C, Western Approaches

Admiral Sir Percy Noble	to Nov 42
Admiral Sir Max Horton	from Nov 42

Chief of Staff
    Commodore J. Mansfield   to Jan 43
    Captain A.S. Russell   from Jan 43
Deputy Chief of Staff (Operations)
    Captain R.W. Ravenhill   from Feb 42
Staff Officer (Anti-Submarine)
    Commander Honourable
    G.D. Howard-Johnston   from June 42
Commodore (D), Western Approaches
    Commodore G.W.G. Simpson   from Apr 41

APPENDIX 2

Summary of C and A 3 Group Compositions
July 1942–May 1943

C 1

ONS 112   *Assiniboine, St Croix, Battleford, Chambly, Chilliwack, Dianthus* (RN), *Nasturtium* (RN), *Orillia, Primrose* (RN)

SC 94   *Assiniboine, Battleford, Chilliwack, Dianthus* (RN), *Nasturtium* (RN), *Orillia, Primrose* (RN). *Chambly* detached to Halifax with damaged ship; *St Croix* on A/S exercises in Conception Bay.

ONS 123   *Broke* (RN), *Battleford, Chilliwack, Eyebright, Orillia. Assiniboine* and *Dianthus* (RN) in UK following heavy damage due to ramming attacks of previous operations; *Broke* (RN) temporarily assigned; *Eyebright* joined after working up at Tobermory. *Nasturtium* reassigned to A 3; *Primrose* did not sail.

SC 99   *St Francis, Battleford, Chambly, Chilliwack, Eyebright, Napanee, Orillia, Rosthern. St Francis* reassigned from C 4; *Chambly* returned from detached duty; *Napanee* from refit; *Rosthern* from refit.

ON 133   *St Laurent, Battleford, Chambly, Chilliwack, Eyebright, Napanee, Orillia. St Francis* in Londonderry with defects; *St Laurent* from refit; *Rosthern* reassigned to A 3.

HX 211   *Battleford, Chambly, Chilliwack, Eyebright, Napanee, Orillia. St Laurent* and *Orillia* (returned after sailing) in St John's with defects; *Dauphin* joined for the passage to make up numbers.

ON 143   *Battleford, Chambly, Chilliwack, Eyebright, Kenogami, Napanee, Shediac. Kenogami* and *Shediac* assigned to C 1 from WLEF.

SC 110   *St Laurent, Battleford, Chilliwack, Eyebright, Kenogami, Napanee, Shediac. St Laurent* defects repaired; *Chambly* to refit.

DEPLOYMENT OF THE OCEAN ESCORT GROUPS April 1942 to May 1943

ESCORT GROUP		APRIL	MAI	JUNI	JULI	AUGUST	SEPTEMBER	OKTOBER	NOVEMBER	DE
B.1	24.1.15		HX 187	ONS 96 · HX 193	ONS 108	ON·HX 119/201 · ON·HX 124	ONS 206	SC 134 · SC 105	HX 215	
B.2	24.1.16	SC 81	ONS 97	HX 86 · SC 87	HX 198 · HX 110	SC 92 · ONS 118	HX 208	ONS 138 · SC 106	HX 213	ONS 148
B.3	24.1.17		HX 188	ONS 98	ONS 107 · HX 109	SC 93 · ON 120	ON 207 · ONS 130	ON 136 · ONS 140	ONS 146	
B.4	24.1.18		SC 82	ON 99 · SC 87	ON 109 · HX 111	HX 199 · ONS 122	DNS 126 · ON 204	HX 209 · SC 104	HX 214 · ONS 144	ONS 150
B.6	24.1.4		ONS 94	HX 101 · HX 192	SC 88 · ONS 106	HX 200 · ON 117	HX 205 · ONS 132	SC 103	ONS 142	HX 217
B.7	24.1.5	HX 186	ONS 189	ONS 100	SC 91 · HX 185	SC 94 · ON 123	SC 99 · ON 129	SC 102 · HX 211	ON 143 · SC 108	HX 216
C.1	24.1.11		SC 84	ONS 103	UNS 112 · SC 89	B7	ON 129	ON 139	SC 110	ON 149
C.2	24.1.12		ON 93 · HX 191	ONS 104	HX 113 · HX 90	HX·ON 201/119 · 202/121	SC 131 · ON 141	HX 210 · SC 108	SC 109	
C.3	24.1.13		ON 95	SC 85 · ON 105	ON 115 · HX 197	ONS 115 · SC 96	SC 98 · ON 127	ON 137 · SC 107	ON 147	
C.4	24.1.14		ONS 92 · HX 190	ONS 102	ONS 105 · HX 196	ONS 116 · SC 95	ON 125	ON 135 · HX 212	HX 145	
A.3	24.1.3	HX 185								SC 111

TASK UNIT		DEZEMBER	JANUAR	FEBRUAR	MÄRZ	APRIL	MAI	JUNI	JULI	AU
B.1	24.1.15	ON 151	SC 114	ON 162	ONS 171	ON 178	HX 236			
B.2	24.1.16	148 · HX 219	ON 159	SC 118	ON 170 · SC 123	ONS 4	ONS 129 · ONS 9			
B.3	24.1.17	HX 218	HX 220	SC 117	HX 228 · ON 174	HX 232	ON 181			
B.4	24.1.18	ONS 150	ON 161		ONS 169 · HX 229	HX 234	HX 183 · HX 241			
B.5	24.1.19				ON 168	ON 176	ONS 7			
B.6	24.1.4	HX 217	ON 155	ONS 165	SC 122	SC 126 · SC 125	DNS 6 · SC 131			
B.7	24.1.5	246 · ON 153		ON 164	ON 227 · SC 120	HX 231	ONS 5 · SC 130			
C.1	24.1.11	ONS 154		SC 118	ON 173	ONS 2 · SC 127	ON 184			
C.2	24.1.12	249 · SC 113	ONS 160 · HX 222	HX 225	ON 172	ON 179 · ON 180	HX 237			
C.3	24.1.13	ONS 152	HX 221 · ONS 158	ONS 163 · HX 224	ONS 169	SC 124 · ON 177	HX 238 · HX 235	ONS 8		
C.4	24.1.14	SC 112			HX 226	HX 233	ON 182 · HX 240			
C.5	–									
A.3	24.1.3	SC 111	HX 223	ON 166	SC 121 · HX 229A	HX 175				
EG.40	–				ONS 3		SC 128			

ONS 154   *St Laurent, Battleford, Chilliwack, Kenogami, Napanee, Shediac. Eyebright* in St John's with defects; *Burnham* (RN) assigned to the group but unable to sail owing to defects.

HX 222   *Chesterfield* (RN), *Vansittart* (RN), *St Croix, Battleford, Chilliwack, Kenogami, Napanee, Shediac. St Laurent* to Halifax with defects; two RN destroyers temporarily assigned; *St Croix* from refit.

KMS 10   *Burwell* (RN), *St Croix, Battleford, Kenogami, Napanee, Shediac. Chilliwack* in Halifax for repairs; *St Laurent* and the RN frigate *Itchen*, both members of C 1, stayed in the UK during this convoy.

MKS 9   *St Croix, Battleford, Kenogami, Napanee, Shediac. Burwell* in Gibraltar with defects.

ONS 2   *St Laurent, St Croix, Battleford, Kenogami, Napanee, Shediac. Burwell* still in Gibraltar; *Itchen* in the UK; returning TORCH corvettes *Camrose, Kitchener, Moose Jaw,* and *Ville de Quebec* sailed with the group.

SC 127   *St Laurent, St Croix, Itchen* (RN), *Agassiz, Napanee, Woodstock. Itchen* (RN) joined at St John's; *Agassiz* from refit; *Woodstock,* ex-TORCH, from very brief refit at Halifax; *Kenogami* delayed with defects.

ON 184   *St Laurent, St Croix, Itchen* (RN), *Agassiz, Sackville, Woodstock. Sackville* from refit; *Napanee* in St John's with defects.

C 2

ON 113   *Burnham* (RN), *St Croix, Brandon, Dauphin, Drumheller, Polyanthus* (RN)

HX 201   *Burnham* (RN), *Brandon, Dauphin, Drumheller, Polyanthus* (RN). *St Croix* to A/S exercises in Conception Bay.

ON 119   *Broadway* (RN), *Burnham* (RN), *St Laurent, Brandon, Dauphin, Drumheller, Polyanthus* (RN), *Sorel, Broadway* from refit; *St Laurent* on temporary assignment; *Sorel* joined in mid-ocean.

SC 97   *Broadway* (RN), *Burnham* (RN), *Brandon, Dauphin, Drumheller, Morden. St Laurent* to C 1, *Sorel* to WLEF; *Morden* from refit.

ON 129   *Burnham* (RN), *Winchelsea* (RN), *Brandon, Dauphin, Drumheller, Morden, Polyanthus* (RN). *Broadway* in UK with defects; *Winchelsea* assigned from RN forces to replace her; *Polyanthus* back following repairs.

SC 102   *Burnham* (RN), *Winchelsea* (RN), *Drumheller, Morden, Pictou, Polyanthus* (RN). *Brandon* and *Dauphin* to refit; *Pictou* from refit.

ON 139 *Broadway* (RN), *Sherwood* (RN), *Winchelsea* (RN), *Drumheller, Morden, Primrose* (RN), *Polyanthus* (RN), *Pictou. Broadway* from refit; *Burnham* to refit; *Sherwood* assigned to the group, as was *Primrose.*

SC 108 *Broadway* (RN), *Sherwood* (RN), *Morden, Orillia, Polyanthus* (RN), *Primrose* (RN). *Winchelsea* reassigned elsewhere; *Pictou* and *Drumheller* on detached duty; *Orillia* reassigned from C 1 as partial replacement.

ON 149 *Broadway* (RN), *Sherwood* (RN), *Morden, Orillia, Polyanthus* (RN), *Primrose* (RN)

SC 113 *Broadway* (RN), *Sherwood* (RN), *Morden, Orillia, Pictou, Polyanthus* (RN), *Primrose* (RN). *Pictou* returned from detached duty.

ON 160 *Sherwood* (RN), *Lagan* (RN), *Waveney* (RN), *Morden, Orillia, Polyanthus* (RN), *Primrose* (RN). *Broadway* in UK for repairs; *Pictou* returned to NS for refit, replaced by two new RN frigates, *Lagan* and *Waveney.*

HX 225 *Sherwood* (RN), *Lagan* (RN), *Waveney* (RN), *Drumheller, Morden, Polyanthus* (RN), *Primrose* (RN). *Drumheller* from refit; *Orillia* to refit.

KMS 11 *Broadway* (RN), *Sherwood* (RN), *Lagan* (RN), *Chambly, Drumheller, Morden, Primrose* (RN). *Broadway* back from repairs; *Waveney* reassigned; *Chambly* arrived direct from Halifax after refit; *Polyanthus* refitting.

MKS 10 *Broadway* (RN), *Sherwood* (RN), *Lagan* (RN), *Chambly, Drumheller, Morden, Primrose* (RN)

ON 179 *Broadway* (RN), *Lagan* (RN), *Amherst, Drumheller, Morden, Primrose,* and the TORCH corvettes *Algoma* and *Calgary. Sherwood* repairing defects, as was *Chambly; Amherst,* ex C 1, en route to refit; TORCH corvettes en route to Halifax.

HX 237 *Broadway* (RN), *Lagan* (RN), *Chambly, Drumheller, Morden, Primrose* (RN). *Chambly* rejoined independently from UK.

C 3

ON 115 *Saguenay, Skeena, Agassiz, Galt, Louisburg, Sackville, Wetaskiwin*
HX 202 *Saguenay, Skeena, Galt, Louisburg, Sackville, Wetaskiwin. Agassiz* to Halifax for repairs.
ON 121 *Saguenay, Skeena, St Francis, St Laurent, Galt, Louisburg, Sackville, Wetaskiwin. St Francis* and *St Laurent* temporarily assigned.

SC 98   *Saguenay, Skeena, Agassiz, Galt, Sackville, Wetaskiwin. Louisburg* assigned to TORCH, in Halifax making preparations for sailing to UK.

ON 131   *Saguenay, Skeena, Agassiz, Anenome* (RN), *Galt, Sackville, Wetaskiwin. Anenome* attached for one convoy.

HX 210   *Saguenay, Skeena, Witherington* (RN), *Agassiz, Galt, Sackville, Wetaskiwin. Witherington* from WLEF, temporarily assigned.

SC 109   *Saguenay, Skeena, Agassiz, Galt, Sackville, Wetaskiwin. Winchelsea* (RN) attached following heavy damage to *Saguenay* in collision early on.

ONS 152   *Burnham* (RN), *Skeena, Agassiz, Galt, Sackville, Wetaskiwin. Burnham* from refit to replace *Saguenay*.

HX 221   *Assiniboine, Burnham* (RN), *Bittersweet, Buttercup* (RN), *Columbine* (RN), *Eyebright, La Malbaie. Assiniboine* fresh from long refit, as was *Bittersweet; La Malbaie* (RPV) a new commission; *Eyebright,* ex C 1, laid over in St John's with defects for several weeks; *Buttercup* and *Columbine* attached for one passage; *Skeena, Galt, Agassiz, Sackville, Wetaskiwin* to refit in NS.

ONS 163   *Assiniboine, Burnham* (RN), *Jed* (RN), *Bittersweet, La Malbaie, Eyebright. Jed,* RN frigate, assigned to the group.

HX 226   *Burnham* (RN), *Jed* (RN), *Eyebright, La Malbaie, Bittersweet, Mayflower. Assiniboine* to repair following damage in last operation; *Mayflower* from refit.

ONS 172   *Burnham* (RN), *Jed* (RN), *Bittersweet, Eyebright, La Malbaie, Mayflower.* The TORCH corvettes *Port Arthur, Summerside,* and *Woodstock* were temporarily attached.

SC 124   *Burnham* (RN), *Jed* (RN), *Bittersweet, Eyebright, La Malbaie, Mayflower*

ON 180   *Burnham* (RN), *Skeena, Bittersweet, Eyebright, La Malbaie, Mayflower. Jed* reassigned; *Skeena* from refit.

HX 238   *Burnham* (RN), *Skeena, Bittersweet, Eyebright, La Malbaie, Mayflower, Pictou. Pictou* from refit.

C 4

ON 116   *Ottawa, St Francis, Amherst, Arvida, Celandine* (RN), *Pictou, Sherbrooke*

SC 96   *Ottawa, St Croix, Amherst, Arvida, Sherbrooke, Celandine* (RN). *Pictou* damaged in collision, to Halifax for repairs; *St Francis* reassigned to C 3; *St Croix* assigned from C 2.

ON 127   *Ottawa, St Croix, Amherst, Arvida, Celandine* (RN), *Sherbrooke*

SC 101   *Restigouche, St Croix, Amherst, Arvida, Celandine* (RN), *Sherbrooke*. *Ottawa* lost to enemy action with ON 127; *Restigouche* from refit assigned to replace her.

ON 137   *Restigouche, St Croix, Amherst, Arvida, Celandine* (RN), *Sherbrooke*

SC 107   *Restigouche, Amherst, Arvida, Celandine* (RN), *Sherbrooke, St Croix* to refit; TORCH corvettes *Algoma* and *Moose Jaw* attached for the passage to the UK.

ON 147   *Restigouche, St Francis, Amherst, Arvida, Celandine* (RN), *Dauphin, Sherbrooke*. *St Francis* assigned after duty with C 1; *Dauphin* from refit.

SC 112   *Churchill* (RN), *Restigouche, Amherst, Brandon, Celandine* (RN), *Collingwood, Sherbrooke*. *Churchill* assigned from RN forces; *Arvida* to refit after ON 147; *Brandon* and *Collingwood* from refit.

ONS 158   *Churchill* (RN), *Restigouche, Amherst, Brandon, Collingwood, Sherbrooke*. *Celandine* delayed with defects.

HX 224   *Churchill* (RN), *Restigouche, Amherst, Brandon, Celandine* (RN), *Collingwood, Sherbrooke*

KMF 10B   *Churchill* (RN), *Restigouche, Amherst, Brandon, Celandine* (RN), *Collingwood*. *Sherbrooke* temporarily assigned to B 4.

MKF 10B   *Churchill* (RN), *Restigouche, Amherst, Brandon, Celandine* (RN), *Collingwood*

ON 177   *Churchill* (RN), *Restigouche, Amherst, Brandon, Collingwood*. *St Albans*, Norwegian destroyer, attached for the crossing.

HX 235   *Churchill* (RN), *Restigouche, Baddeck, Brandon, Collingwood*. *Amherst, Celandine* to refit; *Baddeck*, ex TORCH corvette, from brief refit.

A 3

SC 95   *Schenck* (US), *Spencer* (US), *Bittersweet, Collingwood, Mayflower, Snowflake* (RN), *Trillium, Wallflower* (RN)

ON 125   *Babbitt* (US), *Spencer* (US), *Bittersweet, Collingwood, Mayflower, Nasturtium* (RN), *Trillium*. *Nasturtium* reassigned from C 1.

SC 100   *Campbell* (US), *Spencer* (US), *Bittersweet, Mayflower, Nasturtium* (RN), *Trillium, Rosthern*. *Collingwood* to refit; *Rosthern* from refit; the TORCH corvettes *Lunenburg* and *Weyburn* assigned for passage to UK.

ON 135   *Campbell* (US), *Spencer* (US), *Bittersweet, Mayflower, Rosthern, Trillium*. *Nasturtium* assigned to TORCH.

HX 212   *Badger* (US), *Campbell* (US), *Dianthus* (RN), *Rosthern,*
Trillium. Bittersweet and *Mayflower* refitting; TORCH corvettes
Alberni, Summerside, and *Ville de Quebec* assigned for passage to
UK; *Dianthus* from repairing defects.

ON 145   *Badger* (US), *Burza* (POL), *Campbell* (US), *Dianthus* (RN),
Rosthern, Trillium

SC 111   *Badger* (US), *Spencer* (US), *Dauphin, Dianthus* (RN), *Rosthern,*
Trillium. Dauphin from refit.

ONS 156   *Badger* (US), *Spencer* (US), *Dauphin, Dianthus* (RN), *Rosthern,*
Trillium

HX 223   *Campbell* (US), *Spencer* (US), *Dauphin, Dianthus* (RN), *Napanee,*
Rosthern, Trillium. Napanee in passage to join C 1.

ON 166   *Campbell* (US), *Spencer* (US), *Chilliwack, Dauphin, Dianthus*
(RN), *Rosthern, Trillium. Chilliwack* en route to Halifax for refit.

SC 121   *Greer* (US), *Spencer* (US), *Dauphin, Dianthus* (RN), *Rosthern,*
Trillium

ON 175   *Greer* (US), *Spencer* (US), *Dauphin, Dianthus* (RN), *Rosthern,*
Trillium

HX 234   *Greer* (US), *Spencer* (US), *Skeena, Arvida, Dianthus* (RN),
Wetaskiwin. Dauphin and *Trillium* to refit; *Rosthern* temporarily
attached to B 4; *Skeena, Arvida, Wetaskiwin* from refit.

A 3 was dissolved following convoy HX 234; the corvette nucleus was
reassigned to the new group C 5.

Notes

PROLOGUE

1 See G.N. Tucker, *The Naval Service of Canada*, I, and J.A. Boutilier, ed, *The RCN in Retrospect*, chaps 1–7, for details of the RCN's early period.
2 D.C. Gordon, *The Dominion Partnership in Imperial Defence, 1870–1914* (Baltimore: John Hopkins Press 1965), 267
3 Tucker, *Naval Service of Canada*, I, 342
4 See W.A.B. Douglas, 'Conflict and Innovation in the Royal Canadian Navy,' 210–32.
5 Tucker, *Naval Service of Canada*, I, 366–8
6 See A.J. Marder, *From the Dreadnought to Scapa Flow*, IV (Oxford: Oxford University Press 1964), chap 10.
7 Capt S.W. Roskill, *Naval Policy between the Wars*, II
8 'Defence of Trade,' CNS memorandum, 12 Feb 1937, Public Archives, Canada (PAC), MG 27, III, B5, V 37, file D-26
9 'Chiefs of Staff Committee, Plan for the Defence of Canada,' as amended to May 1939, PAC, RG 24, 2696, HQS 5199, F,V 1
10 Roskill, *Naval Policy*, II, 226
11 'Defence of Trade,' CNS memo, 12 Feb 1937
12 Tucker, *Naval Service of Canada*, I, 351–3
13 Director, Naval Intelligence and Plans, to Director, Naval Personnel, 29 Oct 1938, PAC, RG 24, 3852, NSS 1018-6-8, V 1
14 CNS to C-in-C, A&WI, 24 Mar 1939, PAC, RG 24, 3852, NSS 1018-6-8, V 2

CHAPTER I: THE ROAD TO THE ISLES

1 Grand Admiral Karl Dönitz, *Memoirs*, chap 5
2 Adm Sir R. Bacon and F.E. McMurtrie, *Modern Naval Strategy* (London: Frederick Muller 1940), 148–9
3 F.M. McKee, *Volunteers for Sea Service*, 40

4 'Development of Canadian Naval Policy,' Plans Division memorandum, 9 Dec 1943, Directorate of History (DHist), National Defence Headquarters, Ottawa, NS 1440–5

5 DHist interview with RAdm L.W. Murray, RCN, May 1970, PAC, MG 30, E 307, V 4

6 J.W. Pickersgill, *The Mackenzie King Record*, I, 76

7 [Angus L. Macdonald], *Speeches*, 127

8 Tucker, *Naval Service of Canada*, II, chap 1; M. Milner, *Canadian Naval Force Requirements*

9 'Manpower Problems of the Royal Canadian Navy during the Second World War,' Army Historical Section report, no 71, 20 Sept 1954, DHist

10 Naval Staff Minutes, 29 Apr 1940, DHist

11 Ibid, 22 Jan 1940

12 'Summary of War Effort – Naval,' 19 Jan 1940, DHist, NS 1440 / 10, and Milner, *Canadian Naval Force Requirements*, 19–23

13 CNS to minister, 29 Jan 1940, DHist, NSH 1700–193 / 96

14 DNP to CNS, 29 Jan 1940, DHist, NSH 1700–193 / 96

15 CNS to minister, 29 Jan 1940

16 See Tucker, *Naval Service of Canada*, II, chaps 2–4, for details of ship acquisition.

17 Naval Council Minutes, 9 Apr 1940, PAC, RG 24, 4044, NS 1078-3-4, V I

18 A.L. Macdonald Papers, 'Shipbuilding in N.S.,' contains correspondence on this subject, Public Archives of Nova Scotia (PANS), MG 2, cabinet 2, F 1221. *Report of Royal Commission on Provincial Development and Rehabilitation*, V 1–2

19 Macdonald to C.D. Howe, 30 Apr 1941, Macdonald Papers, F 1222 / 10

20 'Development of Canadian Naval Policy,' DHist, NS 1440–5

21 Pickersgill, *Mackenzie King Record*, I, 76

22 Joseph Schull, *The Far Distant Ships*, 32

23 Pickersgill, *Mackenzie King Record*, 136–7

24 Interview with Adm H.G. DeWolf, RCN, 10 July 1981

25 F.H. Hinsley, *British Intelligence in the Second World War*, I, 334–5

26 Capt S.W. Roskill, *The War at Sea*, I, 134–5, 351–3

27 All correspondence related to this matter is found in PAC, RG 24, 11065, NSS 41-1-7, V I and II.

28 COAC to Naval Secretary, 10 Feb 1941, ibid, and Admiralty to NSHQ, 4 Apr 1941, ibid

29 Ibid

30 Interview with Capt E.S. Brand, RCN, 10 July 1981

31 Naval Staff Minutes, 11 Feb 1941

32 'Appreciation. The Nature of the Canadian Military Effort Midsummer 1941 to Spring 1942,' Chiefs of Staff Committee, 28 May 1941, DHist, NS 1650-1, V 2

33 Naval Council Minutes, 30 Oct 1940

34 CNS to First Sea Lord, 14 Nov 1941, DHist, NSH 1700–193 / 96

35 CNS to minister, 4 Jan 1941, DHist, NSH 1700–193 / 96

36 Commodore Commanding, Halifax Force to Naval Secretary, 7 Jan 1941, DHist, NDHQ NSS 8020-476

37 Naval Staff Minutes, 14 Jan 1941, 29 Jan 1941, 11 Feb 1941; Naval Council
   Minutes, 30 Jan 1941; correspondence in DHist, NDHQ NSS 8020-476
38 Tucker, *Naval Service of Canada*, II, appendix 1
39 'Review of the Development of Canadian Naval Policy,' nd, DHist, NS 1650-1,
   V II, 2–3
40 DNO to ACNS and CNS, 15 Aug 1940, DHist, NS 8000, HMCS *Captor*
41 Roskill, *War at Sea*, I, 451–2
42 C.P. Stacey, *Arms, Men and Governments*, 310–15, 357–67
43 Col S.W. Dziuban, *Military Relations between the United States and Canada*,
   101–8
44 'History of North Atlantic Convoy Escort Organization and Canadian Participation
   Therein, 9 / 39–4 / 43,' Plans Division narrative, 1 May 1943, DHist, 81 / 520,
   9; W.A.B. Douglas, 'The RCN and RCAF in the Battle of the Atlantic,' 164–75, 167
45 Stacey, *Arms, Men and Governments*
46 P. Bridle, ed, *Documents on Relations between Canada and Newfoundland*,
   1935–1949, doc no 550
47 Naval Staff Minutes, 3 Sept 1940
48 'Modernization of Armament and Equipment,' DHist, NS 8060, 4
49 Ibid
50 Naval Staff Minutes, 11 Mar 1941

CHAPTER 2: THE STRUGGLE BEGINS

1 DOP to CNS, 21 Dec 1942, DHist, M-11
2 Hinsley, *British Intelligence in the Second World War*, II, 167–79, 169
3 'Review of Methods of Dealing with the U-Boat Menace,' Admiralty Report,
   Feb 1940, V-Adm A.G. Talbot, RN, Papers, Imperial War Museum, London, 282
4 Hinsley, *British Intelligence in the Second World War*, II, 168
5 Tucker, *Naval Service of Canada*, II, 186–203; 'NOIC St John's Report on Existing
   Facilities St John's, June 1941,' DHist, NS 1440–166 / 25; 'The Royal Canadian
   Navy in Newfoundland, 1940–44,' narrative by Lt S. Keate, RCNVR, 1944, DHist,
   NS 8000, HMCS *Avalon*
6 Macdonald Papers, diary entry, 6 Aug 1941, F 390
7 Tucker, *Naval Service of Canada*, II, 193–4; *Jane's Fighting Ships*, 1941
8 RAdm J.C. Hibbard to author, 21 Nov 1981; RAdm H.F. Pullen to author, 16 Oct
   1981; David Zimmerman to author, 31 Aug 1981; interview with Mr L.C. Audette
   (numerous occasions); DHist, career profile; interview with Mrs J.D. Prentice,
   8 Nov 1982
9 'Royal Canadian Navy in Newfoundland'
10 Ibid; J.D. Prentice to G.N. Tucker, 15 Jan 1947, DHist, NS 8000 HMCS *Chambly*
11 In Captain (D), Greenock, to C-in-C, WA, 10 June 1941, PAC, RG 24, 6909, NSS
   8970–300
12 DHist interview with RAdm Murray, May 1970, PAC, MG 30, E 207, V 4
13 RAdm H.G. DeWolf to author, 15 Oct 1981
14 Navy List, Nov 1941, DHist library

15 Lt E.N. Clarke (Eng) to Captain (D), Newfoundland, 6 Dec 1942, PAC, RG 24, 11115, 61-1-3

16 CCNF to C-in-C, WA, and others, 28 July 1941, DHist, NS 8440-70

17 Milner, *Canadian Naval Force Requirements*

18 Admiralty to CNS, 12 July 1941, DHist, NS 8440-70

19 Naval Council Minutes, 14 July 1941

20 Schull, *Far Distant Ships*, 78; Monthly Anti-Submarine Report, Aug 1941, DHist library

21 CCCS to NSHQ, 6 July 1941, PAC, RG 24, 11065, 41-1-1, V I

22 Secretary of the Admiralty to CNS, 16 July 1941, PAC, RG 24, 6909, NSS 8970-3000

23 CNS to Secretary of the Admiralty (draft), 19 Aug 1941, PAC, RG 24, 6909, NSS 8970-3000

24 CCCS to NSHQ, 6 July 1941

25 Reports from NOIC Sydney to COAC, Aug–Sept 1941, PAC, RG 24, 11065, 41-1-1, V I

26 Captain (D), Newfoundland, to CCNF, 2 Sept 1941, PAC, RG 24, 3892, NSS 1033-6-1

27 Prentice to Tucker, 15 Jan 1947

28 J.R.M. Butler, *Grand Strategy*, III, pt 2, chap 5

29 Stacey, *Arms, Men and Governments*, 310–15; Dziuban, *Military Relations between the United States and Canada*, 242–52

30 W.A.B. Douglas and B. Greenhous, *Out of the Shadows*, 71

31 'Personal Appreciation of Situation for RCN Ships in United Kingdom,' Lt Cdr W.E.S. Briggs, RCNR, 23 Apr 1943, PAC, RG 24, 11960, CS 34

32 Western Approaches Convoy Instructions, pt 300, General Instructions for Escorts, Naval Historical Branch (NHB), London, N / NHB / 10 / 70; Escort-of-Convoy Instructions, pt V, Primary Duties of Escorts, Naval Historical Center (NHC), Operational Archives Branch, Washington Naval Yard, Washington, DC

33 'History of North Atlantic Convoy Escort Organization ...,' Plans Division narrative, 1 May 1943, 11–12

34 'Progress of Analysis of the Value of Escort Vessels and Aircraft in the Anti-U-Boat Campaign,' Public Record Office (PRO), Kew, UK, PREM 3 414 / 3

35 Report of Proceedings, SOE, SC 41, 6 Sept 1941, PRO, ADM 199 / 55

CHAPTER 3: BETWEEN A ROCK AND A HARD PLACE

1 Dönitz, *Memoirs*, 18–24

2 'U-Boat Methods of Combined Attack on Convoys. From February 1st to October 1st, 1941,' RN intelligence report, 10 Nov 1941, DHist, ADM 223 / 1; Dr J. Rohwer to the author, 30 Sept 1982

3 Account of SC 42 based on 'Analysis of U-Boat Attacks on Convoy SC 42, 9th–16th September, 1941,' DA/SW analysis, PRO, ADM 199 / 1489; Commodore's report, SC 42, PRO, ADM 237 / 219; Prentice to Tucker, 15 Jan 1947, DHist, NS 8000, HMCS *Chambly*; J. Rohwer and G. Hummelchen, *Chronology of the War*

at Sea, I; W.A.B. Douglas and J. Rohwer, 'The Most Thankless Task Revisited';
Schull, *Far Distant Ships*, 79–86; HMCS *Chambly*, Report of Proceedings, 14 Sept
1941, PAC, RG 24, 6901, NS 8910-339 / 21

4 Naval Council Minutes, 15 Sept 1941

5 Cdr F.H. Houghton to CNS, 23 Sept 1941, DHist, NSH 1700-193 / 96c; Naval
Council Minutes, 22 Sept 1941; Admiralty Pink Lists, Sept 1941 to Apr 1942,
PRO, ADM 187, V 15–18; CNS to Admiralty, 8 Oct 1941, PAC, RG 24, 3875, NSS
1048-48-31, V I.

6 Prentice to Tucker, 15 Jan 1947; HMCS *Chambly*, Report of Proceedings, 14 Sept
1941

7 E.F. Burton, ed, *Canadian Naval Radar Officers*

8 Correspondence on early naval radar policy and the development of manpower can
be found in PAC, RG 24, 5678, NSS 101-1-11, and in Naval Staff and Naval
Council minutes.

9 W.E. Knowles Middleton, *Radar Development in Canada*, chap 7

10 'Report on the Sea Trials of 271 Radar, HMS *Orchis*, April–May 1941,' PRO, ADM
1 / 11063, also in Cdr H.J. Fawcett, RN, Papers, Churchill College, Cambridge,
FWCT 2 / 4 / 2

11 'Design of a 214 WC Yagi for CSC,' NRC Radio Branch report, PRA-28, Nov 1941;
'SWIC Apparatus Approval Tests,' NRC Radio Branch report, PRA-23, NRC library

12 'Summary of Naval War Effort, Oct–Dec 41,' DHist, NS 1440-10, V 2

13 'Summary of Analysis of U-Boat Attacks on Atlantic Convoys, August 1940 to
February 1942,' DA/SW analysis, 21 June 1942, PRO, ADM 199 / 1490

14 Houghton to CNS, 23 Sept 1941; Roskill, *War at Sea*, I, 471

15 Prentice to Tucker, 15 Jan 1947

16 Captain (D), Newfoundland, to CCNF, 16 Oct 1941, PAC, RG 24, 3892,
NSS 1033-6-1; CCNF to A/CNS, 15 Oct 1941, PAC, RG 24, 11979, NS 15-15

17 USN Administrative History of WW II, no 139, C-in-C, U.S. Atlantic Fleet and
Commander Task Force Twenty-Four, 87

18 C-in-C, US Atlantic Fleet, to CCNF, 9 Oct 1941, US National Archives (USNA),
Washington, DC, RG 80, box 232, file A4-1 (Aug–Oct); Director, Trade Division,
Admiralty, minute, 26 Nov 1941, DHist, NS 8440-70; DA/SW to CCNF, 22 Dec
1941, PAC, RG 24, 11940, NS 8910-20

19 Patrick Abazzia, *Mr. Roosevelt's Navy*, 116–17

20 HMS *Veteran*, Report of Proceedings, as repeated by C-in-C, WA, to CCNF, 17 Oct
1941, PAC, RG 24, 11505, MSI-2-6

21 HMCS *Shediac*, Report of Proceedings, and C-in-C, WA, Minutes, Convoy Cover,
SC 48, PRO, ADM 237 / 187

22 Account of SC 52 based on BdU War Diary, DHist; Eastern Air Command, RCAF,
weekly intelligence reports, DHist, 181.003 (D3091); and Rohwer and
Hummelchen, *Chronology of the War at Sea*, I

23 Roskill, *War at Sea*, I, 475

24 CO, HMCS *St Laurent*, to Captain (D), Newfoundland, 18 Oct 1941, and related
correspondence, PAC, RG 24, 11938, NSS 8440-2, V I

25 Captain (D), Newfoundland, to Lt Graham, RN, 29 Dec 1941, PAC, RG 24, 11940, NRC 4935, 15-0
26 CO, HMCS *Chambly*, to Captain (D), Newfoundland, 4 Nov 1941, PAC, RG 24, 11929, NSS 1033-6-1
27 Captain (D), Newfoundland, to CCNF, 5 Nov 1941, PAC, RG 24, 11929, NSS 1033-6-1
28 CCNF to Naval Secretary, 14 Aug 1941, PAC, RG 24, 11929, MSOO 220-3-6; CCNF to A/CNS, 15 Oct 1941, PAC, RG 24, 11979, 15-15; CCNF to Naval Secretary, 6 Nov 1941, PAC, RG 24, 11929, MSOO 220-3-6
29 'Training and Manning Policy,' memorandum to senior officers from the Naval Secretary, 24 Dec 1941, PAC, RG 24, 3892, NSS 1033-7-2
30 NSHQ to CCNF, 16 Oct 1941, PAC, RG 24, 11941, NRC 6951
31 Pink Lists, Dec 1941, PRO, ADM 197, V 16
32 FONF to Naval Secretary, 7 Dec 1941, PAC, RG 24, 11929, MSOO 220-3-6
33 Naval Secretary to FONF, 27 Dec 1941, PAC, RG 24, 11929, MSOO 220-3-6
34 H. Lawrence, *A Bloody War*, 74
35 W. Pugsley, *Saints, Devils and Ordinary Seamen* (Toronto: Collins 1945), 53
36 Interview with Cdr Harry Shorten, RCN, DHist
37 C-in-C, US Atlantic Fleet, to CNO, 17 Nov 1941, USNA, RG 80, box 232, file A4-1 (Nov–Dec) 1941
38 Discussed in Ibid
39 War Diary, USS *Prairie*, NHC, Op Archives
40 S.E. Morison, *The History of U.S. Naval Operations in the Second World War*, I, 117–19
41 USN Administrative History of WW II, no 139, 105
42 Prentice to Tucker, 15 Jan 1947
43 W. Sclater, *Haida* (Toronto: Oxford University Press 1946)
44 Interview with Mr L.C. Audette, Jan 1982; Captain E.S. Brand to author, 20 Oct 1981; RAdm H.G. DeWolf to author, 15 Oct 1981; RAdm H.N. Lay to author, 8 Oct 1981

CHAPTER 4: NEW PRIORITIES AND A CERTAIN BALANCE

1 Plans Division memorandum, 29 Jan 1942, PAC, RG 24, 3844, NSS 1017-10-39, V 1
2 Milner, *Canadian Naval Force Requirements*, 56–8
3 CO, USS *Nicholson* to A/S officer, Atlantic Coast (USN), 19 May 1942, NHC, Op Archives, 10th Fleet files, ASM Division, box 23, HMS *Osprey*
4 K. Macpherson and J. Burgess, *The Ships of Canada's Naval Forces, 1910–1981*, app 8; Pink Lists, PRO, ADM 187, V 16–17
5 COAC to CNS, 21 Dec 1942, PAC, RG 24, 6796, NS 8375-4
6 Commander, Eastern Sea Frontier, to C-in-C, U.S. Atlantic Fleet, 14 Feb 1942, USNA, RG 80, box 308, file A14-1 (14 Feb–Apr); interview with Dr P.K. Lundeburg, 5 May 1982
7 Board on the Organization of East Coast Convoys, Report to C-in-C, U.S. Fleet, nd, PRO, ADM 205 / 19

8 Compiled from Daily Location of Ships and Aircraft, NHC, Op Archives
9 Captain (D), Newfoundland, to FONF, 31 Mar 1942, and FONF to NSHQ, 1 Apr 1942, PAC, RG 24, 11929, MSOO 220-3-6
10 HMCS *Chambly*, log, Apr–Aug 1942, PAC, RG 24, 7184
11 'Training at St John's,' Naval Historian's narrative, June 1945, DHist, NS 8000, HMCS *Avalon*
12 Chiefs of Staff Committee, Special Session in Washington, Minutes, 2–3 Jan 1942, DHist, 193.009 (D53)
13 Rohwer and Hummelchen, *Chronology of the War at Sea*, I, 210–11
14 Atlantic Convoy Instructions, NHB, N / NHB / 10 / 70; DA/SW, comments on ONS 92, 28 Sept 1942, PRO, ADM 199 / 1338
15 ACNS(T) to FSL, 26 May 1942, PRO, ADM 205 / 23
16 Macpherson and Burgess, *Ships of Canada's Naval Forces*, app 8
17 NSHQ to FONF and COAC, 29 May 1942, PAC, RG 24, 11929, MSOO 220-3-6
18 COAC to NSHQ, 30 May 1942, and FONF to NSHQ, 30 May 1942, PAC, RG 24, 11929, MSOO 220-3-6
19 Monthly reports, Training Office, Halifax, May 1942 to June 1943, PAC, RG 24, 11988, 4–6
20 Churchill to Harry Hopkins, 12 May 1942, PRO, Ministry of Transport (MT), 62 / 36
21 Roskill, *War at Sea*, II, 94–104
22 Fuehrer Conference on Naval Affairs, 14 May 1942, Capt J. Cresswell Papers, Churchill College, Cambridge, CRES 104 / 5 / 1
23 Tucker, *Naval Service of Canada*, II, app 10
24 C-in-C, U.S. Fleet, via COMNAVEU to FSL, 11 May 1942, ACNS(T) to FSL, 17 May 1942, COMINCH to FSL, 20 May 1942, and FSL to COMINCH, 21 May 1942, PRO, ADM 205 / 19
25 'History of North Atlantic Convoy Escort Organization ...,' Plans Division narrative, 1 May 1943, 14–15
26 'Minutes of Ottawa Conference on Trade and Escort Matters,' 23–24 July 1942, PAC, RG 24, 3975, NS 1048-48-31
27 Compiled from Macpherson and Burgess, *Ships of Canada's Naval Forces*, app 8
28 'Battle of the Atlantic Review, 18 May 1942,' ACNS(T) to FSL, PRO ADM 1 / 12062
29 FONF to Secretary, Naval Board, 17 July 1942, DHist, NSHQ, NSC 7401-430-7
30 FONF to Secretary, Naval Board, 29 Apr 1942, and Secretary, Naval Board, to FONF, 1 June 1942, DHist, NS 1000-198
31 Anthony Watts, *The U-Boat Hunters*, 148–9
32 *The U-Boat War in the Atlantic*, II, *January 1942–May 1943*, Admiralty Restricted Book, BR 305(2) (hereinafter referred to as BR 305[2]), DHist and NHB
33 Account of ONS 92 based on BR 305(2); Convoy Cover, PRO, ADM 237 / 120; DA/SW comments, PRO, ADM 199 / 1338; A/SW unit, U.S. Atlantic Fleet, analysis, NHC, Op Archives; Rohwer and Hummelchen, *Chronology of the War at Sea*, I
34 BR 305(2)
35 Account of ONS 100 based on BR 305(2); Convoy Cover, PRO, ADM 237 / 86; Rohwer and Hummelchen, *Chronology of the War at Sea*, I

36 Account of ONS 102 based on BR 305(2); SOE's Report of Proceedings, 28 June
   1942, PRO ADM 199 / 1338; HMCS *Chambly*, log, PAC, RG 24, 7184; Rohwer and
   Hummelchen, *Chronology of the War at Sea*, I
37 BR 305(2)
38 Naval Staff Minutes, 14 May 1942
39 President, Halifax Shipyards, to C.D. Howe, 6 Jan 1942, Macdonald Papers,
   F 1222 / 53
40 Naval Staff Minutes, 29 June, 6, 9, 13 July 1942; 'Modernization of Armament
   and Equipment,' DHist, NS 8000, 11–15
41 FONF to NSHQ, 16 June 1942, PAC, RG 24, 11114, NS 61-1-1
42 Interview with RAdm H.G. DeWolf, RCN, DHist biography file
43 Naval Historian's notes, DHist, NSH 1700–193 / 96
44 Account of ON 113 based on BR 305(2); Convoy Cover, PRO, ADM 237 / 87 and 88;
   A/SW unit, analysis, 16 Sept 1942, NHC, Op Archives; Rohwer and Hummelchen,
   Chronology of the War at Sea, I

CHAPTER 5: AN ACCEPTABLE RATE OF EXCHANGE

1 Marc Milner, 'Canadian Escorts in the Mid Atlantic,' app 7
2 Minutes of conference, 25 July 1942, PAC, RG 24, 3975, NS 1048-48-31, V I
3 DOD to minister, CNS, and VCNS, 19 June 1942, PAC, RG 24, 3842, NSS
   1017-10-22
4 Account of ON 115 based on BR 305(2); Convoy Cover, PRO, ADM 237 / 88;
   DHist, NS 8280, ON 115; Rohwer and Hummelchen, *Chronology of the War at
   Sea*, I
5 SOE's Report of Proceedings, DHist, NS 8280
6 CO, HMCS *Sackville*, Report of Proceedings, DHist, NS 8280
7 CTF-24 to C-in-C, U.S. Fleet, 4 Aug 1942, PAC, RG 24, 11929, MSOO 220-3-6
8 All WA comments from minutes sheets in PRO, ADM 237 / 88
9 Admiralty to BAD, 20 Aug 1942, PRO, ADM 237 / 88
10 SO(A/S) Minutes, PRO, ADM 237 / 88; CO, HMCS *Chambly*, to Captain (D), Newfoundland, 1 Aug 1942, PAC, RG 24, 11938, NS 8100-1, V I
11 Captain (D), Newfoundland, minutes on copy of above, nd, PAC, RG 24, 11940,
   5298, NRC 308-0
12 CO, HMCS *Chambly*, to Captain (D), Newfoundland, 1 Aug 1942
13 Account of SC 94 based on BR 305(2); DA/SW analysis, PRO, ADM 199 / 2007; DHist,
   NS 8280, SC 94; Roskill, *War at Sea*, II, 209–10; Captain D. Macintyre,
   The Battle of the Atlantic, 150–6; Rohwer and Hummelchen, *Chronology
   of the War at Sea*, I
14 Interview with CPO C.P. Van der Hagen, RCN, DHist
15 DASW analysis, app 4
16 BR 305(2)
17 Ibid; Rohwer and Hummelchen, *Chronology of the War at Sea*, I

18 Account of ONS 122 based on BR 305(2); DASW analysis, PRO, ADM 199 / 2010; Convoy Cover, PRO, ADM 237 / 124; DHist, NS 8280, ONS 122; Rohwer and Hummelchen, *Chronology of the War at Sea*, I
19 Lt Col N. Borchgrevink, Norwegian Research Centre for Defence History, to author, 22 Sept 1981
20 Account of SC 97 based on BR 305(2); DA/SW analysis, PRO, ADM 199 / 1710; DHist, NS 8280, SC 97; Rohwer and Hummelchen, *Chronology of the War at Sea*, I
21 See Lawrence, *Bloody War*.
22 CO, HMS *Walker*, to COAC, Sept 1942, PAC, RG 24, 11567, DO-24-1
23 Naval Staff Minutes, 20 Aug 1942
24 Navy Lists, Nov 1942
25 'Operational Training,' DHist, NS 4900
26 The precise links between events at sea and staff reaction are difficult to determine because the Staff's minuted copies of reports of proceedings were destroyed after the war.
27 Naval Staff Minutes, 20 and 31 Aug 1942
28 Secretary, Naval Board, to COAC, FONF, Captains (D), and other senior officers, 11 Nov 1942, PAC, RG 24, 11988, G-21-1-2
29 Brand interview, 10 July 1981

CHAPTER 6: THE DISQUIET GROWS

1 FSL to Sir Arthur Slater, 13 July 1942, Roskill Papers, Churchill College, Cambridge, ROSK 5 / 12
2 Hinsley, *British Intelligence in the Second World War*, II, 228–32
3 BR 305(2)
4 Dönitz, *Memoirs*, 241
5 Account of ON 127 based on BR 305(2); SOE's Report of Proceedings, 17 Sept 1942, DHist, NS 8280, ON 127; Convoy Cover, PRO, ADM 237 / 90; J. Rohwer, *Die U-Boot Erfolge der Achsenmächte*; ASW unit analysis, NHC, Op Archives; SOE's Report of Proceedings and staff comments, PRO, ADM 199 / 1338; Commodore's report, nd, PRO, ADM 199 / 1710; Narrative 'A,' DHist; Rohwer and Hummelchen, *Chronology of the War at Sea*, I
6 FONF to NSHQ, 16 Sept 1942, DHist, NSHQ 7400-300
7 SO(A/S) minute, 20 Oct 1942; C-in-C, WA, to Admiralty, 29 Nov 1942; and DCOS (Operations) minute, 20 Oct 1942, PRO, ADM 237 / 90
8 NSHQ to Admiralty, 15 Sept 1942, PAC, RG 24, 3975, NS 1048-48-31
9 Tucker, *Naval Service of Canada*, II, 74–6; P. Elliot, *Allied Escort Ships of World War II*, 357–71
10 Naval Staff Minutes, 1 Oct 1942; Naval Board Minutes, 5 Oct 1942
11 FONF to NSHQ, 10 Sept 1942, DHist, NSH 7400-300
12 CTF-24 to FONF, 21 Sept 1942, PAC, RG 24, 11114, NS 61-1-1, V 2
13 COAC to Secretary, Naval Board, 10 Nov 1942, PAC RG 24, 11114, NS 61-1-1, V 2;

comments of CNEC, A/Engineer-in-Chief, Director of Engineering, Director of Personnel, and FONF can be found in PAC, RG 24, 3844, NS 1017-10-35.

14 As quoted in COAC to Secretary, Naval Board, 10 Nov 1942

15 Lt E.N. Clarke (E) to Captain (D), Newfoundland, 6 Dec 1942, PAC, RG 24, 11115, NS 61-1-3

16 DOD to Secretary, Naval Board, 3 Dec 1942, and attached correspondence, DHist, NS 1650-DS

17 'Summary of RCN Wardroom Grouses,' Lt J. George, Historical Records officer, RCN, Spring 1943, DHist, M-11

18 FONF to NSHQ, 18 Sept 1942, PAC, RG 24, 3975, NS 1048-48-31

19 'History of North Atlantic Convoy Escort Organization ...,' Plans Division narrative, 1 May 1943, 16

20 Allied Anti-Submarine Survey Board Minutes, 11 Apr 1943, PRO, ADM 1 / 13756

21 BR 305(2); Rohwer and Hummelchen, *Chronology of the War at Sea*, I

22 Account of SC 100 based on BR 305(2); SOE's Report of Proceedings, 30 Sept 1942, PRO, ADM 199 / 714; DA/SW analysis, PRO, ADM 199 / 1710; Convoy Cover, PRO, ADM 237 / 197; CTF-24 to C-in-C, U.S. Fleet, 5 Nov 1942, PRO, ADM 199 / 714; Rohwer and Hummelchen, *Chronology of the War at Sea*, I

23 Accounts of RB 1 and ON 131 based on BR 305(2); SOE's Report of Proceedings, ON 131, PRO, ADM 199 / 1338; ASW unit analysis, ON 131, PAC, RG 24, 11940; DHist, NS 8280, ON 131; Rohwer and Hummelchen, *Chronology of the War at Sea*, I

24 BR 305(2)

25 Account of SC 104 based on BR 305(2); DA/SW analysis, PRO, ADM 199 / 2011; SOE's Report of Proceedings, PRO, ADM 199 / 714; Rohwer and Hummelchen, *Chronology of the War at Sea*, I; Macintyre, *Battle of the Atlantic*, 162–5

26 Accounts of ON 137, ONS 138, and ON 139 based on BR 305(2); SOE's Report of Proceedings, ON 137, PRO, ADM 199 / 1338; ASW unit analysis, ON 137, PAC, RG 24, 11940; Convoy Cover, ONS 138, PRO, ADM 237 / 126; DA/SW analysis, ONS 138, PRO, ADM 199 / 2012; ASW unit analysis, ONS 138, NHC, Op Archives; various reports of proceedings, ON 139, PRO, ADM 199 / 1338; Rohwer and Hummelchen, *Chronology of the War at Sea*, I

27 BR 305(2); account of HX 212 based on BR 305(2); DA/SW analysis, PRO, ADM 199 / 1710; SOE to C-in-C, WA, DA/SW 2 Nov 1942, PRO ADM 199 / 1710; Rohwer and Hummelchen, *Chronology of the War at Sea*, I

28 K. Poolman, *Escort Carriers*

29 Report of Proceedings, EG 20, 22 Sept to 3 Oct 1942, PRO, ADM 199 / 618

30 Account of SC 107 based on BR 305(2); documents in PRO, ADM 199 / 715 and 716; 'The Battle against Convoy SC 107 – October 30 to November 5, 1942,' by J. Rohwer, DHist, NS 8280, SC 107; J.M. Waters, *Bloody Winter*; Douglas and Rohwer, 'The Most Thankless Task,' 210–21; Roskill, *War at Sea*, II, 215–16; Rohwer and Hummelchen, *Chronology of the War at Sea*, I

31 Account of ONS 144 based on BR 305(2); DA/SW analysis, PRO, ADM 188 / 1710; CO, HNorMS *Rose*, to Captain (D), Liverpool, and Convoy Cover, PRO, ADM 237 / 129

32 Air Officer, C-in-C, Coastal Command, to Anti–U-Boat Warfare Committee, British Cabinet, 22 Mar 1943, PRO, ADM 199 / 1787

33 CO, HMCS *Skeena*, Report of Proceedings, 1 Dec 1942, app 2, DHist, NS 8280, SC 109

34 British and American comments on Major Hoople in PRO, ADM 199 / 715; see also 'Hints on Escort Work,' memorandum from Captain (D), Halifax, 30 Mar 1943, PRO, ADM 1 / 13749, now at DHist under same reference.

35 BR 305(2); SOE's Report of Proceedings, PRO, ADM 199 / 715; DHist, NS 8280; Rohwer and Hummelchen, *Chronology of the War at Sea*, I

36 Schull, *Far Distant Ships*, 107–9, 115–22; interview with Dr M. Hadley, Victoria, BC, 9 Nov 1982

37 Secretary, Naval Board, to COAC, FONF, and other senior officers, 21 Nov 1942, PAC, RG 24, 11503, SMS-001

CHAPTER 7: THE RECKONING

1 Roskill, *War at Sea*, II, app O

2 C.B.A. Behrens, *Merchant Shipping and the Demands of War*, chap 14; see also R.M. Leighton, 'US Merchant Shipping and the British Import Crisis,' 199–223.

3 See M. Howard, *Grand Strategy*, IV, 301–11, for a discussion of the importance of this body; original documents in PRO, PREM 3, 414 / 1, and CAB 86 / 4.

4 Secretary of State, Dominion Affairs, to Secretary of State, External Affairs, 23 Nov 1942, PAC, MG 26, J 1, V 334

5 Admiralty to CONNAV, NSHQ, and others, 18 Nov 1942, DHist, NSH 8440-140

6 CTF-24 to C-in-Clant and others, 26 Nov 1942, DHist, NSH 8440-140

7 All correspondence related to WSF used here is found in DHist, NSH 8440-140

8 W.G. Lund, 'The Royal Canadian Navy's Quest for Autonomy,' 138–57

9 Minute, Director of Operations (Home), RN, 2 Jan 1943, and other related minutes, PRO, ADM 199 / 715

10 P.M.S. Blackett, *Studies of War*, app B

11 RAdm W.S. Chalmers, *Max Horton and the Western Approaches*, 162–3

12 Minutes, 2 Dec 1942, PRO, PREM 3, 414 / 1

13 V-Adm E.L.S. King, ACNS(T), to Nelles, 5 Dec 1942, DHist, NS 8440

14 V-Adm V.G. Brodeur, NMCS, to NSHQ, 2 Dec 1942, DHist, M-11

15 FONF to CNS, 2 Dec 1942, DOD to CNS, 6 Dec 1942, DNP minute, 5 Dec 1942, CNEC to VCNS, 6 Dec 1942, DHist, M-11

16 Secretary of State, External Affairs, to Secretary of State, Dominion Affairs, 5 Dec 1942, PAC, MG 26, J 1, V 334

17 Account of HX 217 based on BR 305(2); DHist, NS 8280, HX 217; DA/SW analysis of HX 217, PRO, ADM 1 / 3671; Rohwer and Hummelchen, *Chronology of the War at Sea*, I

18 First Lord to Churchill, 15 Dec 1942, PRO, PREM 3, 331 / 8

19 Secretary of State, Dominion Affairs, to Secretary of State, External Affairs, 17 Dec 1942, PAC, MG 26, J 1, V 334

20 S.E. Boyd-Shannon to a Mr Chapman, 22 Dec 1942, PRO, ADM 1 / 12564

21 Capt E.S. Brand to author, 2 Oct 1978
22 DSD to CNS, 24 Dec 1942, DOP to CNS, 21 Dec 1942, and SO(A/S) to DOD, 24 Dec 1942, DHist, M-11; DOD to CNS 26 Dec 1942, DHist, NS 8780; compilation of signals from FONF, 23 Dec 1942, and COAC, 25, 27 Dec 1942, DHist, NS 8440-60
23 Minutes, 24 Dec 1942, PAC, C-4875
24 SO(A/S) to DOD, 24 Dec 1942
25 FONF to CNS, 21 Dec 1942, PAC, RG 24, 6796, NS 8375-4
26 COAC to CNS, 21 Dec 1942, PAC, RG 24, 6796, NS 8375-4
27 Captain (D), Halifax, to COAC, 23 Dec 1942, PAC, RG 24, 11940, (D)-1-1
28 COAC to Secretary, Naval Board, 24 Dec 1942, PAC, RG 24, 3995, NS 1057-1-27
29 DOD to CNS, 28 Dec 1942, DHist, NS 1440-5
30 COMNAVEU to COMINCH, 29 Nov 1942, NHC, Op Archives, CON-COMINCH Papers, COMNAVEU-Admiralty dispatches, box 51
31 Roosevelt to Churchill, 18 Dec 1942, PAC, RG 24, 6796, NS 8375-4
32 Churchill to Lord Leathers, FSL, and Mr G. Lloyd, 19 Dec 1942, PRO, MT 63 / 70
33 BAD to Admiralty, 23 Dec 1942, PRO, MT 63 / 70
34 FSL to CNS, 18 Dec 1942, PAC, RG 24, 6796, NS 8375-4; Brand to author, 2 Oct 1978
35 Interview with RAdm R.P. Welland, RCN, DHist biography file
36 'Report of Conference on Fuel Supply to UK and Africa and Related Escort Matters,' Washington, 29–31 Dec 1942, attached to DOP's report to CNS, 4 Jan 1943, PAC, RG 24, 6796, NS 8375-4
37 DOP to CNS, 21 Dec 1942, DHist, M-11
38 CNS to minister, nd, attached to CNS to minister, 5 Jan 1943, PAC, RG 24, 6796, NS 8375-4
39 Account of ONS 154 based on BR 305(2); DHist, NS 8280, ONS 154; Naval War Diary, RN, PRO, ADM 199 / 2253 and 4; DA/SW analysis and other RN officers' comments, PRO, ADM 199 / 356; various reports of proceedings in PRO, ADM 199 / 1274; H. Revely, *The Convoy That Nearly Died*; Rohwer and Hummelchen, *Chronology of the War at Sea*, I; Schull, *Far Distant Ships*, 139; Narrative 'A,' DHist; COS to FONF, 7 Jan 1943, PAC, RG 24, 11335, 8280, SC 107; Douglas and Rohwer, 'The Most Thankless Task,' 221
40 CNS to minister, 5 Jan 1943, PAC, RG 24, 6796, NS 8375-4
41 CNS to FSL, 7 Jan 1943, DHist, NS 8440-60
42 Mackenzie King to Churchill, 9 Jan 1943, DHist, NS 8440
43 Churchill to Mackenzie King, 18 Jan 1943, DHist, NS 8440; original drafts in PRO, ADM 205 / 26
44 Narrative 'A,' DHist

CHAPTER 8: THE VIEW FROM THE SIDELINES

1 'Battle of Canada,' Lt P.E. Evans, RCNVR, Mar 1943, NHC, Op Archives, Heineman Papers, box 4, ONS 166, additional information
2 Captain (D), Halifax, to C-in-C, CNA, minute 2 of Capt R.E.S. Bidwell, COS, to C-in-C, CNA, 22 June 1943, Macdonald Papers, F276 / 13

3 'Report on Anti-Submarine Warfare, North Western Atlantic Area,' Allied Anti-Submarine Survey Board, 18 May 1943, PRO, ADM 1 / 13756
4 'Comments on the Operation and Performance of HMC Ships, Establishments, and Personnel in the Battle of the Atlantic,' A/Lt Cdr D.W. Piers to Captain (D), Newfoundland, 1 June 1943, and staff remarks, PAC, RG 24, 3997, NS 1056-3-24
5 Correspondence relating to possible exchange of MOEF and WLEF groups, PAC, RG 24, 3893, NS 1033-6-1
6 'US Naval Repair Base, Londonderry,' report by Lt J. George, Historical Records officer, RCNVR, 24 Dec 1943, PAC, RG 24, 11695, DH 1003-2-13
7 'Proposed Methods of Increasing Facilities for the Refit of HMC Ships,' Supervising Naval Engineer, Maritimes (SNEM), 13 Jan 1943, PRO, ADM 1 / 13756
8 Correspondence on manpower can be found in the file 'Enlistment of Skilled Labour,' PAC, RG 24, 5619, NSS 30-2-9
9 SNEM, 13 Jan 1943
10 Correspondence between F.J. Horne, CNO's Office, USN, and BAD in early 1943, and RCN reaction, in PAC, RG 24, 11695, DH 1003-2-13
11 COAC to FONF, 16 Jan 1943, PAC, RG 24, 11979, COAC 1-3-6
12 Lt E.N. Clarke to Captain (D), Newfoundland, 19 Feb 1943, PAC, RG 24, 11960, CENF 1000-112 / 4
13 War Diary, USS Prairie, NHC, Op Archives
14 RN Maintenance Office, Argentia, 13 Feb 1943, PAC, RG 24, 11960, CENF 1000-112 / 4
15 DTD minute, 21 Dec 1942, PRO, ADM 1 / 12564
16 C-in-C, WA, to NSHQ, 28 Mar 1943, PAC, RG 24, 3995, NSS 1057-1-27; interview with V-Adm Sir Peter Gretton, 26 Apr 1981
17 CNS to FSL, 28 Jan 1943, PRO, ADM 1 / 12564
18 See J. Rohwer, The Critical Convoy Battles of March 1943, 39
19 Rohwer and Hummelchen, Chronology of the War at Sea, II
20 HMCS Kenogami, log, PAC, RG 24, 7428 and 9; following account based on details from all available logs held by PAC
21 Account of KMS 10 based on BR 305(2); DA/SW analysis, PRO, ADM 199 / 2018; reports of proceedings, PRO, ADM 199 / 975; Commodore's report, PRO, ADM 199 / 727; Rohwer and Hummelchen, Chronology of the War at Sea, II
22 Operational reports, Newfoundland Command, Jan–Feb 1943, PAC, RG 24, 11505; NEF and MOEF war diaries
23 Rohwer and Hummelchen, Chronology of the War at Sea, II
24 Account of SC 118 based on BR 305(2); Pink Lists, vols 19–24; Dönitz, Memoirs, 321; Roskill, War at Sea, II, 356–7, Rohwer and Hummelchen, Chronology of the War at Sea, II; Hinsley, British Intelligence in the Second World War, II, 560–1
25 Roskill, War at Sea; Dönitz, Memoirs, 322–3
26 Chalmers, Max Horton, 165
27 'Progress of Analysis of the Value of Escort Vessels and Aircraft in the Anti U-Boat Campaign,' P.M.S. Blackett, 5 Feb 1943, PRO, PREM 3, 414 / 1
28 Chalmers, Max Horton, 162–3

29 Howard, *Grand Strategy*, IV, 305–11
30 Rohwer and Hummelchen, *Chronology of the War at Sea*, II
31 Hinsley, *British Intelligence in the Second World War*, II, app I pt ii
32 Dönitz, *Memoirs*, 310; Roskill, *War at Sea*, II, 353–4
33 Account of ONS 166 based on BR 305(2); reports and minutes in PRO, ADM
   199 / 365; Waters, *Bloody Winter*, 178–92; Roskill, *War at Sea*, II, 357;
   Heineman Papers, NHC, Op Archives
34 Adm A. Andrews to COMINCH, 5 Jan 1943, USNA, RG 80, box 661,
   A 14 / EF-A14-1, Mar 1943
35 Minutes, 6 Jan 1943, PRO, PREM 3, 414 / I
36 'History of North Atlantic Convoy Escort Organization ...,' Plans Division narrative, I May 1943, 19
37 Operational report for Feb 1943, Newfoundland Command, PAC, RG 24, 11505
38 DOP to Admiralty and FSL, 15 Feb 1943, PRO, ADM 205 / 27
39 P.K. Lundeberg, 'American Anti-Submarine Operations in the Atlantic,' NHC,
   Op Archives, Privileged Manuscript Collection, box 28, L, 3–5
40 Lund, 'Royal Canadian Navy's Quest for Autonomy'
41 Tucker, *Naval Service of Canada*, II, chap 14; Minutes of the Atlantic Convoy
   Conference, PRO, ADM 199 / 1148
42 'Unified Control in Western Atlantic,' DTD, RN, memorandum, 4 Feb 1943, PRO,
   ADM I / 12663
43 FSL to Churchill, 10 Apr 1943, PRO, ADM 205 / 27
44 VCNS to FSL, 9 Mar 1943, Roskill Papers, ROSK 5 / 14
45 Lund, 'Royal Canadian Navy's Quest for Autonomy'
46 Admiralty to BAD, 20 Feb 1943, NHC, Op Archives, 10th Fleet, Convoy and
   Routing Division, box 249, 2-2-11, Atlantic Convoys; Tucker, *Naval Service of
   Canada*, II, chap 14
47 Appendix A to ACC 4, Training and Material Readiness of Operational Escort
   Groups (Surface Craft and Air Craft), PRO, ADM 199 / 1148
48 Howard, *Grand Strategy*, IV, 306
49 Hinsley, *British Intelligence in the Second World War*, II, 561–2
50 Account of SC 121 based on BR 305(2); Rohwer and Hummelchen, *Chronology of
   the War at Sea*, II; Waters, *Bloody Winter*, 195–216
51 See especially Rohwer, *Critical Convoy Battles*, and M. Middlebrook, *Convoy*.
52 The groups are listed in Roskill, *War at Sea*, II, 367.
53 Howard, *Grand Strategy*, IV, 307
54 Ibid, 310; Hinsley, *British Intelligence in the Second World War*, II, 567–8
55 'Battle of the Atlantic: Adverse Factors,' FSL to Anti–U-boat Warfare Committee,
   30 Mar 1943, PRO, CAB 86 / 4
56 Account of ONS 5 based on BR 305(2); V-Adm Sir P. Gretton, *Crisis Convoy*;
   Douglas and Rohwer, 'The Most Thankless Task'; Rohwer and Hummelchen,
   Chronology of the War at Sea, II; Hinsley, *British Intelligence in the Second World
   War*, II, 568–70
57 'The First Year of Canadian Operational Control in the Northwest Atlantic,' Plans
   Division narrative, DHist

58 Rohwer and Hummelchen, *Chronology of the War at Sea*, II; Hinsley, *British Intelligence in the Second World War*, II, 570
59 Report on operations of support groups, DA/SW, 15 June 1943, PRO, ADM 199 / 2020

CHAPTER 9: SUMMER OF DISCONTENT

1 Pickersgill, *Mackenzie King Record*, II, 466
2 Dönitz, *Memoirs*, 406–8
3 Douglas, 'Conflict and Innovation'
4 RAdm D.W. Piers, RCN, interview, June 1978
5 'Summary of Wardroom Grouses,' Lt George, Spring 1943
6 'Comments on the Operation and Performance of HMC Ships, Establishments and Personnel,' A/Lt Cdr Piers, 1 June 1943
7 Anti-Submarine Warfare Summary, no 7, app I, Anti-Submarine Warfare Operational Research, report no 3, COAC, Apr 1943, NHC, Op Archives, 10th Fleet files, ASW Analysis and Statistics Section, ser 15, box 262, A16-3(5)
8 'Hints on Escort Work,' Captain (D), Halifax, 30 Mar 1943, PRO, ADM 1 / 13749, also at DHist under same reference
9 Captain (D), Newfoundland, to FONF, 1 May 1943, Macdonald Papers, F276 / 10
10 FONF to Secretary, Naval Board, 13 May 1943, Macdonald Papers, F276 / 9
11 Capt R.E.S. Bidwell to C-in-C, CNA, 22 June 1943, Macdonald Papers, F276 / 13
12 Captain (D), Halifax, to C-in-C, CNA, minute 2 to Bidwell to C-in-C, CNA, 22 June 1943, and C-in-C, CNA, to Secretary, Naval Board, minute 3
13 RDFO to DSD, 20 May 1943, Macdonald Papers, F276 / 8, DSD minute attached to above, nd; Secretary, Naval Board, to FONF, 18 July 1943, Macdonald Papers, F276 / 14
14 CNS to minister, 27 Nov 1943, Macdonald Papers, F276 / 34
15 Ibid
16 Gp Capt P.F. Canning to Air Marshal Slessor, 27 May 1943, PRO, ADM 1 / 13746
17 AA/SSB Minutes, 11 Apr 1943, PRO, ADM 1 / 13746
18 AA/SSB Minutes, 17 Apr 1943, PRO, ADM 1 / 13746
19 FSL to Mansfield, nd, PRO, ADM 1 / 13746
20 AA/SSB Minutes, 11 May 1943, PRO, ADM 1 / 13746
21 See J.N. Kennedy, *History of the Department of Munitions and Supply*, I.
22 AA/SSB Minutes, PRO, ADM 1 / 13746
23 Mansfield to FSL, nd, PRO, ADM 1 / 13746
24 Stacey, *Arms, Men and Governments*, 315–18; V-Adm Sir Peter Gretton to author, 5 Aug 1982
25 Macdonald diary, 23 Dec 1942, Macdonald Papers, F390
26 Ibid, 26 May 1943
27 Ibid, 11 Aug 1943
28 Capt W. Strange to minister, as quoted in minister to CNS, nd (actually ca 20 Nov 1943), Macdonald Papers, F276 / 3, minister to CNS, 21 Aug 1943, PAC, RG 24, 3995, NSS 1057-1-27

29 Admiralty to NSHQ, 24 Aug 1943, Macdonald Papers, attached to F276 / 23
30 CNS to minister, 1 Sept 1943, with enclosures, DHist, M-11
31 'Report of Mr. J.J. Connolly's Trip to UK in one of HMC Corvettes [sic],' Naval Staff Minutes, 15 Nov 1943, and Nelles Papers, DHist, folder B
32 'Canadian Naval Construction Programme,' no author, nd, Macdonald Papers, F276 / 45
33 DOD to CNS, 16 Nov 1943, Macdonald Papers, F276 / 26 and 27; VCNS to CNS, 10 Nov 1943, Macdonald Papers, F276 / 22; CNEC to CNS, 11 Nov 1943, Macdonald Papers, F276 / 23
34 Minutes of meeting in the office of the CNEC, 16 Nov 1943, DHist, NSHQ, NSS 6101-1
35 'Equipping the Canadian Navy,' interview with Mr J.J. Connolly, executive assistant to the minister for Naval Services, London, 26 Jan 1945, DHist, 8780, NSMS 1057-1-35
36 Minister to CNS, nd, Macdonald Papers, F276 / 3
37 CO, HMCS *Assiniboine*, to Captain (D), Newfoundland, 9 Aug 1943, PAC, RG 24, 3997, NSS 1057-3-24; Stacey, *Arms, Men and Governments*, 317; Nelles Papers, DHist
38 Minister to CNS, 25 Nov 1943, Macdonald Papers, F276 / 28
39 CNS to minister, 26 Nov 1943, with enclosures, Macdonald Papers, F276 / 33
40 CNS to minister, 27 Nov 1943, Macdonald Papers, F276 / 34
41 See 'Correspondence with Commodore Simpson,' Macdonald Papers, F1067.
42 DWT to CNS, 2 Dec 1943, Nelles Papers, DHist
43 CNS to minister, 4 Dec 1943, Macdonald Papers, F276 / 39
44 Minister to CNS, 10 Dec 1943, Macdonald Papers, F276 / 47
45 Connolly interview, 26 Jan 1945
46 DeWolf interview, 14 July 1981
47 Connolly interview, 26 Jan 1945
48 CNS to minister, 5 Jan 1943, PAC, RG 24, 6796, NS 8375-4
49 Minutes of Anti–U-boat Warfare Committee, 24 Feb 1943, memo from FSL on result of hedgehog, PRO, ADM 199 / 1787
50 'The Case for Unified Control in the Atlantic,' DTD memo, 11 Jan 1943, PRO, ADM 1 / 12663
51 'Personal Appreciation of Situation for RCN Ships in United Kingdom,' Lt Cdr W.E.S. Briggs, 23 Apr 1943, PAC, RG 24, 11960, CS 34
52 'Report of Visit of Commodore Superintendent, Halifax, to United Kingdom,' Commodore G. Hibbard, 13 Dec 1943, PAC, RG 24, 11695, DH 1003-2-18
53 Admiralty to OPNAV, 29 Jan 1942, NHC, Op Archives, CNO-COMINCH Papers, box 51, COMNAVEU-Admiralty Dispatches

EPILOGUE

1 'The First Year of Canadian Operational Control in the Northwest Atlantic,' Plans Division narrative, 18 Aug 1944, DHist

2 Lundeberg, 'American A/S Operations in the Atlantic'; Morison, *History of USN Operations in the Second World War*, x

3 Eberhard Rössler, *The U-Boat*, chap 8

4 Dönitz, *Memoirs*, 406–30

5 Elliott, *Allied Escort Ships*, 456, 356–69

6 Ibid, 245

7 'First Year of Canadian Operational Control,' Plans Division narrative, 18 Aug 1944

8 DA/SW paper, 15 May 1943, and minutes, PRO, ADM I / 12589

9 'First Year of Canadian Operational Control,' Plans Division narrative, 18 Aug 1944

10 Howard, *Grand Strategy*, IV, 302

11 'First Year of Canadian Operational Control,' Plans Division narrative, 18 Aug 1944

12 Account of ONS 18–ON 202 based on 'Analysis of U-Boat Operations in the Vicinity of Convoys ONS 18 and ON 202,' Anti–U-boat Division, DHist, 81 / 520 / 8280 ON 202; Narrative 'A', DHist; Roskill, *War at Sea*, III; Rohwer and Hummelchen, *Chronology of the War at Sea*, II

13 W.A.B. Douglas, 'Conflict and Innovation in the Royal Canadian Navy'

14 'First Year of Canadian Operational Control,' Plans Division narrative, 18 Aug 1944

15 Macpherson and Burgess, *Ships of Canada's Naval Forces*, app 8

16 'First Year of Canadian Operational Control,' Plans Division narrative, 18 Aug 1944

17 Ibid

18 Milner, *Canadian Naval Force Requirements*, 47

19 Roskill, *War at Sea*, II, app O

Bibliography

PRIMARY SOURCES, CANADA

Public Archives, Canada

MG 26   William Lyon Mackenzie King Papers
MG 30   Rear Admiral L.W. Murray, RCN, Papers
RG 2   War Cabinet Committee Papers and Minutes
RG 24   NSHQ Central Registry Files
        COAC Files
        FONF Files
        Captain (D), Halifax, Files
        Captain (D), Newfoundland, Files
        Naval Council Minutes

Directorate of History, National Defence Headquarters

General:
Naval Historian's Files
Naval Board Minutes
Naval Staff Minutes
Summaries of Naval War Effort
Newfoundland Command, War Diaries
Convoy Records
Chiefs of Staff Committee Papers and Minutes
Vice-Admiral P.W. Nelles, RCN, Papers
Captain E.S. Brand, RCN, Papers
A.L. Macdonald Papers (copies)
BdU War Diary
Daily States (of RCN and Allied ships operating with the RCN)

Principal narratives:
Narrative 'A' (Operations)
History of North Atlantic Convoy Escort Organization and Canadian Participation
    Therein 9 / 39–4 / 43
The First Year of Canadian Operational Control in the Northwest Atlantic
The RCN in Newfoundland 1939–1944
Modernization of Armament and Equipment
Outline History of the Trade Division
Manpower Problems of the Royal Canadian Navy during the Second World War
Operational Training

Published primary sources consulted at DHist:
Admiralty BR 305(2) (*The U-Boat War in the Atlantic*, II, *January 1942–May 1943*),
    Naval Staff, 1952
– *Monthly Anti-Submarine Reports*, Naval Staff, 1939–45
Behrens, C.E. *Effects on U-Boat Performance of Intelligence from Decryption of
    Allied Communications*, Center for Naval Analysis, Office of the Chief of Naval
    Operations, USN, 1954
Navy Lists (RCN and RN)
Janes Fighting Ships

Public Archives, Nova Scotia

Angus L. Macdonald Papers

PRIMARY SOURCES, BRITAIN

Public Record Office, Kew

ADM 1	General Subject Files
ADM 187	Pink Lists
ADM 199	Naval Historian's Files
ADM 205	First Sea Lord's Papers
ADM 217	Western Approaches Command Files
ADM 219	Director, Naval Operational Studies, Files
ADM 223	U-boat Situation Reports
	U-boat Appreciations
ADM 237	Convoy Covers
PREM 3	Prime Minister's Papers
PREM 4	Prime Minister's Papers
WT 62	Private Office Papers, Minister of War Transport

Churchill College, Cambridge

A.V. Alexander Papers
Captain Sir John Creswell, RN, Papers
Vice-Admiral Sir John H. Edelsten, RN, Papers
Commander H.J. Fawcett, RN, Papers
Captain S.W. Roskill, RN, Papers

Imperial War Museum, London

Rear Admiral Sir Oswald Dawson, RN, Papers
Vice-Admiral D. Egerton, RN, Papers
L. Marshland Gander, papers
S.A. Kerslake, RNVR, Papers
Commander F. Poole, RCNVR, Papers
Vice-Admiral A.G. Talbot, RN, Papers

Naval Historical Branch, London

Atlantic Convoy Instructions
BdU War Diary
BR 305(2)
Convoy covers not held by PRO
Various convoy records
Western Approaches Convoy Instructions

PRIMARY SOURCES, UNITED STATES

Naval Historical Center, Operational Archives, Washington

CNO–Double Zero Files
CNO-COMINCH Papers
CNO-COMNAVEU-Admiralty Dispatches
CTF-24 War Diary
Tenth Fleet, Convoy and Routing Division Files
Tenth Fleet, Anti-Submarine Measures Division Files
Tenth Fleet, ASW Analysis and Statistics Section
U.S. Atlantic Fleet, ASW Unit Analyses
USN Administrative Histories, Second World War
NOB Argentia, War Diary
NOB Londonderry, War Diary
USS *Prairie*, War Diary
USS *Vulcan*, War Diary
Daily Location of Ships and Aircraft
Composition of Task Forces

Escort-of-Convoy Instructions (Lantflt 9A)
Captain P. Heineman, USCG, Papers
P.K. Lundeberg 'American Anti-Submarine Operations in the Atlantic, May 1943–
May 1945,' unpublished PH D dissertation (Columbia University), Privileged
Manuscript Collection

United States National Archives, Washington

RG 80 USN ASW, Convoy and Escort Files
RG 313 CTF-24 Files (unavailable to researchers due to loss of finding aid)
USS *Prairie*, Log
USS *Denebola*, Log
USS *Vulcan*, Log

Library of Congress, Manuscript Division

Fleet Admiral E. King, USN, Papers
Frank Knox Papers

OTHER PRIMARY SOURCES, PUBLICATIONS

Bridle, P., ed. *Documents on Relations between Canada and Newfoundland*, I,
1935–1949. Ottawa: Department of External Affairs 1974
British Vessels Lost at Sea 1939–45. Cambridge: Patrick Stephens 1976
Rohwer, J. *Die U-Boot Erfolge der Achsenmachte 1939–45*. Munich: J.F. Lehmans 1968
Rohwer, J., and G. Hummelchen. *Chronology of the War at Sea, 1939–1945*. 2 vols,
London: Ian Allan 1972

SECONDARY SOURCES, SELECT BIBLIOGRAPHY

Abbazia, P. *Mr. Roosevelt's Navy*. Annapolis, Md: U.S. Naval Institute Press 1975
Baker, R. *The Terror of Tobermory*. London: W.H. Allen 1972
Beesley, P. *Very Special Intelligence*. London: Hamilton 1977
Behrens, C.B.A. *Merchant Shipping and the Demands of War*. London: HMSO and
Longmans Green 1955
Bekker, C. *Hitler's Naval War*. Garden City, NJ: Doubleday and Co 1974
Blackett, P.M.S. *Studies of War*. London: Oliver and Boyd 1962
Bothwell, R., and W. Kilbourne. *C.D. Howe*. Toronto: McClelland and Stewart 1979
Boutilier, J.A., ed. *The RCN in Retrospect*. Vancouver: University of British Columbia
Press 1982
Buell, T.B. *Master of Sea Power, A Biography of Fleet Admiral Ernest J. King*.
Boston: Little Brown and Co 1980
Burton, E.F., ed. *Canadian Naval Radar Officers*. Toronto: University of Toronto
Press 1946
Butler, J.R.M., ed. *Grand Strategy*. 6 vols, London: HMSO 1956–76

Cameron, J.M. *Murray the Martyred Admiral*. Hantsport, NS: Lancelot Press 1981
Chalmers, RAdm W.S. *Max Horton and the Western Approaches*. London: Hodder and Stoughton 1954
Dönitz, Grand Admiral Karl. *Memoirs: Ten Years and Twenty Days*, trans R.H. Stevens. London: Weidenfeld and Nicholson 1959
Douglas, W.A.B. 'Conflict and Innovation in the Royal Canadian Navy, 1939–1945,' in G. Jordan, ed, *Naval Strategy in the Twentieth Century*, 210–32. New York: Crane Russack 1977
– 'The RCN and RCAF in the Battle of the Atlantic,' in S. Aster, ed, *The Second World War as a National Experience*. Ottawa: The Canadian Committee for the History of the Second World War 1981
Douglas, W.A.B., and B. Greenhous. *Out of the Shadows*. Toronto: Oxford University Press 1977
Douglas, W.A.B., and J. Rohwer. 'The Most Thankless Task Revisited: Convoys, Escorts and Radio Intelligence in the Western Atlantic,' in J.A. Boutilier, ed, *The RCN in Retrospect*. Vancouver: University of British Columbia Press 1982
Dziuban, Col S.W. *Military Relations between the United States and Canada, 1939–1945*. Washington: Department of the Army 1959
Easton, A.H. *50 North: Canada's Atlantic Battleground*. Toronto: Ryerson 1966
Elliott, P. *Allied Escort Ships of World War II*. London: Macdonald Janes 1977
Granatstein, J.G.L. *Canada's War*. Toronto: Oxford University Press, 1975
Granatstein, J.G.L., and J. Hitsman. *Broken Promises*. Toronto: Oxford University Press 1977
Gretton, V-ADm Sir Peter. *Convoy Escort Commander*. London: Cassell 1964
– *Crisis Convoy*. London: P. Davis 1974
Hadley, Michael L. *U-Boats against Canada: German Submarines in Canadian Waters*. Kingston and Montreal: McGill-Queen's University Press 1985
Henry, D. 'British Submarine Policy 1918–1939,' in B. Ranft, ed, *British Naval Policy 1860–1939*. London: Hodder and Stoughton 1977
Hinsley, F.H. *British Intelligence in the Second World War*, vols I & II. Cambridge: Cambridge University Press 1979–81
Howard, M. *Grand Strategy* (ed J.R.M. Butler, 6 vols, London: HMSO 1956–76) IV, *August 1942–September 1943*
Hughes, T., and J. Costello. *The Battle of the Atlantic*. New York: Dial Press 1977
Kennedy, J.N. *A History of the Department of Munitions and Supply*. Ottawa: King's Printer 1950
Lamb, J. *Corvette Navy*. Toronto: Macmillan 1977
Lawrence, H. *A Bloody War*. Toronto: Macmillan 1979
Lay, RAdm H.N. *Memoirs of a Mariner*. Stittsville, Ont: Canada's Wings 1982
Leighton, R.M. 'US Merchant Shipping and the British Import Crisis,' in K.R. Greenfield, ed, *Command Decisions*, 199–223. Washington: Office of the Chief of Military History, U.S. Army 1960
Leighton, R.M., and R.W. Coakley. *Global Logistics and Strategy, 1940–43*. Washington: Department of the Army 1968
Lenton, H.T. *German Warships of the Second World War*. New York: Arco 1976

Lund, W.G. 'Command Relationships in the North Atlantic: The Canadian Perspective,' unpublished Masters thesis, Queen's University 1972
– 'The Royal Canadian Navy's Quest for Autonomy in the Northwest Atlantic,' in J.A. Boutilier, ed., *The RCN in Retrospect.* Vancouver: University of British Columbia Press, 1982
[Macdonald, Angus L.] *Speeches of Angus L. Macdonald.* Toronto: Longmans Green 1960
Macintyre, Capt D. *U-Boat Killer.* London: Weidenfeld & Nicholson 1956
– *The Battle of the Atlantic.* London: B.T. Batsford 1961
McKee, F.M. *Volunteers for Sea Service: A Brief History of the Royal Canadian Navy Volunteer Reserve.* Toronto: Houstons Standard 1973
Macpherson, K., and J. Burgess. *The Ships of Canada's Naval Forces, 1910–1981.* Toronto: Collins 1981
March, E.J. *British Destroyers.* London: Seeley Service and Co 1966
Middlebrook, M. *Convoy.* London: Allen Lane 1976
Middleton, W.E. Knowles. *Radar Development in Canada: The Radio Branch of the National Research Council of Canada, 1939–1946.* Waterloo, Ont: Wilfrid Laurier University Press 1981
Milner, Marc. 'Canadian Escorts in the Mid Atlantic 1941–43,' unpublished Masters thesis, University of New Brunswick 1979
– *Canadian Naval Force Requirements.* Operational Research and Analysis Establishment, National Defence Headquarters, Ottawa: extramural paper no. 20, 1981
– 'Royal Canadian Navy Participation in the Battle of the Atlantic Crisis of 1943,' in J.A. Boutilier, ed, *The RCN in Retrospect.* Vancouver: University of British Columbia Press 1982
– 'Canada's Naval War,' *Acadiensis* 12, no. 2 (Spring 1983)
– 'Convoy Escorts: Tactics Technology and Innovation in the Royal Canadian Navy 1939–1943,' *Military Affairs* 48, no. 1 (Jan 1984)
Morison, S.E. *The History of US Naval Operations in the Second World War*, vols I and X. Boston: Little Brown and Co 1947 and 1962
Pickersgill, J.W. *The Mackenzie King Record.* 4 vols, Toronto: University of Toronto Press 1960–70
Poolman, K. *Escort Carriers.* London: Ian Allan 1972
Postan, M.M. *British War Production.* London: HMSO and Longmans Green 1952
Postan, M.M., D. Hay, and J.D. Scott. *Design and Development of Weapons.* London: HMSO and Longmans Green 1964
Preston, A., and Alan Raven. *Flower Class Corvettes*, ensign no 3. London: Bivouac Books 1973
Price, A. *Aircraft versus the Submarine.* London: Kimber 1973
Raven, A., and J. Roberts. *'V' and 'W' Class Destroyers*, Man O'War 2. London: Arms and Armour Press 1979
Rayner, Cdr D.A. *Escort.* London: Kimber 1953
Report of the Royal Commission on Provincial Development and Rehabilitation. Halifax, NS: King's Printer 1944
Revely, H. *The Convoy That Nearly Died.* London: Kimber 1979

Rohwer, J. 'La Radiotelegraphie Auxiliare du Commandement dans la Guerre Sous Marine,' *Revue D'Histoire de la Deuxieme Guerre Mondiale* no. 69 (June 1968)
– *The Critical Convoy Battles of March 1943.* Annapolis, Md: U.S. Naval Institute Press 1977
Roskill, Capt S.W. *The War at Sea.* 3 vols, London: HMSO 1954–61
– *A Merchant Fleet at War.* London: Collins 1962
– *Naval Policy between the Wars.* 2 vols, London: Collins 1968–77
– *Churchill and the Admirals.* London: Collins 1977
Rössler, Eberhard. *The U-Boat.* London: Arms and Armour Press 1981
Schull, J. *The Far Distant Ships.* Ottawa: Queen's Printer 1952
Showell, J.M. *The German Navy in World War Two.* London: Arms and Armour Press 1979
Stacey, Col C.P. *Arms, Men and Governments.* Ottawa: Department of National Defence 1970
– *Canada and the Age of Conflict*, vol 2. Toronto: Macmillan 1979
Sternhell, C.M., and A.M. Thorndike. *Anti-submarine Warfare in World War II.* Washington: Office of the Chief of Naval Operations 1946
Tucker, G.N. *The Naval Service of Canada.* 2 vols, Ottawa: King's Printer 1952
Waddington, C.H. *O.R. in World War 2: Operational Research against the U-Boat.* London: Elek Science 1973
Waters, J.M. *Bloody Winter.* Princeton, NJ: Van Nostrand 1967
Watts, Anthony. *The U-Boat Hunters.* London: Macdonald Janes 1976
Young, G. *The Short Triangle.* Lunenburg, NS: Lunenburg County Press 1975

Index

Picture Credits

Public Archives of Canada: PM King visiting *Assiniboine*, PA-104223; Nelles and Grant, PA-134539; the nerve-centre of the early corvettes, PA-136247; depth charge and carrier leaving *Pictou*, PA-116838; Hvalfjordhur, PA-135968; *Battleford* in Nov 1941, PA-135970; Prentice, 0-753; *Arrowhead*, PA-136840; *U210*, 0-4447; RCN officers aboard *Chambly*, PA-134538; Rowland and Mainguy, M-563; DeWolf, PA-135972; hedgehog, PA-112918

Canadian Forces Photographic Unit: St John's harbour, PMR 84-731; survivors aboard *Shediac*, PMR 83-1247; *Belgian Soldier*, PMR 84-75 (courtesy Joe Rolland); *Regina*, PMR 84-242; sinking the *Vestfold*, PMR 83-941; AA/SSB leaving Ottawa, PL 16280; *Trillium*, CN 6142; *Battleford* in spring 1943, RE 83-1242

Kenneth R. Macpherson: *Assiniboine* after her battle with *U210*; *Algoma*; *St Croix*; *Sackville*; *Churchill*; *Arvida*; *Shediac* after modernization

Bibliothek für Zeitgeschichte, Stuttgart: *U124*; *U221*; *U94*

Maritime Command Museum, Halifax: destroyers and escorts berthed at Halifax

Other photographs in the collection of the Directorate of History, National Defence Headquarters, Ottawa

This book was designed by

A N T J E L I N G N E R

and was printed by

University of Toronto Press